GERMAN

The Easy Way

SECOND EDITION

PAUL G. GRAVES
Former Instructor of German
University of Colorado
Boulder, Colorado

and

HENRY STRUTZ
Former Associate Professor of Languages
SUNY Technical College at
Alfred, New York

BARRON'S

All inquiries should be addressed to:
Barron's Educational Series, Inc.
250 Wireless Boulevard
Hauppauge, New York 11788

Library of Congress Catalog Card No. 96-83182

International Standard Book No. 0-8120-9145-0

PRINTED IN THE UNITED STATES OF AMERICA

9 8 7 6 5 4 3

CONTENTS

Introduction

INTRODUCTION

Teacher (to little Tommy): Don't say 'I ain't coming.' You must say 'I am not coming, he is not coming, we are not coming...'

Little Tommy: Ain't nobody coming?

Soon Tommy will learn how to say it correctly. Most children speak as if they knew their grammar—at least they're not concerned with it. Self-consciousness afflicts mainly grown-ups. To enter into the realm of a foreign language, it helps to "become as little children." It is a sad fact that a minimum of grammar is essential for the proper study of a foreign language. But grammar in this book is not the bugaboo of yesterday. You will be eased into it without pain. Please keep in mind, this book wants to make friends with you; it tries to be neighborly, lively, and humorous.

The topics, as outlined in the table of contents, are relevant to everyday situations and problems. There is a storyline (sort of), not exactly a cliff-hanger, yet designed to keep you interested. And there are characters in the story itself that you will recognize, a friend, a relative, maybe yourself. Anecdotes, jokes, and brain teasers are interspersed throughout the text to lend it variety. There are loads of exercises also—not too hard, you'll find—following each section. The answer key at the back of the book will enable you to verify your responses. There are German-English and English-German Vocabularies, a list of strong and irregular verbs, and a pronunciation guide.

You probably know that German is spoken today by over ninety million people in Germany, Austria, Switzerland, and Liechtenstein. German is used and understood by millions elsewhere in Europe and around the world. It is recognized as one of the great international languages and is particularly useful in the fields of science, technology, the arts, and commerce. Germany is one of the world's leading industrial countries.

Knowing German will give you access to some of the world's finest literature, and, in works of non-fiction, to outstanding reference works and textbooks on every conceivable subject. Visiting one of the German-speaking countries as a tourist, your pleasure will be vastly enhanced if you are able to talk with the Germans, the Austrians, and the Swiss in their native tongue.

Here's how to get the most out of this book. Set aside half an hour each day or one to two hours three times a week for its study; then stick to your schedule. Read each lesson aloud, and repeat what you have read. Repetition in language study is half the battle. Try to form a mental picture of each new word you learn. Test yourself daily on the vocabulary that you have just learned. Your stock of words will grow by leaps and bounds. Some of them will be identical with their English counterparts, others will strike you as quite similar; this fact alone should give you a head start. Since German is closely related to English, you will know a great number of words even before you get going. You will notice that German is largely a phonetic language, which means that you will pronounce most words the way they are spelled. German-language radio and TV programs offered by *Deutsche Welle* are widely available in the United States and worldwide via satellite, cable, and shortwave. Speak and listen at any opportunity to German-speaking people here or abroad. Don't be afraid to speak. Nobody is going to laugh at you. People will usually help and respect you for the effort.

There are some native speakers of German whose grammar will be worse, sometimes far worse, than yours. For example, some replace the forms of the definite article, "the," with *de,* all the time, instead of bothering with **der, die, das,** etc. We don't recommend that you do that. Strive for perfection. But if you make mistakes at first, don't worry. If you can't say something one way, try to express it differently, with words you know. Remember Mark Twain's quip: "As for the adjective, when in doubt, leave it out."

CHAPTER 1

Auf dem Weg zum Schwimmbad
On the Way to the Pool

How to Pronounce It Properly

It is hot in the city. There is only one thought that occupies the mind of Anton Gruber, an employee of the Schmidt Advertising Agency, just back from the office in his apartment where the air conditioning has broken down. It is 5 p.m.:

> **Schwimmen!**
> Shvĭmĕn!
> To swim!
> **Ich muß schwimmen gehn.**
> Ĭch mооss shvĭmĕn gāyn.
> I must swimming go.

(Pardon the word order.)

The *i* in **schwimmen** is short as in most vowels that are followed by two or more consonants. The ˘ on top of the vowel *i* shows you that it is a short vowel. But the ¯ on top of the *a* in **gāyn** means that here we have a long vowel. In this chapter a short vowel (*ă, ĕ, ĭ, ŏ, ŭ*) or umlaut (*ă̈, ŏ̈, ŭ̈*) is marked by the symbol ˘, and a long vowel or umlaut by the symbol ¯. German **ich** isn't pronounced like *itch, ish,* or *ik.* It's a very breathy sound, like the *h* in *hula-hoop.* To learn it, try playing Santa Claus and proffer a few hearty "Ho-Ho-Ho's," saying them as fast as you can and exaggerating the *h.* Then you can throw in some "Ha-Ha-Ha's!" and "Heh, Heh, Heh's." You can also think of "Hartford, Hereford, Hampshire," and similar places where "hurricanes hardly happen," as Henry Higgins instructed Liza Doolittle in *My Fair Lady.* The *i* before it is short, as in *nitwit.* The *u* in **muß** is also short and sounded as in *puss.* And look again at the word **schwimmen.** Germans have to put a *c* between the *s* and the *h,* but it's still pronounced *sh.* Watch out for the German *w.* This is always pronounced like the English *v.*

Anton needs company, so he says to himself:

> **Ich glaube, ich geh mit Susie.**
> Ĭch gloubĕ ĭch gāy mĭt Zūzēē
> I think I (will go) go with Susie.

The *au* in **glaube** should remind you of *Ouch!!* Anyway, he calls his girlfriend:

> **Susie, willst du schwimmen gehn?**
> Zūzēē vĭlst dōо shvĭmĕn gāyn?
> Susie, wilt thou swimming go? (Do you want to go swimming?)

Actually, the word is **gehen,** but when you speak you often skip the second *e.* The Germans, being a very poetic people, ask a question the way William Shakespeare would. Apparently she agrees because he continues:

> **Gut, ich komme um zehn Uhr.**
> Gōōt, ĭch kŏmĕ ōōm tsāyn ōōr.
> Good, I come (will come) at ten o'clock.

The *u* in the German **gut** rhymes with *loot* or *boot,* so it's long. The *u* in **um** is also short as in *my foot!* The *z* in **zehn** must be pronounced like *ts.* Think of the last Tsar of Russia (or the next one, if the monarchy is restored). On a less lofty level, you can remember that German *z* is sounded like the *zz* in *pizza,* as in "He eats in Pete's pizza parlor." To get back to the even more lofty, remember **Mozart.** Most speakers of English say **Mozart** as the Germans do, sounding the *z* like *ts.* Most people also pronounce the *z* in his opera *Die Zauberflöte (The Magic Flute)* correctly, with a *ts* sound. The *h* in **zehn** merely tells you to lengthen the vowel. It does the same after an *a,* an *o,* or a *u.* Therefore, the sound of the *u* in **Uhr** is long. If for the rest of this chapter you are to pronounce the *oo* as a *long* sound, it will have a bar over it like this: $\overline{oo}$. You'll remember it if you think of the $\overline{oo}$ sound in the verb *to ooze.* So Anton picks her up, and on the way to the pool they talk:

ANTON **Schönes Wetter heute, nicht wahr?**
Shōnĕs vĕttĕr hoitĕ, nĭcht vāhr?
Nice weather today, isn't it?

In **schönes** we have the *ö* which, because of the funny little dots on top of the *o,* is called an umlaut *($\overline{oo}$mlout).* Please practice this sound in front of a mirror. You cannot produce it correctly unless you look funny, with your lips rounded and pushed forward forcefully. Imagine that you are whistling a tune (make it a happy one), or blowing up a balloon (maybe a bright red one). The *eu* in **heute** sounds like the *oy* in *boy.* The umlaut of *au* is *äu* as in **Sau, Säue** *(sow, sows,* the adult female swine), likewise pronounced like an *oy (soy).* Now the **nicht wahr.** This expression is most practical. Literally it means "not true?" It could be translated "no?" or "Isn't that so?" But it's more idiomatic to use whatever English phrase best fits the context, such as isn't it, aren't you (they), don't you, doesn't she, etc.

SUSIE **Absolut! Ich freu mich aufs Schwimmen.**
Ăbsŏlūt! Ĭch froi mĭch oufs shvĭmĕn.
Absolutely! I look forward to the swim.

Dann können wir ein Boot mieten.
Dăn kŏnĕn vīr ein bōt mēetĕn.
Then we can a boat rent.

The *a* in **dann** is not like the *a* in English *pat* but more like the *o* in *pot.* Every vowel if doubled is long. Please try a straight *o* without the off-glide into the *oa* (as in the English *boat).*

ANTON **Was tust du später?**
Văs tōost dōo shpāytĕr?
What dost thou (are you doing) later? (Shakespeare again)

The *a* in **was** is short, as in *cop.* In **später** you pronounce the *sp* like *shp.* The same is true with other words that start with an *sp.* Words starting with an *st* are likewise sounded as if they began with *sht,* like **Stadt** (city): **shtăt.** The *ä* in **später** sounds exactly like an *e;* it usually sounds like an ordinary *e,* pronounced *āy,* as in *gehen.*

SUSIE **Ich muß meine Mutter besuchen.**
Ich mŏoss meinĕ mŏottĕr bĕzōochĕn.
I must my mother visit.

As you can see again, the Germans use a different word order. Quite often the verb stands at the end of the sentence. We'll talk about this later. The *ei* in **meine**—be sure to pronounce the *e* at the end of the word—and any other *ei* (or *ai*) always sound like the *ei* in *kaleidoscope.* The *u* in **Mutter** is short because it is followed by a double consonant. That is true for every vowel *(a, e, i, o, u)* followed by a double consonant. **Besuchen** has the accent on the second syllable, which is true of every verb starting with *be-* or *ge-.*

ANTON **Warum mußt du sie besuchen?**
Vărōŏm mōōst dōō zēē bĕzōōchĕn?
Why must thou her visit?

   In *warum* you accent the second syllable. The *e* in *sie* merely serves to lengthen the *i*. *Sie* rhymes with Robert E. *Lee*.

SUSIE **Sie ist krank. (*Krank* rhymes with *honk*.)**
Zēē ĭst krănk.
She is ill.

ANTON **Was fehlt ihr? (*Ihr* rhymes with *here*.)**
Văs fāylt ēēr?
What ails her? (What's wrong with her?)

SUSIE **Nicht viel. Aber sie fühlt sich nicht wohl.**
Nĭcht fēēl. Aabĕr zēē fūlt zĭch nĭcht vōl.
Not much. But she feels not well.

   The *ch* in *nicht* sounds exactly like the one in *ich* that we had before. *Viel* is pronounced like *feel*. The German *v* (almost) always sounds like an *f*. In *Vogel* (bird) or in *Feder* (feather) you hear the same *f* sound. You will insult them by calling their favorite car a *Vokswagen*. It is a *Folksvagen*. The *l* in this word must be pronounced, and the *a* is a straight *a*, as in *Saab*, the Volkswagen's Swedish competitor. The *ü* in *fühlt* is, you guessed it, an umlaut. Kindly refer to what was said in the case of the *ö*. Round your lips and push them forward even more vigorously so that the sound comes out through a little round hole.

ANTON **Was sagt der Doktor?**
Văs zāāgt dĕr dŏctōr?
What says the doctor?

SUSIE **Sie soll im Bett bleiben und Medizin nehmen.**
Zēē sŏl ĭm bĕt bleibĕn ōōnd mĕdĭtsēēn nāymĕn.
She should in bed stay and medicine take.

ANTON **Braucht sie jemanden?**
Broucht zēē yāymăndĕn?
Needs she somebody?

   The *j* in *jemanden* is always pronounced like the *y* in *yodel*, never like the *j* in *jackass*.

SUSIE **Nein, sie hat ja kein Fieber.**
Nine, zēē hăt yā kine fēēbĕr.
No, she has no fever.

   Here, *ja* doesn't mean "yes." It's a filler or "flavoring particle" used to reinforce Susie's conviction that her mother is not all that sick.

ANTON **Soll ich dich morgen vom Büro abholen?**
Zŏl ĭch dĭch mŏrgĕn fŏm būrō ăphōlĕn?
Shall I you tomorrow from the office pick up?
Ich komme gern.
Ĭch kŏme gĕrn.
I (will) come gladly.

   The *g* in *morgen* and the *g* in *gern* both sound like the *g* in *go*. The *g* (almost) always sounds that way in German, never never like the *g* in *gin*. The accent in *Büro* is on the *o*. The *o* in *abholen* is long, as in *hole*.

SUSIE **Ja, natürlich. Vielleicht können wir tanzen gehn.**
Yā, nătürlĭch. Fĭleicht kŏnĕn vīr tăntsĕn gāyn.
Yes, naturally (of course). Maybe can we dancing go.

Don't get wires crossed; that is, don't mix up German *ei* and *ie* in words like *vielleicht.* English pronunciation of these combinations varies. Remember the song "You say neither" *(neether)* and "I say neither" *(neyether).* Some pronounced Leonard Bernstein's name *Bernsteen.* But he preferred *Bernstine.* In German, there is no choice, and therefore no confusion. *Ei* is always pronounced *eye.* Although Albert Einstein had a great sense of humor, he probably wouldn't have been amused by the pronunciation *Eensteen.* Vienna sausages **(Wiener Würstchen),** or *wieners,* is a word sometimes seen with variant spellings (*ei* or *ee*) in English. It shouldn't be. German *ie* is always pronounced as in *Marie Curie, Diesel, Dietrich,* and *Grieg.* Think of *chiefs* and *priests* in their *briefs,* roasting *wieners* and enjoying **Wein** (wine) and **Bier** (beer). We won't say anything about **Schnaps** because there's no *ie* or *ei* in it.

ANTON **In der Stadt oder am Strand?**
Ĭn dĕr shtăt ōdĕr ăm shtrănd?
In the city or at the beach?

SUSIE **In der Stadt.** (*Stadt* rhymes with *pot.*)
Ĭn dĕr shtăt.
In the city.

Vielleicht können Karl und Nora mitkommen.
Fīleicht kŏnĕn Kărl ōŏnd Nōră mĭtkŏmĕn.
Maybe can Karl and Nora come along.

Er ist ein guter Tänzer, und
Air ĭst ein gōōtĕr tĕntsĕr ōŏnd
He is a good dancer and

sie ist eine nette Frau.
zēē ĭst einĕ nĕtĕ frow. (**Frau** rhymes with *now.*)
she is a nice woman.

Pronouncing *r* and *l*: German *r* often sounds quite a bit different from its English counterpart. Most of the time the Germans roll it in the throat as in Parisian French or (chiefly in Austria and Bavaria) trill it with the tongue as in Scottish and Irish brogues. Many German actors and singers are very accomplished at rolling the *r* both in the throat and on the tongue. Try practicing both. German *l* should sound like the flat *l* in *William.* Germans have difficulties with English *r* and *l.* It will take time for you to master *r* and *l,* and you may be told how charming your American accent is. We hope you'll pronounce every word correctly when you read the complete dialog now. If you've forgotten one word or another, look it up in the vocabulary at the end of the book.

ANTON **Schwimmen! Ich muß schwimmen gehn. Ich**
Shvĭmĕn! Ĭch mōōss shvĭmĕn gāyn. Ĭch

glaube, ich geh mit Susie.—Susie, willst du schwimmen gehn?—Gut, ich
gloubĕ, ĭch gāy mĭt Zūzēē.—Zūzēē, vĭlst dōō shvĭmĕn gāyn? —Gōōt, ĭch

komme um zehn Uhr.—Schönes Wetter heute, nicht wahr?
kŏmĕ ōŏm tsāyn ōōr.—Shōnĕs vĕttĕr hoitĕ, nĭcht vāhr?

SUSIE **Absolut. Ich freu mich aufs Schwimmen.**
Ăbsŏlūt. Ĭch froi mĭch oufs shvĭmĕn.

Dann können wir ein Boot mieten.
Dăn kŏnĕn vīr ein bōt mēētĕn.

ANTON **Was tust du später?**
Văs tōōst dōō shpāyter?

SUSIE **Ich muß meine Mutter besuchen.**
Ĭch mōōss meinĕ mōōttĕr bĕzōōchĕn.

ANTON **Warum mußt du sie besuchen?**
Vărōōm mōōst dōō zēē bĕzōōchĕn?

SUSIE   **Sie ist krank.**
Zēē ĭst krănk.

ANTON   **Was fehlt ihr?**
Văs fāylt ēēr?

SUSIE   **Nicht viel. Aber sie fühlt sich nicht wohl.**
Nĭcht fēēl. Aabĕr zēē fūlt zĭch nĭcht vōl.

ANTON   **Was sagt der Doktor?**
Văs sāagt dĕr dŏctōr?

SUSIE   **Sie soll im Bett bleiben und Medizin nehmen.**
Zēē sŏl ĭm bĕt bleibĕn ōōnd mĕdĭtsēēn nāymĕn.

ANTON   **Braucht sie jemanden?**
Broucht zēē yāymăndĕn?

SUSIE   **Nein, sie hat ja kein Fieber.**
Nine, zēē hăt yā kein fēēbĕr.

ANTON   **Soll ich dich morgen vom Büro abholen?**
Sŏl ĭch dĭch mŏrgĕn fŏm bŭrō ăbhōlĕn?

Ich komme gern.
Ĭch kŏme gĕrn.

SUSIE   **Ja, natürlich. Vielleicht können wir tanzen gehn.**
Yā, nătürlĭch. Fīleicht kŏnĕn vīr tăntsĕn gāyn.

ANTON   **In der Stadt oder am Strand?**
Ĭn dĕr shtăt ōder ăm shtrănd?

SUSIE   **In der Stadt. Vielleicht können Karl und**
Ĭn dĕr shtăt. Fīleicht kŏnĕn Kărl ōōnd

Nora mitkommen. Er ist ein guter Tänzer,
Nōră mĭtkŏmĕn. Air ĭst ein gōōter tĕntsĕr

und sie ist eine nette Frau.
ōōnd zēē ĭst eine nĕtĕ frow.

Please note: All nouns and words used as nouns are capitalized in German.

When is a German vowel long? When is it short?

später	**Boot**	**zehn**	**mieten**
shpāyter	bōt	tsāyn	mēēten
later	boat	ten	to rent

A vowel (or umlaut) is long if it is followed by a single consonant (*t* in *später*); if it is doubled (*oo* in *Boot*); if it is followed by a silent *h* (*h* in *zehn*); if it is followed by a silent *e* (*e* in *mieten*).

schwimmen	**Wetter**	**tanzen**
shvĭmĕn	vĕttĕr	tăntsĕn
to swim	weather	to dance

A vowel is short if it is followed by more than one consonant; it is also short if it is an *e* in the last syllable of a word that ends with an *-en* or *-er,* as shown.

Sometimes the German *e* sound was transcribed with an *ay,* as in *geh* (*gay*—go) or the German *o* sound with an *ō.* As mentioned before, there is no off-glide sound.

Also, there is no *y* sound in front of the German *u.* Examples: The German word *Uhr* (watch, clock) is pronounced *oor,* not *yoor.* The German verb *fuhr* (drove) sounds like *foor,* not *fyoor.*

The letter *ß,* or *scharfes s,* is pronounced like *ss,* as in *Kuß* (kiss). Although you will still see it, this letter is being phased out. Traditionally it replaced *ss* before consonants and at the end of a word. It is now acceptable to write *ss* instead.

The combination *chs* is pronounced *ks* in words like **sechs** (six) or **Luchs** (lynx).

In words with a *gn* or a *kn* *both* consonants are sounded, as in the German **Knie** (knee) or **Gnade** (mercy). Do not say **Kenie** or **Genade.** There is no pause between the *K* and the *n,* or between the *G* and the *n. Do not* insert a vowel (like a short *e*) between the consonants.

The *ck* sounds exactly like a *k,* as in **Sack** (sack).

Das deutsche Alphabet
Dăs doitche ălfăbāyt
The German alphabet

German letter	pronounced like
a	ah (as in *father*)
b	bay
c	tsay (today used mostly in words with a *ch* or *sch*)
d	day
e	eh (no off-glide sound)
f	ef
g	gay
h	haa (rhymes with *baa*)
i	ee (rhymes with *sea*)
j	yot
k	kaa (rhymes with *blah*)
l	el
m	em
n	en
o	oh (no off-glide sound; pronounced as in *old*)
p	pay
q	koo
r	err (roll it most of the time)
s	ess (voiced before vowels, it is pronounced "z," as in *zeal*)
t	tay
u	oo (rhymes with *boo*)
v	fou (as in *foul*; rhymes with *sow*)
w	vay
x	iks (rhymes with *six*)
y	üpsilon (accent on the first syllable)
z	tsett

Y is a rare letter in German. It should always be pronounced like an *ü* as in **Zylinder** (*tsülinder,* top hat) or **Ägypten** (*āygüpten,* Egypt). It also occurs as the end vowel in first names like *Anny, Fanny, Pauly,* etc. It is then pronounced like a long *i.*

There is a Pronunciation Guide at the end of the book.

The following tongue twister provides good practice for the student struggling with the *v*'s and *w*'s. Remember, the German *w* sounds like the English *v.*

Wir Wiener Waschweiber würden weiße Wäsche
Vēēr vēēněr văshveiběr vŭrděn veisse věshě
We Viennese washerwomen would white laundry

waschen, wenn wir wüßten, wo warmes, weiches
văshěn, věn vēēr vŭssten, vō vărměs, veichěs
wash, if we knew where warm, soft

Wasser wäre.
văsser văyrě.
water was.

Jokes featuring Germans pronouncing English *w* like a *v* as in "Vitch vay vent de vest vint?", were for a long time the stock-in-trade of vaudeville comedians. Here is an example:

A young housewife who did not have much money to spend asked a German butcher the price of some hamburger steak. "Vitch von?" he wanted to know. "Zis von or zat von?" She pointed it out to him.

"A dollar a pound," he said.

"But," she replied, "at the store across the street they charge only fifty cents."

"Vel," asked Franz, "vy don't you buy it from zem?"

"They are out of it," she explained.

"Aha," answered the butcher. "Ven I am out of it, I sell it for tventy-fife cents."

EXERCISES: Try to do them on your own. If you get desperate, look up the answers in the key at the end of the book.

1. The *ch* in **ich** sounds like the first letter of
     a. kind   b. huge   c. chop
2. The *w* in **schwimmen** is pronounced like the first letter of
     a. wisdom   b. whether   c. vain
3. The *au* in **glaube** sounds like the vowel sound in
     a. mouse   b. taught   c. food
4. The *z* in **zehn** reminds you of
     a. zip   b. pizza   c. silk
5. The *u* in **Uhr** is like the sound in
     a. lure   b. unit   c. unload
6. The *eu* in **heute** reminds you of the sound in
     a. road   b. boy   c. Hugh
7. The *ch* in **besuchen** is the sound that you hear in
     a. loch   b. Hugo   c. macho
8. The *ei* in **meine** reminds you of
     a. keen   b. mean   c. fine
9. The *a* in **krank** rhymes with
     a. crank   b. honk   c. song
10. The *eh* in **fehlt** rhymes with
      a. mailed   b. field   c. held
11. The *v* in **viel** is the same as the first letter of
      a. veal   b. foal   c. will
12. The *j* in **jemanden** sounds like the first letter of
      a. John   b. gypsy   c. yonder
13. The *g* in **gern** is pronounced like the g in
      a. goose   b. gentle   c. ginger
14. The *st* in **Stadt** sounds like
      a. *sht*   b. *st*   c. *ts*
15. The *ö* in **können** reminds you of the sound in
      a. gone   b. pen   c. curse
16. The name of the German letter *x* is:
      a. *iks*   b. eggs   c. *aks*
17. The *chs* in **Büchse** (box) sounds like
      a. *sh*   b. *gs*   c. *ks*
18. The German *y* in **Zypern** (Cyprus) is pronounced like
      a. *ü*   b. *i*   c. *u*
19. You pronounce the word **Knödel** (dumpling) like
      a. **Nödel**   b. **Knödel**   c. **Kenödel**
20. You pronounce the word **Gnom** (gnome, a dwarf) like
      a. noun   b. genoum   c. gnohm

CHAPTER 2

Anton und seine nette Nachbarin, Frau Müller
Anton and His Nice Neighbor, Mrs. Müller

The Article (*the* book, *a* book)

1. The Definite Article—*der, die, das*, etc. (the)

Abbreviations:

Genders

m   masculine (man)
f   feminine (woman)
n   neuter (thing)

Numbers

sing.   singular (one man)
pl.   plural (two or more men)

Cases

nom.	nominative	subject or predicate nominative: *The man* (subject) is tall. He is *a tall man*. (predicate nominative)
gen.	genitive	(in English, also called possessive): the face *of the man* or *the man's* face (possessive: belonging to the man)
dat.	dative	(better known in English as the indirect object): He gives it *to the man*. (To whom does he give it?)
acc.	accusative	(better known in English as the direct object): He sees *the man*. (Whom does he see?)

At this point we should also mention the fact that the prepositions (such as *in, at, on, for;* in German: *in, an, auf, für* etc.) control the case forms of their objects. In Chapter 6 you will learn that prepositions govern cases other than the nominative.

In German all nouns (words that are the names of something) are either masculine, feminine, or neuter. Male persons are naturally masculine; female persons, feminine (there are a few exceptions that can, for the time being, safely be ignored); things can be either masculine, feminine, or neuter. Please try to memorize the article along with the noun: *der Mann,* the man; *die Frau,* the woman; *das Ding,* the thing; *der Strand, die Stadt.* The last two are things, yet one is masculine, the other feminine.

Die Wohnung   (The Apartment) I

Der Eisschrank **(m)** (ice shronk)
  in der Küche **(f)** *des* Mannes ist
  immer voll.
In *dem* großen Kasten **(m)** im
  Wohnzimmer **(n)** sind
  viele Bücher **(n)**.
Den kleineren Raum **(m)**
  benutzt er als
  Schlafzimmer **(n)**.

The refrigerator
  in the kitchen of the man (in the
  man's kitchen) is always full.
In the big cabinet in the
  living room there are
  many books.
The smaller room
  he uses as
  a bedroom.

Please note: **Eisschrank** is a compound noun: **Eis** (n) and **Schrank** (m). The last noun, **Schrank,** determines the gender of the whole word. Wherever the natural gender is obvious, the notation *m, f,* or *n* has often been omitted.

These are the four cases of the masculine singular (m. sing.):

nom.:	*der* Eisschrank	the refrigerator (subject)
gen.:	*des* Mannes	of the man
dat.:	*dem* Kasten	(in) the cabinet
acc.:	*den* Raum	the room (direct object)

Die Wohnung   (The Apartment) II

Die Küche ist klein,
  aber nett.
Das Bild *der* Mutter
  hängt an *der* Wand **(f)**.
Von ihr bekam er *die*
  Geschirrspülmaschine **(f)**
  (geshirrshpülmasheene).
Seine Mutter ist leider
  tot.

The kitchen is small
  but nice.
The picture of the mother
  hangs on the wall.
From her he received the
  dishwasher.

His mother unfortunately
  is dead.

These are the four cases of the feminine singular (f. sing.):

nom.:	*die* Küche	the kitchen (subject)
gen.:	*der* Mutter	of the mother
dat.:	*der* Wand	(on) the wall
acc.:	*die* Geschirrspülmaschine	the dishwasher (direct object)

die Wohnung   (The Apartment) III

Das Fenster in der Küche
  ist immer offen, auch das
  des Badezimmers **(n)**. *Dem*
  Putzmädchen **(n)** öffnet er
  die Hauseingangstür **(f)**
  (houseingongstür) **von**
  oben. Man betritt *das*
  Wohnzimmer vom
  Flur **(m)**.

The window in the kitchen
  is always open, also that
  of (the one in) the bathroom.
  For the cleaning girl he
  opens the house entrance
  door from above. One
  enters the living room
  from the corridor.

These are the four cases of the neuter singular (n. sing.):

nom.:	*das* Fenster	the window (subject)
gen.:	*des* Badezimmers	of the bathroom
dat.:	*dem* Putzmädchen	for the cleaning girl
acc.:	*das* Wohnzimmer	the living room (direct object)

Die Wohnung   (The Apartment) IV

Die **Preise (m)** *der*
   **Wohnungen (f) sind hier
   ziemlich hoch. Anton zahlt
   Frau Müller und** *den*
   **Besitzern (m) die Miete (f)
   am Anfang (m) des
   Monats (m). Dann bezahlt
   er auch** *die* **Rechnungen (f)
   für Strom (m), Gas (n)
   und Telephon (n).**

The prices of the
   apartments are here
   rather high. Anton pays
   Mrs. Müller and the
   owners the rent at the
   beginning of the month.
   Then he pays also the
   bills for electricity,
   gas, and telephone.

These are the four cases of the plural. Please note that the same four forms are used for all three genders.

nom.:	*die* **Preise**	the prices (subject)
gen.:	*der* **Wohnungen**	of the apartments
dat.:	*den* **Besitzern**	(to) the owners
acc.:	*die* **Rechnungen**	the bills (direct object)

Anton und Frau Müller, I

2. The Indefinite Article—*ein, eine, einen,* etc. (a, an)

In English we have only one form for the indefinite article, *a* or *an*, which is used for somebody or something that is not specified. Examples: *A* man was here. He gave him *an* answer.

Anton ist *ein* **netter
   Mensch und er macht auch
   den Eindruck (m)** *eines*
   netten Kerls. *Einem* **Mann
   wie ihm ist man immer
   gewogen; er hat**
   einen **guten Sinn (m) für
   Humor.**

Anton is a nice
   man and he gives also
   the impression of a
   nice guy. To a man
   like him one is always
   kindly disposed; he has
   a good sense of humor.

Masculine

nom.:	*ein* **Mensch**	a man (predicate nom.)
gen.:	*eines* **Kerls**	of a guy
dat.:	*einem* **Mann**	(to) a man
acc.:	*einen* **Sinn**	a sense (direct object)

Anton und Frau Müller, II

Frau Müller ist *eine* **sehr
   hilfsbereite Nachbarin.
   Sie hat das Benehmen (n)**
   einer **liebenswürdigen Dame.
   Sie klopft an und betritt
   Antons Wohnung mit**
   einer **herzlichen Miene (f)
   und bringt ihm** *eine*
   **Zeitung (f). Sie behandelt
   ihn wie einen Sohn.**

Mrs. Müller is a very
   cooperative neighbor.
   She has the manners
   of a kind lady.
   She knocks and enters
   Anton's apartment with
   an affectionate look
   and brings him a
   newspaper. She treats
   him like a son.

Feminine

nom.:	*eine* Nachbarin	a neighbor (predicate nom.)
gen.:	*einer* Dame	of a lady
dat.:	*einer* Miene	(with) a look
acc.:	*eine* Zeitung	a newspaper (direct object)

Anton und Frau Müller, III

Ein Buch liegt auf dem Frühstückstisch (m), auch das Bild *eines* Mädchens. Mit *einem* höflichen Nicken (n) steht er auf und bietet ihr *ein* Glas (n) Tee (m) an.	A book lies on the breakfast table, also the picture of a girl. With a polite nod he gets up and offers her a glass of tea.

Neuter

nom.:	*ein* Buch	a book (subject)
gen.:	*eines* Mädchens	of a girl
dat.:	*einem* Nicken	(with) a nod
acc.:	*ein* Glas	a glass (direct object)

Please note: **Antons Wohnung** (Anton's apartment) = **die Wohnung des Anton.** There is *no* apostrophe (') in the German version.

Additional Vocabulary

was ist, was sind?	what is, what are?
wie ist, wie sind?	how is, how are?
wo ist, wo sind?	where is, where are?
wer hat?	who has?
wer ist, wer sind?	who is, who are?
wie heißt?	what is the name of?
wann waren Sie?	when were you?

EXERCISE 1 Fill in the missing articles.

1. _____ kleineren Raum benutzt er als Schlafzimmer.
   the
2. **Das Bild** _____ **Mutter hängt an der Wand.**
   of the
3. _____ **Fenster ist offen.**
   the, sing.
4. **In** _____ **großen Kasten sind Bücher.**
   the
5. **Von ihr bekam er** _____ **Geschirrspülmaschine.**
   the
6. **In der Küche** _____ **Mannes**
   of the
7. **Das Bild an** _____ **Wand**
   the
8. **Die Preise** _____ **Wohnungen**
   of the
9. **Anton zahlt** _____ **Besitzern** _____ **Miete.**
   to the   the
10. **Man betritt** _____ **Wohnzimmer.**
    the
11. **Anton hat** _____ **guten Sinn für Humor.**
    a
12. **Mit** _____ **höflichen Nicken**
    a

13. **Er macht den Eindruck** _____ **netten Kerls.**
                                                   of a
14. **Das Benehmen** _____ **liebenswürdigen Dame**
                                of a
15. **Anton bietet ihr** _____ **Glas Tee an.**
                                    a

EXERCISE 2 Fill in the correct _definite_ article (nom. sing.).

1. _____ **Mann**   7. _____ **Wohnzimmer**
2. _____ **Mutter**   8. _____ **Mädchen**
3. _____ **Kasten**   9. _____ **Dame**
4. _____ **Wand**   10. _____ **Kerl**
5. _____ **Fenster**   11. _____ **Glas**
6. _____ **Raum**   12. _____ **Eisschrank**

EXERCISE 3 Fill in the correct _indefinite_ article (nom. sing.)

1. _____ **Geschirrspülmaschine**
2. _____ **Küche**
3. _____ **Badezimmer**   6. _____ **Mutter**
4. _____ **Dame**   7. _____ **Kasten**
5. _____ **Eisschrank**   8. _____ **Putzmädchen**

EXERCISE 4 Answer in German.

1. **Wo ist der Eisschrank?**
2. **Wo sind viele Bücher?**
3. **Was ist immer offen?**
4. **Was zahlt er den Besitzern?**
5. **Wie heißt die Nachbarin?**
6. **Wer hat einen Sinn für Humor?**

EXERCISE 5 Write the following sentences in German.

1. There are many books in the cabinet.
2. He received the dishwasher from the mother.
3. The refrigerator is in the kitchen.
4. Anton pays the rent.
5. The prices are high.
6. Mrs. Müller is a cooperative neighbor.
7. He opens the house entrance door.
8. The window is always open.
9. He enters the livingroom.
10. He offers her a glass of tea.

EXERCISE 6 Finish the following sentences with the missing word.

1. **Im Kasten sind viele** _____.
2. **Die Küche ist klein, aber** _____.
3. **Er betritt das Zimmer vom** _____.
4. **Er bezahlt die** _____.
5. **Er öffnet die** _____.
6. **Die Preise der Wohnungen sind** _____.
7. **Von ihr bekam er die** _____.
8. **Den kleineren Raum benutzt er als** _____.
9. **Das Fenster ist immer** _____.
10. **Der Eisschrank ist immer** _____.

EXERCISE 7 Choose the correct word.

1. **Frau Müller bringt ihm**
   a. **eine Zeitung**   b. **ein Glas Tee**   c. **Bücher**
2. **Auf dem Frühstückstisch liegt**
   a. **ein Putzmädchen**   b. **ein Bild**   c. **eine Rechnung**
3. **Von Mutter bekam er**
   a. **Bücher**   b. **einen Kasten**   c. **die Geschirrspülmaschine**

4. **An der Wand hängt ein Bild**
   a. **des Wohnzimmers** b. **der Mutter** c. **der Hauseingangstür**
5. **Sie betritt die Wohnung vom**
   a. **Flur** b. **Badezimmer** c. **Schlafzimmer**
6. **In der Küche**
   a. **sind viele Bücher** b. **ist der Eisschrank**
   c. **ist ein großer Kasten**

EXERCISE 8 True or false?   T / F

1. **In dem großen Kasten sind viele Bilder.** ——
2. **Der Eisschrank ist in der Küche.** ——
3. **Das Bild der Mutter hängt an der Geschirrspülmaschine** ——
4. **Er bezahlt die Rechnung für die Bücher.** ——
5. **Er hat einen guten Sinn für Humor.** ——
6. **Frau Müller bringt ihm Medizin.** ——
7. **Das Fenster im Badezimmer ist immer offen.** ——
8. **Er bezahlt den Besitzern die Miete.** ——
9. **Den kleineren Raum benutzt er als Küche.** ——
10. **Sie klopft an und betritt das Badezimmer.** ——

Ein Dialog

(A Dialog)

FRAU MÜLLER Guten Morgen (m), Herr Anton. Haben Sie gut geschlafen?

Good morning, Mr. Anton. Did you sleep well?

ANTON Danke, sehr gut. Und Sie?

Thank you, very well. And you?

FRAU MÜLLER Ausgezeichnet. Aber ich schlafe immer gut.

Fine. But I always sleep well.

ANTON Ich auch; besonders heute.

Me too; especially today.

FRAU MÜLLER Sie meinen, weil es Samstag (m) ist? Kein Büro?

You mean because it is Saturday? No office?

ANTON Genau.

Exactly.

FRAU MÜLLER Das Wetter ist sehr schön. Die Sonne scheint und keine Wolke (f) am Himmel (m).

The weather is very beautiful. The sun is shining, and there's not a cloud in the sky.

ANTON Wunderbar.

Wonderful.

FRAU MÜLLER Ich bin sehr froh. Die letzten paar Tage (m) hat es zuviel geregnet.

I am very glad. The last few days it has rained too much.

ANTON Stimmt.

That's true.

FRAU MÜLLER Trinken Sie, bitte, den Tee; der wird sonst kalt.

Please drink the tea; it'll get cold otherwise.

ANTON Richtig. Vielen Dank (m) für die Zeitung.

Right. Many thanks for the paper.

FRAU MÜLLER Keine Ursache (f).

Don't mention it.

ANTON Etwas Neues (n) drin?

Any news in it?

FRAU MÜLLER Nicht der Rede (f) wert.

Nothing worth talking about.

Please note: another word for **Samstag** is **Sonnabend**.

Ein and *kein*

kein Büro (n)	no office	**kein Besitzer (m)**	no owner
keine Wolke (f)	no cloud	**keine Zeitung (f)**	no paper

The endings are the same as in *ein/eine/ein*. There is also a plural: *keine,* **keiner, keinen. Keine Büros, Wolken,** etc.

Additional Vocabulary

Ich schlafe schlecht.	I sleep badly.
Ich bin sehr traurig.	I am very sad.
Ich trinke Kaffee (m) oder Milch.	I drink coffee or milk.
Ich schlafe kaum.	I hardly sleep.
Ich bin guter Laune (f).	I am in a good mood.

EXERCISE 9 Fill in the missing words.
1. **Guten** _____, **Herr Anton.**
   morning
2. **Das** _____ **ist sehr schön.**
   weather
3. **Die** _____ **Tage hat es geregnet.**
   last few
4. **Ich bin** _____.
   very glad
5. **Sie meinen, weil es** _____ **ist?**
   Saturday
6. **Keine Wolke am** _____
   sky
7. _____ **für die Zeitung**
   Many thanks
8. **Ich bin sehr** _____.
   sad

EXERCISE 10 Complete each sentence or phrase with one of the words listed here: **ist, Sonne, Tage, keine, Rede, zuviel, sehr, bitte.**
1. **Das Wetter** _____ **sehr schön.**
2. _____ **Wolke am Himmel**
3. **Die letzten** _____
4. **Trinken Sie** _____ **den Tee.**
5. **Nicht der** _____ **wert**
6. **Es hat** _____ **geregnet.**
7. **Danke,** _____ **gut**
8. **Die** _____ **scheint.**

EXERCISE 11 Write the following in German:
1. I always sleep well.
2. The sun is shining.
3. Many thanks for the paper.
4. Don't mention it.
5. Please, drink the tea.
6. No office?
7. Nothing worth talking about
8. Because it is Saturday?
9. Exactly
10. I am very glad.

EXERCISE 12 Translate the following into English.
1. **Ausgezeichnet**
2. **Besonders heute**
3. **Trinken Sie, bitte, den Tee.**
4. **Etwas Neues drin?**

5. **Keine Wolke am Himmel**
6. **Danke, sehr gut**
7. **Wunderbar**
8. **Guten Morgen, Herr Anton**

EXERCISE 13 Fill in the missing letters.
1. **AUSGE__EIC__NET**
2. **K__INE __OLKE**
3. **SAM__TAG**
4. **KE__N B__RO?**
5. **W__NDERB__R**
6. **DAS WET__ER IST SC__ÖN**
7. **DIE LET__TEN TA__E**
8. **DIE SON__E SCH__INT**
9. **ET__AS N__UES?**
10. **NI__HT DER RE__E WE__T**

EXERCISE 14 Choose the correct article.
1. _____Sonne scheint.
2. _____Tee wird kalt.
3. _____Wetter ist schön.
4. _____Büro ist nett.
5. _____Zeitung ist hier.
6. _____letzten Tage hat es geregnet.

EXERCISE 15 Answer in complete German sentences.
1. **Wie ist das Wetter?**
2. **Wo ist keine Wolke?**
3. **Was trinkt Anton?**
4. **Wie heißt die Nachbarin?**
5. **Was scheint am Himmel?**
6. **Wer bringt die Zeitung?**

EXERCISE 16 Construct sentences using the cue words.
1. **Haben / geschlafen?**
2. **Sonne / Wolke / Himmel**
3. **Danke / Zeitung**
4. **Tage / geregnet**
5. **Ich / froh**
6. **weil / Samstag**

EXERCISE 17 Choose the correct word according to the text.
1. **Heute ist**
   a. **kein Samstag**   b. **kein Büro**   c. **keine Zeitung**
2. **Vielen Dank für**
   a. **die Wolke**   b. **das Wetter**   c. **die Zeitung**
3. **Frau Müller ist sehr**
   a. **schön**   b. **froh**   c. **genau**
4. **Anton trinkt**
   a. **Kaffee**   b. **Tee**   c. **Milch**

EXERCISE 18 True or false?   T / F
1. **Frau Müller schläft immer schlecht.** _____
2. **Sie ist immer traurig.** _____
3. **Am Samstag geht er ins Büro.** _____
4. **Heute trinkt Anton Tee.** _____
5. **Die letzten Tage hat es nicht geregnet.** _____
6. **Das Wetter ist heute sehr schlecht.** _____
7. **Keine Wolke am Himmel** _____
8. **Anton hat kaum geschlafen.** _____
9. **Die Sonne scheint.** _____

Ein Witz

ANTON Soll ich Ihnen etwas von dem Buchhalter in unserem Büro erzählen?

FRAU MÜLLER Ja, bitte.

ANTON Also gestern tritt er plötzlich auf unsere hübsche Stenotypistin zu, packt sie und küßt sie. In dem Augenblick kommt der Chef herein und sagt: "Dafür zahle ich Ihnen?" Was glauben Sie, Frau Müller, antwortet ihm der Buchhalter?

FRAU MÜLLER Ich bin gespannt.

ANTON "Nein, das tue ich umsonst."

(A Joke)

Shall I tell you something about the bookkeeper in our office?

Yes, please.

Well, yesterday suddenly he steps up to our pretty typist, grabs her, and kisses her. At this moment the boss enters and says: "For this I'm paying you?" What do you think, Mrs. Müller, does the bookkeeper tell him?

I am anxious to know.

"No, this I do for free."

Note: We admit that the dialog between Anton and his landlady is less than brilliant—not exactly the stuff headlines are made of. Nevertheless, exchanging banalities about the weather, one's job, how one has slept, etc., affirms a common humanity and establishes rapport. Remember, we have to start somewhere. You can't expect these characters to be witty, complex, or intriguing if you know only 100 words of German, can you? When you've learned more German, you can give your imagination free rein and devise lurid, grotesque, or uplifting variations on the characters' doings. Then, for instance, you can transform Mrs. Müller into an axe-murderess with a cellar full of former tenants' corpses, or into a kind of angel or saint who guides, inspires, and ennobles her roomers in all aspects of their lives.

CHAPTER 3

Die Kusine aus Denver
The Cousin from Denver

The Noun

Nouns: words that are the names of persons, places, ideas, or things.

Kristy, Susie's American cousin, is her guest tonight along with Mother, Anton, and the Bauers (Nora and Karl).

Die Gäste kommen

The guests are coming

Kristy ist Susie Brauns
  Kusine aus Denver. Sie
  ist in Deutschland auf Besuch
  und wohnt bei Susie und
  ihrer Tante. Für heute Abend
  hat man Nora und Karl Bauer
  eingeladen und
  natürlich auch Susies Freund,
  Anton Gruber.
  Susies *Mutter* stellt die
  Teller (m) auf den Tisch (m).
  „Wo sind die Messer (n) und
  die Löffel (m)?" fragt Kristy.
  Da erinnert sie sich an einen
  Witz (m). „Frau Braun,
  womit rühren Sie
  Ihren Kaffee (m) um?" „Mit
  meiner rechten Hand." "Das ist
  komisch," erwidert Kristy.
  „Ich benutze einen Löffel."
  Die *Mädchen* (n) helfen den
  Tisch decken. Das *Wetter*
  ist schön, die *Fenster* (n)
  sind weit offen. Man hört
  einen *Wagen* (m) vorfahren.

Kristy is Susie Braun's
  cousin from Denver. She
  is in Germany on a visit
  and lives at Susie's and
  her aunt's. For this evening
  they have invited Nora and
  Karl Bauer and,
  naturally, also Susie's
  boyfriend, Anton Gruber.
  Susie's mother puts the
  plates on the table.
  "Where are the knives and
  the spoons?" asks Kristy.
  Then she remembers a
  joke. "Mrs. Braun, with
  what do you stir
  your coffee?" "With
  my right hand." "That is
  funny," replies Kristy.
  "I use a spoon."
  The girls help to set
  the table. The weather
  is beautiful, the windows
  are wide open. One hears
  a car drive up.

Most English nouns add *-s* or *-es* to the singular to form the plurals: *book, books, grass, grasses.* In terms of forming plurals, German nouns belong to one of five groups. The nouns printed in italics in the foregoing text belong to Group 1.

Masculine Nouns

	SINGULAR	PLURAL
nom.:	der Teller	die Teller
gen.:	des Tellers	der Teller
dat.:	dem Teller	den Teller*n*
acc.:	den Teller	die Teller

17

Feminine Nouns

	SINGULAR	PLURAL
nom.:	die Mutter	die Mütter
gen.:	der Mutter	der Mütter
dat.:	der Mutter	den Müttern
acc.:	die Mutter	die Mütter

Neuter Nouns

	SINGULAR	PLURAL
nom.:	das Mädchen	die Mädchen
gen.:	des Mädchens	der Mädchen
dat.:	dem Mädchen	den Mädchen
acc.:	das Mädchen	die Mädchen

Most of these nouns end with *-chen, -lein, -er, -el* or *-en;* they do not change in the plural, except for adding *-n* in the dative (unless they end with it to begin with: *den Mädchen*). Some nouns take an umlaut in the plural: *Mutter/Mütter; Tochter/Töchter* (daughter); *Bruder/Brüder* (brother); *Vater/Väter* (father); *Mantel/Mäntel* (overcoat) (m).
Note: das Fräulein/die Fräulein (Miss).

EXERCISE 1 Fill in the missing German words.
1. **Wo sind** _____?
   the knives and the spoons
2. _____ **sind weit offen.**
   The windows
3. **Sie stellt** _____ **auf den Tisch.**
   the plates
4. **Susie hat** _____.
   a car
5. **Sie ist Frau** _____.
   Braun's daughter
6. _____ **helfen.**
   The girls
7. _____ **Kristy hat blaue Augen.**
   Miss

EXERCISE 2 Write the following sentences in German.
1. Kristy spends a month in Germany.
2. Where are the plates and the spoons?
3. Susie has a boyfriend.
4. She is Mrs. Braun's daughter.
5. Kristy has two brothers.
6. That is funny.
7. The weather is very beautiful.
8. One hears a car.
9. Mrs. Braun is the mother of a girl.

EXERCISE 3 Answer in complete German sentences.
1. **Wo verbringt Kristy ihre Ferien?**
2. **Wer ist Frau Brauns Tochter?**
3. **Wie heißt Susies Freund?**
4. **Was stellt Susies Mutter auf den Tisch?**
5. **Was hört man vorfahren?**
6. **Wer hilft Frau Braun?**
7. **Wer erzählt einen Witz?**

EXERCISE 4 Choose the correct word or words.
1. **Kristy ist die Kusine von**
   - a. **Susie**
   - b. **Anton**
   - c. **Frau Braun**
2. **Die Teller liegen auf dem**
   - a. **Wagen**
   - b. **Eisschrank**
   - c. **Tisch**
3. **Für kaltes Wetter benutzt man**
   - a. **einen Mantel**
   - b. **einen Löffel**
   - c. **ein Messer**
4. **Wer ist Frau Brauns Tochter?**
   - a. **Kristy**
   - b. **Susie**
   - c. **Nora**
5. **Kristy ist auf Ferien in**
   - a. **England**
   - b. **Schweden**
   - c. **Deutschland**

Vor der Mahlzeit

Nora und Karl sind
  Susies Freunde. Sie und
  Anton sind gerade
  angekommen.

NORA (to Kristy) **Sehr nett,**
  Sie wiederzusehen.
  Wann waren Sie zuletzt
  in Deutschland?

KRISTY **Vor dreizehn *Jahren* (n).**

KARL **Sie sprechen sehr gut**
  Deutsch.

KRISTY **Finden Sie? Aber ich**
  habe doch einen
  amerikanischen *Akzént* (m).

ANTON **Behalt ihn! Er klingt**
  sehr nett.

SUSIE **Darf ich Euch etwas**
  Wein (m) anbieten? Oder
  ein *Stück* Obst (n)?

KRISTY (to Nora and Karl) **Haben**
  Sie noch die zwei *Hunde* (m)?

NORA **Sie meinen Pipsi und Putzi,**
  die weißen Pudel (m)?

KRISTY **Die waren so herzig.**

NORA **Ja, die sind tot.**

KRISTY **Schade, ich hab' sie so**
  gern im Arm (m)
  gehalten.

Before the Meal

Nora and Karl are
  Susie's friends. She and
  Anton have just
  arrived.

Very nice to
  see you again.
  When were you in
  Germany last?

Thirteen years ago.

You speak German
  very well.

Do you think so? But
  I have an American
  accent.

Keep it! It sounds
  very nice.

May I offer you
  some wine? Or
  a piece of fruit?

Do you still have
  the two dogs?

You mean Pipsi and Putzi,
  the white poodles?

They were so cute.

Yes, they are dead.

That's a pity. I
  liked to hold them
  in my arms.

The italicized nouns belong to Group 2. They add *-e* to the singular to form the plural. Some of them use the umlaut (like ***Frucht, Früchte*** (f), fruit). Many consist of only one syllable.

Additional Vocabulary

die Hand, Hände	hand
der Sohn, Söhne	son
der Zug, Züge	train

Here are three examples representative of nouns that belong to Group 2:

Masculine Nouns

	SINGULAR	PLURAL
nom.:	**der Freund**	**die Freunde**
gen.:	**des Freundes**	**der Freunde**
dat.:	**dem Freund**	**den Freunden**
acc.:	**den Freund**	**die Freunde**

Feminine Nouns

	SINGULAR	PLURAL
nom.:	**die Hand**	**die Hände**
gen.:	**der Hand**	**der Hände**
dat.:	**der Hand**	**den Händen**
acc.:	**die Hand**	**die Hände**

Neuter Nouns

	SINGULAR	PLURAL
nom.:	**das Jahr**	**die Jahre**
gen.:	**des Jahres**	**der Jahre**
dat.:	**dem Jahr**	**den Jahren**
acc.:	**das Jahr**	**die Jahre**

EXERCISE 5 Answer with complete sentences in German.
1. **Wer sind Susies Freunde?**
2. **Wo sind Noras Pudel?**
3. **Wie hießen sie?**
4. **Wann war sie zuletzt in Deutschland?**
5. **Wie waren die Hunde?**

EXERCISE 6 Complete the following sentences.
1. **Nora, Karl und Anton sind gerade _____.**
2. **Susies Mutter stellt die Teller auf den _____.**
3. **Darf ich Ihnen etwas Wein _____?**
4. **Die Hunde sind leider _____.**
5. **Sie hat einen amerikanischen _____.**
6. **Behalt ihn! Er klingt sehr _____.**
7. **Sehr nett, Sie _____.**

EXERCISE 7 Fill in the correct endings.
1. **Vor vielen Jahr_____**
2. **Er hat zwei Hund_____.**
3. **Er tut es mit den Händ_____.**
4. **Die Söhn_____ sind hier.**
5. **Sie kommen mit den Züg_____.**
6. **Sie hat zwei Stück_____ in der Hand.**

EXERCISE 8 Fill in the missing letters in the German words.
1. **VOR DRE__ZE__N JA__REN**
2. **EIN STÜ__K OBS__**

3. SIE SP__ECHEN GUT D__UTSCH
4. GER__DE ANGE__OMMEN
5. SUSIES FRE__NDE
6. SIE WI__DERZUSE__EN
7. MIT KEINEM A__ZENT

EXERCISE 9 Write the following in German.
1. Thirteen years ago
2. Do you think so?
3. They were so cute.
4. Nice to see you again.
5. That's a pity.
6. Keep it.
7. Anton has just arrived.

Nach dem Essen

**Nach dem Essen (n) gehen
Susie und ihre Gäste (m) ins
Wohnzimmer (n) und machen
es sich bequem. Mutter
Braun wäscht indessen das
Geschirr (n) und die
Gläser (n) in der Küche.
Die *Männer* rauchen, Anton eine
Zigarette (f), Karl eine
Pfeife (f). Die Damen rauchen
nicht, außer Kristy.**

KARL (to Susie, pointing at the
wall) **Sind das neue *Bilder*?**

SUSIE **Ja, ich habe sie vorige
Woche (f) gekauft. Auch
diese *Bücher* (n). Einen
Roman (m) über japanische
Kinder (n) und einen über
mexikanische *Götter* (m),
beide sehr interessant.**

ANTON (to Kristy) **Wie lange
bleibst du hier?**

KRISTY **Ich weiß noch nicht.
Wahrscheinlich bis
Dezember (m).**

ANTON **Hier ist es kälter
als in Amerika.
Hast du genug
Winterkleider (n)
mitgebracht?**

KRISTY **Ich glaube schon.
Vielleicht kaufe ich mir
hier noch einen Pullover
(m).**

SUSIE ***Kinder*, wollt ihr etwas
spielen oder wollen wir
ein paar *Lieder* (n)
singen?**

After the Meal

After dinner Susie and
her guests go to the
living room and make
themselves comfortable.
Mother Braun meanwhile
washes the dishes and
glasses in the kitchen.
The men smoke, Anton a
cigarette, Karl a pipe.
The ladies do not smoke,
except Kristy.

Are these new
pictures?

Yes, I bought them
last week. Also
these books. A
novel about Japanese
children and one
about Mexican gods,
both very interesting.

How long will
you stay here?

I don't know yet.
Probably until
December.

Here it is colder
than in America.
Have you enough
winter clothing
taken along?

I think so.
Maybe I buy myself
here another pullover.

Children, do you want
to play something,
or shall we sing a
few songs?

The italicized nouns in the foregoing text belong to Group 3. They add *-er* to the singular to form the plural. They all take the umlaut in the plural.

Masculine Nouns

	SINGULAR	PLURAL
nom.:	**der Mann**	**die Männer**
gen.:	**des Mann**es	**der Männer**
dat.:	**dem Mann**	**den Männer**n
acc.:	**den Mann**	**die Männer**

Neuter Nouns

	SINGULAR	PLURAL
nom.:	**das Bild**	**die Bilder**
gen.:	**des Bild**es	**der Bilder**
dat.:	**dem Bild**	**den Bilder**n
acc.:	**das Bild**	**die Bilder**

Note: There are no feminine nouns in this group.

Additional Vocabulary

Haus, Häuser (n)   house
Volk, Völker (n)   people
Land, Länder (n)   country, land

EXERCISE 10 Choose the correct answer.
1. **Nach dem Essen gehen die Gäste**
   a. **in die Küche**   b. **ins Schlafzimmer**   c. **ins Wohnzimmer**
2. **Karl raucht**
   a. **nicht**   b. **eine Pfeife**   c. **eine Zigarette**
3. **Frau Braun wäscht**
   a. **Susies Bücher**   b. **ihre Hände**   c. **das Geschírr**
4. **Susie hat einen Roman über**
   a. **japanische Kinder**   b. **amerikanische Kinder**   c. **deutsche Kinder**
5. **Kristy kauft sich hier vielleicht**
   a. **ein Winterkleid**   b. **einen Pullover**
   c. **eine Geschirrspülmaschine**

EXERCISE 11 Match the following sentences:
1. **Karl raucht eine Pfeife.**   _____ Are those new pictures?
2. **Sind das neue Bilder?**   _____ Kristy has enough
3. **Die Romane sind**   winter clothing.
   interessant.   _____ Karl smokes a pipe.
4. **Kristy hat genug**   _____ She probably stays
   Winterkleider.   till December.
5. **Sie bleibt wahrscheinlich**   _____ The novels are
   bis Dezember.   interesting.

EXERCISE 12 Fill in the missing letter.
1. **Die GL__SER**
2. **Die B__CHER**
3. **Die KLE__DER**
4. **Die MÄN__ER**
5. **VIELLEI__HT**

EXERCISE 13 Write the following in German.
1. The guests make themselves comfortable.
2. I bought two books last week.
3. The men smoke.
4. I think so.
5. I don't know yet.

EXERCISE 14 True or false?   T / F
1. **Susie raucht.**   _____
2. **Frau Braun wäscht indessen das Geschirr.**   _____
3. **Karl raucht eine Pfeife.**   _____
4. **Nach dem Essen geht man in den Flur.**   _____
5. **Anton raucht nicht.**   _____

Anders in Amerika

Different in America

Nach dem Kartenspiel (n) sprechen sie über verschiedene Themen (n).

After the card game they speak about various topics.

KARL **Kristy, vergleich doch bitte die amerikanischen Männer mit den deutschen.**

Kristy, please compare the American men with the German ones.

KRISTY **In Deutschland sind die älteren Herren höflicher als in Amerika. Sie bringen den *Damen* oft *Blumen* (f) und Bonbons (n), verbeugen sich und küssen ihnen die Hand (f). Aber die alten *Herren* und die alten Bräuche (m) sterben langsam aus. Heute arbeiten und studieren mehr *Frauen* als früher, in allen Bereichen (m). Sie sind auch unternehmungslustiger und selbständiger in jeder *Hinsicht* (f). Die *Welt* (f) ist anders. Der Handkuß (m) ist zwar ganz kontinental, wie es im bekannten amerikanischen Lied (n) heißt. Aber damit kann man die *Miete* (f) nicht bezahlen. Viele junge *Menschen,* besonders die *Studenten* und *Studentinnen* auf den *Universitäten* (f), sind fast so wie in Amerika. Es gibt aber einige faszinierende Unterschiede (m).**

In Germany the older gentlemen are more polite than in America. They often bring the ladies flowers and candy, bow, and kiss their hand. But the old gentlemen and the old customs are slowly dying out. Today, more women work and study than formerly, in all fields. They are also more enterprising and more independent in every respect. The world is different. A kiss on the hand is certainly quite continental, as the well-known American song puts it. But you can't pay the rent with it. Many young people, especially the students (of both sexes) at the universities, are almost the same as in America. But there are some fascinating differences.

The italicized nouns of the above text belong to Group 4. They add -*n* or -*en* to the singular to form the plural.

Masculine Nouns

	SINGULAR	PLURAL
nom.:	**der Mensch**	**die Menschen**
gen.:	**des Menschen**	**der Menschen**
dat.:	**dem Menschen**	**den Menschen**
acc.:	**den Menschen**	**die Menschen**

Feminine Nouns

	SINGULAR	PLURAL
nom.:	die Blume	die Blumen
gen.:	der Blume	der Blumen
dat.:	der Blume	den Blumen
acc.:	die Blume	die Blumen

Neuter Nouns (irregular)

	SINGULAR	PLURAL
nom.:	das Herz (heart)	die Herzen
gen.:	des Herzens	der Herzen
dat.:	dem Herzen	den Herzen
acc.:	das Herz	die Herzen

Additional Vocabulary

Antwort (f)	answer	**Schwester (f)**	sister
Katze (f)	cat	**Straße (f)**	street
Präsident (m)	president	**Stunde (f)**	hour
Präsidentin (f)	president	**Tante (f)**	aunt
Schule (f)	school	**Tür (f)**	door

Note that some masculine nouns denoting persons form corresponding feminine nouns that end in -*in* (plural -*innen*). **Präsident,** shown above, is one of these nouns. Others are:

der Lehrer	die Lehrerin, -innen	teacher
der Freund	die Freundin, -innen	friend
der Student	die Studentin, -innen	student
der Photograph	die Photographin, -innen	photographer

EXERCISE 15 Fill in the missing German word endings.
1. **Wie sind die amerikanischen Zeitung_____?**
2. **Student_____ sind auf den Universität_____.**
3. **Die älteren Herr_____ sind höflicher.**
4. **Wir haben einen Präsident_____.**
5. **Die Tür_____ sind offen.**

EXERCISE 16 True or false?   T / F
1. **Frau Braun und Susie singen nach dem Kartenspiel.**   ____
2. **Die älteren Herren bringen den Damen oft Bonbons.**   ____
3. **Die Amerikaner küssen den Damen immer die Hand.**   ____
4. **Die Damen bringen den Herren Blumen.**   ____
5. **Viele ältere deutsche Männer verbeugen sich.**   ____

EXERCISE 17 Finish the sentences with the missing words.
1. **Die jungen Menschen in Deutschland sind so wie in _____.**
2. **Die älteren Herren in Deutschland sind _____.**
3. **Vergleichen Sie die deutschen Frauen mit den _____.**
4. **Studenten sind auf den _____.**
5. **Meine Damen und _____!**

EXERCISE 18 Translate the following into English.
1. **Nach dem Kartenspiel**
2. **Bitte vergleichen Sie.**
3. **Die Studenten auf den Universitäten**
4. **Die Schulen in Deutschland**
5. **Sie sprechen über verschiedene Themen.**

EXERCISE 19 Write the following in German.
1. They bow.
2. We have sisters.

3. She has two cats.
4. They often bring flowers.
5. The schools in America

Leben in Amerika   Life in America

KARL (to Kristy) **Du bist Lehrerin, nicht wahr?**
You are a teacher, aren't you?

KRISTY **Ja, schon seit sechs Jahren.**
Yes, for six years already.

KARL **Sind *Jobs* (m) jetzt in Amerika schwer zu finden?**
Are jobs hard to find in America now?

KRISTY **Ziemlich schwer. Besonders für Lehrerinnen. Ich habe Glück (n). Meine Stellung (f) ist relativ sicher.**
Pretty hard. Especially for (female) teachers. I am lucky. My position is relatively secure.

ANTON **Wohnst du allein?**
Do you live by yourself?

KRISTY **Mit einer Freundin. Wir teilen die Kosten. Die Wohnung ist sehr bequem, mit *Sofas* (n), *Radios* (n) und Fernsehern (m) in, praktisch gesprochen, jedem Zimmer, und einer herrlichen Aussicht (f) auf zwei *Parks* (m) und die Berge.**
With a girl friend. We share the costs. The apartment is very comfortable, with sofas, radios and TV sets in, practically speaking, every room, and a marvelous view of two parks and the mountains.

KARL **Das klingt wunderbar.**
That sounds wonderful.

KRISTY **Ja, ich bin sehr zufrieden.**
Yes, I am very satisfied.

ANTON **Hast du *Fotos* (n)?**
Do you have photos?

KRISTY **Jawohl; einen Moment (m). Hier.**
Yes, indeed; just a moment. Here.

KARL **Großartig!**
Excellent!

KRISTY **Danke. Ich photographiere sehr gern. Habe drei *Kameras* (f).**
Thank you. I like taking pictures very much. Have three cameras.

FRAU MÜLLER **Habt ihr auch eine Garage (f)?**
Do you have a garage, too?

KRISTY **Klar. Für zwei Autos.**
Sure. For two cars.

Fotos can also be spelled **Photos.**

The italicized nouns belong to Group 5. They are of foreign origin and add *-s* to the singular to form the plural.

Masculine Nouns

	SINGULAR	PLURAL
nom.:	**der Job**	**die Jobs**
gen.:	**des Jobs**	**der Jobs**
dat.:	**dem Job**	**den Jobs**
acc.:	**den Job**	**die Jobs**

Feminine Nouns

	SINGULAR	PLURAL
nom.:	die Kamera	die Kameras
gen.:	der Kamera	der Kameras
dat.:	der Kamera	den Kameras
acc.:	die Kamera	die Kameras

Neuter Nouns

	SINGULAR	PLURAL
nom.:	das Radio	die Radios
gen.:	des Radios	der Radios
dat.:	dem Radio	den Radios
acc.:	das Radio	die Radios

Additional vocabulary

Bar (f)   bar
Hotel (n)   hotel

Some nouns of foreign (usually Greek) origin end in *-en* in the plural.

Thema (n), Themen   topics, themes
Firma (f), Firmen   firms
Drama (n), Dramen   dramas

Watch out for: **Name (m), des Namens, die Namen** (names)

EXERCISE 20 Answer with whole sentences in German.
1. **Wer wohnt mit einer Freundin?**
2. **Wo sind Sofas, Radios und Fernseher?**
3. **Was ist Kristys Job?**
4. **Was ist in der Garage?**
5. **Was teilen die Freundinnen?**

EXERCISE 21 Write the following in German.
1. The names are Kristy and Susie.
2. A wonderful view
3. A garage for two cars
4. I am lucky.
5. I am very satisfied.

EXERCISE 22 Fill in the missing German words.
1. **Die Wohnung ist sehr _____.**
   comfortable
2. **Das _____ herrlich.**
   sounds
3. **Besonders interessante _____**
   topics
4. **Zwei große _____**
   firms
5. **Sie hat zwei _____.**
   names

EXERCISE 23 Fill in the missing letters.
1. **KRISTY IST EI__E LE__RERIN.**
2. **FERNS__HER UND RA__IOS**
3. **ICH HABE Z__EI K__M__RAS.**
4. **BON__ONS UND BL__MEN**
5. **SEIT S__CHS JA__REN**

Fliegende Untertassen

Flying Saucers

**Nora und Karl sind
glücklich verheiratet. Aber
sie haben einen Freund, der
schon seit drei Jahren
geschieden ist.
Unlängst waren sie mit ihm
beisammen. Karl fragte ihn:
"Sag mal, glaubst du
wirklich an fliegende
Untertassen (f)?"
"Absolut", antwortete er.
"Tatsächlich? Hast du schon
je eine gesehen?"
"Nicht seit meiner Scheidung
(f). Oft warf sie das ganze
Geschirr (n) nach mir,"
erwiderte er.**

Nora and Karl are
happily married. But
they have a friend who
has been divorced
for three years.
Recently they met.
Karl asked him:
"Say, do you really
believe in flying
saucers?"
"Absolutely," he replied.
"Really? Have you
ever seen one?"
"Not since my divorce.
Often she threw all the
dishes at me," he
retorted.

Notes on nouns and "things": We know that grammar isn't fascinating to everyone, and we realize that keeping noun groups straight can be tedious. In a popularity contest with math, grammar probably runs a close second. But if you become proficient in grammar or in math, you will see a certain beauty and order in patterns. Language is closely connected with life, with people; therefore the patterns are never rigid or boring. The five groups are not strait-jackets, and exceptions do exist. Nevertheless, learning plurals according to groups will help you understand nouns better. If your mind resists thinking in terms of groups, you may find it less daunting to remember the following pointers:

1. Whenever you meet a new German noun, learn its gender *(der, die, das)* and its plural right away.

2. Some German nouns don't change. In such instances, pay attention to the definite article and the verb, i.e., *der Lehrer ist hier* (the teacher is here) as distinct from *die Lehrer sind hier* (the teachers are here). (Johann Strauss's *Kaiserwalzer* refers to "Waltzes of the Emperors," although most people think it means "Emperor Waltz" because *Kaiser* and *Walzer* are the same, singular and plural. The waltzes were written for a meeting of the German and Austrian emperors in the 1880s in Berlin, no doubt a more colorful "summit conference" than most contemporary ones.)

3. Many, but by no means all German nouns take an umlaut in the plural. Except for the umlaut, the plural form may be the same as the singular, or it may add an ending.

4. Plurals can end in *e, -en, -er, n,* or *-s.* English has some distinctive noun plurals, such as oxen, geese, mice, (wo)men, children, phenomena, memoranda, and lice. Just think of German as having more distinctive noun plurals than English.

Nouns in Group 5 are a piece of cake, since all you do is add an *-s,* never an umlaut or an *-n* in the dative. Take a word like *der Computer.* What's the plural? *Die Computers.* You've got it. The same with *der Countdown, der Boom, die Party, das Baby, die Story,* and many other words. The Germans have even simplified things for themselves, since both *die Partys* and *die Parties, die Babys* and *die Babies, die Storys* and *die Stories* are acceptable.

German used to be more inventive, more creative when coining words. Nowadays though, many Germans (and lots of others too, except for Icelanders and some of the French) have taken to swallowing foreign words whole (mostly from American English), even when perfectly good words for the same things already exist in their own language. Some Germans glibly call it *Neudeutsch* (New German), although it isn't *neu* (German immigrants to English-speaking countries have been fracturing English and German for centuries) and it isn't really *Deutsch.* But by their linguistic laziness (which they think stylish) they've made things easy for themselves—and, more important—for you.

Cousin Kristy can be thought of as a young, attractive advocate of equal rights for women. She dislikes being patronized and opposes patriarchy in every context, including language and religion. Grudgingly she accepts the grammatical fact that all nouns ending in **-chen** or **-lein,** including *Mädchen* (girl) and *Fräulein* (Miss), are neuter. But it's harder for her to understand why *Weib* (woman, wife) should be neuter. Kristy knows that *Weib* is used in both a highly laudatory and a pejorative sense. She thinks that raising up or putting down women, seeing women, as better or worse than the male half of humanity, is the worst sort of sexism. She's glad the word is used infrequently nowadays, although it persists in phrases like *Weib und Kind* and *ein tolles Weib* (a terrific woman). Though she's not a vegetarian, she's a staunch, if inconsistent, supporter of animal rights, as we'll see later. She is also a proponent of children's rights and objects to the use of the pronoun "it" to denote an infant (or sometimes an older child) in English, and to the grammatical fact that in German *das Kind, das Baby,* and *das Tier* (animal) are neuter. *Das Ding* (the thing) is neuter, logically enough. But *Weib, Baby, Kind,* and *Tier* certainly are not things. Why are they neuter? Well, we disclaim any responsibility for this state of "things," and leave it to philologists to provide reasons. Kristy can take consolation however, in the fact that in German, "John Q. Public" or the "man in the street" can be either the male *Otto Normalverbraucher* (Otto Ordinary Consumer) or the female *Lieschen Müller.*

CHAPTER 4

Abends bei den Bauers: Sprachspiele und Fernsehen
An Evening with the Bauer Family: Word Games and TV

The Adjective; Comparisons; the Adverb

An adjective modifies a noun to denote a quality, to indicate a quantity, or to specify something, e.g., **der** *nette* **Mensch.**

Adverbs are explained later in this chapter.

Die Familie Bauer	The Bauer Family
Nora und Karl Bauer sind besonders *nette Menschen* **und überall sehr** *beliebt.* **Sie haben zwei** *junge Kinder.* **Gretchen hat** *blondes Haar* **und** *blaue Augen,* **Peter** *dunkles Haar* **und** *braune Augen.* **Die** *glänzende Erziehungsmethode* **der Eltern resultiert in** *den guten Manieren der braven Kinder.*	Nora and Karl Bauer are especially nice people and very popular everywhere. They have two young children. Gretchen has blond hair and blue eyes, Peter dark hair and brown eyes. The splendid educational method of the parents results in the good manners of the well-behaved (good) children.

Adjective-noun combinations without preceding articles take "strong" endings:

	MASCULINE SINGULAR	FEMININE SINGULAR
nom.:	**jung*er* Sohn** young son	**glänzend*e* Erziehungsmethode** splendid educational method
gen.:	**jung*en* Sohn*es*** of the young son	**glänzend*er* Erziehungsmethode** of the splendid educational method
dat.:	**jung*em* Sohn** to the young son	**glänzend*er* Erziehungsmethode** to the splendid educational method
acc.:	**jung*en* Sohn** young son	**glänzend*e* Erziehungsmethode** splendid educational method

NEUTER SINGULAR	PLURAL
nom.: **blondes Haar**	**brave Kinder**
blond hair	good children
gen.: **blonden Haares**	**braver Kinder**
of blond hair	of good children
dat.: **blondem Haar**	**braven Kindern**
to blond hair	to good children
acc.: **blondes Haar**	**brave Kinder**
blond hair	good children

Because they do the job of indicating case, the endings of the adjectives above are called "strong." Most strong endings are the same as those of the definite article. Adjectives preceded by definite articles (*der*-words) take "weak" endings (*-en*):

MASCULINE SINGULAR	FEMININE SINGULAR
nom.: **der nette Mensch**	**die schöne Tochter**
the nice man	the pretty daughter
gen.: **des netten Menschen**	**der schönen Tochter**
of the nice man	of the pretty daughter
dat.: **dem netten Menschen**	**der schönen Tochter**
to the nice man	to the pretty daughter
acc.: **den netten Menschen**	**die schöne Tochter**
the nice man	the pretty daughter

NEUTER SINGULAR	PLURAL
nom.: **das junge Kind**	**die blauen Augen**
the young child	the blue eyes
gen.: **des jungen Kindes**	**der blauen Augen**
of the young child	of the blue eyes
dat.: **dem jungen Kind**	**den blauen Augen**
to the young child	to the blue eyes
acc.: **das junge Kind**	**die blauen Augen**
the young child	the blue eyes

Adjectives preceded by indefinite articles (*ein*-words):

MASCULINE SINGULAR	FEMININE SINGULAR	NEUTER SINGULAR
nom.: **ein alter Mann**	**eine kleine Frau**	**ein neues Bild**
an old man	a little woman	a new picture
gen.: **eines alten Mannes**	**einer kleinen Frau**	**eines neuen Bildes**
of an old man	of a little woman	of a new picture
dat.: **einem alten Mann**	**einer kleinen Frau**	**einem neuen Bild**
to an old man	to a little woman	to a new picture
acc.: **einen alten Mann**	**eine kleine Frau**	**ein neues Bild**
an old man	a little woman	a new picture

Predicative adjectives are used after a verb, and never take an ending: **Die Bauers sind** *beliebt.*

Adjectives can also be used as nouns. A great German writer once said: **Es ist viel Gutes und Neues in diesem Buch. Aber das Gute ist nicht neu and das Neue ist nicht gut.**

EXERCISE 1 Fill in the endings.
1. **Ich treffe einen nett_____ Menschen.**
2. **Das ist ein jung_____ Kind.**
3. **Er hat eine brav_____ Tochter.**
4. **Sie hat schön_____ Augen.**

5. Die klein_____ Kinder sind gut.
6. Wo ist das blond_____ Mädchen?
7. Ich spreche mit der alt_____ Frau.
8. Er ist ein gut_____ Mann.
9. Schön_____ Wetter ist heute.
10. Der nett_____ Mensch ist Herr Bauer.
11. Die Farbe des groß_____ Tisches ist braun.
12. Mit blond_____ Haar ist man beliebt.

EXERCISE 2 Fill in the missing German adjectives.

1. **Das Buch** _____ **Sohnes**
                    of the young
2. **Ich wohne** _____ **Haus.**
                    in the new
3. **Die Nase** _____ **Frau ist groß.**
                    of the little
4. **Ich gebe** _____ **Mann zwei Mark.**
                    to the old
5. **Wo ist die Mutter** _____ **Mädchens?**
                    of the good
6. **Wer bringt** _____ **Kind?**
                    the little

EXERCISE 3 Choose the correct answer according to the text.

1. **Das Haar des Mädchens ist**
   a. **grau**   b. **braun**   c. **blond**
2. **Peters Augen sind**
   a. **grün**   b. **braun**   c. **blau**
3. **Die Kinder haben**
   a. **kurze Haare**   b. **gute Manieren**   c. **nette Kleider**
4. **Nora und Karl haben jetzt**
   a. **zwei junge Kinder**   b. **einen Hund**   c. **keine Kinder**

EXERCISE 4 Write the following sentences in German.

1. They are nice people
2. The parents have good manners.
3. They are popular everywhere.
4. The children are well-behaved.
5. Who has a splendid educational method?

Das Haus

**Die Bauers haben ein
kleines, aber nettes Haus in
einem Vorort. Es besteht
aus Wohnzimmer, Eßzimmer,
Diele, zwei Schlafzimmern,
Küche, Badezimmer und
Toilette. Das Haus hat einen
Balkon, eine Garage und
einen kleinen Garten. Kristy
findet das Haus sehr
gemütlich.**

The House

The Bauer family has a
small but nice house in
a suburb. It consists of a
living room, dining room,
den, two bedrooms,
kitchen, bathroom, and
toilet. The house has a
balcony, a garage, and
a little garden. Kristy
finds the house very
cozy.

Peter

Wenn Peter als kleiner
Junge auf die Toilette (f)
gehen mußte, sagte er: „Ich
muß auf die kleine Seite (f)",
oder manchmal „auf die
große Seite", (je nachdem).
Heute sagt er wahrscheinlich:
„Ich muß aufs Klo (n)."

Peter

When Peter as a little
boy had to go to the
toilet, he said: "Got to
go number one"
or sometimes "number two,"
depending.
Today he probably says:
"I've gotta go to the can."

Gretchen am Telephon

GRETCHEN (am Telephon in der Diele):
Hallo? Guten Abend (m),
Frau Körner. Ist Erika
dort? Kann ich mit ihr
sprechen? Erika? Ist *dein*
Telephon (n) kaputt? Oder
deine Leitung (f)? *Unser*
Telephon ist O.K. War in
eurer Gegend (f) ein
Gewitter (n)? Nein? Sag,
hast du gestern diesen
herrlichen Film (m) mit
Jürgen Kaiser gesehen?
Also, dieser Mann ist *mein*
ganz großes Ideal (n)!—
Aber *meine* teure Erika—
wie kannst du nur so
etwas sagen? Jürgen
Kaiser ist doch viel
schöner als Hans
Hinnemann.—Was sagst du?
—Also ich habe viele andere
Männer gesehen, aber ich kann
dir versichern, Jürgen ist der
schönste von allen! Ich muß
jetzt auflegen. Grüße (m) an
deinen Bruder Paul.
Wiederhören!

Gretchen on the Phone

Hello? Good evening,
Mrs. Körner. Is Erika
there? May I talk to
her? Erika? Is your
phone out of order? Or
your line? Our
phone is O.K. Was there
a thunderstorm in your
area? No? Say,
did you see
this marvelous movie with
Jürgen Kaiser yesterday?
Well, this man is my
great big idol!—
But my dear Erika—
how can you say
something like that?
Jürgen Kaiser is much
handsomer than Hans
Hinnemann. What is that?

—Well, I have seen many
other men, but I can
assure you, Jürgen is the
handsomest of all! I have
to hang up now. Regards
to your brother Paul.
See you. (Actually: "Until
I hear from you again.")

Please note: Usually Gretchen and Erika stay on the phone a long time, discussing the relative attractiveness of movie stars, the likes of Tom Cruise and Brad Pitt. They spend even more time commenting on the physical and personal traits of all their classmates. But we'll give you more useful information about "*der*-words" and "*ein*-words."

Der-words take the same endings as the definite article. Some *der* words are: *dieser* (this), *jeder* (each), *jener* (that), and *welcher* (which).

Dieser kleine Junge, diese schöne Frau, dieses kleine Kind; jener nette Mann; jener gute Vater, jene gute Mutter, jenes neue Bild; welcher herrlicher Film? welche deutsche Zeitung? welches neue Haus?

The following is a list of possessive adjectives, called "*ein*-words," because they take the same endings as the indefinite article *ein* (see pages 10–11).

SINGULAR		PLURAL	
mein	my	**unser**	our
dein	your	**euer**	your
sein	his		
ihr	her	**ihr**	their
sein	its (n)	**Ihr**	your (polite form, always capitalized)

Possessive adjective, adjective and noun combinations

dein interessant*es* Buch	your interesting book
mein*e* teur*e* Erika	my dear Erika
mein groß*es* Ideal	my great idol
unser*e* nett*en* Gäste	our nice guests
eur*e* schön*en* Frau*en*	your beautiful women
ihr*e* brav*en* Kind*er*	her (or their) well-behaved children

Adjective-noun combinations preceded by *viele* (many), *wenige* (few), *andere* (other), *einige* (some), or *mehrere* (several) keep their strong endings: **viele andere Mädchen, wenige amerikanische Kinder, andere neue Häuser, einige alte Gläser, mehrere nette Frauen.**

EXERCISE 5 Answer in German.
1. **Wer hat ein kleines, nettes Haus?**
2. **Woraus besteht es?**
3. **Wie findet Kristy das Haus?**
4. **Wer spricht mit Gretchen am Telephon?**
5. **Wer ist schöner als Hans Hinnemann?**

EXERCISE 6 Construct sentences using these cue words.
1. **Haus / klein / Vorort**
2. **kann / Erika / sprechen**
3. **gesehen / Film / Kaiser**
4. **kaputt / Telephon**
5. **Gewitter / Gegend**
6. **Grüße / Bruder**

EXERCISE 7 Fill in the missing endings.
1. **Dies____ klein____ Junge geht schwimmen.**
2. **Dein____ Leitung ist kaputt.**
3. **Ich habe dies____ herrlich____ Film gesehen.**
4. **Unser____ Mädchen sind nett.**
5. **Ich besitze viel____ schön____ Häuser.**
6. **Ich treffe wenig____groß____Männer.**

EXERCISE 8 Translate the following into English.
1. **Das Haus hat auch eine Diele.**
2. **Erika spricht mit ihrer Freundin.**
3. **Das Telephon ist kaputt.**
4. **Das ist ein ausgezeichneter Film.**
5. **Das Gewitter war in meiner Gegend.**
6. **Ich muß jetzt abhängen.**

EXERCISE 9 Choose the correct answers according to the text.
1. **Das Haus ist**
   a. **in der Stadt** b. **auf dem Land** c. **in einem Vorort**
2. **Gretchens Telephon ist**
   a. **O.K.** b. **kaputt** c. **nicht dort**

3. **Erikas Bruder heißt**
   a. **Uwe**   b. **Paul**   c. **Fritz**
4. **Erika spricht am Telephon mit**
   a. **Gretchen**   b. **Nora**   c. **Peter**

EXERCISE 10   Write the following sentences in German.
1. My house is new.
2. His daughters are beautiful.
3. This nice woman is my mother.
4. Which girl has blond hair?
5. I saw many good films.
6. We had some great presidents.

Wer ist schöner?

Who Is More Handsome?

NORA   (coming into the hall):
Du warst schon wieder am Telephon (n). Mit deiner Busenfreundin?

You were on the phone again. With your bosom friend?

GRETCHEN   **Ich hab' mich mit Erika zerstritten.**

I had an argument with Erika.

NORA   **Warum? O, ich weiß. Über den Jürgen Kaiser.**

Why? Oh, I know. About Jürgen Kaiser.

GRETCHEN   **Natürlich. Sie hat gesagt, Hans Hinneman ist *schöner*.**

Of course. She said Hans Hinnemann is handsomer.

NORA   **Also, das ist doch Geschmacksache (f).**

Well, that's a matter of taste.

GRETCHEN   **Mutter!**

Mother!

NORA   **Ich glaube auch, daß Jürgen *der schönste* ist.**

I also believe that Jürgen is the handsomest.

GRETCHEN   **Mutti!** (embracing her) **Ich hab' dich lieb.**

Mommy! I love you.

Please note: **Betty ist so gut wie ich.**
Betty is as good as I.

Comparisons

The comparative form of the adjective adds *-er* or *-r* to its stem, and the superlative *-est* or *-st*.

Jürgen ist schön*er* als (than) Hans.
Jürgen ist der schön*ste*.

Note: In the superlative we can say either "Jürgen is the handsomest" or "the most handsome." *Schön* is usually translated "beautiful" for women, "handsome" for men. The poetic "fair" is used for both sexes.

Wer ist die Schönste?

Who Is the Fairest?

Schneewittchens Stiefmutter, die böse Königin, fragte, "Spieglein Spieglein an der Wand, wer ist die schönste im ganzen Land?"

Snow White's step mother, the wicked queen, asked "Mirror, mirror on the wall, who is the fairest of them all?" (the most beautiful in the whole country)

Most adjectives consisting of one syllable take an umlaut in the comparative and the superlative.

> **das kalte Wetter, das kältere Wetter, das kälteste Wetter**
> **die junge Frau, die jüngere, die jüngste**
> **die lange Oper, die längere Oper, die längste Oper**

Wagners Opern sind lang. *Lohengrin* **ist länger als** *Der fliegende Holländer. Die Götterdämmerung* **ist die längste.**	Wagner's operas are long. *Lohengrin* is longer than *The Flying Dutchman. The Twilight of the Gods* is the longest.

When the definite article (the) is omitted in the superlative, German uses a form with *am*, as in *am schönsten* (most beautiful).

> *Die Götterdämmerung* **ist am längsten.**
> *The Twilight of the Gods* is longest.

Some of the forms are irregular: **gut, besser, best-; viel, mehr, meist-.**

Mehr über das Haus

More About the House

Das Haus ist schön eingerichtet, weil Nora guten Geschmack (m) hat. Im Wohnzimmer haben die Bauers ein großes Sofa, zwei Polstersessel (m), einen Couchtisch (m), auch eine Stereoanlage (f) und an den Wänden (f) Regale (n) mit vielen Büchern. Im Eßzimmer steht ein Tisch mit sechs Stühlen (m) und einer Zimmerpflanze (f). Leider hat das Haus bloß zwei Schlafzimmer. Die Eltern schlafen in dem einen und Gretchen in dem anderen. Peter schläft auf dem Sofa im Wohnzimmer. Die Diele ist sehr gemütlich möbliert.

The house is beautifully decorated because Nora has good taste. In the living room the Bauers have a large sofa, two easy chairs, a coffee table, also a stereo set, and on the walls bookshelves with many books. In the dining room is a table with six chairs and a house plant. Unfortunately, the house has only two bedrooms. The parents sleep in the one, and Gretchen in the other. Peter sleeps on the sofa in the living room. The den is furnished very cozily.

Wokurka

Wherespa

KARL	(comes into the den, sits down) **Was geht da vor? Krieg' ich nicht auch ein Busserl (n)?**	What's going on here? Don't I get a little kiss, too?
GRETCHEN	**Aber sicher!**	You bet!
KARL	(taking the newspaper) **Wo ist Peter?**	Where is Peter?
GRETCHEN	**Spielt im Garten (m). Da kommt er.**	Playing in the yard. There he comes.
PETER	**Vati, weißt du einen Satz (m) mit WOKURKA?**	Daddy, do you know a sentence with WHERESPA in it?

KARL WOKURKA? Das gibt's doch nicht. Oder meinst du Workuta, die russische Stadt, wo so viele Zwangsarbeiter ums Leben gekommen sind?

WHERESPA? There is no such word. Or do you mean Vorkuta, the Russian city where so many forced laborers lost their lives?

PETER Nein! Wiesbaden ist eine Stadt (f), WO KURKApellen *fleißig* spielen.

No! Wiesbaden is a city WHERE SPA bands play diligently.

KARL, NORA, GRETCHEN Schrecklich!

Terrible!

GRETCHEN Ich weiß ein Rätsel (n).

I know a riddle.

NORA Ja?

Yes?

GRETCHEN Was ist das: es hängt am Baum (m), ist grün und bellt *wütend?*

What is this: It hangs on a tree, is green, and barks furiously?

NORA Keine Idee (f).

No idea.

GRETCHEN Weißt du's, Vati?

Do you know, Daddy?

KARL Nein.

No.

GRETCHEN Ein Hering.

A herring.

PETER Ein Hering hängt doch nicht am Baum.

But a herring doesn't hang on a tree.

GRETCHEN Ich hab' ihn dort hingehängt.

I've hung it there.

NORA Ein Hering ist doch nicht grün.

But a herring is not green.

GRETCHEN Ich hab' ihn grün angestrichen.

I painted it green.

KARL Und er bellt *wütend?*

And he barks furiously?

GRETCHEN Das hab' ich nur gesagt, damit du es nicht so *leicht* errätst.

This I only said so you wouldn't guess the answer so easily.

KARL Was die Kinder mir heute antun!

What I have to put up with from the children today!

Note: Did you know that English "buss," as in "Give me a buss," derives from the South German/Austrian **Busserl?** In most German-speaking areas, **Küßchen** (diminutive of **Kuß**) is more common for "little kiss," as in the proverb **Ein Küßchen in Ehren kann niemand verwehren** (No one can forbid a well-intentioned little kiss) or, more freely, "A little kiss can do no harm."

Die Philosophie über Alles

Philosophy Above All

Als Studentin in Wien interessierte sich die berühmte Kernphysikerin Lise Meitner so sehr für die Werke des Philosophen Edmund Husserl, daß die Leute von ihr sagten: "Lise denkt nie an Busserl, nur an Husserl."

As a student in Vienna the famous nuclear physicist Lise Meitner was so interested in the works of the philosopher Edmund Husserl, that people said of her, "Lise never thinks of **Busserl**, just of Husserl."

Der Fernseher

Karl sieht sich das Fernsehprogramm (n) *gründlich* an und ist sehr unzufrieden.

KARL Das ist doch *wirklich* arg.

NORA Was?

KARL Kein anständiges Programm (n)! Und dafür muß man noch zahlen! Die sollten *uns* bezahlen, daß wir uns ihren Mist ansehen! Da: *Die Straß*en (f) *von San Franzisko; Mord* (m) *auf dem Hausboot* (n); *Daisys Geburtstag* (m), Zeichentrickfilm (m) von Walt Disney; *Immer Ärger* (m) *mit Pop*, Spaß (m) für Spaßvögel (m) mit Professor Paul Popwitz; *Popeye, kleine Lulu und sechs Babys* (n).

NORA Was ist um acht?

KARL *Die Abenteuer von Tom Sawyer und Huckleberry Finn.*

PETER Vati—kann ich das sehen? Bitte ...

KARL Vielleicht sollten wir die Heublers einladen und Bridge spielen.

PETER Der Lehrer hat gesagt ...

KARL Aber um acht schläfst du doch schon *fest!*

The TV

Karl looks at the TV program carefully and is very dissatisfied.

That really is bad.

What?

No decent program. And for that you have to pay. They should pay *us* for watching their garbage! Just look! *The Streets of San Francisco; Murder on the Houseboat; Daisy's Birthday*, an animated film by Walt Disney; *Always Trouble with Pop*, fun for jokesters with Professor Paul Popwitz; *Popeye, Little Lulu and Six Babies*.

What is at eight?

The Adventures of Tom Sawyer and Huckleberry Finn.

Daddy—can I see that? Please ...

Maybe we should invite the Heublers and play bridge.

The teacher said ...

But by eight you're going to be fast asleep!

Grammar Bits

Good news: In English we usually add **-ly** to form adverbs: nice (adjective), nicely (adverb). But in German, nothing at all is added to an adverb. What a relief after all those noun cases and adjective endings! In the foregoing text there were several adverbs modifying verbs: **Das Haus ist *schön* eingerichtet; die Kurkapelle spielt *fleißig;* er bellt *wütend;* damit du es nicht so *leicht* errätst; sieht sich das Programm *gründlich* an; das ist doch *wirklich* arg; du schläfst schon *fest*.**

Here are some frequently used adverbs not connected to an adjective:

damals	at that time	**oben**	upstairs
draußen	outside	**unten**	downstairs
drinnen	inside	**nie**	never
hoffentlich	it is to be hoped	**nun**	now

EXERCISE 11 Fill in the proper German form.
1. **Anna ist** _____ **als ihr Bruder. (groß)**
2. **Fritz ist** _____ **von allen. (stark)**
3. **Bonbons sind** _____ **als Zigaretten. (gut)**
4. **Gretchen ist** _____ **von allen. (gut)**
5. **Hans ist** _____ **als Rudi. (alt)**

EXERCISE 12 Fill in the missing adverb.
1. **Das Haus ist** _____ **möbliert.**
                     beautifully
2. **Der Hering bellt** _____.
                        furiously
3. **Er kann das** _____ **lernen.**
                    easily
4. **Das ist** _____ **gut.**
               really
5. **Er kommt** _____.
                it is to be hoped
6. **Ich habe ihn** _____ **gesehen.**
                    never
7. _____ **waren wir in Deutschland.**
    At that time
8. **Sie hat** _____ **Kleider als ich.**
               more

EXERCISE 13 Complete the sentences.
1. **Gretchen spricht am Telephon mit ihrer** _____.
2. **Sie hat sich mit ihr** _____.
3. **Im Wohnzimmer sind Regale mit vielen** _____.
4. **Leider haben die Bauers bloß zwei** _____.
5. **Karl ist mit dem Fernsehprogramm sehr** _____.
6. **Um acht schläft Peter schon** _____.

EXERCISE 14 True or false?   T / F
1. **Die Diele ist sehr gemütlich.**   _____
2. **Gretchen schläft im Wohnzimmer.**   _____
3. **In der Küche ist eine Stereoanlage.**   _____
4. **Die Zimmerpflanze ist im Eßzimmer.**   _____
5. **Gretchen weiß ein Rätsel.**   _____
6. **Karl kriegt ein Busserl.**   _____

EXERCISE 15 Translate the following sentences into English.
1. **Ich hab' dich lieb.**
2. **Das ist Geschmacksache.**
3. **Ich spreche mit meiner Busenfreundin.**
4. **Was geht da vor?**
5. **Aber sicher!**
6. **Da kommt er.**
7. **Das gibt's doch nicht.**
8. **Kein anständiges Programm!**

Zwei Zungenbrecher
Two Tongue Twisters

P.S.: Since there were fun and games on the agenda at the Bauers' tonight, despite the shadow of Vorkuta, the children could also have suggested to their dad that he try a couple of tongue twisters. In German they are called *Zungenbrecher* because you can break your tongue (*Zunge,* f.) doing them. Here are a couple of them:

Der Potsdamer Postkutscher putzt den Potsdamer Postkutschkasten.
The Potsdam postman cleans Potsdam's postal coach.

Sieben zerquetschte Zwetschgen.
Seven squashed plums.

CHAPTER 5

Anton sieht sich nach einem anderen Job um
Anton Looks for Another Job

Pronouns

A pronoun is a word that is used as a substitute for a noun, e. g., Anton **kommt;** *er* **kommt.**

Personal Pronouns

1st Person

	SINGULAR		PLURAL	
nom.:	**ich**	I	**wir**	we
dat.:	**mir**	to me	**uns**	to us
acc.:	**mich**	me	**uns**	us

2nd person

	SINGULAR		PLURAL	
nom.:	**du**	you	**ihr**	you
dat.:	**dir**	to you	**euch**	to you
acc.:	**dich**	you	**euch**	you

3rd person

	SINGULAR		PLURAL	
nom.:	**er**	he	**sie**	they
	sie	she		
	es	it		
dat.:	**ihm**	to him	**ihnen**	to them
	ihr	to her		
	ihm	to it		
acc.:	**ihn**	him	**sie**	them
	sie	her		
	es	it		

A capitalized *Sie* is the polite form to be used instead of *du* (the ancient *thou*). To a stranger you say: "***Bringen Sie* mir Tee,**" instead of "***Bring* mir Tee,**" or "***Du, bring* mir Tee.**" Another polite form is the capitalized *Ihnen*. "**Ich bringe** *Ihnen* **Tee,**" instead of the familiar "**Ich bringe** *dir* **Tee.**"

Anton in Deutschland

Anton and Susie meet at a **Café-Konditorei,** one of those places where you can sit, read newspapers, and chat as long as you like and no one will bother you.

Vocabulary

beehren	to honor
beim Kommen	when coming
bewundern	to admire
Charme (m)	charm
damit	with it
Du wirst mich schon nicht ändern.	You won't change me.
er kam	he came
geboren	born
Geschlecht (n)	sex
"gnädige Frau"	"gracious lady", madam
hänseln	to tease
Höflichkeit (f)	politeness
Ich red', wie mir der Schnabel gewachsen ist.	I don't mince words; *here:* That's just the way I talk.
die meisten Mitglieder (n)	most members
neun	nine
noch immer	still
respektieren	to respect
Servus!	Hello!, Goodbye!
Sie haben ihn gern.	They like him.
weiblich	female
Wien	Vienna
wienerisch	Viennese

Anton ist in Wien geboren. *Er* kam vor neun Jahren nach Deutschland und spricht noch immer mit einem wienerischen Akzent. Zu seinen Freunden sagt *er* „Servus" beim Kommen oder Gehen. Die meisten Mitglieder des weiblichen Geschlechtes beehrt *er* mit „Küß die Hand, gnädige Frau" (oder „gnädiges Fräulein"). Susie hat *ihn* oft damit gehänselt. „*Ich* red', wie *mir* der Schnabel gewachsen ist", sagt *er* dann immer. „*Du* wirst *mich* schon nicht ändern." Die Leute haben *ihn* gern. Sie respektieren seine Höflichkeit und bewundern seinen Charme.

Note: Idioms are ways of saying things in one language that can't be translated word for word into another. Idioms often lend savor and spice to speech. When Anton says, „**Ich red', wie mir der Schnabel gewachsen ist,**" he's saying literally, "I talk the way my beak has grown." Some idioms (like **gern haben** or the one with **Schnabel**) are used by German speakers everywhere. Others are associated with a particular region. In the South you're not likely to hear **Tschüs** (so long!, Bye now!) too often. It's a cheerful North German transformation of the rather solemn French *adieu.* On the other hand, Anton's **Servus** and **Küß die Hand, gnädige Frau,** as well as **Grüß Gott,** are salutations not usually heard in northern areas. Concerning **küssen,** remember **Busserl** (little kiss) in the last chapter? It, like many other southern forms, is understood and even sometimes used by Northerners. Standard German for "a little" is **ein bißchen.** But Southern forms like **bißl** and **bisserl,** as well as **nix** for **nichts,** are heard elsewhere. Just as many Americans find a Southern accent charming (Southern belles living outside the South have been known to work at keeping it), many Germans find some Southern accents delightful, and are much attracted to picturesque Alpine areas and captivated by proverbial "Viennese charm." Some Viennese have maliciously alleged that charm to be a mere painted façade, the gilding on a nest of vipers. The American South's fabled grace and charm has its darker sides too, witness all those "Southern Gothic" novels. There are even similarities between Southern accents in the United States and in German-speaking areas. In both, the vowel *i* as in *I* or *eye* is sounded softly. *Eins, zwei, drei* sounds snappy, "Prussian" in the North. In the South it's more languid, taking on the same coloration as the Southern American *i*, as in "nice white rice," with the *i* sounded a little like the *a* in *nap*.

As to Anton, our Austrian immigrant to Germany: Because there is no language problem, despite differing accents and idioms, many Germans have lived and worked in Austria. The most famous are Beethoven (born in Bonn) and Brahms (born in Hamburg), now buried near each other in Vienna's *Zentralfriedhof* (Central Cemetery). The best known of the many Austrian immigrants to Germany is Adolf Hitler, who became dictator of Germany. Like that other Austrian, Maria Antonia von Habsburg, better known as Marie Antoinette, Queen of France, he had a turbulent political career away from Austria that came to a violent, catastrophic end. Anton is a much more ordinary sort. He's *gemütlich* (easy-going, convivial), the way Austrians are usually thought of—the way they see themselves.

EXERCISE 1 Fill in the missing pronouns.

1. _____ ist in Wien geboren.
          He
2. **Susie hat** _____ **oft gehänselt.**
             him
3. **Du wirst** _____ **nicht ändern.**
            me
4. **Ich red', wie** _____ **der Schnabel gewachsen ist.**
           to me
5. **Ich bringe** _____ **den Tee.**
        to you (familiar)

EXERCISE 2 Answer in German.

1. **Wer ist in Wien geboren?**
2. **Wo wohnt er jetzt?**
3. **Was sagt er zu seinen Freunden?**
4. **Was bewundern die Leute an ihm?**
5. **Was sagt er zu manchen Damen?**

EXERCISE 3 Translate into English.

1. **Sie bewundern ihn.**
2. **Er kommt aus Wien.**
3. **Susie hat ihn damit gehänselt.**
4. **Er spricht mit einem wienerischen Akzent.**
5. **Bitte, bring mir Kaffee.**

EXERCISE 4 Fill in the missing letters.

1. **WEIBLI__HES GESC__LECHT**
2. **DIE L__UTE HAB__N IHN G__RN.**
3. **ER SAGT "SER__US."**
4. **ER IST JETZT IN DE__TSCHLA__D.**
5. **SIE HAT I__N GEH__NSELT.**

In der Café-Konditorei

Vocabulary

Café-Konditorei (f.)	a combination café and pastry shop
deliziös	delicious
geben	to give
hausgemacht	homemade
Kellner, -in	waiter, waitress
Kipfel (n.)	croissant
Mehlspeiskoch (m.)	pastry cook
mit Schlag	with whipped cream
nennen	to name, call
Österreicher (m.)	Austrian
Platz (m.)	*here:* seat
Tasse (f.)	cup

Heute finden wir *ihn* in der Café-Konditorei Walser.

„Habt *ihr* die *Münchener Neuesten*?'' fragt *er* die Kellnerin.

„Leider nicht'', antwortet *sie*. „Soll *ich Ihnen* vielleicht die *Süddeutsche Zeitung* bringen?''

„Gut. Geben *Sie sie mir*, bitte.''

Hier kommt Susie.

„Servus'', sagt *er*, steht auf und bietet *ihr* einen Platz an.

„Schön von *dir* zu kommen.—Herr Ober! „Bringen *Sie uns*, bitte, zwei Tassen Kaffee mit Schlag und einige von *euren* deliziösen Kipfeln.'' Und zu Susie sagt *er*: „Der Mehlspeiskoch hier ist Österreicher. Alles hausgemacht.''

Note: A head waiter is an *Oberkellner.* Perhaps to get better service, Germans flatteringly call all waiters *Herr Ober!*

Anton calls the croissants *deliziös.* He could have said **schmackhaft, lecker,** or even **himmlisch** (heavenly). A propos of "heavenly": Unleavened bread (matzoth) has religious significance for Jews. Hot cross buns bear a Christian symbol. Croissants, French for "crescents," represent the Muslim symbol of the crescent moon. (In Islamic countries the Red Crescent engages in activities similar to those of the Red Cross.) Croissants were introduced to Vienna when Muslim Turkish armies abandoned their provisions after their siege of the city failed. Austrian Anton calls them *Kipfel.* Elsewhere they're known as *Hörnchen.*

Ein kleiner Witz

„Guten Tag'', sagt Fritz am Kiosk, „haben Sie noch die Zeitung von gestern?''

„Leider nicht; aber kommen Sie doch morgen und holen Sie sich (*get*) die Zeitung von heute.''

EXERCISE 5 Choose the correct word.
1. **Wo finden wir Anton heute?**
   a. **in England** b. **in der Café-Konditorei** c. **in Wien**
2. **Dort trifft Susie**
   a. **ihn** b. **ihm** c. **ihr**
3. **Er steht auf und bietet**
   a. **ihm einen Platz an** b. **ihr einen Platz an**
   c. **uns einen Platz an**
4. **Schön von dir zu**
   a. **kommen** b. **gehen** c. **finden**

5. Sie bringt ihm
   a. **eine amerikanische Zeitung**   b. **die** *Münchener Neuesten*
   c. **die** *Süddeutsche Zeitung*

EXERCISE 6   Insert the missing words.
   1. **Er steht auf und bietet ihr einen**_____.
   2. **Der Mehlspeiskoch ist ein**_____.
   3. **Bringen Sie uns Kaffee mit**_____.
   4. **„Habt ihr die Zeitung'', fragt er die**_____.
   5. **Heute finden wir ihn in einer**_____.

EXERCISE 7   True or false?   T / F
   1. **„Habt ihr die Zeitung?'' fragt er Kristy.**   _____
   2. **Er nennt den Kellner „Herr Ober''.**   _____
   3. **Sie bringt deliziöse Kipfel.**   _____
   4. **Heute ist er im Café Wunderlich.**   _____
   5. **Sie haben die** *Süddeutsche Zeitung.*   _____

EXERCISE 8   Fill in the missing pronouns.
   1. **Habt** _____ **Kaffee mit Schlag?**
                       you
   2. **Soll ich** _____ **die Zeitung geben?**
                  to you (formal)
   3. **Bringen Sie** _____ **Kipfel.**
                           to us
   4. **Ich bringe** _____ **Blumen.**
                    to you (familiar)
   5. **„Leider nicht'', antwortet** _____.
                                            she

EXERCISE 9   Write the following in German.
   1. He asks the waitress.
   2. Nice of you to come
   3. Two cups of coffee with whipped cream
   4. The pastry cook is excellent.
   5. All homemade

Ein anderer Job?

Vocabulary

anderseits	on the other hand
Arbeitslosigkeit (f)	unemployment
aufgeben	to give up
Aussicht	*here:* opportunity, chance
derselben Ansicht	of the same opinion
du hast angedeutet	you have hinted
eine Menge	lots of
entscheiden	to decide
für dich selbst	for yourself
gewinnen	to win
heutzutage	nowadays

Inserat (n)	ad
meinen	to think
Nimm dich in Acht.	Watch out.
nichts	nothing
rät mir davon ab	advises me not to
recht haben	to be right
schau dir an	look at
verdienen	to earn
wagen	*here:* to take a chance
wechseln	to change
Zukunft (f)	future

SUSIE   Also *du* hast angedeutet, daß *du* deinen Job aufgeben willst.

ANTON   Ja, Susie. *Ich* verdiene dort nicht genug und *ich* habe auch keine Aussichten für die Zukunft. Aber *es* ist schwer, heutzutage etwas zu finden. Eine Menge Inserate, aber nichts Besonderes für *mich.*—Ah, der Kaffee!
Mein Vater rät *mir* davon ab, Jobs zu wechseln. „Nimm *dich* in acht", meint *er.* „Schau *dir* die Arbeitslosigkeit an."
Viele Leute sind derselben Ansicht und *sie* haben wahrscheinlich recht. Anderseits, wer nicht wagt, gewinnt nicht.

SUSIE   Das mußt *du* für *dich* selbst entscheiden.

EXERCISE 10   Fill in the missing pronouns.

1. _____ verdiene nicht genug.
        I

2. _____ ist schwer heutzutage.
        It

3. Susie sagt, _____ haben recht.
                they

4. Das mußt _____ für dich selbst entscheiden.
            you

5. Wenn _____ nicht wagt, gewinnt sie nicht.
        she

EXERCISE 11   Write in German.

1. I don't earn enough there.
2. No opportunities for the future
3. Lots of delicious croissants
4. It is hard nowadays.
5. On the other hand, my job is good.

EXERCISE 12   Complete each sentence with a word or phrase listed here: **aufgeben, derselben Ansicht, wunderbar, davon ab, acht.**

1. Die Kipfel sind _____.
2. Ich und Susie sind _____.
3. Er will den Job _____.
4. Er rät mir _____.
5. Nehmt euch in _____.

EXERCISE 13   Fill in the missing German words.

1. Ich verdiene dort nicht _____.
                              enough

2. Sie haben _____ recht.
              probably

3. Schau dir die _____ an.
                  unemployment

4. Wer nicht _____, gewinnt nicht.
              gambles

5. Das mußt du für dich selbst _____.
                              to decide

EXERCISE 14 Translate the following into German.
1. I have no opportunities.
2. Watch out.
3. We are of the same opinion.
4. You have hinted.
5. I like coffee with whipped cream.

EXERCISE 15 Rewrite the italicized nouns with the proper pronouns.
1. *Anton* kam vor neun Jahren nach Deutschland._____
2. *Susie* wird ihn nicht ändern._____
3. Er bietet *Susie* einen Platz an._____
4. Sie essen *Kipfel*._____
5. Wir sehen das *Kind*._____

Inserate (Ads)

Vocabulary

bankrott	bankrupt
bereits	already
Bernhardiner (m)	St. Bernard dog
Erfahrung (f)	experience
es wird sich zeigen	it'll show itself; we'll see
fressen	to eat (like an animal)
führender Werbefachmann (m)	advertising executive
Führungskraft (f)	executive
Gehalt (n)	salary
gesucht	*here:* wanted
Heim (n)	home
liebevoll	affectionate
Postwurfsendung (f)	direct mail advertising
Schau!	Look here!
Schmeichelkätzchen (n)	"snuggle cat" (*schmeicheln*—to flatter; the ending *-chen* is a diminutive ending.)
steril	sterile; *here:* neutered (of an animal)
suchen	to look for
süß	sweet
sich täuschen	to deceive oneself
Tierfreund (m)	animal lover
verschenken	to give away
verschmust	cuddly
warten	to wait
zimmerrein	housebroken

ANTON   Hast du nicht unlängst gesagt, du willst eine Katze? Hör dir das an: Schöne schwarze Katze, steril, freundlich, verschmust, ein richtiges Schmeichel-kätzchen, nur an liebevollen Tierfreund zu verschenken.

SUSIE   Schau, da ist ein Hund, der reden kann; er sagt: Suche neues Heim. Bin ein süßer, kleiner Bernhardiner, zwei Monate alt und zimmerrein. Ich koste nicht viel.

ANTON   Wart nur, bis der ein Jahr alt ist. Der frißt dich bankrott.—Aber schau hier: Das ist vielleicht ein Job für mich.
Führender Werbefachmann gesucht (Postwurfsendung). Sehr gutes Gehalt, glänzende Aussichten. Minimum: sechs Jahre Erfahrung. AWC 52-34-81.
Was glaubst du, Susie?

SUSIE Klingt gut.

ANTON Wenn *ich mich nicht täusche*, ist das die größte Werbefirma hier.

SUSIE Ich glaube, *du siehst dich* bereits als Führungskraft.

ANTON *Das wird sich zeigen.*

Reflexive Pronouns

Reflexive pronouns are used if, in the same sentence, the subject is identical with the object; example: *ich* täusche *mich* (I deceive myself).

More Examples

Du siehst dich.	You see yourself.
Er zeigt sich.	He shows himself.
Sie zeigt sich.	She shows herself.
Es zeigt sich.	It shows itself.
Wir waschen uns.	We wash ourselves.
Ihr rasiert euch.	You shave yourselves.
Sie verletzen sich.	They hurt themselves.

EXERCISE 16 Complete each sentence with a word listed here: **Katze, reden, Erfahrung, gut, Tierfreund.**
1. **Der Job ist für einen Mann mit sechs Jahren _____.**
2. **Der Hund in dem Inserat kann _____.**
3. **Man verschenkt sie an einen liebevollen _____.**
4. **Susie will eine schwarze _____.**
5. **Das Gehalt ist sehr _____.**

EXERCISE 17 Answer in complete German sentences.
1. **Was will der Hund?**
2. **Wie alt ist er?**
3. **Wer wird für Postwurfsendungen gesucht?**
4. **Was tut der Bernhardiner, wenn er ein Jahr alt ist?**
5. **Was sehen sich die beiden in der Zeitung an?**

EXERCISE 18 True or false?   T / F
1. **Der Hund kostet sehr viel.**   _____
2. **Ein Werbefachmann wird gesucht.**   _____
3. **Die Katze ist unfreundlich.**   _____
4. **Der Bernhardiner ist zwei Jahre alt.**   _____
5. **Susie will ein Krokodil.**   _____

EXERCISE 19 Translate into German.
1. He deceives himself.
2. It will show itself.
3. We shave ourselves.
4. They wash themselves.
5. She sees herself.

EXERCISE 20 Fill in the missing reflexive pronouns.
1. **Es zeigt _____ in seinem Benehmen.**
2. **Er verletzt _____ beim Schwimmen.**
3. **Ich täusche _____ nie.**
4. **Du siehst _____ nicht so.**
5. **Ihr wascht _____ am Morgen.**

Antons Bekannter

Vocabulary

arbeiten	to work
(ein) Bekannter (m)	an acquaintance
beneiden	to envy
brauchen	to need
Jacke (f)	jacket
jetzig	present
Karriere machen	to be quickly promoted
kennen	to know
lieh, *past tense of* **leihen**	to lend (to somebody)
Schule (f)	school
Schulkollege (m)	schoolmate
verdanken	to owe
Werbefachleute (pl.)	advertising executives
zurückgeben	to return

ANTON Kennst du den Mann, *der* dort steht? Das ist ein Bekannter, *dessen* Frau bei uns arbeitet. Er ist auch der Mann, *dem* ich meine jetzige Stellung verdanke, den Job, *den* ich jetzt nicht mehr haben will.

SUSIE Ist das die Frau, *die* so schön ist und *deren* Tochter mit Gretchen in die Schule geht? Die Dame, *der* ich einmal eine Jacke lieh, *die* sie mir nie zurückgegeben hat?

ANTON Richtig. Die Tochter ist das Mädchen, *das* Gretchens Schulkollegin ist, *dessen* grüne Augen sie beneidet, und mit *dem* sie gern Tennis spielt. Vicky ist ein Mädchen, *das* jeder liebt.

SUSIE Die Firmen, *die* Werbefachleute brauchen, sind hauptsächlich in München, nicht wahr?

ANTON Du meinst die Firmen, *deren* Hauptsitze in München sind?

SUSIE Ja, die großen Firmen, bei *denen* man Karriere machen kann.

ANTON Leider ja. Mit den Organisationen, *die* ich kenne, stimmt das.

Relative Pronouns

Relative pronouns introduce a clause that modifies, explains, elaborates on a noun (or pronoun); example:

Kennst du den *Mann* (ihn), *der* dort steht?
Do you know the man (him) who is standing there?

Forms of ***der*** and, much less frequently, ***welcher,*** are used as relative pronouns.

MASCULINE SINGULAR	FEMININE SINGULAR
nom.: **der (welcher)**	**die (welche)**
gen.: **dessen**	**deren**
dat.: **dem (welchem)**	**der (welcher)**
acc.: **den (welchen)**	**die (welche)**

NEUTER SINGULAR	PLURAL
nom.: **das (welches)**	**die (welche)**
gen.: **dessen**	**deren**
dat.: **dem (welchem)**	**denen (welchen)**
acc.: **das (welches)**	**die (welche)**

The word to which the pronoun relates determines its gender and number:

> *Die Frau, die* **so schön ist (f. sing.)**
> The woman who is so beautiful
> *Die Firmen, deren* **(f. pl.) Hauptsitze in München sind**
> The firms whose home offices are in Munich

The relative clause is always set off from the main clause by a comma. In a relative clause, verb forms always stand last:

> **Die Frau, deren Tochter mit Gretchen in die Schule geht**

Demonstrative Pronouns

Demonstrative pronouns point to a particular person (or thing); example: *Dieser* **Mensch ist nett** (This person is nice). Or: *Jenes* **Haus ist klein** (That house is small).

The forms of the *der*-words can also be used as *demonstrative pronouns:*

> *Der* **ist ein netter Mensch;** *das* **ist sehr schön;**
> **ich treffe** *den* (this one); *dem* (to this one) **gebe ich nichts.**

Interrogative Pronouns

Interrogative pronouns are used to inquire after a person, thing, place, idea, or action.

We are already familiar with many of the forms of the *interrogative pronoun:* **wer, wessen** (of whom), **wem, wen, welcher, warum,** etc.

Note also: **womit** (with what), **worauf** (on what), **was für ein** (what kind of).

Drei Witze

HERR SCHMIDT (am Telephon)
Bezahlen Sie uns heute die Rechnung?

HERR KRAUSE Noch nicht.

HERR SCHMIDT Wenn Sie sie nicht jetzt bezahlen, dann sage ich allen Ihren Gläubigern (creditors), **daß Sie uns bezahlt haben.**

„**Nein, ich brauche den Job nicht. Der hat keine Zukunft für mich. Die Tochter des Chefs** (of the boss) **ist bereits verheiratet** (married).‟

„**Herr Schultz, meine Frau hat gesagt, ich soll Sie um eine Gehaltserhöhung** (a raise in salary) **bitten.**‟
„**Gut. Ich frage meine Frau, ob** (whether) **ich Ihnen eine geben soll.**‟

EXERCISE 21 Fill in the proper relative pronouns:
1. **Er kennt den Mann, _____ dort steht.**
2. **Das ist die Frau, _____ Tochter ich kenne.**
3. **Vicky ist ein Mädchen, _____ sehr schön ist.**
4. **Karl Bauer hat einen Sohn, _____ Name Peter ist.**
5. **Peter ist der Junge, _____ ich das Buch gebe.**
6. **Anton ist der Mann, _____ euch lieb hat.**
7. **Das ist die Frau, _____ dort steht.**
8. **Die Firmen, _____ Werbefachleute brauchen, sind in München.**
9. **Das sind die Männer, mit _____ man arbeiten soll.**
10. **Ich spreche von den Frauen, _____ Söhne hier sind.**

EXERCISE 22 Answer in complete German sentences.
1. **Was lieh Susie der Frau des Bekannten?**
2. **Was spielt Gretchen mit ihrer Schulkollegin?**
3. **Wo sind die Hauptsitze der Werbefirmen?**
4. **Wem verdankt Anton seine jetzige Stellung?**
5. **Was für einen Job hat Kristy?**

EXERCISE 23 Insert the missing demonstrative pronouns, *der, die, das,* etc.
1. **Ich kaufe** _____.
      this one, (m.)
2. **Was geben wir** _____?
             to this one (f)
3. _____ **ist alles sehr schön.**
      That
4. **Hast du** _____ **gesehen?**
             these
5. _____ **ist sehr fleißig.**
      This one (m.)

EXERCISE 24 Translate into English.
1. **Die Firma, die ihren Hauptsitz in München hat, ist groß.**
2. **Der Mann, den ich kenne, ist klein.**
3. **Die grünen Augen, die sie hat, sind schön.**
4. **Die Frau, die so schön ist, ist meine Freundin.**
5. **Der Freund, dem ich meine Stellung verdanke, ist Konrad.**

EXERCISE 25 Complete the following sentences.
1. **Ich verdanke ihm die** _____.
2. **Gretchens Schulkollegin hat grüne** _____.
3. **Vicky ist ein Mädchen, das jeder** _____.
4. **Damals lieh ich der Dame eine** _____.
5. **Das ist eine große Firma, bei der man Karriere** _____.

CHAPTER 6

Heute gehen wir ins Gasthaus und nachher ins Kino
Tonight We Are Going to a Restaurant and Then to the Movies

Prepositions; Direct and Indirect Object

A preposition is a word that combines with a noun or pronoun to form a phrase, e.g., *on* the table, *for* me; *auf* dem Tisch, *für* mich.

Tonight Nora, Karl, and Gretchen will eat some traditional German dishes at a popular place near their home. Afterwards they will take in a movie. Kristy comes along too.

Einer von uns ist telepathisch.

Vocabulary

angenehm	agreeable
anrufen	to call (by telephone)
denken	to think
durch	through
Ecke (f)	corner
es wäre doch nett	it would be nice
gegen	*here:* (at) about
Kopf (m)	head
ohne	without
erst	only
Spaziergang (m)	walk, stroll
die Straße entlang	along or down the street (Notice the noun *preceding* the preposition.)
um	*here:* around
vor zehn Minuten	ten minutes ago

Note: 37.5° Centigrade equals 99.5° Fahrenheit

Prepositions Taking the Accusative

entlang, um, durch, gegen, ohne, für

It is Saturday afternoon at the Bauers. Karl, just coming home from a walk, enters the livingroom. Nora looks up from a book she has been reading.

NORA Schön draußen?
KARL Ein herrlicher Tag.
NORA Wie war der Spaziergang (m)

KARL Sehr angenehm. Wie ich da die Straße *entlang um* die Ecke gehe, denke ich, es wäre doch nett, Kristy einzuladen.

NORA Du meinst, ins Gasthaus?

KARL Genau. Und dann ins Kino.

NORA Weißt du was? Ich habe sie gerade angerufen.

KARL Und eingeladen?

NORA Ja.

KARL Aber mir ist das erst vor zehn Minuten *durch* den Kopf gegangen. Einer von uns muß telepathisch sein.

NORA Sie ist *gegen* fünf Uhr hier. Aber leider müssen wir *ohne* den Jungen gehen.

KARL Hat er noch immer Fieber?

NORA Nicht viel. 37,5 (siebenunddreißig-fünf). Frau Schulze bleibt bei ihm *für* den Abend.

KARL Schade. Peter geht so gern essen.

NORA In welches Restaurant sollen wir gehn?

KARL Obermayer vielleicht? Oder etwas Besseres?

NORA Nein. Obermayer ist nett und gemütlich.

Grammar Again (but rather painless)

Please note: In time expressions *gegen* also means *around, at about*.
Die Kinder kommen gegen fünf (Uhr). The children are coming around five (o'clock).

Er ist gegen das Fernsehen.   He is against television.

Some prepositions contract with the article *das:* **ins Restaurant** instead of **in das Restaurant.** The same is true in the case of *fürs (für das)* and *ums (um das).*

EXERCISE 1 Insert the missing words in German.
1. **Es geht ihm _____ den Kopf.**
                    through
2. **Ich bin _____ den Krieg (war).**
              against
3. **Sie sind im Restaurant _____ den Jungen.**
                              without
4. **Sie gehen die Straße _____.**
                        along
5. **Karl kommt _____ neun.**
                  around

EXERCISE 2 Answer in German.
1. **Warum kann Peter nicht mitkommen?**
2. **Wann ist Kristy hier?**
3. **Wie lange (how long) bleibt Frau Schulze bei Peter?**
4. **Wann ist ihm das durch den Kopf gegangen?**
5. **In welches Gasthaus gehen sie?**

EXERCISE 3 Complete each sentence.
1. **Ich habe Kristy gerade _____.**
2. **Einer von uns muß _____.**
3. **Peter geht so gern _____.**
4. **Ich gehe die Straße entlang um die _____.**
5. **Wir müssen leider ohne den Jungen _____.**

EXERCISE 4 Write the following sentences in German.
    1. He goes down the street.
    2. I just called her.
    3. He must go without the boy.
    4. It is about seven o'clock.
    5. I buy it for him.
    6. She comes around the corner.
    7. I get it through him.

EXERCISE 5 Translate into English.
    1. **Schön draußen?**
    2. **Es wäre nett, sie einzuladen.**
    3. **Vielleicht etwas Besseres?**
    4. **Mir ist das durch den Kopf gegangen.**
    5. **Ich gehe die Straße entlang.**

Das Gasthaus Obermayer

Vocabulary

außer	aside from
begrüßen	to greet
dauern	*here:* to take (time)
entfernt	distant, away; *here:* "twenty minutes *away* from . . ."
entgegenkommen	*here:* to come toward . . .
es gibt	there are (is)
Gasthaus (n)	restaurant
Gebäude (n)	building
gegenüber	opposite (Here, too, the noun often precedes the preposition.)
Händedruck (m)	handshake
Kino (n)	movie theater, cinema
Konzertsaal (m)	concert hall
läuft	runs, is running
man betritt	one enters
Menu (n)	menu (in German pronounced *Menü*)
mitkommen	to come along
nach	after
Platz nehmen	to take a seat
seit	since, for
Speisekarte (f)	bill of fare, menu
Stammgast (m)	regular guest
Tafel (f)	blackboard
ungefähr	approximately
zu Fuß (m)	on foot

Prepositions Taking the Dative

von, zu, gegenüber, außer, nach, seit, aus, bei, mit

    Das Gasthaus des Herrn Obermayer ist ungefähr zwanzig Minuten *vom* Haus Herrn Bauers entfernt. *Mit* dem Auto dauert das wahrscheinlich nur vier Minuten. Aber sie gehen *zu* Fuß. Es ist in einem alten Gebäude, dem Zentralkino *gegenüber*. *Außer* diesem gibt es noch zehn andere Kinos in der Stadt, auch ein Stadttheater und einen Konzertsaal. *Nach* dem Essen wollen

sie sich den letzten Jürgen Kaiser Film ansehen, der *seit* fünf Tagen im Zentralkino läuft. Kristy, die junge Dame *aus* Amerika, die *bei* ihrer Kusine Susie wohnt, ist mitgekommen. Man betritt das Gasthaus. Nora und Karl sind Stammgäste. Herr Obermayer kommt ihnen entgegen und begrüßt sie *mit* einem freundlichen Händedruck. Sie nehmen Platz und er zeigt ihnen die Speisekarte, eine große Tafel, auf der man das heutige Menu sehen kann.

Please note:

vom Haus	= *von dem* Haus
zum Haus	= *zu dem* Haus (with a neuter noun)
zur Universität	= *zu der* Universität (with a feminine noun)
beim Lehrer	= *bei dem* Lehrer

EXERCISE 6 Insert the missing words in German.

1. **Außer** _____ **Zentralkino gibt es zehn andere.**
   the
2. **Gegenüber** _____ **Haus des Herrn Bauer ist ein Garten.**
   the
3. **Kristy kommt** _____ **anderen Land.**
   from a
4. **Herr Obermayer kommt** _____ **Speisekarte.**
   with the
5. **Sie wohnt bei** _____ **Kusine.**
   the
6. **Von** _____ **Haus** _____ **Kino geht man 20 Minuten.**
   the   to the
7. **Er weiß es seit** _____ **Jahr.**
   a
8. **Nach** _____ **Essen gehen sie ins Kino.**
   the

EXERCISE 7 Translate into English.

1. **Außer dem Zentralkino gibt es zehn andere.**
2. **Herr Obermayer kommt mit der Speisekarte.**
3. **Sie sind Stammgäste seit vielen Jahren.**
4. **Sie gehen zu Fuß ins Restaurant.**
5. **Dem Konzertsaal gegenüber ist das Theater.**

EXERCISE 8 Choose the correct words.

1. **Nach dem Essen gehen sie**
   a. **tanzen** b. **schwimmen** c. **ins Kino**
2. **Gegenüber dem Kino ist**
   a. **das Gasthaus** b. **eine Garage** c. **das Stadttheater**

3. **Kristy kommt**
   a. **aus England** b. **aus Berlin** c. **aus Amerika**
4. **Vom Haus des Herrn Bauer geht man**
   a. **drei Minuten** b. **zwanzig Minuten** c. **eine Stunde**
5. **Herr Obermayer kommt mit**
   a. **der Speisekarte** b. **der Rechnung** c. **der Tochter**

EXERCISE 9 Write the following in German.

1. They go on foot.
2. Aside from Obermayer's restaurant
3. Today's menu is on a big blackboard.
4. With the car it takes four minutes.
5. They are regular guests.

Some Culinary Notes: At Obermayer's our friends are probably enjoying a hearty German soup. One, a strong beef consommé, is called a *Kraftbrühe* (strength broth). The "fine broth of a boy" the Irish speak of has probably consumed lots of it and other staples such as *Erbsensuppe* (pea soup) and *Linsensuppe* (lentil soup), which often contain pork or other meat. Soups like *Aalsuppe* (eel), *Biersuppe* (beer), and *Ochsenschwanzsuppe* (oxtail) are not everyone's cup of tea or, rather, soup. Since our friends are in Southern Germany, in Bavaria, they might be savoring *Rumfordsuppe,* named for famed inventor Benjamin Thompson of Woburn, Massachusetts, created Count of Rumford by the Elector of Bavaria. Rumford ran the army and became the country's most powerful official. Wanting the Bavarians, especially the army, to be well nourished, he invented the soup that bears his name. It consists of potatoes, barley, peas, meat scraps, bread crusts, and, sometimes, stale beer. Most Bavarians are too proud of their fine beers to let them get stale. Some would rather skip soup and drink beer, also known as *flüßiges Brot* (liquid bread).

Another famous foreigner who made it big in Bavaria, for a while at least, was the dancer Lola Montez. Her lover, King Ludwig I, made her "Countess of Landsfeld." Because she was a pioneer in the fight for women's rights, Kristy thinks highly of Lola. After a brief but eventful career in Munich, Lola acted on the stage in America and died in poverty in New York.

But let's get back to our subject. Our friends select *gekochtes Rindfleisch* (boiled beef). More unusual regional dishes are also found in Germany. Chancellor Helmut Kohl is particularly partial to *Pfälzer Saumagen* (stuffed pig's stomach, Palatinate style) and invites visiting dignitaries to sample it. Despite its unlovely name, hog belly *à la* Palatinate might please your palate too. Much farther north, *Zwischenahner Smoortaal* is eel smoked with a variety of woods (exactly which ones is a secret) and doused in *Schnaps.* You eat it with your hands, which are then rinsed in more *Schnaps.* Not for teetotalers *(Abstinenzler).*

The guests at Obermayer's finish up with eclairs, *Liebesknochen* (love bones). Eat too many and you'll develop "love handles" *(Hüftpolster)* and plenty of pounds all over.

Die schlimme° Katze   naughty

Vocabulary

an	at, to
auf	*here:* on
belästigen	to bother
Boden (m)	floor
Brot (n)	bread
das spielt doch keine Rolle	it doesn't matter
entschuldigen Sie	excuse me
frischgebacken	freshly baked
hängen	to hang
hinter	behind
in Ordnung	O.K.
Kirche (f)	church
Komm her!	Come here!
Korb (m)	basket
lachen	to laugh
mit gerunzelter Stirn	with a frown
mittelalterlich	medieval
neben	beside, next to
nicht weiter	not anymore
ruhig	quiet(ly)
plötzlich	suddenly

schlimm	*here:* naughty
schwarz	black
sitzen	to sit
springt auf (aufspringen)	jumps up
stellen	to put
Suppenterrine (f)	soup tureen
über	over
um	*here:* in order to
unter	under
Vollmond (m)	full moon
wieder zurück	back again
zwischen	between

Prepositions Taking the Dative or the Accusative:

auf, an, neben, unter, über, zwischen, in, vor, hinter

Die Kellnerin kommt mit einer großen Suppenterrine und stellt sie *auf den* Tisch, *an dem* die Gäste sitzen. *Neben die* Terrine stellt sie einen großen Korb mit frischgebackenem Brot. Die schöne, schwarze Katze des Herrn Obermayer sitzt *unter dem* Tisch. Plötzlich springt sie *über den* Sessel, der *zwischen der* Amerikanerin und Gretchen steht, und dann wieder zurück *unter den* Tisch. Die Gäste lachen. Herr Obermayer kommt mit gerunzelter Stirn.

OBERMAYER   Bitte entschuldigen Sie. Komm her. Du bist sehr schlimm heute. (Er nimmt die Katze *auf den* Arm.) Weißt du nicht, daß du ruhig *unter dem* Tisch *auf dem* Boden liegen mußt?

KARL   Aber bitte, das spielt doch keine Rolle.

GRETCHEN   Sie ist so herzig.

OBERMAYER   Die belästigt Sie nicht weiter. Ist die Suppe in Ordnung?

ALLE   Ausgezeichnet.

Heute sind viele Touristen *in der* Stadt. Sie sind *in die* Stadt gekommen, um die mittelalterliche Architektur zu bewundern, und auch die Statuen *vor* und *hinter der* Kirche. *Über der* Stadt hängt ein wunderschöner Vollmond.

Grammar the Easy Way

Die Katze sitzt unter   *where / wo?*
dem Tisch

The cat's LOCATION is described: we use the DATIVE.

Die Katze springt   *where to / wohin?*
(jumps) über *den*
Sessel.

The cat's DESTINATION is described, the motion toward some goal: we use the ACCUSATIVE.

EXERCISE 10   Fill in the missing articles with the proper endings.
1. **Sie stellt einen Korb neben** _____ **Terrine.**
2. **Der Mond hängt über** _____ **Stadt.**
3. **Die Katze springt über** _____ **Tisch.**
4. **Die Touristen sind in** _____ **Kirche.**
5. **Sie sind in** _____ **Stadt gekommen.**
6. **Die Katze spielt auf** _____ **Boden.**

7. Der Sessel steht zwischen ＿＿＿＿＿＿ **Kellner und mir.**
8. Der Hund liegt unter ＿＿＿＿＿＿ **Tisch.**
9. Er läuft vor ＿＿＿＿＿＿ **Haus.**
10. Sie geht in ＿＿＿＿＿＿ **Museum.**

EXERCISE 11 Write the following sentences in German.
1. Please excuse me.
2. It doesn't matter.
3. You are very naughty today.
4. We eat freshly baked bread.
5. The cat sits on the floor.

EXERCISE 12 Translate into English.
1. **Die wird Sie nicht weiter belästigen.**
2. **Sie geht hinter die Kirche.**
3. **Die Kellnerin bringt einen großen Korb.**
4. **Die Suppe ist in Ordnung.**
5. **Wir bewundern die mittelalterliche Architektur.**

EXERCISE 13 Answer in complete German sentences.
1. **Wohin sind viele Touristen gekommen?**
2. **Wo sitzt die Katze?**
3. **Wo ist die Suppe?**
4. **Wohin stellt die Kellnerin den Korb?**
5. **Wo sind die Statuen?**

Ein Witz (?)

GAST **Kellner, diese Suppe ist kalt.**

KELLNER **Was wollen Sie von mir? Soll ich mir die Finger verbrennen** (burn my fingers)?

Rindfleisch° und Liebesknochen° beef, eclairs

Vocabulary

(an)statt	instead of
aufessen	to eat up
beginnen	to begin
bestellen	to order
denn	for
dick	fat
es schmeckt ihnen gut	it tastes good; they like it
Portion (f)	portion, helping
sich beeilen (be-eilen)	to hurry up
sie ißt	she eats
Spinat (m)	spinach
trotz	in spite of
während	during
wegen	because of
zum Dessert (n) (pronounce *desér*)	for dessert

Prepositions Taking the Genitive

statt, trotz, während, wegen

Die Gäste haben das gekochte Rindfleisch und zum Dessert Liebeskno-
chen bestellt, und es schmeckt ihnen allen sehr gut. Nora ißt Spinat *statt der*
Salzkartoffeln. Kartoffeln, sagt sie, machen sie zu dick. *Trotz der* großen
Portionen essen sie alles auf. *Während des* Desserts sieht Karl auf die Uhr.
Wegen des Kinos müssen sie sich beeilen, denn es beginnt in zehn
Minuten.

Gretchen und Jürgen Kaiser

Vocabulary

Anisplätzchen (n)	anise cookies
Besuch (m)	visit
dafür	for it
das tropft (tropfen)	that drips
der (die) Erwachsene	the adult
geben	to give
Gefrorenes (n)	ice cream
gefüllte Datteln (f. pl.)	stuffed dates
Geld (n)	money
Gib! (geben)	give
gleich	right away
Hat Ihnen der Film gefallen?	Did you like the film?
Hör doch damit auf!	Stop this!
ein Hundertmarkschein (m)	a hundred-mark bill
Karte (f)	ticket
Kasse (f)	ticket window
kein Wunder	no wonder
Kontrollabschnitt (m)	stub
Naseputzen (n)	blowing of noses
Platzanweiser (m)	usher
Programm (n)	program
sammeln	to collect
Schlange (f)	*here*: line
Schmachtfetzen (m)	tearjerker
schnell	fast
Seufzen (n)	sighing
sei so gut	be so kind
die Süßigkeiten (f. pl.)	sweets
Taschentuch (n)	handkerchief
total	*here*: totally
überlassen	to relinquish
unerhört!	*here*: terrific!
vergessen	to forget
vierzehn	fourteen
wieviel?	how much?
zum Andenken (n)	for a souvenir
Zuschauerraum (m)	auditorium
zwanzig	twenty

Direct and Indirect Objects

In front of the ticket window at the movies:

NORA **Schau dir die Schlange an!**

KRISTY **Unerhört!**

NORA **Kein Wunder. Kaiser ist der populärste Filmstar in Deutschland.**

GRETCHEN **Er ist herrlich!**

KARL **Habt ihr euch genug Taschentücher mitgenommen?**

NORA **Geh, hör doch auf damit!**

KRISTY **Aber es geht ziemlich schnell. Wir sind gleich an der Kasse.**

KARL **Vier Karten, bitte; drei für Erwachsene, eine für ein Mädchen unter vierzehn. Wieviel ist das?**

KASSIERER **Zwanzig Mark, bitte.**
(They enter the theater.)

KRISTY (to Karl) **Wollen Sie** *mir*, **bitte,** *die Karten* **geben? Zum Andenken an unseren Kinobesuch?**

KARL (He does.) **Sie sammeln** *die Kinokarten?* **Gretchen sammelt** *die Programme.* **Besonders von Filmen mit Jürgen. Aber Sie müssen** *dem Platzanweiser den Kontrollabschnitt* **überlassen.**

NORA **Die Süßigkeiten!**

KARL **Total vergessen! Nora, sei so gut und gib** *Gretchen das Geld* **dafür. Ich habe bloß einen Hundertmarkschein bei mir.**

GRETCHEN **Was soll ich kaufen? Gefrorenes?**

NORA **Nein, das tropft. Vielleicht Anisplätzchen oder gefüllte Datteln.**

Eine halbe Stunde später hört man im Zuschauerraum viel Seufzen und Naseputzen. Nora gibt *Gretchen ein Taschentuch.*

KARL (to Kristy) **Hat Ihnen der Film gefallen?**

KRISTY **Soso. Und Ihnen?**

KARL **Ein Schmachtfetzen!** (to Gretchen) **Gretchen?**

GRETCHEN **Er ist herrlich!**

This is a good rule: If the direct object is a noun, it follows the indirect object; if the direct object is a pronoun, it precedes the indirect object.

Dative nouns usually precede accusative nouns.

	INDIRECT OBJECT DATIVE	DIRECT OBJECT ACCUSATIVE
Sie sammelt		**die Programme.**
Sie gibt	**mir** (to me)	**die Karten.**
Sie überläßt	**dem Platzanweiser** (to him)	**den Kontrollabschnitt.**
Gib	**ihr** (to her)	**das Geld.**
Die Kellnerin bringt den Gästen (to them)		**das Essen.**

Accusative pronoun objects precede dative pronoun objects.

	DIRECT OBJECT ACCUSATIVE	INDIRECT OBJECT DATIVE
Er gibt	**es** (the handkerchief)	**ihr** (to Gretchen).
Sie gibt	**ihn** (the stub)	**ihm** (to the usher).
Sie bringt	**es** (the food)	**ihnen** (to the guests).

EXERCISE 14 Insert the missing prepositions and definite articles.

1. **Ich esse Brot** _____ **Spinats.**
   instead of the

2. _____ **Ferien bin ich in Deutschland.**
   During the

3. _____ schlechten Wetters sind die Fenster offen.
      In spite of the
4. **Er beeilt sich** _____ **Kinos.**
          because of the

EXERCISE 15 Choose the right words.
1. **Zum Dessert bestellen sie**
  a. **Brot** b. **Anisplätzchen** c. **Liebesknochen**
2. **Das Kino beginnt in**
  a. **zehn Minuten** b. **zwei Minuten** c. **einer Stunde**
3. **Was hat Karl vergessen?**
  a. **seine Uhr** b. **die Süßigkeiten** c. **die Kinokarten**
4. **Warum will Nora kein Gefrorenes?**
  a. **weil es tropft** b. **weil es süß ist**
  c. **weil es gut schmeckt**
5. **Nora gibt ihrer Tochter**
  a. **fünf Mark** b. **ein Taschentuch** c. **einen Mantel**

EXERCISE 16 Complete each sentence with a word listed below:
Uhr, Kinobesuches, Rindfleisch, Schmachtfetzen, Platzanweiser.
1. **Sie essen das gekochte** _____.
2. **Karl sieht auf die** _____.
3. **Zum Andenken unseres** _____.
4. **Der Kontrollabschnitt ist für den** _____.
5. **Karl sagt, der Film ist ein** _____.

EXERCISE 17 Write the following in German.
1. Potatoes make Nora fat.
2. Did you take enough handkerchiefs along?
3. Karl says the film is a tearjerker.
4. Stop it!
5. Terrific!
6. No wonder
7. How much is that?

EXERCISE 18 True or false?   T / F
1. **Kaiser ist sehr populär.**   _____
2. **Karl kauft sechs Karten.**   _____
3. **Die Karten kosten fünfzehn Mark.**   _____
4. **Gretchen kauft Gefrorenes.**   _____
5. **Er gibt Kristy die Karten.**   _____

EXERCISE 19 Insert the correct German words.
1. **Er gibt** _____ **die Karten.**
      to the usher
2. **Gib dem Karl** _____.
      the program
3. **Er zeigt** _____ **die Stadt.**
      to the tourists
4. **Sie bringt** _____ _____.
      to the mother   the bread
5. **Gib** _____ _____.
    to the sister   the watch

EXERCISE 20 Replace the nouns of Exercise 19 with the correct German pronouns.
1. **Er gibt** _____ _____.
2. **Gib** _____ _____.
3. **Er zeigt** _____ _____.
4. **Sie bringt** _____ _____.
5. **Gib** _____ _____.

CHAPTER 7

Susie, Nora und Kristy gehen einkaufen
Susie, Nora, and Kristy Go Shopping
Off to Brandstätter's Department Store

Verbs—Present Tense

sein, haben, werden

A verb is a word that expresses an act or occurrence, e.g., Karl *rises, eats* breakfast; *steht auf, ißt* **Frühstück,** etc. Verbs can also express states of being, e.g., Kristy *is, becomes, remains (**ist, wird, bleibt**).*

Familienangelegenheiten

Nora, Susie, and Kristy enter the store talking. Nora has apparently had some trouble at home, but no details are given.

Vocabulary

Absicht (f)	intention
ausgehen	to go out
ausreichend	sufficient
Beisammensein (n)	togetherness
Biber (m)	beaver
du solltest	you should
erklären	to explain
Familienangelegenheiten (f.pl.)	family matters
gelangweilt (langweilen)	bored
genauso	just as
Heute wird nicht gespart.	Today I'm not going to skimp.
hoffen	to hope
Ich bin schlechter Laune (f).	I am in a bad mood.
ich nehme an (annehmen)	I suppose (to suppose)
im Grunde genommen	actually
innerhalb (preposition, takes genitive)	within

Kaufhaus, Warenhaus (n)	department store
Konfliktstoff (m)	subject of conflict
Kredit (m)	credit
Kreditkarte (f)	credit card
Kunstleder (n)	artificial (imitation) leather
Kunstpelz (m)	artificial (fake) fur
ledig	unmarried
Nerven (m. pl.)	nerves
Nerz (m)	mink
Nerzmäntel (m. pl.)	mink coats
Pelzmantel (m)	fur coat
Pelzwaren (f. pl.)	furs
Problem (n)	problem
Schlußverkauf (m)	final bargain sale
schützen	to protect
Silberfuchs (m)	silver fox
Tiere (n. pl.)	animals
töten	to kill
wäre nicht schlecht	would not be bad
Was ist passiert?	What happened?
Welt (f)	world

NORA *Ich bin* schlechter Laune . . .

SUSIE Was ist passiert?

NORA *Du bist* noch ledig, Susie. Familienangelegenheiten . . . *er ist* ein netter Junge . . .

KRISTY Du meinst Peter?

NORA Ja. *Er ist* ein guter Junge, und Gretchen—also, *sie ist* ein braves Mädchen, nicht wahr? Wie soll ich das erklären? Karl und ich, *wir sind* sehr glücklich mit den Kindern—*ihr seid* nicht gelangweilt mit meinen Problemen? *Sie sind* im Grunde genommen . . .

SUSIE . . . die besten Kinder in der Welt. Du solltest mehr ausgehen. Wie heute. Zu viel Beisammensein innerhalb der Familie ist schlecht für die Nerven.

Grammar Again

These are the present tense forms of the verb *sein* (to be):

PERSON	SINGULAR		PLURAL	
1st	**ich bin**	I am	**wir sind**	we are
2nd	**du bist**	you are	**ihr seid**	you are
3rd	**er, sie, es ist**	he, she, it is	**sie sind**	they are
			Sie sind	you are (formal)

Try to find the conjugated forms of *sein* in the dialog you just read.

The familiar *du* (sing.) and *ihr* (pl.) are used when talking to friends, relatives, children, pets, saints, or deities. If Nora had addressed a stranger, she would have started out like this:

Sie sind noch ledig . . .

The pronoun *Sie,* when addressing someone formally, is always capitalized. *Sie* is both singular and plural.

Ein neuer Pelzmantel?

SUSIE *Ich habe* die Absicht—also heute wird nicht gespart.

NORA Ich nehme an, *du hast* genug Geld bei dir oder auf deiner Kreditkarte.

KRISTY *Sie hat* gestern ihr Gehalt bekommen.

NORA	Ein neuer Pelzmantel wäre nicht schlecht.
VERKÄUFERIN	(saleslady) *Wir haben* heute einen Schlußverkauf in Pelzwaren.
KRISTY	Ich hoffe, *ihr habt* hier ausreichenden Kredit zum Ankauf von Nerzmänteln. Führen die auch Nerz?
SUSIE	Nerz, Silberfuchs, Biber—*sie haben* alles.
KRISTY	Aber ach, die armen Tiere! Wir sollten sie schützen, nicht töten. Wir sollten eigentlich nur Kunstpelze tragen. Die sind genauso schön. Glaubst du nicht?
NORA	Das ist ein kleiner innerer Konfliktstoff für dich. Ich habe aber ganz andere Probleme.

Grammar You Cannot Do Without

These are the present tense forms of *haben* (to have):

PERSON	SINGULAR		PLURAL	
1st	**ich habe**	I have	**wir haben**	we have
2nd	**du hast**	you have	**ihr habt**	you have
3rd	**er, sie, es hat**	he, she, it has	**sie haben**	they have
			Sie haben	you have (formal)

Now try to spot the forms of *haben* in the dialog above.

The third indispensable verb in this group of verbs is **werden**. It means *to become,* but notice the many idiomatic translation possibilities in:

Ich werde Arzt.	I become a doctor.
Du wirst böse.	You get angry.
Er wird blind.	He goes blind.
Sie werden (ein) Schriftsteller.	You turn out to be a writer.

Plural of werden

wir werden	we become
ihr werdet	you become
sie werden	they become

EXERCISE 1 Fill in the missing verbs (present tense).
1. Er _____ ein guter Mann. (to be)
2. Wir _____ viel Geld. (to have)
3. _____ du zufrieden? (to be)
4. Frau Bauer, Sie _____ eine gute Mutter. (to be)
5. Er _____ ein neues Haus. (to have)
6. Nora und Susie, ihr _____ genug Geld. (to have)
7. Du _____ Ärztin in einem Jahr. (to become)
8. Leider _____ er leicht böse. (to get)
9. Ihr _____ große Männer. (prove to be)

EXERCISE 2 Answer the questions in complete German sentences.
1. Wie heißt das Warenhaus?
2. Was sollte Nora mehr tun?
3. Was ist schlecht für die Nerven?
4. Was hat Susie gestern bekommen?
5. Was für Pelze führt das Kaufhaus Brandstätter?

EXERCISE 3 Write the following sentences in German.
1. I am not bored with your problems. (familiar)
2. This is hard for me to understand.
3. What happened?
4. A mink coat would not be bad.
5. I am in a bad mood.

EXERCISE 4 Change both verbs and nouns (where possible) from singular to plural.
1. **Du hast ein neues Auto.**
2. **Er wird Arzt.**
3. **Sie ist schlechter Laune.**
4. **Ich werde böse.**
5. **Wirst du es kaufen?**

Grammar You'll Love to Hear About

Basic Forms and Stem Changes

It will please you to hear that in German we have only one form in which to express the present tense: *ich höre,* whereas in English you have three to contend with: I hear, I do hear, I am hearing.

Infinite means "without ending." Infinitives don't have personal endings. In English they're sometimes called the "to do" form. To find out who's doing what, when, we have to add endings. You've seen many regular verbs. In the present tense they add the endings *-e, -st, -t, -en, -t,* and *-en* to the stem (what's left after you remove *-en* from the infinitive). The stem of *glauben* is thus *glaub-.*

PERSON	SINGULAR	PLURAL
1st	ich glaub*e*	wir glaub*en*
2nd	du glaub*st*	ihr glaub*t*
3rd	er, sie, es glaub*t*	sie glaub*en*
		Sie glaub*en* (polite form)

Conjugating the many regular verbs you've seen is a cinch. Take verbs like: *bringen, brauchen, fragen, kriegen, machen, rauchen, sagen, suchen, spielen,* and *zeigen.* Start with the *ich* form and continue with the other persons.

Now we have some verbs whose stem ends in *-s, -ss, -ß, -tz* and *-z.* The only change here occurs in the second person singular: **ich tanze, du tanzt;** or **ich grüße, du grüßt.** Since the stem of these words ends with an *s*-sound anyway, to insert an additional *s* would be superfluous. Thus, the ending in the second person is simply *-t.*

There are verbs whose stem ends in *-d* or *-t,* such as *arbeiten* (to work) or *baden* (to bathe). In Southern Germany and Austria, where Kristy is visiting, many people informally say **du arbeitst** or **du wartst.** But the standard German forms, which insert an *e* before the *-st* of the *du* form, and an *e* before the *-t* of the third person singular and the second person plural (the *ihr* form), are really much easier to pronounce. Look at *arbeiten* conjugated for you in the present tense and observe the extra *-e* in the second person (singluar and plural) and in the third person singular.

PERSON	SINGULAR	PLURAL
1st	**ich arbeit***e*	wir arbeit*en*
2nd	**du arbeit***est*	ihr arbeit*et*
3rd	**er arbeit***et*	sie arbeit*en*
		Sie arbeiten (polite)

Or, **ich bad***e* (bathe), **du bad***est,* **er bad***et.*

We have had verbs like this before: *antworten, mieten,* and *reden.* You'll meet a few other verbs like *finden* (to find) and *warten* (to wait) that require insertion of an *e* to make easy pronunciation possible, but they won't cause much trouble.

Susie und ihr Chef (pronounced "sheff")

This is not about Susie's favorite cook but about her obnoxious boss.

Vocabulary

beschäftigt	busy
billig	cheap
darum	*here:* for it
Dort will ich auch hin.	I'd like to go there, too.
Es paßt mir.	It suits me.
Flasche (f)	bottle
Geschäft (n)	business
gesprächig	talkative
Handtasche (f)	pocketbook
Hast du (et)was dagegen?	Do you mind?
Kölnischwasser (n)	cologne
Kostüm (n)	*here:* tailored suit
Lederwarenabteilung (f)	leather goods department
mitbringen	to bring along
miteinander	together
noch immer	still
Parfümerie (f)	cosmetics department
schreiben	to write
Unterbrechung (f.)	interruption
zuhören (with dative)	to listen

NORA   Arbeit*est* du auch manchmal am Samstag, Susie?

SUSIE   Nur wenn wir sehr beschäftigt sind und mein Chef mich darum bitt*et*. Leider ist er sehr gesprächig. Du red*est* zu ihm, aber er hört dir nicht zu; er red*et* und red*et* ohne Unterbrechung. Aber genug vom Geschäft.

NORA   Tanz*t* du gern?

SUSIE   Ja, sehr. Und Anton tanzt sehr gut, wie du weiß*t*.

NORA   Vielleicht können wir wieder einmal miteinander ausgehen.

SUSIE   Das wäre nett.—Wo ist Kristy?

NORA   In der Lederwarenabteilung.

SUSIE   Dort will ich auch hin. Also wir treffen uns später.

Important Vowel Changes

Some verbs change the stem-vowel from E to I:

ich spreche, du sprichst, er spricht
ich treffe, du triffst, er trifft
ich gebe, du gibst, er gibt

(Imperative singular: **sprich! gib!**)

from *a* to *ä* or from *au* to *äu*:

ich schlafe, du schläfst, er schläft
ich trage, du trägst, er trägt
ich laufe, du läufst, er läuft

These changes take place in the second and third person singular only.

Kristy und Susie kaufen ein

Susie trifft Kristy, die ihrer Mutter in Amerika etwas mitbringen will.

KRISTY Mutti *trägt* noch immer ihre alte Handtasche. Ich glaube, sie braucht eine neue. Vielleicht diese hier aus Kunstleder.

SUSIE *Sprichst* du mit ihr am Telephon? Das ist jetzt viel billiger.

KRISTY Nein, aber ich schreibe ihr jede Woche.—*Läufst* du mit mir zur Parfümerie? Ich brauche eine Flasche Kölnischwasser.

SUSIE Ich muß mir ein neues Kostüm kaufen. Glaubst du nicht auch, daß mir ein Kostüm besser paßt als ein Kleid?

KRISTY Genau. Hast du was dagegen, wenn ich mitkomme?

EXERCISE 5 Choose the correct words.
1. **Susies Chef ist sehr**
    a. **gesprächig** b. **nett** c. **schön**
2. **Er redet**
    a. **nie** b. **manchmal** c. **ohne Unterbrechung**
3. **Susie trifft Kristy**
    a. **in der Lederwarenabteilung** b. **in der Parfümerie**
    c. **im Restaurant**
4. **Was sich Susie kaufen will, ist**
    a. **eine Handtasche** b. **ein Kostüm** c. **ein Buch**
5. **Kristy kauft etwas für**
    a. **ihren Bruder** b. **ihren Vater** c. **ihre Mutter**

EXERCISE 6 Insert the German verb in its correct form.
1. **Susie** _____ **gern.** (to dance)
2. **Er** _____ **oft.** (to bathe)
3. _____ **du am Samstag?** (to work)
4. _____ **mir bitte die Handtasche!** (to give)
5. **Sie** _____ **ein neues Kostüm.** (to wear)

EXERCISE 7 Change the subjects and verbs from plural to singular.
1. **Ihr trefft ihn später.**
2. **Ihr schlaft während des Tages.**
3. **Die Mädchen laufen schnell.**
4. **Die Jungen helfen** (to help) **mir.**
5. **Sprecht mit ihm!**

EXERCISE 8 Write the following sentences in German.
1. We are very busy.
2. They go out together.
3. He talks without interruption.
4. He doesn't listen to me.
5. Do you mind?

"Teufelsbalg"

When conjugated, these verbs show a number of irregularities: **sammeln, tun, raten, halten, schelten, nehmen, wissen, lesen.**

Vocabulary

angeblich	supposedly
bei weitem	by far
Bierflasche (f)	beer bottle
blöd(e)	stupid
Briefmarke (f)	stamp

Flammenwerfer (m)	flame thrower
Freude bereiten (f)	to give joy, pleasure
Hältst du mich . . .?	Do you think I am. . .?
Hausaufgabe (f)	homework
Kapitalanlage (f)	investment
Konkurrenz (f)	competition
Krieg spielen	to play war
kurzen Prozeß (m) machen (mit jemandem/etwas)	to give short shrift (to someone/something)
Lederhosen	leather shorts
lesen	to read
Münze (f)	coin
(er) nimmt sich jemanden vor (sich vornehmen)	he deals with someone
raten	to advise
Saison (f) (pronounce "zezón")	season
sammeln	to collect
selten	rare(ly)
(er) schilt mich (schelten)	he scolds me
sein möglichstes	his utmost
Silbermünze (f)	silver coin
Spiel (n)	game
Teufelsbalg (m)	devil's brat
typisch	typical
Verkaufsschlager (m)	popular item; one that sells well
(er) verbrennt jemanden (verbrennen)	he burns someone up (literally!)
Welt (f)	world
wieso?	why? how come?
wissen	to know
zuerst	first

Kristy and Nora pass the coin and stamp counter.

KRISTY Sammelt Peter Briefmarken? Die meisten Jungen tun das.

NORA Natürlich. Wir alle sammeln etwas. Karl sammelt alte Bierflaschen. Ich *sammle* Münzen. Besonders Silbermünzen. Das ist angeblich eine gute Kapitalanlage.
(They walk over to men's wear.)

KRISTY Was, *rätst* du mir, soll ich für meinen Freund in Amerika kaufen?

NORA Etwas typisch Deutsches? Vielleicht Lederhosen?

KRISTY Gute Idee.

NORA Ich gehe indessen zur Computerwelt. (She takes the escalator there and asks the sales lady)
Was is das Neueste in Software für Computerspiele?

VERKÄUFERIN „Teufelsbalg" ist bei weitem der größte Verkaufsschlager der Saison. Der hat mit der Konkurrenz kurzen Prozeß gemacht. „*Hältst* du mich für blöd, daß ich immer noch 'Pac-Man' spielen soll?" *schilt* mich mein Junge. „ 'Teufelsbalg,' der *nimmt* sich seine Feinde vor, einen nach dem anderen, und verbrennt sie mit Flammenwerfern. Wieso *weißt* du das nicht?"

NORA Ihr Sohn muß Ihnen große Freude bereiten.

VERKÄUFERIN Er *tut* sein möglichstes.

NORA *Liest* er auch manchmal etwas?

VERKÄUFERIN Sehr selten. Aber er *weiß*, daß er zuerst seine Hausaufgaben machen muß; dann kann er Krieg spielen.

NORA Geben Sie mir einen „Teufelsbalg."

Grammar That Will Help

sammeln: ich sammle Briefmarken, du sammelst, er sammelt
tun: ich tue, du tust, er tut, wir tun, ihr tut, sie tun
raten: Was rätst du mir? Er rät mir.
halten: Hältst du mich für blöd? Er hält mich für blöd.
schelten: ich schelte ihn, du schiltst mich, er schilt mich
nehmen: ich nehme mir ihn vor, du nimmst dir . . ., er nimmt sich . . .
wissen: ich weiß, du weißt, er weiß, wir wissen, ihr wißt
lesen: ich lese, du liest, er liest, wir lesen

EXERCISE 9 Put into the third person singular (**Er** _____ **Briefmarken**).
1. **Ich sammle Briefmarken.**
2. **Du schiltst Nora.**
3. **Wir wissen alles.**
4. **Was tun wir heute?**
5. **Wir nehmen das Buch.**
6. **Was haltet ihr in der Hand?**
7. **Was rätst du mir?**
8. **Wir lesen viel.**

EXERCISE 10 Fill in the missing letter in the German words.
1. **ICH SAMM__E M__NZEN.**
2. **PETER IST NIC__T BL__D.**
3. **EINE GUT__ KA__ITALAN__AGE**
4. **ET__AS T__PISCH D__UTSCHES**
5. **DANN KAN__ ER KRI__G SP__ELEN.**

EXERCISE 11 Write the following in German.
1. This is a good investment.
2. Leather shorts are typically German.
3. This is the biggest seller of the season.
4. The competition is very strong (**stark**).
5. He does his utmost.

EXERCISE 12 Choose the correct words.
1. **Karl sammelt**
    a. **Zeitungen** b. **Münzen** c. **alte Bierflaschen**
2. **Teufelsbalg**
    a. **verbrennt seine Feinde** b. **macht Hausaufgaben**
    c. **schläft immer**
3. **Was Kristy vielleicht kauft, sind**
    a. **Uhren** b. **Lederhosen** c. **Briefmarken**
4. The second person singular of *halten* is
    a. **hältst** b. **haltest** c. **haltst**
5. The third person singular of *nehmen* is
    a. **nehmt** b. **nehm** c. **nimmt**

Noras Pläne

Vocabulary

Amulett (n)	amulet, charm
Ankündigung (f)	announcement
dabei	in doing so
dreißig	30
dreizehn	thirteen
Einkauf (m)	purchase
fünfmal	five times
goldener, -e, -es	golden
gratulieren	to congratulate
Geburtstag (m)	birthday
Hals (m)	neck
jetzig	present
Laß sehen!	Let me see!
leben	to live
Mir ist das Geld ausgegangen.	I ran short of money.
Möbel (pl.)	furniture
möglicherweise	possibly
Monogramm (n)	initials
noch nicht	not yet
so ziemlich	pretty much
übersiedeln	to move
undenkbar	unthinkable
wir sind umgezogen (umziehen)	we moved
Zauberpyramide (f)	magical pyramid
Zuwachs (m)	addition to the family

Nora, Susie and Kristy meet in the furniture department.

NORA Habt ihr alle eure Einkäufe gemacht?

KRISTY So ziemlich.

SUSIE Mir ist das Geld dabei ausgegangen. Kein Nerz, aber ein Amulett für Anton.

NORA Laß sehen!

SUSIE Ich hab's noch nicht. Wegen des Monogramms. Eine goldene Zauberpyramide, um den Hals zu tragen.

KRISTY Das klingt super.

NORA Der wird sich sehr freuen. Geburtstag?

SUSIE Ja.—(to Nora) Kaufst du neue Möbel?

NORA Möglicherweise. *Ich habe meine jetzigen schon seit dreizehn Jahren.*

KRISTY *Wie lange wohnst du schon hier?*

NORA Ich bin hier geboren.

KRISTY Meine Eltern *leben seit dreißig Jahren in Amerika* und sind fünfmal umgezogen.

NORA Ich brauche neue Möbel, wenn wir übersiedeln. Das jetzige Haus ist zu klein. Peter *schläft schon seit zwei Jahren im Wohnzimmer.* Und wer weiß?

SUSIE Ist das eine Ankündigung?

NORA Vielleicht bekommen wir Zuwachs.

SUSIE, KRISTY Wir gratulieren!

One can hear the singing of children from the children's day care center nearby.

Action Starting in the Past and Continuing into the Present

German, like many other languages, uses the present tense for something that started in the past but is still going on. You may have heard foreigners say in unidiomatic, but quite comprehensible English, "I am in this country since (for) 20 years" or "We are waiting already (for) six months for an answer." German uses *seit* (since, for) or *schon* (already) or both in this construction. Please take another look at the examples of this construction we just saw in the preceding dialog.

Ich habe meine jetzigen Möbel schon seit dreizehn Jahren.
I have had my present furniture for thirteen years.
(I got it thirteen years ago, and I still have it.)

Wie lange wohnst du schon hier?
How long have you been living here?

Meine Eltern leben seit dreißig Jahren in Amerika.
My parents have been living in America for 30 years. (And they still are.)

Peter schläft schon seit zwei Jahren im Wohnzimmer.
Peter has been sleeping in the living room for two years.

EXERCISE 13 Write the following sentences in German.
1. We have been living in Germany for twenty years.
2. He has been here for two hours.
3. She has been working for three months.
4. I was born in New York.
5. Who knows?

EXERCISE 14 Choose the correct words.
1. **Susie kauft Anton**
   a. **einen Nerzmantel**   b. **ein Amulett**   c. **ein Auto**
2. **Nora hat ihre Möbel schon seit**
   a. **dreizehn Jahren**   b. **einem Jahr**   c. **sechs Monaten**
3. **Ihr jetziges Haus ist**
   a. **zu groß**   b. **zu klein**   c. **zu schön**
4. **Sie bekommt vielleicht**
   a. **Zuwachs**   b. **eine Geschirrspülmaschine**   c. **ein Buch**
5. **Susie fragt Nora: „Kaufst du neue Möbel?" Nora antwortet:**
   a. **„Natürlich."**   b. **„Absolut nicht."**   c. **„Möglicherweise."**

EXERCISE 15 Translate into English.
1. **Ich lebe hier schon zehn Jahre.**
2. **Ist das eine Ankündigung?**
3. **Das ist undenkbar.**
4. **Möglicherweise**
5. **So ziemlich**

EXERCISE 16 True or false?   T / F
1. **Die Zauberpyramide ist für Karls Geburtstag.**   _____
2. **Noras Haus ist zu klein.**   _____
3. **Kristys Eltern sind nie umgezogen.**   _____
4. **Nora ist in Amerika geboren.**   _____
5. **Vielleicht bekommt Nora Zuwachs.**   _____

EXERCISE 17 Answer in complete German sentences.
1. **Wo ist Nora geboren?**
2. **Wo leben Kristys Eltern?**
3. **Wie lange wohnt Nora in ihrem Haus?**
4. **Wo schläft Peter seit zwei Jahren?**
5. **Was trägt Anton bald (soon) um den Hals?**

CHAPTER 8

Anton findet einen neuen Job
Anton Finds a New Job

Verbs—Past and Future Tenses

Das Interview
The Present Perfect of *sein, haben, werden,* and of Weak Verbs

Vocabulary

(w) = weak verb

anständig	decent
früher	previous
gleichzeitig	at the same time
Ich kann Besseres leisten.	I can do better.
Ich weiß das zu schätzen.	I appreciate that.
kündigen (w)	to give notice
Laß ihn kommen!	Let him come!
Lohnschreiber (m)	hack writer
marktschreierische Reklame (f)	ballyhoo, advertising hype
Möglichkeit (f)	opportunity, possibility
schicken (w)	to send
schöpferisch	creative(ly)
Schreiben (n)	letter
Sie haben recht.	You are right.
Stellengesuch (n)	job application
tätig	active
Teilhaber (m)	partner
versichern (w) *(here with dative)*	to assure
wertlos	worthless
Wie geht's?	How are you?

ANTON   (in his new office, on the phone with Susie) **Susie, wie geht's? —*Bist du* gestern im Kino *gewesen?* —War's schön? —Hast du ein paar Minuten? Gut. Also, wie du weißt, den Job, über den *wir* im Café *geredet haben, habe ich* nicht *gekriegt. Ich bin* zu spät dort *gewesen.* Aber ich habe einen anderen. Das ist so passiert:**

(Flashback; Schelling's office in the advertising firm Schelling & Holz.)

SCHELLING   **Bitte nehmen Sie Platz, Herr Gruber. *Sie haben* uns vor zehn Tagen ein Stellengesuch *geschickt. Ich habe* das Schreiben meinem Teilhaber *gezeigt,* und *er hat gesagt,* laß ihn kommen.**

ANTON   **Ich weiß das zu schätzen, Herr Schelling.**

SCHELLING   **Wie lange *haben Sie* für Ihre frühere Firma *gearbeitet?***

ANTON   **Sieben Jahre; ich arbeite dort noch immer. Aber *ich habe gekündigt* und meinem Chef gleichzeitig *versichert,* daß ich bleibe, bis er jemand anders findet.**

SCHELLING   Sehr anständig. Warum *haben Sie gekündigt?*
ANTON   *Ich habe* dort keine Möglichkeit *gehabt*, schöpferisch tätig zu sein.
SCHELLING   Was meinen Sie damit?
ANTON   Sie kennen die Firma.
SCHELLING   Marktschreierische Reklame für wertlose Produkte.
ANTON   Diese Reklame *hab' ich gemacht.*
SCHELLING   Ich glaube, Sie sind ein Idealist.
ANTON   *Ich bin* ein Lohnschreiber *geworden.* Aber ich kann Besseres leisten.
SCHELLING   Ich glaube, Sie haben recht.

More Grammar

English and German use the past participle with a helping verb to form tenses called *perfect* (from the Latin for "finished, done").

> *Bist du* im Kino *gewesen?*

Have you been at the movies? (More idiomatically: Were you at the movies?) Add the past participle *gewesen* to the present tense of *sein* (**ich bin, du bist,** etc.) and you have the present perfect: *ich bin gewesen.* Note that sometimes a German present perfect can be translated by an English present perfect. But very often an English past tense must be used instead. Sometimes you have a choice, as in:

> *Ich habe* dort keine Möglichkeit *gehabt.*
> I have had (had) no opportunity there.

Add the past participle *gehabt* to the present tense of *haben* (**ich habe, du hast,** etc.) and you have the present perfect: **ich habe gehabt.**

> *Ich bin* ein Lohnschreiber *geworden.*
> I have become (became) a hack writer.

Add the past participle *geworden* to the present tense of *sein* (**ich bin, du bist,** etc.) and you have the present perfect: **ich bin geworden.**

You may have noticed that German uses *sein* and *haben* as helping verbs to form the present perfect. We'll talk about that a little later in this chapter. *Werden* and *sein* itself use the auxiliary *sein.*

We speak of regular or weak verbs if there is no change in the stem vowel. In order to form the present perfect of most weak verbs—from now on marked (w)—we use the present tense of *haben* plus the past participle. This we get by adding the prefix *ge-* to the third person of the verb.

Ich kriege den Job.	I get the job.
Ich habe den Job *gekriegt.*	I got the job.
schicken	*Sie haben* ein Stellengesuch *geschickt.*
zeigen	*Ich habe* es meinem Teilhaber *gezeigt.*
sagen	. . . und *er hat gesagt* . . .

Please notice the word order.

> *Ich habe* den Job nicht *gekriegt.*

The past participle (**gekriegt**) stands at the end of the sentence.

EXERCISE 1   Fill in the proper German words

1. **Bist du im Theater** _____?
                       been

2. **Ich hab' den Job** _____.
                       got

3. **Er hat ihm ein Stellengesuch** _____.
                       sent

4. **Hat er Reklame** _____?
                made

5. **Er ist ein Lohnschreiber** _____.
                     become

6. **Wie lange hat er für die Firma** _____?
                         worked

7. **Warum haben Sie** _____?
                given notice

EXERCISE 2 Choose the correct words.
1. **Bist du gestern im Kino**
     a. **geworden?**   b. **gewesen?**   c. **gehabt?**
2. **Der Job, über den wir geredet**
     a. **haben**   b. **sind**   c. **gewesen**
3. **Sie haben uns ein Stellengesuch**
     a. **schickt**   b. **geschickt**   c. **schicken**
4. **Sind Sie heute im Büro**
     a. **gehabt?**   b. **gearbeitet?**   c. **gewesen?**
5. **Anton hat seiner früheren Firma**
     a. **gekündigt**   b. **gearbeitet**   c. **gehabt**

EXERCISE 3 Put the following sentences into the present perfect.
1. **Hast du ein paar Minuten?**
2. **Ich kriege einen Job.**
3. **Ich kündige ihm.**
4. **Er arbeitet sehr viel.**
5. **Er zeigt ihm das Schreiben.**

EXERCISE 4 Answer in complete German sentences.
1. **Wie lange hat Anton für seine frühere Firma gearbeitet?**
2. **Warum kündigt er?**
3. **Was nennt ihn Herr Schelling?**
4. **Wo ist Susie gestern gewesen?**
5. **Wann hat Anton das Schreiben geschickt?**

EXERCISE 5 Write the following in German.
1. Ballyhoo
2. Let him come!
3. What do you mean by that?
4. You are an idealist.
5. Susie, how are you?

Please note: In everyday conversations the Germans prefer using the present perfect. In English the past tense is preferred.

         Sie haben uns ein Schreiben geschickt.
         You sent us a letter.
         Ich habe gekündigt.
         I gave notice.

The German past tense is mostly used in narration.

Die wirksame Schlagzeile

Past Tense; Strong Verbs; Verbs Ending with _-ieren;_ Verbs with Prefixes

Vocabulary

	Abitur (n)	final high school exam
	Annonce (f)	ad
er	**aß (essen, ißt, aß, gegessen)**	he ate

man	**bat (bitten, bittet, bat, gebeten)**	he asked
er	**beschloß (beschließen, beschloß, beschlossen)**	he decided
	bis Mitternacht	till midnight
er	**blieb (bleiben, bleibt, blieb, ist geblieben)**	he stayed
die	**eigenen**	his own
er	**fand (finden, findet, fand, gefunden)**	he found
er	**gestand (gestehen, gestand, gestanden)**	he confessed
	Gewicht (n)	weight
er	**ging (gehen, ging, ist gegangen)**	he went
das	**half (helfen, hilft, half, geholfen)**	that helped
er	**hatte (haben, hat, hatte, gehabt)**	he had
	Konkurrenz (f)	*here*: the competitors
	musikalisches Reimgeklingel (n)	jingles
	probieren (w) *	to try
	sang (singen, sang, gesungen)	he sang
	Schlagzeile (f)	headline; *here*: ''catchy first line''
er	**schlief (schlafen, schläft, schlief, geschlafen**	he slept
er	**schrieb (schreiben, schrieb, geschrieben)**	he wrote
er	**trank (trinken, trank, getrunken)**	he drank
	Sonntagsausgabe (f)	Sunday edition
	studieren (w) *	to study
	verfassen (w) *	to compose, write
er	**verließ (verlassen, verläßt, verließ, verlassen)**	he left
er	**verlor (verlieren, verlor, verloren)**	he lost
	Volkswirtschaftslehre (f)	economics
er	**war (sein, ist, war, gewesen)**	he was
	Werbeagentur (f)	advertising agency
	Werbespot (m)	commercial (for radio and TV)
	wirksam	effective
er	**wußte (wissen, weiß, wußte, gewußt)**	he knew

* refers to explanatory remarks that follow the story.

    Als Anton Wien *verließ*, um sich in Deutschland eine Stellung zu suchen, war es gerade nach dem Abitur. Er *ging* in München auf die Universität and *studierte* Volkswirtschaftslehre. Dann *beschloß* er, in eine kleinere Stadt zu übersiedeln. Dort *fand* er einen Job in einer Werbeagentur. Er hatte immer schon ein Talent fürs Schreiben und das *half* ihm natürlich. Zuerst *bat* man ihn, Werbespots fürs Radio, musikalisches Reimgeklingel und Inserate zu verfassen. ,,Damals habe ich mehr Inserate geschrieben, mehr Annoncen verfaßt, als du in zehn Sonntagsausgaben findest,'' *beichtete* er Susie einmal. Er *wußte*, eine wirksame Schlagzeile ist alles. Er *blieb* oft bis Mitternacht im Büro, *aß*, *trank* und *schlief* im Büro, *verlor* Gewicht, *studierte* die Schlagzeilen und ,,Jingles'' der Konkurrenz, dann *probierte* und *sang* er die eigenen.

Important Information on Verbs

*(w) means that these are ''weak'' verbs which add the following endings to their stems (the stem of a German verb is what remains after you shorten the infinitive by dropping the *-en* endings): the stem of *fragen* (to ask) is *frag-*.

	SINGULAR	PLURAL
1st person	**ich frag -te**	**wir frag -ten**
2nd person	**du frag -test**	**ihr frag -tet**
3rd person	**er, sie, es frag -te**	**sie frag -ten**

If the stem ends in *-d*, *-t*, *-dn*, *tm*, *-chn*, *-fn*, or *-gn* an additional *-e* must be inserted, between the stem and the endings shown above, to make pronunciation easier, e.g. *er arbeitete* (he worked) or *er öffnete* (he opened).

We mentioned before that the past participle of the weak verb is formed by adding the prefix *ge-* to the third person singular of the verb: *er hat gefragt* (he has asked). The prefix *ge-* is used to form the past participle of strong verbs too. Therefore, when you see forms beginning with *ge-* they're usually past participles, e.g., the weak *gesagt, geraucht, gespielt* or the strong *gekommen, getrunken, geschlafen.* But note that verbs beginning with the inseparable prefixes *be-, ge-, emp-, er-, ver-,* and *zer-* add no *ge-* to the past participle. Examples are *er hat beschlossen, verkauft, gestanden* (he has decided, sold, confessed). Note that *gestanden* is the past participle of *gestehen,* a verb which has *ge-* (one of the inseparable prefixes) in every form. No extra *ge-* is added to form the past participle. Inseparable prefixes are never stressed.

The weak *schmieren* (to smear, lubricate) and the strong *frieren* (to freeze) are of Germanic origin and their past participles are *geschmiert* and *gefroren.* But most verbs ending in *-ieren,* including *studieren, telefonieren,* and *interessieren,* are weak verbs of foreign origin. They add no *ge-* to the participle either: *sie hat studiert, telefoniert* (she has studied, telephoned).

Learning strong or irregular verbs in any language, including English, is a bit of a chore. Try to memorize their four basic forms, the infinitive, the 3rd person singular of the present, the past, and the past participle. These four forms are known as the principal parts. For quick reference you can find these difficult verbs listed in alphabetical order in the back of the book. Some of them aren't all that hard. Here are some principal parts that won't give you much trouble.

kommen	**kommt**	**kam**	**gekommen**
to come	comes	came	come
sehen	**sieht**	**sah**	**gesehen**
to see	sees	saw	seen
singen	**singt**	**sang**	**gesungen**
to sing	sings	sang	sung
trinken	**trinkt**	**trank**	**getrunken**
to drink	drinks	drank	drunk

There are many other verbs as easy as these, and numerous others where the relationship to English may be a bit more difficult to spot, but is nevertheless there.

EXERCISE 6 Put the following into the past tense.
1. **Anton findet einen neuen Job.**
2. **Damals hat er viele Briefe geschrieben.**
3. **Er ist bis Mitternacht im Büro geblieben.**
4. **Er arbeitet dort lange.**
5. **Dann hat er Wien verlassen.**
6. **Das Talent fürs Schreiben hilft ihm.**
7. **Er hat Susie darum gebeten.**
8. **Manchmal ißt er im Büro.**
9. **Er hat meistens Wasser getrunken.**
10. **Das Kind singt gern.**

EXERCISE 7 Fill in the correct words.
1. **Er hat mir den Arzt** _____. (to recommend)
2. **Sie hat das Kleid** _____. (to tear)
3. **Wir haben das Spiel** _____. (to lose)
4. **Er hat die Schlagzeile** _____. (to compose)
5. **Das Kind hat die Bonbons** _____. (to try)

EXERCISE 8 Answer in complete German sentences.
1. **Welche Stadt verließ Anton?**
2. **Was suchte er in Deutschland?**
3. **Wo studierte er Volkswirtschaftslehre?**
4. **Was verfaßte er mehr als alles andere?**
5. **Was half ihm dabei?**

EXERCISE 9 Finish the following sentences:
1. **Er blieb oft bis Mitternacht im** _____.
2. **Er beschloß, in eine kleinere Stadt zu** _____.
3. **Er fand einen Job in einer** _____.
4. **Er hatte immer schon ein Talent fürs** _____.
5. **„Damals habe ich mehr Inserate** _____."

Ich bin geflogen, *ich habe* gezählt.

Vocabulary

	am Ende (n)	in the end
	daß ich nicht schlafen konnte	that I couldn't fall asleep
	es fiel mir ein (fallen, fällt, fiel, ist gefallen)	it occurred to me
	es ist mir im Kopf herumgegangen	it went around in my head
	Futter (n)	*here:* lining
ist	**geflogen (past participle of fliegen, flog)**	has flown
ist	**gekommen (kommen, kam)**	has come
sind	**gelaufen (laufen, läuft, lief)**	have run
habe	**geschoren (scheren, schor)**	have shorn
sind	**gewachsen (wachsen, wächst, wuchs)**	have grown
	gräßlich	horrible
sind	**herumgesprungen (-springen, sprang herum)**	have jumped about
	hin und her	back and forth
	Schaf (n)	sheep
	Schlafproblem (n)	sleeping problem
	schließlich	finally
	sechs tausend (6 000)	six thousand

versuchen (w)	to try
(sich) vorstellen (w)	to imagine
waren es	there were
Wolle (f)	wool
zählen (w)	to count
züchten (w)	to raise

Vorige Woche *ist* Anton nach Bonn zu einem Freund *geflogen*, **der ein Schlafproblem hat.**

"Gestern *habe* ich wieder sehr schlecht *geschlafen*; ich weiß nicht, was ich tun soll."

"Warum zählst du nicht Schafe?" meint Anton.

"Auch das *habe* ich *versucht*. Ich *habe* mir *vorgestellt*, daß ich Schafe züchte. Am Ende waren es 6 000; die *sind* sehr schnell *gewachsen*, immer mehr von ihnen *sind gekommen*, *sind* hin und her *gelaufen* und *herumgesprungen*, und ich *habe* sie alle *gezählt*. Dann *habe* ich sie alle *geschoren*. Schließlich *habe* ich aus der Wolle 6 000 Mäntel *gemacht* und sie wieder *gezählt*. Aber dann hatte ich ein gräßliches Problem. Es fiel mir ein, daß ich doch Futter für die 6 000 Mäntel brauche. Das *ist* mir dann so im Kopf *herumgegangen*, daß ich nicht einschlafen konnte."

The Grammar of *haben* and *sein*

In most cases you can form the present perfect tense with the auxiliary verb **haben**: Ich habe sie gezählt; ich habe sie geschoren; ich habe Mäntel gemacht.

However, there are some verbs that take the auxiliary **sein**. How do we know when to use **haben** and when to use **sein**? Luckily, there is a rule that can be relied on:

Sein is to be used when two conditions are met:

1. The verb in question must express motion to a place or change of condition.
2. The verb must be intransitive (which means that it cannot take a direct object).

Er hat Mäntel gemacht.

Machen is transitive.

Sie sind gekommen.

Kommen is intransitive; it also expresses motion.

Er ist gestorben (he has died). **Sterben** (to die) is intransitive; though there obviously is no motion, there certainly is a most radical change of condition.

Of course, there always are exceptions to the rule, as is the case with:

bleiben (to stay): **Er *ist* geblieben**

geschehen (to happen): **Es *ist* geschehen.**

If you've been brushing up your Shakespeare lately, you'll remember forms like *they are come* and *she is fled*, similar to German **sie sind gekommen** and **sie ist geflohen**. The use of *to be* as a helping verb in English is old-fashioned. In German, however, it is very much part of the living language. So learn your "*sein* verbs."

EXERCISE 10 Fill in the correct auxiliary verbs.

1. Wir _____ die Studenten gezählt.
2. Er _____ ins Kino gelaufen.
3. Wir _____ in der Stadt geblieben.
4. Ihr _____ gut geschlafen.
5. Die Kinder _____ herumgesprungen.

EXERCISE 11 Answer in complete German sentences.
1. **Wann ist Anton nach Bonn geflogen?**
2. **Wieviele Schafe hat er gezählt?**
3. **Was hat er aus der Wolle gemacht?**
4. **Was war das Problem?**

EXERCISE 12 Match the following.
1. **Auch das habe ich versucht.**
2. **Ich habe wieder schlecht geschlafen.**
3. **Sie sind hin und her gelaufen.**
4. **Ich habe mir vorgestellt . . .**
5. **Immer mehr sind gekommen.**
6. **Es ist mir im Kopf herumgegangen.**

_____ I imagined . . .
_____ More and more of them came.
_____ It went around in my head.
_____ This, too, I tried.
_____ They ran back and forth.
_____ I slept badly again

EXERCISE 13 Translate into German.
1. The sheep grew very fast.
2. It occurred to me.
3. They ran back and forth.
4. I made 6,000 coats.
5. I had a horrible problem.

Big Shot Anton

Future Tense

Vocabulary

Abendkleid (n)	evening gown
anziehen	to put on
behandeln (w)	to treat
Es sieht gut aus.	It looks good.
Gehaltsaufbesserung (f)	raise in salary
hohes Tier (n)	big shot
im Ernst	seriously
Teilhaberschaft (f)	partnership
zeitig	early
zu Hause	at home

Anton continues his telephone conversation with Susie.

ANTON **Ob ich mit meinem jetzigen Job zufrieden bin? Sehr.** _Ich werde_ **wahrscheinlich einige Jahre hier** _bleiben_**. Schelling** _wird_ **mir in sechs Monaten eine Gehaltsaufbesserung** _geben_**. In ein oder zwei Jahren bekomme ich vielleicht eine Teilhaberschaft. Was sagst du? Ein hohes Tier? Klar.** _Wirst du_ **mich dann mit mehr Respekt** _behandeln_**? Im Ernst, es sieht gut aus.—Was machst du heute?—Ich hole dich ab. Essen und tanzen.** _Wirst du_ **dir dein rotes Abendkleid** _anziehen_**?—Du mußt morgen zeitig aufstehen?—Wir sind vor zwölf zu Hause.** (The phone rings.) **Das** _wird_ **der neue Klient** _sein_**. Servus.**

Note: _**Auf Wiederhören**_ is what most Germans, and even most Austrians, use when saying goodbye on the telephone. But Anton, never failing to assert his Austrian identity, always says _**Servus.**_

More Interesting Information

The future tense is formed by the present tense of the auxiliary verb **werden** plus an infinitive.

Ich werde hier bleiben.

Er wird mir eine Gehaltsaufbesserung geben.

Wirst du dir dein rotes Abendkleid anziehen?

When using the future tense in a simple sentence, put the infinitive at the end of the sentence.

By using a word like *wahrscheinlich* or *vielleicht* together with the present tense, you can imply futurity:

In ein oder zwei Jahren *bekomme*   ***werde ich vielleicht***
***ich vielleicht* eine Teilhaberschaft**   **eine Teilhaberschaft *bekommen*.**

The future can be used to suggest a probability in the present:

Das wird der neue Klient sein.

That's probably the new client.

EXERCISE 14   True or false?   T / F
1. **Anton ist mit seinem jetzigen Job unzufrieden.** _____
2. **Er wird eine Gehaltsaufbesserung kriegen.** _____
3. **Eine Teilhaberschaft bekommt er nie.** _____
4. **Sie werden heute abend Bridge spielen.** _____
5. **Susie wird morgen zeitig aufstehen.** _____

EXERCISE 15   Choose the correct words.
1. **Wie lange wird Anton bei Schelling bleiben?**
   a. **ein Jahr**   b. **zehn Jahre**   c. **einige Jahre**
2. **Wenn das Telephon läutet, glaubt Anton, es ist**
   a. **Karl**   b. **der neue Klient**   c. **Kristy**
3. **Er bekommt die Gehaltsaufbesserung wahrscheinlich**
   a. **in sechs Monaten**   b. **in zwei Jahren**   c. **nie**
4. **Am Ende der Konversation sagt er zu Susie**
   a. **Auf Wiederhören**   b. **Guten Tag**   c. **Servus**

EXERCISE 16   Construct sentences using the cue words.
1. **Schelling / geben / Gehaltsaufbesserung**
2. **Bald / vielleicht / Teilhaberschaft**
3. **Susie / anziehen / Abendkleid**
4. **Abends / essen / tanzen**
5. **Anton / zufrieden / Job**

EXERCISE 17   Write the following sentences in German.
1. Anton is satisfied with his present job.
2. She will treat him with more respect.
3. He will get a raise in salary.
4. Seriously, it looks good.
5. That is probably the new client.

EXERCISE 18   Answer in complete German sentences.
1. **Wie lange wird Anton wahrscheinlich bei Schelling & Holz bleiben?**
2. **Was wird sich Susie abends anziehen?**
3. **Was bekommt Anton vielleicht in zwei Jahren?**
4. **Was bekommt er in sechs Monaten?**
5. **Wann werden sie wieder zu Hause sein?**

CHAPTER 9

Morgens im Hause Bauer
Eine Reifenpanne auf dem Weg nach Hause
Starting the Day at the Bauers
A Flat Tire on the Way Home

Reflexive and Modal Verbs; Double Infinitives; Imperatives

Nora und die Waage

Reflexive Verbs Taking the Accusative

Reflexive verbs are forms whose subject reflects on or refers to itself; example: **Karl wäscht sich** (Karl washes himself).

Vocabulary

abnehmen (nimmt ab, nahm ab, abgenommen)	to lose weight
angezogen	dressed
bereiten (w)	to prepare
Brot (n)	bread
sich erinnern (w)	to remember
sich erkälten (w)	to catch cold
sich gehen lassen	to lose control of oneself
gesund	healthy
Honig (m)	honey
ich müßte sein	I would have to be
Kalorien (f. pl.)	calories
Liebling (m)	darling
nach der Tabelle (f)	according to the table or chart
noch nicht einmal	not yet
Pfund (n)	pound
Selbstdisziplin (f)	self-discipline
sich setzen (w)	to sit down
sofort	right away
sorgen (w)	to worry

streichen (strich, gestrichen)	to spread
Waage (f)	scales
sich wundern (w)	to be surprised
zunehmen (nimmt zu, nahm zu, zugenommen)	to gain weight

Karls Tag beginnt sehr zeitig. Er steht auf, *wäscht sich, rasiert sich* und ist angezogen, und es ist noch nicht einmal sieben Uhr. Dann *setzt* er *sich am* Frühstückstisch. Nora hat das Frühstück bereitet und *setzt sich* zu ihm.

NORA   *Ich wundere mich,* **daß du so wenig Schlaf brauchst.**

KARL   **Manche Menschen haben mit sechs Stunden genug.**

NORA   **Aber du ißt so wenig. Streich dir doch etwas von dem Honig aufs Brot.**

KARL   **Nein danke. Zu viele Kalorien.**

NORA   **Voriges Jahr,** *ich erinnere mich,* **hast du dich um diese Zeit** *erkältet.* **Nimmst du deine Vitamine?**

KARL   *Sorg dich* **nicht, Liebling. Ich fühle mich stark und gesund. Aber wenn** *ich mich gehen lasse,* **nehme ich sofort zu.**

NORA   **Ich bewundere deine Selbstdisziplin. Ich bin gerade auf die Waage gestiegen . . .**

KARL   **Und hast ein paar Pfund zu viel?**

NORA   **Nein; mein Gewicht ist normal. Nach der Tabelle müßte ich bloß um zehn Zentimeter größer sein.**

Something to Reflect on

One of the so-called genuine reflexive verbs is *sich wundern:* **ich wundere mich, du wunderst dich, er, sie, es wundert sich, wir wundern uns, ihr wundert euch, sie (Sie) wundern sich.**

Other verbs may relate back to the subject, but they can also relate to somebody (something) else: *er wäscht sich,* but also: *er wäscht Peter, er wäscht den Tisch.*

Other Reflexive Verbs

sich amüsieren	to amuse oneself
sich entschuldigen	to apologize
sich aufregen	to get excited

EXERCISE 1   Insert the correct German verbs and pronouns.

1. **Karl** _____ _____ **daran.**
   remembers

2. **Sie** _____ _____ **sehr oft.**
   catches cold

3. _____ _____ _____ **stark genug?**
   Do you feel (familiar)

4. _____ _____ **bei deiner Mutter!**
   Apologize (familiar)

5. **Wir** _____ _____ **sehr gut.**
   amuse ourselves

EXERCISE 2   Answer in complete German sentences.

1. **Wer bereitet das Frühstück?**
2. **Worüber** (about what) **wundert sich Nora?**
3. **Warum streicht sich Karl keinen Honig aufs Brot?**
4. **Was bewundert Nora?**
5. **Was fragt Karl seine Frau?**

EXERCISE 3 True or false?   T / F
   1. **Karls Tag beginnt spät.**   ___
   2. **Er ißt immer allein.**   ___
   3. **Karl fühlt sich stark und gesund.**   ___
   4. **Nora hat zugenommen.**   ___
   5. **Karl erkältet sich nie.**   ___

EXERCISE 4 Translate into English.
   1. **Es ist noch nicht einmal sieben.**
   2. **Nora setzt sich zu ihm.**
   3. **Um diese Zeit erkältest du dich.**
   4. **Ich bin gerade auf die Waage gestiegen.**
   5. **Nach der Tabelle ist mein Gewicht normal.**

EXERCISE 5 Complete each sentence with a word listed here:
ihm, Frühstück, gestiegen, Vitamine, normal, Schlaf
   1. **Karl braucht wenig _____.**
   2. **Nimmst du deine _____?**
   3. **Nora setzt sich zu _____.**
   4. **Sie bereitet das _____.**
   5. **Ich bin gerade auf die Waage _____.**
   6. **Mein Gewicht ist _____.**

Peter und der Zahnarzt

Reflexive Verbs Taking the Dative

Vocabulary

Aspirinbüchse (f)	box of aspirin
sich **beklagen (w)**	to complain
bürsten (w)	to brush
dasselbe	the same
ein bißchen	a little
es tut mir weh	it hurts me
Gejammer (n)	wailing, complaining
holen (w)	to get, fetch
immer noch	still
Notiz (f)	note, memo
Protest (m)	protest
putzen (w)	*here:* to brush
sich **vorstellen (w)**	to imagine
wach	awake
Zahn (m)	tooth
Zahnarzt (m)	dentist
Zahnweh (n)	toothache

   Die Kinder sind nun wach und wollen ihr Frühstück. Nora fragt sie jeden Morgen dasselbe:
(to Peter): „Hast du dir die Zähne geputzt?"
(to Gretchen): „Hast du dir das Haar gebürstet?"
   Gestern hat sich Peter über Zahnweh beklagt.
„Tut dir der Zahn immer noch weh, Peter?"
„Ja, ein bißchen."
„Aber nicht genug, um zu Hause zu bleiben?"
„Leider nicht."
   „Karl", sagt Nora, „bitte hol mir die Aspirinbüchse. Ich mache mir eine Notiz, daß ich den Zahnarzt anrufe. Kein Protest, Peter? Stell dir vor, Karl; Peter wird ohne Gejammer zum Zahnarzt gehen."

Please practice the following:

Ich habe mir die Zähne geputzt.	I brushed my teeth.
Putz dir die Zähne!	Brush your teeth!
Ich habe mir das Haar gebürstet.	I brushed my hair.
Bürste* dir das Haar!	Brush your hair!
Der Zahn tut mir weh.	The tooth hurts me.
Hol mir das!	Get that for me.
Ich mache mir eine Notiz.	I make a note for myself.

*Since the stem of the verb ends with a -*t*, the -*e* in the imperative is retained for easier pronounceability.

EXERCISE 6 Choose the correct words.
1. **Die Kinder wollen**
   a. **nichts** b. **ihr Frühstück** c. **ihr Abendessen**
2. **Nora fragt Peter, „Hast du dir die Zähne**
   a. **geputzt?"** b. **gewaschen?"** c. **gemacht?"**
3. **Weil Peter Zahnweh hat, bekommt er**
   a. **ein Bonbon** b. **einen Hering** c. **Aspirin**
4. **Der Zahn tut Peter weh**
   a. **ein bißchen** b. **sehr** c. **manchmal**
5. **Nora wird den Zahnarzt**
   a. **treffen** b. **anrufen** c. **einladen**

EXERCISE 7 Which is the better German?
Check the correct sentence.
1. a. **Ich habe meine Füße gewaschen.** ——
   b. **Ich habe mir die Füße gewaschen.** ——
2. a. **Sie hat ihr Haar getrocknet.** ——
   b. **Sie hat sich das Haar getrocknet.** ——
3. a. **Er hat sich den Arm verletzt** (hurt). ——
   b. **Er hat seinen Arm verletzt.** ——
4. a. **Sie hat ihren Kopf gewaschen.** ——
   b. **Sie hat sich den Kopf gewaschen.** ——
5. a. **Er hat seinen Mantel genommen.** ——
   b. **Er hat sich den Mantel genommen.** ——

Please note that in German we use the dative reflexive pronouns (**er hat** *sich*, etc.) in referring to parts of the body or clothing.

EXERCISE 8 Write the following sentences in German.
1. Nora asks each child the same (thing).
2. Did you brush your hair?
3. Do you have a toothache?
4. Peter won't stay at home.
5. Go, wash your hands.

EXERCISE 9 Complete each sentence with the German equivalent of the words listed here: toothache, box of aspirin, awake, memo, stay
1. **Die Kinder sind nun** —————.
2. **Karl, bitte hol mir die** —————.
3. **Nicht genug, um zu Hause zu** —————.
4. **Peter beklagt sich über** —————.
5. **Ich mache mir eine** —————.

EXERCISE 10 Answer in complete German sentences.
1. **Was fragt Nora Gretchen?**
2. **Was holt Karl für Nora?**
3. **Worüber hat sich Peter beklagt?**
4. **Tut ihm der Zahn sehr weh?**
5. **Was macht sich Nora, damit sie nicht vergißt?**

Die Reifenpanne

Modal Verbs

dürfen, können, mögen, müssen, sollen, wollen

Modal verbs describe the facts of a situation, also indicate an attitude; example: **Wir** *müssen* **den Reifen wechseln** (We have to change the tire), or: **Sie** *können* **Platz nehmen** (You can take a seat).

Vocabulary

anbieten (bietet an, bot an, angeboten)	to offer
ansonsten	otherwise
Auspuffrohr (n)	exhaust pipe
Batterie (f)	battery
bis auf . . .	except for . . .
da gibt's	there is, there are
dürfen	to permit
fahren (fährt, fuhr, gefahren)	to drive
festmachen (w)	to fasten
Hebebühne (f)	hydraulic platform, lift
heutzutage	nowadays
ich soll nicht . . . (sollen, soll, sollte, gesollt)	I am not supposed to . . .
inspizieren (w)	to inspect
kein Wunder (n)	no wonder
Keks (m or n)	cookies
klagen (w)	to complain
können (kann, konnte, gekonnt)	to be able to
Kühler (m)	radiator
Magengeschwür (n)	stomach ulcer
mögen Sie nicht . . . (mag, mochte, gemocht)	don't you like . . .
Öl (n)	oil
Panne (f)	*here*: flat tire
Platz nehmen	to take a seat
sieht ganz so aus	looks that way
Stoßdämpfer (m)	shock absorber
Tankstelle (f)	service station
Tankwart (m)	service station attendant
überprüfen (w)	to check
Vorderreifen (m)	front tire
wackeln (w)	to wobble
wollen (will, wollte, gewollt)	to want to
Zigarre (f)	cigar

KARL (fährt zur Tankstelle auf dem Weg nach Hause) *Wollen* Sie sich bitte den rechten Vorderreifen ansehen. Ich glaube, ich habe eine Panne.

TANKWART Sieht ganz so aus. Wir *müssen* ihn wechseln. Sie *können* indessen drinnen Platz nehmen. Da gibt's Kaffee und Keks.

KARL (drinnen)

MANAGER Wie geht's, Herr Bauer?

KARL Bis auf die Panne, nicht schlecht. Und Ihnen?

MANAGER Kann nicht klagen. Darf ich Ihnen eine Zigarre anbieten?

KARL Nein, danke. Ich *soll* nicht rauchen. Magengeschwüre.

MANAGER Kein Wunder, heutzutage. Ist Ihr Wagen ansonsten in Ordnung? *Sollen* wir ihn inspizieren? Stoßdämpfer? Er hat ihn jetzt auf der Hebebühne.

KARL   Bitte.

MANAGER   (inspiziert sie) Stoßdämpfer sind in Ordnung. Aber das Auspuffrohr *müssen* wir festmachen, das wackelt. *Mögen* Sie nicht mehr Kaffee?

KARL   Ich *soll* auch keinen Kaffee trinken. Wenn Ihr Mann fertig ist, *kann* er die Batterie überprüfen, auch das Öl und das Wasser im Kühler.

MANAGER   Sehr gut.

How to Use Modal Verbs

Wollen Sie sich den rechten Vorderreifen ansehen? Ich will mir ihn ansehen (du willst, er will, ich wollte).

Wir *müssen* ihn wechseln. Ich muß ihn wechseln (du mußt, er muß, ich mußte).

Sie *können* drinnen Platz nehmen. Ich kann Platz nehmen (du kannst, er kann, ich konnte).

Darf ich Ihnen eine Zigarre anbieten? (du darfst, er darf, wir *dürfen*, wir durften)

Ich soll nicht rauchen (du sollst, er soll). Wir *sollen* nicht rauchen (wir sollten).

Mögen Sie nicht mehr Kaffee? (Ich mag keinen, du magst, er mag, ich mochte keinen Kaffee.)

Most of the time modal verbs are used with a complementary (completing) infinitive, one that completes the meaning. But sometimes they are used alone. **Ich muß zur Schule gehen** is idiomatically shortened to **Ich muß zur Schule.** Also: **Er kann Englisch. Sie will ins Theater.** In these uses, an infinitive such as **gehen** is understood or implied, as is the case in English with *go* in the poetic, old-fashioned *I must away.*

EXERCISE 11   Fill in the correct German forms.

1. Er _____ den Reifen wechseln. (können)
2. _____ du schon rauchen? (dürfen)
3. Ich _____ keinen Tee. (mögen)
4. _____ er ins Kino gehen? (wollen)
5. _____ sie zu Hause bleiben? (sollen)
6. _____ ihr heute arbeiten? (müssen)

EXERCISE 12   Complete each sentence with a word listed here. **Panne, Stoßdämpfer, Auspuffrohr, Hebebühne, Kühler**

1. Der Manager sagt, die _____ sind in Ordnung.
2. Der Tankwart inspiziert den _____.
3. Er hat das Auto auf der _____.
4. Karls Wagen hat eine _____.
5. Man muß das _____ festmachen.

EXERCISE 13   Answer in complete German sentences.

1. Warum will Karl keine Zigarre?
2. Welcher Reifen hat die Panne?
3. Was soll der Tankwart noch überprüfen?
4. Wo ist das Wasser in einem Auto?
5. Wo inspiziert er die Stoßdämpfer?

EXERCISE 14   Translate into English.

1. Karl hat eine Reifenpanne.
2. Er muß das Auspuffrohr festmachen.
3. Darf ich Ihnen eine Zigarette anbieten?
4. Überprüfen Sie bitte das Wasser im Kühler.
5. Soll er sich nicht die Stoßdämpfer ansehen?
6. Kann nicht klagen.
7. Bis auf die Magengeschwüre, nicht schlecht.
8. Sieht ganz so aus.

EXERCISE 15 True or false?   T / F
1. **Der Manager bietet ihm Tee an.**   ——
2. **Karl raucht eine Zigarre in der Tankstelle.**   ——
3. **Der Tankwart trinkt indessen Kaffee.**   ——
4. **Man hat den Wagen auf der Hebebühne.**   ——
5. **Er muß den Reifen wechseln.**   ——

Double Infinitives

The past participles of modal verbs (*gedurft, gekonnt, gemocht, gemußt, gesollt,* and *gewollt*) are used only when there is no complementary infinitive, as in:

Der Kaiser hat den Krieg nicht gewollt.
The emperor didn't want the war.

Vor Jahren hat sie Russisch gekonnt.
Years ago she knew Russian.

But, as we've seen, most of the time modals are used with a complementary infinitive. Then, in the perfect or past perfect the infinitive takes the place of the past participle. With a complementary infinitive the above are:

Der Kaiser hat den Krieg nicht erklären wollen.
The emperor didn't want to declare war.

Vor Jahren hat sie Russisch sprechen können.
Years ago she could speak Russian.

There are several examples of this "double infinitive construction" in the perfect tenses in the dialog below. They are printed in italics. A few other verbs such as *sehen, hören,* and *helfen* also use this construction, in which the infinitive serves grammatically as a past participle in the perfect tenses. Read the dialog now and note that it's **Haben Sie die Auspuffklappe ersetzen *müssen*** (not *gemußt*)?—Did you have to replace the exhaust valve? And: **Haben Sie den Wagen schmieren *wollen*** (not *gewollt*)?—Did you want to lubricate the car?

Alles in Ordnung

Vocabulary

anfüllen (w)	to fill up
Aufsatz (m)	essay, composition
kalter Aufschnitt (m)	cold cuts
Auspuffklappe (f)	exhaust valve
Benzin (n)	gasoline
Butter (f)	butter
ersetzen (w)	to replace
das Ganze	the whole thing
Ich habe ihn anfüllen lassen.	I caused it to be filled up.
Käse (m)	cheese
Kunde (m)	customer
niemand	nobody
notwendig	necessary
Ölwechsel (m)	oil change
schmieren (w)	to lubricate
Schmierung (f)	lubrication
selbstverständlich	of course, by all means

Soll ich den Wagen hierlassen?	Shall I leave the car here?
Sonst noch etwas?	Anything else?
Tank (m)	tank
vorgestern	day before yesterday
Windschutzscheibe (f)	windshield
wünschen (w)	to wish

TANKWART   **Alles in Ordnung, Herr Bauer. Sonst noch etwas?**

KARL   **Haben Sie die Auspuffklappe** *ersetzen müssen*?

TANKWART   **Nein, das war nicht notwendig.**

KARL   **Haben Sie den Wagen** *schmieren wollen*?

TANKWART   **Heute habe ich nicht daran** *arbeiten können*. **Aber ich empfehle Schmierung und Ölwechsel für nächste Woche. Ich wasche noch die Windschutzscheibe. Brauchen Sie Benzin?**

KARL   **Ich habe mir den Tank erst vorgestern** *anfüllen lassen*. **Soll ich den Wagen für Ölwechsel nächste Woche hierlassen?**

TANKWART   **Wie Sie wünschen, Herr Bauer. Das Ganze dauert eine halbe Stunde, wenn niemand vor Ihnen da ist.—Ich sehe einen Kunden kommen. Entschuldigen Sie, bitte.**

KARL   (inside, to manager) **Darf ich Ihr Telephon benutzen?**

MANAGER   **Selbstverständlich.**

KARL   (dials) **Nora? Wie fühlst du dich? Ich hatte eine Reifenpanne.—Ich höre Gretchen singen; ja, mit dem Radio. Hilfst du Peter den englischen Aufsatz schreiben? Brauchst du etwas? Kalten Aufschnitt, Butter und Käse? Dann werde ich nicht vor sechs nach Hause** *kommen können*. **Auf Wiederhören.** (He pays his bill and leaves.)

Notice the two infinitives at the end of the sentences:

> **Der Tankwart hat einen Kunden** *kommen sehen*.
> **Karl hat Gretchen** *singen hören*.
> **Nora hat ihrem Sohn** *schreiben helfen*.

EXERCISE 16   Rewrite the following in the past tense.

> Example: **Ich habe nicht schreiben können.**
> **Ich konnte nicht schreiben.**

1. **Haben Sie das Auspuffrohr ersetzen müssen?**

_____

2. **Hat er den Wagen schmieren wollen?**

_____

3. **Hast du den Tank anfüllen lassen?**

_____

4. **Hat sie Gretchen sprechen hören?**

_____

5. **Hat er nach Hause kommen können?**

_____

EXERCISE 17   Choose the correct words.

1. **Nächste Woche läßt Karl den Wagen**
   a. **schmieren**   b. **versichern**   c. **verkaufen**
2. **Auf dem Weg nach Hause kauft Karl**
   a. **ein Kostüm**   b. **ein Bild**   c. **Aufschnitt**
3. **Gretchen singt zu Hause mit**
   a. **dem Fernseher**   b. **dem Radio**   c. **Peter**
4. **Der Tankwart empfiehlt**
   a. **einen Ölwechsel**   b. **eine neue Auspuffklappe**   c. **nichts**
5. **Schmierung und Ölwechsel dauern vielleicht nur**
   a. **zwei Stunden**   b. **eine Stunde**   c. **eine halbe Stunde**

EXERCISE 18 Match the following:

1. **Wollten Sie einen Ölwechsel?**	_____ He washes the windshield.
2. **Brauchen Sie Benzin?**	_____ Anything else?
3. **Darf ich das Telephon benutzen?**	_____ No, that was not necessary.
4. **Nein, das war nicht notwendig.**	_____ Did you want an oil change?
5. **Er wäscht die Windschutzscheibe.**	_____ Do you need gas?
6. **Sonst noch etwas?**	_____ May I use the phone?

EXERCISE 19 Answer in complete German sentences.
1. **Wann wird der Tankwart den Wagen schmieren?**
2. **Warum hat Karl den Tank anfüllen lassen?**
3. **Warum entschuldigt sich der Tankwart?**
4. **Was für einen Aufsatz muß Peter schreiben?**
5. **Was braucht Nora fürs Abendessen?**

Eine Überraschung?

Familiar Imperatives

Imperative: a grammatical mood that expresses the will to influence the behavior of another, like a hypnotist telling his subject what to do. But very often, giving commands is hardly mind control, since the subjects may not do what you order them to do. Many married people, parents, and teachers constantly complain about noncompliance. Right now, we're going to tell you to learn the imperative and we're sure you'll want to, because it isn't hard at all.

Vocabulary

Abendblatt (n)	evening paper
an die zehn Jahre	about ten years
anspringen	to start
besorgen (w)	to attend to
eigentlich	_here:_ actually
er kann es sich leisten	he can afford it
gebraucht	_here:_ second hand
herkommen (kam her, ist hergekommen)	to come here
hurra!	hooray!
Karosse (f)	coach
kindisch	childish
letzthin	lately
Mittelgebirge (n)	highlands, low mountains
momentan	at the present time
nichts Besonderes	nothing special
noch einmal	once more
rattern (w)	to rattle
rufen (rief, gerufen)	to call
Sonntag (m)	Sunday
taugen (w)	to be of use
Überraschung (f)	surprise
Vorbereitung (f)	preparation
wart einmal (w)	wait a minute

Karl hat seine Einkäufe besorgt und ist wieder zu Hause. Nora ist in der Küche und mit der Vorbereitung des Abendessens beschäftigt. Karl hat es sich bequem gemacht und will das Abendblatt lesen.

KARL   Peter, wo ist die Zeitung?

PETER   Ich glaube, die liegt noch draußen.

KARL   *Geh* und *hol* sie, bitte. Wo ist Gretchen?

PETER   In ihrem Zimmer.

KARL   *Sag* ihr herzukommen!

PETER   Gleich.—Gretchen! *Komm* her.—Sie hört mich nicht.

KARL   *Ruf* sie noch einmal! Oder *schau,* was sie macht. *Sag* ihr, ich will mit ihr sprechen.

PETER   (goes into Gretchen's room; they both come out)

KARL   *Kommt* her, Kinder! Ich muß euch etwas fragen.

GRETCHEN   Eine Überraschung?

KARL   Vielleicht. *Holt* eure Mutter und *bittet* sie, herzukommen.

GRETCHEN   Mutti! Eine Überraschung! *Komm* schnell!

NORA: Was ist passiert?

KARL   *Setzt* euch alle! Wie ihr wißt, komme ich gerade von der Tankstelle. Eine Reifenpanne, nichts Besonderes. Aber letzthin ist immer etwas anderes los mit dem Wagen. Er ist schon ziemlich alt. *Sag,* Nora, sollen wir uns nicht schon einen neuen kaufen?

NORA   *Wart* einmal! Wie lange haben wir ihn eigentlich?

KARL   An die zehn Jahre.

NORA   Und er ist im Grunde genommen noch immer in Ordnung?

KARL   Ja—er rattert ein bißchen . . .

NORA   Ist das alles?

KARL   Und manchmal springt er auch nicht gleich an . . .

PETER   Hurra! Ein neuer Wagen!

NORA   Peter, *sei* nicht kindisch! (to both) *Geht* und *wascht* euch die Hände. Das Essen ist gleich fertig. Und *öffnet* die Fenster. Es ist sehr warm hier. (to Karl) *Fahren wir* einmal ins Mittelgebirge am Sonntag und *sehen wir,* ob die alte Karosse noch etwas taugt. Was kostet denn ein neuer?

KARL   Mehr als wir uns momentan leisten können. *Gib* mir mal die Zeitung. *Schauen wir* uns die Inserate an. Aha! Also einen gebrauchten . . .

NORA   Nein, bitte nicht. Lieber länger *sparen* und dann einen neuen *kaufen!*

KARL   Du hast recht.

Want to influence somebody else's behavior?
Use the imperative.

In conversational German it is perfectly all right to say: **geh, hol** (plural: **geht, holt**) instead of **gehe, hole.** There are some instances where the **-e** must still be used, as in the case of **öffne** or **rette** (save), the reason being that certain combination of letters are hard to pronounce if the **-e** is dropped.

Notice that the **bitte** is often employed to mitigate the harshness of the command, although in dealing with his children Karl does not have to use it.

Komm schnell! Kommt her! These are the familiar forms of the imperative. If you want to use **sein** in the imperative (be so good), you have to say **sei so gut,** or in the plural **seid so gut.** Notice also that the Germans are much more generous in using the exclamation point **(Ausrufungszeichen)!** Psychiatrists or sociologists may decide that means something.

Nora suggests: **Fahren wir** einmal ins Mittelgebirge am Sonntag und **sehen wir, ob** . . . etc. This is the equivalent of the English *let's drive* and *let's see.*

She is against buying a used car and recommends instead: **sparen** und dann **einen neuen kaufen.** Here we have samples of the infinitive being used to express a command. More about this in the following section.

EXERCISE 20 Fill in the missing German words.
1. **Geh und** _____ **die Zeitung!**
      get
2. **Gretchen,** _____ **, herzukommen!**
         ask her
3. **Peter,** _____ **das Fenster!**
         open
4. _____ **, Nora!**
      Tell me
5. **Peter,** _____ **so kindisch!**
         don't be

EXERCISE 21 Write the following sentences in German.
1. Give me the paper, please!
2. Wash your hands!
3. Wait a minute!
4. Tell her to come here!
5. Gretchen, open the door!

EXERCISE 22 Answer in complete German sentences.
1. What does Karl want to read after coming home?
2. Where is Gretchen?
3. What does Karl want to buy?
4. What is wrong with the old car?
5. What does Nora call the old car?

EXERCISE 23 Choose the correct words.
1. **Karl kommt nach Hause and fragt nach**
   a. **dem Buch**   b. **der Zeitung**   c. **dem Essen**
2. **Karl kommt gerade von**
   a. **der Tankstelle**   b. **dem Kino**   c. **Anton**
3. **Nora will am Sonntag**
   a. **zu Hause bleiben**   b. **ins Mittelgebirge**   c. **Susie besuchen**
4. **Karl wird**
   a. **einen neuen Wagen kaufen**   b. **sparen und warten**
   c. **nichts tun**
5. **Karl sagt, der Wagen**
   a. **startet nicht gleich**   b. **startet nie**   c. **startet sofort**

EXERCISE 24 True or false?   T / F
1. **Nora will heute ausgehen.**   _____
2. **Karl will das Morgenblatt lesen.**   _____
3. **Gretchen glaubt, es ist eine Überraschung.**   _____
4. **Nora will nur einen gebrauchten Wagen.**   _____
5. **Der Wagen rattert ein bißchen.**   _____

Die Führerscheinprüfung

Formal Imperatives: Infinitives

Vocabulary

anfangen (fängt an, fing an, angefangen)	to begin
Angelegenheit (f)	matter
(sich) anschnallen (w)	to fasten the seat belt, to buckle up
aufgeregt	excited

aussteigen (stieg aus, ist ausgestiegen)	to get off
belästigen (w)	to bother
bestehen (bestand, bestanden)	*here:* to pass
Bremse (f)	brakes
erleben (w)	to experience
erzählen (w)	to tell, report
Führerscheinprüfung (f)	driver's test
(das) Herumkommandieren (n)	the ordering about
links	left
parken (w)	to park
Prüfer (m)	examiner
Prüfung (f)	test, exam
rasch	fast
rechts	right
Rückspiegel (m)	rearview mirror
schleifen Sie nicht die Kupplung!	Don't let the clutch slip.
stehenbleiben (blieb stehen, ist stehengeblieben)	to stop
Straßenbahn (f)	streetcar
treten (tritt, trat, ist getreten)	*here:* to step
umdrehen (w)	to turn around
vermindern (w)	to reduce
Vorrecht (n)	*here:* right of way
wovon?	of what?
zum Schluß (m)	in the end

German infinitives can be used as nouns and are always neuter. They are always capitalized, like all other nouns.

das Schwimmen	the swimming
das Lesen	the reading
das Rauchen	the smoking

A neighbor comes to the door, enters.

NEIGHBOR Ich bin noch ganz aufgeregt. Habe soeben meine Prüfung bestanden.

KARL Ich gratuliere. Bitte, *nehmen Sie* Platz.

NEIGHBOR Wissen Sie, soviel Herumkommandieren habe ich schon lange nicht erlebt.

KARL Wovon sprechen Sie?

NEIGHBOR Von meiner Führerscheinprüfung. *Entschuldigen Sie,* bitte, ich wollte Sie mit meinen Angelegenheiten nicht belästigen.

KARL Nein, *erzählen Sie* mir!

NEIGHBOR Also. Es fängt an mit bitte *anschnallen! Fahren Sie* links, *fahren Sie* rechts! *Schauen Sie* in den Rückspiegel! *Warten Sie* auf die Straßenbahn, die hat immer das Vorrecht! *Drehen Sie* hier um! Nicht so rasch! *Treten Sie* auf die Bremse! *Schleifen Sie* nicht die Kupplung! Zum Schluß wurde er ganz kurz: das Tempo *vermindern. Stehenbleiben. Parken. Aussteigen.*

More of the Same

„Erzählen Sie mir!" If you want to be polite, you add the *bitte,* as in „Entschuldigen Sie, bitte!" As you can see, the examiner starts out with a polite „Bitte anschnallen" and ends up with a gruff „Aussteigen." We suspect that Karl's neighbor's driving skills may have had something to do with this.

The so-called "impersonal" imperative is quite often used in the case of general instructions, such as: **nicht aufstehen; sitzenbleiben; nicht zum Fenster hinausschauen,** etc. The harshness of the command makes an exclamation point unnecessary.

EXERCISE 25 Answer in complete German sentences.
1. Who comes to the door?
2. What has the neighbor just passed?
3. How does the ordering about start?
4. Which vehicle always has the right of way?
5. What was the examiner's last command?

EXERCISE 26 Translate into English.
1. **Ich habe die Prüfung gerade bestanden.**
2. **Das habe ich schon lange nicht erlebt.**
3. **Ich will Sie mit meinen Angelegenheiten nicht belästigen.**
4. **Schauen Sie in den Rückspiegel!**
5. **Schleifen Sie nicht die Kupplung!**

EXERCISE 27 True or false?   T / F
1. **Der Nachbar war nicht aufgeregt.**   _____
2. **Die Straßenbahn hat immer das Vorrecht.**   _____
3. **Zum Schluß war der Prüfer sehr höflich.**   _____
4. **Der Nachbar mußte sich anschnallen.**   _____
5. **Karl wollte nichts davon hören.**   _____

EXERCISE 28 Match the following sentences.
1. **Er schleifte die Kupplung.**   _____ He looks into the
2. **Zum Schluß wurde er ganz**   rearview mirror.
   kurz.   _____ He buckles up.
3. **Er schaut in den**   _____ Stop.
   Rückspiegel.   _____ He let the clutch slip.
4. **Er schnallt sich an.**   _____ The streetcar has the
5. **Stehenbleiben.**   right of way.
6. **Die Straßenbahn hat das**   _____ In the end he became
   Vorrecht.   quite curt.

EXERCISE 29 Insert the missing words.
1. **Der Nachbar sagt: Ich bin noch ganz _____.**
2. **Soviel Herumkommandieren habe ich schon lange nicht**

   _____.
3. **Ich wollte Sie nicht damit _____.**
4. **Schleifen Sie nicht die _____.**
5. **Treten Sie auf die _____.**

CHAPTER 10

Die Familie Bauer will auf Urlaub fahren
The Bauer Family Wants to Take a Vacation

Prefixes

Prefixes are words or syllables attached to the beginning of a word.

Separable Prefixes

These may be attached to a word but can also stand alone.

ab	an	auf	aus
bei	ein	fort	heim
her	herunter	hin	los
mit	nach	nieder	vor
weg	zu	zurück	zusammen

There are a few others. But don't despair; they are not all that hard to handle.

Der sonnige Süden

Vocabulary

Anfang August	at the beginning of August
anfangen (fängt an, fing an, angefangen)	to start
abwaschen (wäscht ab, wusch ab, abgewaschen)	to wash off
Aufenthalt (m)	stay, sojourn
ausgehen (ging aus, ist ausgegangen)	to go out
Begleitumstände (m. pl.)	accompanying circumstances; side effects
beschreiben (beschrieb, beschrieben)	to describe
bevor	before
bisher	until now
Bündel (n)	bundle, bunch
davon abraten (rät ab, riet ab, abgeraten)	to advise against it
diesmal	this time
Ferienpläne (m. pl.)	vacation plans
Folge (f)	consequence

geschäftshalber	for business reasons
grell	bright, glaring
heimkehren (w)	to come home
Herbst (m)	fall, autumn
herunterkommen (kam herunter, ist heruntergekommen)	*here:* to come off
katastrophal	catastrophic
Kreta	Crete
kümmern sich nicht darum (w)	to pay (no) attention to
Licht (n)	light
Nase (f)	nose
Norden (m)	the north
Nordsee (f)	North Sea
Osten (m)	the East
regnerisch	rainy
Reisebroschüre (f)	travel folder
Skandinavien	Scandinavia
Sonnenbrand (m)	sunburn
Sonnenbrille (f)	sunglasses
sonnig	sunny
Spanien	Spain
(die) strahlende Sonne	the shining sun
Süden (m)	the south
Südeuropa	southern Europe
szenisch	scenic
trüb	cloudy, gloomy
unvermeidlich	unavoidable
unwiderstehlich	irresistible
vor allem deshalb, weil	mainly because
warnen (w)	to warn
Wasserleitung (f), Hahn (m)	water pipe, faucet
wegfahren (fährt weg, fuhr weg, ist weggefahren)	to go away, to leave
weil sie wegzufahren hatten	because they had to leave
Westen (m)	the west
Wunder (n)	wonder
zurückdenken (dachte zurück, zurückgedacht)	to think back

Bisher hat die Familie Bauer ihre Ferien meistens an der Nordsee oder in Skandinavien verbracht, vor allem deshalb, weil sie Anfang August wegzufahren hatte, also zu einer Zeit, wenn es im Süden Europas sehr heiß ist. Diesmal mußte Karl geschäftshalber während des Sommers in der Stadt bleiben und man hat Ferienpläne für den Herbst.

Heute *geht* Nora *aus* und *kehrt* mit einem Bündel Reisebroschüren *heim*, die die szenischen Wunder Südeuropas beschreiben. Das Wetter zu Hause ist trüb, regnerisch und kalt, und die Bilder mit der strahlenden Sonne und dem blauen Himmel der Riviera sind unwiderstehlich.

Denkt sie auch manchmal *zurück* an die unvermeidlichen Begleitumstände eines Aufenthaltes im sonnigen Süden? Sie *geht* im Zimmer *hin und her* und erinnert sich an den Sonnenbrand in Kreta und an das Wasser in Spanien. „Ich *rate* dir *ab*, von der Wasserleitung zu trinken", hat eine Freundin sie gewarnt. „Und *wasch* das Obst gut *ab*, bevor du es ißt." Aber die Kinder haben sich nicht darum gekümmert und die Folgen waren katastrophal. „*Nehmt* euch Sonnenbrillen *mit*, das Licht ist sehr grell." Die Sonnenbrillen *kamen* von ihren Nasen nie *herunter*, dafür sorgte sie.

Please remember:

> **Heute** *geht* Nora *aus.* Sie ist *ausgegangen.*
> Sie *kehrt heim.* Sie ist *heimgekehrt.*
> *Denkt* sie *zurück?* Manchmal wird sie *zurückdenken.*
> Sie *geht hin und her.* Sie ist *hin- und hergegangen.*
> Ich *rate* es dir *ab.* Ich habe es dir *abgeraten.*
> *Nehmt* euch Sonnenbrillen *mit.* Sie haben sie *mitgenommen.*

Separable prefixes are words in their own right and can stand by themselves. When they're attached to verbs, things get more complicated. Just remember that the prefixes can be separated, as in the present, past, and imperative (command form), or attached as in the infinitive and past participle. German for *to turn on* (including the slang sense), is *anmachen.* In English we can say either *She turns (turned) the light on* or *She turns (turned) on the light.* In simple German sentences in the present and past, the prefix is in final position: **Sie macht (machte) das Licht an.** In the present perfect it's **Sie hat das Licht angemacht.**

EXERCISE 1 Put the following sentences into the present tense.
1. **Er ist zurückgekommen.**
2. **Sie ist weggegangen.**
3. **Wir sind auf und ab gegangen.**
4. **Er hat es aufgegessen.**
5. **Sie hat viel Geld ausgegeben.**

EXERCISE 2 Write the following sentences in German.
1. Are you coming along?
2. When is he going to pick us up?
3. When does it start?
4. Are you going back?
5. Do you advise her against it?

EXERCISE 3 Answer in complete German sentences.
1. **Wo hat die Familie Bauer bisher ihre Ferien verbracht?**
2. **Warum ging sie nicht nach Südeuropa?**
3. **Warum mußte Karl während des Sommers in der Stadt bleiben?**
4. **Was bringt Nora heute mit?**
5. **Wie ist das Herbstwetter in Deutschland meistens?**
6. **Wer hat sie vor dem Wasser gewarnt?**
7. **Wie waren die Folgen für die Kinder?**
8. **Warum soll man Sonnenbrillen mitnehmen?**

EXERCISE 4 Choose the correct words.
1. **Die Familie Bauer verbrachte ihre Ferien meistens**
   a. **an der Nordsee** b. **in Spanien** c. **in Amerika**
2. **Heute kam Nora zurück mit**
   a. **kaltem Aufschnitt** b. **Käse und Brot**
   c. **Reisebroschüren**
3. **Wenn sie an Kreta zurückdenkt, erinnert sie sich an**
   a. **den Sonnenbrand** b. **ihre Küche** c. **ihren Fernseher**
4. **Was soll man mit dem Obst machen?**
   a. **es gleich essen?** b. **es abwaschen?**
   c. **sich nicht darum kümmern?**
5. **Das Wetter zu Hause ist im Herbst meistens**
   a. **trüb** b. **schön** c. **heiß**

EXERCISE 5 True or false?   T / F
1. **Manchmal war die Familie Bauer in Skandinavien.**   _____
2. **In Spanien soll man das Wasser immer vom Hahn trinken.**   _____
3. **Obst soll man dort zuerst abwaschen.**   _____
4. **Die Bilder von der Riviera sind sehr schön.**   _____
5. **Während des Sommers ist der Süden Europas zu kalt.**   _____

Hotel mit Wanzen

Separable Prefixes (continued)

Vocabulary

abbezahlen (w)	to pay off
abhalten (hält ab, hielt ab, abgehalten)	*here:* to hold (a conference)
anders	different
abzapfen (w)	to draw off
aufwachen (w)	to wake up
ausbezahlen (w)	to pay in full; *here:* to finish paying for
Blut (n)	blood
erstklassig	first-class
es ist lange her	it is long past
es sieht wunderbar aus	it looks wonderful
Familienkonferenz (f)	family conference
fortfliegen (flog fort, ist fortgeflogen)	to fly away
gierig	greedy
Griechenland	Greece
griechisch	Greek
märchenhaft	''fairy tale-like,'' fabulous
miserabel	miserable
rein	clean
so etwas	something like that
Sonnenaufgang (m)	sunrise
Sonnenuntergang (m)	sunset
vorhaben	to have in mind
vorkommen (kam vor, ist vorgekommen)	to happen, occur
Wanze (f)	bedbug

Nora erinnert sich an die herrliche griechische Insel mit dem märchenhaften Sonnenuntergang und den gierigen Wanzen, die ihr einen Liter Blut *abzapften.* Sie *kommt an,* alles *sieht* wunderbar *aus,* sie sagt: ,,Karl, da ist es herrlich, da *fahre* ich erst nach einem Monat wieder *weg.*'' Dann *schläft* sie *ein, wacht auf* und alles ist anders.

Hat sie das bereits vergessen? Was *hat* sie *vor?*

Anderseits ist das schon sehr lange her, heute verdient Karl viel mehr, sie können sich ein erstklassiges Hotel leisten, dort *kommt* so etwas nicht *vor.* Sie haben zwei Autos in der Garage, eines davon *bezahlt* Karl dieses Jahr *aus,* das andere wird er innerhalb eines Jahres *abbezahlen.* Vielleicht *fliegen* sie im November *fort,* wenn das Wetter miserabel ist. Vielleicht *hält* man heute eine Familienkonferenz darüber *ab.*

Please note these verbs and their separable prefixes, too:
Die Wanzen *zapften* ihr Blut *ab.* Sie haben ihr Blut *abgezapft.*
Sie *kommt an.* Sie ist *angekommen.*
Alles *sieht* wunderbar *aus.* Es hat wunderbar *ausgesehen.*
Da *fahre* ich erst in einem Monat *weg.* Bin erst in einem Monat *weggefahren.*
Sie *schläft ein.* Sie ist *eingeschlafen.*
Sie *wacht auf.* Sie ist *aufgewacht.*
Was *hat* sie *vor?* Was hat sie *vorgehabt?*

Da *kommt* so etwas nicht *vor*. So etwas ist nicht *vorgekommen*.
Eines davon *bezahlt* er *aus*. Er hat es *ausbezahlt*.
Sie *fliegen* im November *fort;* sind *fortgeflogen*.
Man *hält* eine Familienkonferenz *ab;* hat eine *abgehalten*.

EXERCISE 6 Write the following sentences in German.
1. Nora remembers the beautiful sunset.
2. The bedbugs draw off her blood.
3. She happily falls asleep.
4. Maybe they will fly away in November.
5. Karl will finish paying for the other car within a year.
6. In a first-class hotel this does not happen.
7. What does she have in mind?

EXERCISE 7 Translate into English.
1. **Sie können sich ein erstklassiges Hotel leisten.**
2. **Die gierigen Wanzen zapfen ihr das Blut ab.**
3. **Sie wacht auf und alles ist anders.**
4. **Ich fahre erst in einem Monat weg.**
5. **Heute halten wir eine Familienkonferenz ab.**

EXERCISE 8 True or false?   T / F
1. **Das Hotel auf der griechischen Insel war sehr rein.**   ——
2. **Sie haben zwei Autos in der Garage.**   ——
3. **Der Sonnenuntergang war märchenhaft.**   ——
4. **Heute verdient Karl viel mehr.**   ——
5. **Nora erinnert sich an die deutsche Insel.**   ——

EXERCISE 9 Choose the correct words.
1. **Die Wanzen im Hotel waren sehr**
   a. **freundlich** b. **nett** c. **gierig**
2. **Heute verdient Karl**
   a. **mehr** b. **nichts** c. **weniger**
3. **Karl will den anderen Wagen innerhalb eines Jahres**
   a. **verkaufen** b. **abbezahlen** c. **verbrennen**
4. **Der Sonnenuntergang auf der griechischen Insel ist**
   a. **märchenhaft** b. **miserabel** c. **uninteressant**
5. **Die Ferien der Familie Bauer sind dieses Jahr wahrscheinlich im**
   a. **September** b. **November** c. **April**

EXERCISE 10 Complete each sentence with words listed here: **Insel, anders, dieses Jahr, Wanzen, ausbezahlen**
1. ———————— fliegen wir nach Kreta.
2. **Damals waren wir auf einer griechischen** ————————.
3. **Heute ist das alles** ————————.
4. **Er will das Auto** ————————.
5. **Das Hotel hatte leider** ————————.

Wohin?

Some Inseparable Prefixes

Vocabulary

Ägypten	Egypt
(ich habe) Angst (f)	I am afraid
annulieren (w)	to cancel
aufnehmen (nimmt auf, nahm auf, aufgenommen)	to take in
Ausflug (m)	excursion, side trip

auslösen (w)	to trigger, set off
ausrauben (w)	to ransack
Balkan (m)	the Balkans
bemitleiden	to pity
Da leg ich mich lieber nieder	I prefer to lie down.
dreimal	three times
Einfach traumhaft!	A dream!
Ermordung (f)	murder, assassination
Erzherzog (m)	archduke
es reizt mich	it tempts me
Flüchtlinge (m. pl.)	refugees
Flugkarte (f)	airplane ticket
förmlich	practically
Frieden (m)	peace
gefährlich	dangerous
gestehen (gestand, gestanden)	to confess
glühend	burning
Gräfin (f)	countess
herumklettern (w)	to climb around
Heuschrecke (f)	grasshopper
Krieg (m)	war
Kroatien	Croatia
kühl	cool
Leute (pl.)	people
ohne weiteres	readily
Opfer (n)	victim
Plattensee (m)	Lake Balaton
Pulverfaß (n)	powder-keg
Pußta (f)	puszta (Hungarian plain)
Reise (f)	trip
Reisebüro (n)	travel agency
reisen (w)	to travel
Rucksack (m)	backpack
Stechmücke (f)	mosquito
Thronfolger (m)	heir to the throne
Tokaierwein (m)	Tokay wine
Türkei (f)	Turkey
sich etwas anders überlegen (w)	to change one's mind
übersetzen (w)	to translate
Ungarn	Hungary
Unruhen (f. pl.)	unrest, disturbances
(sich) unterhalten (unterhielt, unterhalten)	to converse, talk
ursprünglich	originally
verrückt	crazy
Vertriebene (pl.)	expellees
wie wäre es mit	how would it be with (how about)
Zigeunerlieder (n. pl.)	gypsy songs
zusammenkommen (kam zusammen, ist zusammengekommen)	to get together

(A few hours later)

KARL   Also du hast das Reisebüro besucht und es förmlich ausgeraubt. Alle diese Broschüren!

NORA   Schau dir mal die Bilder von Mallorca an. Einfach traumhaft!

GRETCHEN   Und das, Mutti: „Komm zurück nach Sorrent!''

KARL   Dorthin will ich nicht zurückkommen. Stechmücken so groß wie Heuschrecken.

GRETCHEN   Aber es ist doch so romantisch.

PETER   Schau, Vati, da ist ein Bild von einer Stewardeß, die sagt, „Komm mit nach Wa-ras-din.'' Wo ist das, Vati?

KARL   In Kroatien. Dort waren wir noch nie.

NORA   Aber da gibt es Krieg. Ich habe Angst.

KARL   Es hat schon so viele Kriege auf dem Balkan, dem „Pulverfaß Europas'', gegeben. Die Ermordung in Sarajevo des österreichischen Thronfolgers, Erzherzog Franz Ferdinand, und seiner Frau hat den ersten Weltkrieg ausgelöst. Aber in einigen Teilen von Kroatien gibt es jetzt keinen Krieg. Wir könnten gefährlich leben und es vielleicht riskieren.

NORA   Ach, nein! Denk doch an die Kinder!

GRETCHEN   Warum fahren wir nicht nach Japan, Australien oder Kalifornien?

KARL   Zu teuer! Zu weit!

PETER   Wie wäre es mit Ägypten, Israel oder der Türkei?

NORA   Zu viele Unruhen!

GRETCHEN   Hier sind wunderschöne Bilder vom Plattensee in Ungarn.

KARL   Ungarn kennen wir noch nicht.

NORA   Ich habe total *vergessen*, dir zu *erzählen*, Karl, den Ribars *gefällt* Ungarn sehr gut. Die waren schon dreimal dort.

KARL   Ich *gestehe*, es reizt mich mehr als Italien, Griechenland oder Spanien, die wir schon kennen. Ich denke schon an den Plattensee, an Pußta und Paprika, an Tokaierwein und Zigeunerlieder. Warasdin ist auch nicht weit von Ungarn. "Komm mit nach Warasdin" ist ein schönes Lied aus der Operette *Gräfin Maritza*. Wenn es keinen Krieg gibt, könnten wir vielleicht einen Ausflug dorthin machen.

NORA   Wir *bemitleiden* die Opfer des Krieges, vor allem die Kinder, und die vielen Flüchtlinge und Vertriebenen. Deutschland hat viele von ihnen aufgenommen. Hoffen wir, daß es auf dem Balkan bald Frieden geben wird.

KARL   Fahren wir also nach Ungarn. Ich *bestelle* die Flugkarten. Wir können sie ohne weiteres annullieren, wenn wir es uns anders *überlegen*. Oder wir *verkaufen* sie an jemand anders. Vielleicht reisen wir mit den Ribars.

NORA   Sie ist eine sehr nette Person.

KARL   Und er ein komischer Kerl; mit dem *unterhalte* ich mich immer sehr gut. Warum kommen wir nicht mit ihnen zusammen?

NORA   Gute Idee.

KARL   Seine Familie ist ursprünglich aus Ungarn. Wenn wir etwas nicht *verstehen*, *übersetzt* er es für uns.

NORA   Ausgezeichnet.

KARL   Gut, dann ruf ich ihn morgen an.

GRETCHEN   Schau dir die schönen Bilder an, Vati. Der Plattensee und die Berge.

KARL   Ja, und die verrückten Leute, die mit ihren Rucksäcken in der glühenden Sonne herumklettern. Da leg ich mich lieber nieder und geh am Abend aus, wenn's kühl ist.

Grammar Is Inseparable from Language

Ich vergesse, habe vergessen; ich erzähle, habe erzählt; es gefällt mir, hat mir gefallen; ich gestehe, habe gestanden; ich bestelle, habe bestellt; wir verkaufen, haben verkauft.

Here we have verbs with the inseparable prefixes *ver-, er-, ge-* and *be-*.

There are other inseparable prefixes, such as *ent-* (*entziehen*, to take away) and *zer-* (*zerbrechen*, to crack).

When do we know whether a certain compound verb has a separable or an inseparable prefix? The answer is quite simple: Standing by themselves, *ver-, er-, ge-, be-, ent-* and *zer-* have no meaning. But look at the separable prefixes like *ab, an, auf, zu,* and the rest. Each one is a word in its own right.

You will also have noticed three interesting verbs, *überlegen, unterhalten, übersetzen*. These verbs—in the meaning within the context of the story—have inseparable prefixes; *ich überlege es mir, habe es mir überlegt; ich unterhalte mich, habe mich unterhalten; ich übersetze es, habe es übersetzt.*

EXERCISE 11 Write the following sentences in German.
1. I ransack the travel agency.
2. Look at these beautiful pictures! (formal)
3. I confess, it does not tempt me.
4. Why don't you order the airplane tickets? (formal)
5. He can translate it for us.
6. I prefer to lie down now.
7. I converse with him often.
8. He has changed his mind.
9. Have you forgotten his birthday? (familiar)
10. I am translating it for him.

EXERCISE 12 Answer in complete German sentences.
1. **Wo waren die Stechmücken so groß wie Heuschrecken?**
2. **Wie oft waren die Ribars in Ungarn?**
3. **Wer sagt, „Komm mit nach Warasdin"?**
4. **Was können sie ohne weiteres annulieren?**
5. **Wer klettert in der glühenden Sonne herum?**
6. **An welchen Wein denkt Karl, wenn er an Ungarn denkt?**
7. **Welches Ereignis (event) hat den ersten Weltkrieg ausgelöst?**

EXERCISE 13 Insert the missing words.
1. **Ribars Familie kommt ursprünglich aus _____.**
2. **In Sorrent sind die Stechmücken so groß wie _____.**
3. **Die Flugkarten kann man ohne weiteres _____.**
4. **Nora findet die Bilder von Mallorca _____.**
5. **Peter zeigt seinem Vater das Bild von einer _____.**

EXERCISE 14 Choose the correct words.
1. **Was Nora vom Reisebüro mitnahm, waren**
   a. **Briefmarken** b. **Münzen** c. **Broschüren**
2. **Das Land, nach dem sie wahrscheinlich fliegen werden, ist**
   a. **England** b. **Ungarn** c. **Italien**
3. **Auf dem Bild, das Gretchen Nora zeigt, heißt es: Komm zurück nach**
   a. **Warasdin** b. **Mallorca** c. **Sorrent**
4. **Wen wird Karl morgen anrufen?**
   a. **Herrn Ribar?** b. **Frau Müller?** c. **Frau Braun?**
5. **Nora war heute morgen**
   a. **im Reisebüro** b. **im Museum** c. **im Kino**

EXERCISE 15 Translate into English.
1. **Ich gestehe, das reizt mich.**
2. **Warum bestellst du sie nicht?**
3. **Ich habe vergessen, es dir zu erzählen.**
4. **Hast du es dir anders überlegt?**
5. **Er klettert dort wie verrückt herum.**

CHAPTER 11

Peter hat einen Zögling
Peter Has a Pupil

Numerals; Time of Day; Time Expressions

Einführung: Der kleine Tim

Vocabulary

akzentfrei	without an accent
auskommen (kam aus, ist ausgekommen)	to get by, make do
bestätigen (w)	to confirm
benachbart	neighboring
Betrag (m)	amount
durcheinander	pell-mell
Einführung (f)	introduction
etwas schwach	somewhat weak
Fehler (m)	*here*: shortcoming
fließend	fluent(ly)
gelegentlich	at your convenience
gutmütig	good-natured
Hauslehrer (m)	tutor
Kandiszucker	sugar candy
Kerl	guy
klebrig	sticky
Leidenschaft (f)	passion
nachhelfen (hilft nach, half nach, nachgeholfen)	to assist, tutor
Offizier (m)	officer
(das) Rechnen	arithmetic
rechnen	to do figures
Standort (m)	base
Tasche (f)	pocket
Taschengeld (n)	pocket money
von klein auf	from an early age
Vorrat (m)	supply
wenn auch	if (even though)
wohnhaft sein	to reside
Zögling (m)	pupil

Gretchen und Peter haben schon von klein auf Taschengeld von ihren Eltern bekommen—Beträge, mit denen sie bis zum Ende jeder Woche auskommen sollen. Auch haben sie zeitig damit angefangen, selbst etwas Geld zu verdienen. Gretchen arbeitet als Babysitter und hilft ihrem Vater gelegentlich im Geschäft. Peter arbeitet als Hauslehrer für die Kinder von amerikanischen Offizieren, die in dem benachbarten militärischen Standort wohnhaft sind.

Tim, neun Jahre alt, ist eines von den Kindern, denen Peter nachhilft. Der kleine Junge ist jetzt schon zwei Jahre in Deutschland und ist im allgemeinen ein guter Schüler, wenn auch etwas schwach im Rechnen. Sein Deutsch ist fließend und er spricht beinahe akzentfrei.

Sein Vater bringt ihn zweimal in der Woche zu Peters Haus und die Kinder sind Freunde geworden. Jeder hat Tim gern, er ist ein sehr netter kleiner Kerl.

Er ist sehr gutmütig und brav. Leider hat er einen großen Fehler: er ißt zuviel und alles durcheinander und wahnsinnig schnell. Schokolade ist seine große Leidenschaft; auch Kandiszucker, von dem er immer einen Vorrat in der Tasche trägt, die davon ganz klebrig wird.

EXERCISE 1 Complete each sentence with a word listed here: **Babysitter, Offiziere, Taschengeld, Kandiszucker, Zögling**
1. **Tim macht seine Tasche mit _____ klebrig.**
2. **Sie bekommen _____ von ihren Eltern.**
3. **Gretchen verdient etwas Geld als _____ .**
4. **Der amerikanische Junge ist ein _____ von Peter.**
5. **Amerikanische _____ wohnen dort.**

EXERCISE 2 True or false?   T / F
1. **Gretchen und Peter bekommen kein Taschengeld.**   _____
2. **Tim ist etwas schwach im Rechnen.**   _____
3. **Er kommt zu Peters Haus zweimal in der Woche.**   _____
4. **Peter verdient Geld als Hauslehrer.**   _____
5. **Tim spricht Englisch sehr schlecht.**   _____

EXERCISE 3 Write the following sentences in German.
1. Peter tutors Tim twice a week.
2. Tim is somewhat weak in arithmetic.
3. Tim's father is stationed at the neighboring military base.
4. Tim is a nice little guy.
5. He carries a supply of sugar candy in his pocket.

EXERCISE 4 Choose the correct words.
1. **Was bekommen Gretchen und Peter wöchentlich von ihren Eltern?**
   a. **Bücher** b. **Taschengeld** c. **Bilder**
2. **Wie alt is Tim?**
   a. **zehn Jahre** b. **fünf Jahre** c. **neun Jahre**
3. **Vom Kandiszucker wird Tims Tasche**
   a. **klebrig** b. **voll** c. **rein**
4. **Die Kinder Karls und Noras kriegen ihr Taschengeld**
   a. **jeden Monat** b. **jede Woche** c. **einmal im Jahr**
5. **Tim ißt**
   a. **zu viel** b. **nichts** c. **zu wenig**

EXERCISE 5 Answer in complete German sentences.
1. **Womit verdient Peter Geld?**
2. **Wem hilft er nach?**
3. **Wer spricht Deutsch beinahe akzentfrei?**
4. **Was ist Tims große Leidenschaft?**
5. **Wo trägt er den Kandiszucker?**

Tim rechnet auf deutsch
Cardinal numbers

Vocabulary

Ankunft (f)	arrival
Bahnzeit (f)	railroad time
bereits	already
eher	rather
Eisenbahn (f)	railroad
fremd	strange
gewisse Ziffern (f. pl.)	certain numbers
gewöhnlich	usually
gleichen (glich, geglichen)	to equal
halb	half
Kardinalzahl	cardinal number
Lehrbuch (n)	textbook
mehr und mehr	more and more
Minute (f)	minute
oder was immer	or whatever
Schwierigkeit (f)	difficulty
Sekunde (f)	second
Spaß	fun
Sprache (f)	language
System (n)	system
um 9:25	at 9:25
(ein) Viertel (n)	one quarter
Zahl (f)	number
Zug (m)	train
zum Beispiel (n)	for instance

Die sogenannten **Kardinalzahlen** haben Tim nie **Schwierigkeiten** gemacht. Die wußte er **bereits** zwei Wochen nach seiner **Ankunft** in Deutschland sehr gut:

0	**null**	10	**zehn**	20	**zwanzig**
1	**eins**	11	**elf**	21	**einundzwanzig**
2	**zwei**	12	**zwölf**	22	**zweiundzwanzig**
3	**drei**	13	**dreizehn**	30	**dreißig**
4	**vier**	14	**vierzehn**	40	**vierzig**
5	**fünf**	15	**fünfzehn**	50	**fünfzig**
6	**sechs**	16	**sechzehn**	60	**sechzig**
7	**sieben**	17	**siebzehn**	70	**siebzig**
8	**acht**	18	**achtzehn**	80	**achtzig**
9	**neun**	19	**neunzehn**	90	**neunzig**

100	**hundert**	200	**zweihundert**
101	**hunderteins**	700	**siebenhundert**
102	**hundertzwei**	891	**achthunderteinundneunzig**
110	**hundertzehn**	1000	**tausend**
136	**hundertsechsunddreißig**	1001	**tausendeins**

Sogar eine **Zahl** wie 987 654 wird, weiß er, mit *einem* Wort geschrieben: neunhundertsiebenundachtzigtausendsechshundertvierundfünfzig. Daran hat er viel **Spaß** gehabt.

Warum man nicht so wie im Englischen die **Zahl** 53 fünfzig drei liest, sondern dreiundfünfzig, hat er nie ganz verstanden. Auch die Art, wie man **gewisse Ziffern** schreibt, also 1 , nicht I , und 7 , nicht 7 , war ihm **fremd**.

Dann gibt es natürlich noch die ganz großen Zahlen, wie

1 000 000	eine **Million**
1 000 000 000	eine **Milliarde**
1 000 000 000 000	eine **Billion.**

Die amerikanische Billion ist dasselbe wie die deutsche Milliarde; die amerikanische Trillion gleicht der deutschen Billion. Warum ist das eigentlich in einer Sprache anders als in der anderen?

Poor Tim, struggling with humongous numbers and words. Fortunately, most of us don't have to be concerned with such huge sums, and more fortunately, numbers are usually written numerically, as in English. If Peter had known the nursery rhyme about "four and twenty blackbirds baked into a pie" he could have pointed out to Tim that that quaint old English way of saying numbers is how the Germans say them all the time. Thus twenty-two is *two and twenty* (**zweiundzwanzig**) and sixty-eight is *eight and sixty* (**achtundsechzig**), and so on.

What time is it?

Wenn Tim keine Uhr bei sich hat, wird er vielleicht jemanden fragen:
Wie spät ist es?

oder

Wieviel Uhr ist es?

Die Antwort ist dann gewöhnlich: es ist acht Uhr, oder elf Uhr, oder ein Uhr, oder was immer. Man kann aber das Wort *Uhr* auch weglassen: es ist acht, oder elf, oder eins.

In seinem deutschen Lehrbuch in Amerika hat Tim gelernt, daß 9:15 viertel (oder ein Viertel) nach neun heißt und 9:45 viertel vor zehn. Aber er wohnt jetzt in Süddeutschland, und dort sagt man eher viertel zehn und dreiviertel zehn. Um 9:30 ist es allerdings immer halb zehn. Man kann natürlich auch neun Uhr fünfzehn sagen, oder neun Uhr fünfundvierzig, oder auch: Es ist fünfzehn (Minuten) nach neun, oder fünfzehn (Minuten) vor zehn. Wenn es 9:37 ist, heißt das auch sieben Minuten nach halb zehn, und um 9:25 ist es fünf Minuten vor halb zehn.

Er weiß, daß man jetzt mehr und mehr das 24 Stunden-System benutzt (Bahnzeit), zum Beispiel:

Das Flugzeug kommt um 21:50 an, also um neun Uhr fünfzig abends (P.M.).

Der Zug fährt um 5:10 ab, also um fünf Uhr zehn morgens (A.M.)

EXERCISE 6 Write out the German words (railroad time) of:
1. eight-thirty A.M.
2. twenty to eight P.M.
3. ten past two P.M.
4. a quarter past seven P.M.
5. half past nine A.M.
6. five past three P.M.
7. twelve minutes to six P.M.
8. a quarter past ten A.M.
9. eleven P.M.

EXERCISE 7 Write the following numbers in German words.
1. 387
2. 925
3. 1,011
4. 1,248
5. 17,439

Mehr über Tim

Ordinal Numbers; Fractions

Vocabulary

aufwecken (w)	to wake
Bezirk (m)	district
ebenso wie	just as
entdecken (w)	to discover
pünktlich	punctual, on time
Stunde (f)	*here*: lesson
tagelang	for days
tagsüber	during the day
übermorgen	day after tomorrow
vorgestern	day before yesterday
weitergehen (ging weiter, ist weitergegangen)	to continue

Tim knows a lot already. He has learned that to form ordinal numbers is actually simpler in German than it is in English. All you do is put a period after the number:

1. means *der erste*; *2.*, *der zweite*; *3.*, *der dritte*; etc. *8.* is *der achte*. *1. Mai* is *der erste Mai*. From *20.* on it is *der zwanzigste*. Notice that instead of *-te*, *-ste* has been added to the cardinal number.

Ordinal numbers in German take the same endings as adjectives.

Ich habe eine Wohnung im 9. Bezirk (district). **Das ist ihr 2. Mann. (im neunten Bezirk; ihr zweiter Mann)**

½	**die** *Hälfte*; **aber eine** *halbe* **Stunde** (a half hour)
⅓	**ein drittel** —used as a noun: **ein Drittel**
⅕	**ein fünftel** —used as a noun: **ein Fünftel**
⅞	**sieben achtel**—used as a noun: **sieben Achtel**

Days of the Week

Sonntag	Sunday
Montag	Monday
Dienstag	Tuesday
Mittwoch	Wednesday
Donnerstag	Thursday
Freitag	Friday
Samstag (Sonnabend)	Saturday

Der Tag and *der Abend* are masculine, and all the days of the week, including *Mittwoch*, are masculine, even though *die Woche* is feminine.

Months of the Year

Januar	January
Februar	February
März	March
April	April
Mai	May
Juni	June
Juli	July
August	August
September	September
Oktober	October
November	November
Dezember	December

The Seasons

Frühling	spring
Sommer	summer
Herbst	fall
Winter	winter

All the above are masculine gender as well.

Tim has trouble with some idiomatic German forms, like ***morgen früh*** for *tomorrow morning.* He's also used to English constructions like *In 1989 the Berlin Wall fell* or *Napoleon was decisively defeated in 1815.* German **in** however, is never used alone before dates. We have to say either:

1989 fiel die Berliner Mauer.
or **Die Berliner Mauer fiel im Jahre 1989.**
Napoleon wurde 1815 endgültig besiegt.
or **Im Jahre 1815 wurde Napoleon endgültig besiegt.**

Das Glück° der Katze   good luck

„Vater", sagte er, „komm schnell! Im Speisezimmer ist eine große schwarze Katze."

„Sorg dich nicht," (don't worry) erwiderte sein Vater. „Eine schwarze Katze ist Glück."

„Die hat es, Vati," antwortete Tim. „Sie hat gerade deine Mahlzeit aufgegessen."

Tim hat Peter sehr gern.

Important Time Expressions

If you want to know what date it is, you ask: **Der wievielte ist heute?** or **Den wievielten haben wir heute?** The answer could be: **Heute ist der achtundzwanzigste Februar.** Or it could be: **Heute haben wir den achtundzwanzigsten Februar.**

Am Mittwoch kommt Tim um drei Uhr nachmittags zu Peter und am Sonntag um neun Uhr früh. Letztes Mal ist er um zehn gekommen, seine Mutter hat vergessen, ihn aufzuwecken. Ansonsten ist er sehr pünktlich. Peter arbeitet samstags nicht gern. Vormittags ist er, ebenso wie sein Zögling, in der Schule, und nachmittags macht er seine Aufgaben. Eines Mittwochs kam Tim von der Schule nach Hause und hörte, daß Peter krank ist. „Heute nachmittag hast du keine Stunde", sagte ihm seine Mutter. „Vielleicht übermorgen wieder. Peter hat sich schon vorgestern nicht wohl gefühlt. Tagsüber ist er in Ordnung, aber abends hat er etwas Fieber. Das kann so tagelang weitergehen." Tim war sehr traurig darüber, denn er hat Peter sehr gern.

Please memorize:

vormittags, nachmittags, mittags	in the morning, in the afternoon, at noon
morgens	in the morning
am Morgen	
abends	in the evening
am Abend	
nachts	nights
samstags	Saturdays
mittwochs	Wednesdays
eines Tages	one day

eines Morgens	one morning
eines Mittwochs	one Wednesday
er ist zweimal gekommen; das erste Mal; zum letzten Mal	he has come twice; the first time; for the last time
tagsüber	during the day
tagelang	for days
wochenlang	for weeks

EXERCISE 8 Answer in complete German sentences.
1. **Samstag hat noch einen anderen Namen. Wie ist er?**
2. **Wann fiel die Berliner Mauer?**
3. **Um welche Zeit kommt Tim gewöhnlich zu Peter am Samstag?**
4. **Warum ist er letztes Mal erst um zehn gekommen?**
5. **Wann machen Peter und Tim ihre Aufgaben?**
6. **Warum hat sich Peter vorgestern nicht wohl gefühlt?**
7. **Wie lange kann das Fieber so weitergehen?**
8. **Warum ist Tim traurig darüber?**

EXERCISE 9 True or false?   T / F
1. **Tim kommt jeden Tag zu Peter.**   _____
2. **Peter arbeitet gern am Sonnabend.**   _____
3. **Tims Mutter hat vergessen, ihn aufzuwecken.**   _____
4. **Beide Jungen machen vormittags ihre Aufgaben.**   _____
5. **Während des Tages ist Peter in Ordnung.**   _____

EXERCISE 10 Translate into German.
1. last Sunday
2. tomorrow evening
3. yesterday afternoon
4. every day
5. this morning

EXERCISE 11 Choose the correct words.
1. **Heute ist der**
   a. **5th März**   b. **5. März**   c. **5. des März**
2. **Am Mittwoch kommt Tim immer um**
   a. **5 Uhr**   b. **1 Uhr**   c. **3 Uhr**
3. **Tagsüber ist Peter**
   a. **in Ordnung**   b. **krank**   c. **im Bett**
4. **Vormittags sind Peter und Tim**
   a. **im Schwimmbad**   b. **in der Schule**   c. **zu Hause**

EXERCISE 12 Complete the following sentences.
1. **Letztes Mal ist Tim erst um zehn Uhr _____.**
2. **Abends hat Peter etwas _____.**
3. **Seine Mutter sagt, das kann so tagelang _____.**
4. **Er hat sich schon vorgestern nicht wohl _____.**
5. **Peter arbeitet samstags nicht _____.**

Fünf Paar Hörner

Der Lehrer fragt seine Schüler:
„Sechs Kühe° gehen auf einem schmalen   cows
Feldweg,° eine hinter der anderen.   narrow country lane
Welche kann sich umdrehen und sagen:
‚Ich sehe fünf Paar Hörner?' "°   five pairs of horns
        Tim antwortet: „Die erste Kuh."
        Der Lehrer: „Falsch, Tim. Kühe können nicht
reden."
        Vielleicht können wir die Sprache der Kühe nicht verstehen, dachte Tim
für sich. Aber er sagte nichts.

Witze und Wortspiele°

play on words, puns

Vocabulary

aussprechen (spricht aus, sprach aus, ausgesprochen)	to pronounce
Blatt (n)	*here:* sheet
Buchstabe (m)	letter
ganz am Anfang	right in the beginning
Gedicht (n)	poem
kochen (w)	to cook
Kugelschreiber (m)	ball-point pen
leer	empty
lehren (w)	to teach
Lineal (n)	ruler
Lösung (f)	solution
lustig	amusing
Rübe (f)	turnip
schneiden (schneidet, schnitt, geschnitten)	to cut
Speck (m)	bacon
was ich tun würde	what I would do
wenn ich . . . wäre	if I were . . .
Was würde ich tun?	What would I do?
wenn ich . . . hätte	if I had . . .
Zettel (m)	slip of paper

Manchmal versucht Peter, die Stunde mit Tim etwas lustiger zu machen. Dann erzählt er ihm Witze, zum Beispiel diesen:

-1-

Der Lehrer in der Schule: ,,Was ist weiter entfernt von uns, Deutschland oder der Mond?''

Ein Schüler antwortet: ,,Deutschland.''

,,Wieso?'' fragt der Lehrer.

Der Schüler: ,,Weil wir den Mond sehen können, aber nicht Deutschland.''

(Fortunately, children are less blasé than grownups when it comes to reacting to silly jokes; this one might even have gotten a laugh.)

Oder diesen:

-2-

Die Lehrerin sagte ihren Schülern: ,,Schreibt einen Aufsatz: Was würde ich tun, wenn ich zehn Millionen Mark hätte.''

Jeder Schüler begann sofort zu schreiben, nur Michael nicht. Er spielte die ganze Zeit mit dem Kugelschreiber und seinem Lineal. Nach einer halben Stunde sammelte die Lehrerin die Aufsätze ein. Michael gab ihr ein leeres Blatt.

,,Was ist das, Michael?'' fragte ihn die Lehrerin. ,,Ist das dein Aufsatz? Jeder andere Schüler hat zwei Seiten oder mehr geschrieben.''

,,Frau Lehrerin'', antwortete Michael. ,,Das ist es, was ich tun würde, wenn ich Millionär wäre.''

-3-

Tim weiß natürlich, wie man die Buchstaben des deutschen Alphabets ausspricht. Deshalb kann ihn Peter das Folgende fragen:

,,Tim, wie schreibst du *Kuhhaare* mit nur vier Buchstaben, *Katze* mit zwei und *Zettel* mit zwei?''

Tim weiß das natürlich nicht. Also gibt ihm Peter die Lösung:

Kuhhaare ist QHRE

Katze   ist KC

Zettel   ist ZL

-4-

Ganz am Anfang hat Peter seinen Zögling ein komisches kleines Gedicht gelehrt.

> Eins, zwei, drei, vier, fünf, sechs, sieben,
> eine alte Frau kocht Rüben;
> eine alte Frau kocht Speck,
> schneidet sich den Finger weg.

EXERCISE 13 Answer in complete German sentences.
1. **Womit spielte Michael die ganze Zeit?**
2. **Wie verteidigt** (defends) **der Schüler seine Antwort?**
3. **Was hat jeder andere Schüler geschrieben?**
5. **Was kocht die alte Frau in dem Gedicht?**

EXERCISE 14 True or false?   T / F
1. **Michael schrieb einen langen Aufsatz.**   _____
2. **Er gab der Lehrerin ein leeres Blatt.**   _____
3. **Er spielte mit Kugelschreiber und Lineal.**   _____
4. **Jeder andere Schüler schrieb eine Seite.**   _____
5. **Tim weiß, wie man die Buchstaben ausspricht.**   _____

EXERCISE 15 Complete the following sentences using these words: **Mond, Schule, Aufsatz, Lineal, Gedicht, Seiten**
1. **Michael spielte mit Kugelschreiber und** _____.
2. **Jeder andere Schüler hatte zwei** _____ **oder mehr geschrieben.**
3. **„Was ist weiter entfernt von uns, Deutschland oder der** _____?"
4. **Der Lehrer in der** _____ **fragt seine Schüler.**
5. **Die Schüler schreiben einen** _____.
6. **Peter hat ihn ein komisches kleines** _____ **gelehrt.**

EXERCISE 16 Construct sentences using the cue words.
1. **Was / entfernt / Deutschland / Mond ?**
2. **Was / tun / hätte / zehn Millionen ?**
3. **Lehrerin / Aufsätze / einsammeln**
4. **Tim / wissen / Buchstaben / aussprechen**
5. **Frau / Rüben / kochen**

EXERCISE 17 Fill in the missing letters in the German words.
1. **S__HR__BT E__NEN A__FSA__Z**
2. **K__GELS__R__BER UND LIN__L**
3. **SI__ SA__ELTE DI__ AUFS__TZE EIN**
4. **ER GAB I__R EIN LE__RES BLAT__**
5. **WEN__ ICH EIN MIL__ION__R W__RE**

CHAPTER 12

Die Zukunft der Kinder
The Future of the Children

Conjunctions

A conjunction is a word that joins together sentences, phrases, or words; e. g., **Anton *und* Nora; er weiß, *daß* sie da ist.**

Was Peter wirklich werden will

Coordinating Conjunctions Not Affecting Word Order:

und, denn, oder, aber, sondern

Vocabulary

begabt	talented, gifted
begreifen (begriff, begriffen)	to comprehend
Berufsaussichten (f. pl.)	professional prospects
berufsmäßig	professional
Cellist (m)	cellist
Cello (n)	cello
denn	for
Dirigent (m)	conductor
es bedeutet ihm nichts	it doesn't mean anything to him
Flöte (f)	flute
Geschwister (pl.)	siblings
Kompliment (n)	compliment
Konzert (n)	concert
Musiker (m)	musician
nämlich	namely, that is
Oboe (f)	oboe
Orchester (n)	orchestra
(das) Schönste auf der Welt	the most beautiful thing in the world
seinerseits	on his part
sonderbar	weird, strange
sondern	but, rather, on the contrary
stattdessen	instead
ungern	reluctantly
verraten (verrät, verriet, verraten)	*here*: to disclose, reveal
verstehen (verstand, verstanden)	to understand
zusammenhalten (hält zusammen, hielt zusammen, zusammengehalten)	to stick together

Gestern sprachen Nora *und* Karl über die Zukunft ihrer Kinder. Das Ganze hatte damit angefangen, daß Peter ihnen von seinem Zögling Tim erzählte, der so ungern Violine spielt. Peter kann das nicht verstehen, *denn* die Musik ist für ihn das Schönste auf der Welt. Aber jemand, dem sie nichts bedeutet, wird das seinerseits nicht begreifen.

KARL Wie lange nimmst du jetzt schon Cellostunden?

PETER Seit sieben Jahren.

KARL Das ist eine lange Zeit.

NORA Ich habe unlängst mit seinem Lehrer gesprochen *und* er hat gesagt, daß Peter ungewöhnlich begabt ist.

KARL *Aber* ist er gut genug, um ein berufsmäßiger Musiker zu werden?

PETER Ich bin der erste Cellist in unserem Schulorchester.

NORA Ich glaube, er ist gut, Karl. Am Samstag ist er nicht mit seinen Freunden ins Kino gegangen, *sondern* hat stattdessen beinahe den ganzen Tag Cello geübt.

PETER Wir haben ein Konzert in einer Woche *und* es ist ein sehr schweres Stück. Aber es macht mir wirklich Spaß, es zu üben. Meine Freunde hänseln mich damit und sagen, ich bin sonderbar.

NORA Laß sie reden! Du mach, was *du* willst!

GRETCHEN Peter spielt sehr schön. Er kratzt fast überhaupt nicht.

PETER Danke, Gretchen. von dir ist das ein großes Kompliment.

GRETCHEN Geschwister müssen zusammenhalten.

KARL Das ist alles schön *und* gut. *Aber* weißt du, Peter, wie die Berufsaussichten für Musiker sind?

PETER Ich möchte noch ein anderes Instrument lernen. Vielleicht die Flöte *oder* die Oboe. *Aber* was ich wirklich werden will, hab' ich noch niemandem verraten.

KARL Nämlich?

PETER Ein Dirigent.

Grammar Can Be Easy

Peter kann das nicht verstehen, *denn* die Musik ist für ihn das Schönste auf der Welt.

Aber ist er gut genug?

Er ist nicht ins Kino gegangen, *sondern* hat Cello geübt.

When *but* is used in the sense of *but instead, but on the contrary,* not **aber** but **sondern** is used. As a matter of fact, if we were telling you about *sondern* in German, we'd say: **Im Sinne von anstatt wird nicht aber, sondern sondern gebraucht.** (In the sense *instead* not *aber* but *sondern* is used.) Most of the time, after **nicht** (not), *but* is translated by **sondern**. In the text we read that Peter did *not* go to the movies, *but instead* practiced his cello.

With the conjunctions **und** and **aber** there should be no problems.

EXERCISE 1 Answer in complete German sentences.
1. Worüber sprach man gestern?
2. Was erzählte Peter von Tim?
3. Was ist die Musik für Peter?
4. Wie lange nimmt er schon Cellostunden?
5. Was hat sein Lehrer Nora gesagt?

EXERCISE 2 True or false?   T / F
1. Sie haben ein Konzert in einem Monat.   _____
2. Peter möchte Dirigent werden.   _____
3. Seine Freunde sagen, er ist sonderbar.   _____

4. Er möchte auch singen lernen.
5. Peter übte beinahe den ganzen Tag.

EXERCISE 3 Match the following.

1. **Sie sprachen über die Zukunft der Kinder.**
2. **Peter erzählte von Tim.**
3. **Er ist ungewöhnlich begabt.**
4. **Er kratzt fast überhaupt nicht.**
5. **Seine Freunde hänseln ihn damit.**
6. **Geschwister müssen zusammenhalten.**

_____ Peter talked about Tim.
_____ His friends tease him about it.
_____ Siblings have to stick together.
_____ They talked about the future of the children.
_____ He is unusually gifted.
_____ He hardly scratches at all.

EXERCISE 4 Translate into English.

1. **Er spielt ungern.**
2. **Das Schönste auf der Welt.**
3. **Peter hat fast den ganzen Tag geübt.**
4. **Ich habe ein Konzert in einer Woche.**
5. **Er geht nicht aus, sondern bleibt zu Hause.**

EXERCISE 5 Complete each sentence with a word listed here: **seinerseits, Violine, Zukunft, kratzt, Berufsaussichten, Instrument**

1. **Sie sprachen über die _____ der Kinder.**
2. **Er kann das _____ nicht begreifen.**
3. **Tim spielt ungern _____ .**
4. **Er möchte ein anderes _____ lernen.**
5. **Er _____ fast überhaupt nicht.**
6. **Die _____ sind schlecht.**

Ein General im Frack

Conjunctive Adverbs That _Can_ Affect Word Order

einerseits—ander(er)seits, überdies, außerdem, allerdings, nichtsdesto-weniger, auch, zwar, dennoch

Vocabulary

daraus	(out) of it
dennoch	however
dirigieren	to conduct
einerseits—ander(er)seits	on the one hand—on the other hand
eingehend	thoroughly
Frack (m)	"tails"; full dress coat
Geheimnis (n)	secret
Großonkel (m)	great uncle
Hauptsache (f)	the main thing
Ich werde dir nicht im Wege stehen.	I won't stand in your way.
imstande sein	to be able
Kapellmeister (m)	conductor
kommt darauf an	it depends
(eine) Menge Geld	a lot of money
nichtsdestoweniger	nevertheless

pensioniert	retired
Taktstock (m)	baton
überdies, außerdem	besides
unterrichten (w)	to teach
unterstützen (w)	to support
(ein) Vermögen (n)	*here*: a fortune
weder—noch	neither—nor
zerbrechen (zerbricht, zerbrach, zerbrochen)	to break apart
zornig	angry
zwar	it is true, I admit

KARL Ein Dirigent, sagst du? Das ist wirklich eine Überraschung.

GRETCHEN Wunderbar, Peter. Und sehr romantisch. Ein Dirigent erinnert mich an einen General, aber ohne Uniform.

NORA Ein General im Frack.

PETER Das möchte ich gern sein.

KARL Weißt du, wie lange du da studieren mußt?

PETER Das macht mir nichts aus.

KARL *Einerseits* kostet das zwar eine Menge Geld, *anderseits* ist es vielleicht eine gute Kapitalanlage. Manche von ihnen verdienen ein Vermögen. *Überdies* kann man ja auch unterrichten.

NORA Hauptsache, unser Sohn ist glücklich. *Außerdem* leben Dirigenten angeblich sehr lang.

GRETCHEN Kannst du dir vorstellen, Vati, Peter auf dem Podium. . . . Wirst du mit oder ohne Taktstock dirigieren, Peter?

PETER Kommt darauf an. Zuerst mit, glaube ich. . . . *Allerdings* muß es schöner sein mit den Händen allein.

GRETCHEN Aber dann kannst du den Taktstock nicht zerbrechen, wenn du zornig wirst.

KARL *Nichtsdestoweniger* werde ich mich zuerst mit deinem Lehrer eingehend darüber unterhalten. Mit ihm und *auch* mit deinem Großonkel in Grünau, der, wie du weißt, ein pensionierter Kapellmeister ist. Auch wird es notwendig sein, mit deinem Klassenlehrer darüber zu sprechen.

PETER Der wird mich unterstützen.

KARL Warum hast du so lange ein Geheimnis daraus gemacht? Keiner von uns wußte etwas davon. Natürlich wollen wir das Beste für dich. *Zwar* habe ich mir gedacht, du wirst später imstande sein, mir im Geschäft zu helfen; *dennoch* will ich gern . . .

GRETCHEN Vati, *ich* werde dir im Geschäft helfen; du weißt, ich freue mich schon darauf.

KARL Also gut, Peter; wenn es so weit kommt, werde ich dir nicht im Wege stehen.

Alternatives

On the one hand—on the other

einerseits kostet das. . . , *anderseits* ist es. . . ; *überdies* kann man. . . ; *außerdem* leben. . . ; *allerdings* muß es. . . ; *nichtsdestoweniger* werde ich. . . ; *auch* wird es notwendig sein. . . ; *zwar* habe ich gedacht. . . ; *dennoch* will ich gern. . .

Every one of these examples shows inverted word order after these conjunctive adverbs; that is, *conjunctive adverb + verb + subject*. In a normal, simple sentence the subject stands first, followed by the verb. In the above sentences it is possible to use that word order if you rearrange the words: „**Man kann überdies** (or: **außerdem**) **auch unterrichten**'' is grammatically perfectly respectable.

EXERCISE 6 True or false?   T / F
  1. **Ein Dirigent erinnert Gretchen an einen General.** _____
  2. **Dirigenten verdienen sehr wenig.** _____
  3. **Auch leben sie angeblich lang.** _____
  4. **Peters Großonkel ist ein pensionierter Kapellmeister.** _____
  5. **Karl wird seinem Sohn im Wege stehen.** _____

EXERCISE 7 Translate into English.
  1. **Du wirst imstande sein, mir im Geschäft zu helfen.**
  2. **Er hat ein Geheimnis daraus gemacht.**
  3. **Wir wollen das Beste für dich.**
  4. **Manche von ihnen verdienen sehr viel.**
  5. **Kommt darauf an.**

EXERCISE 8 Choose the correct words.
  1. **Ein Dirigent erinnert sie an einen**
     a. **General**   b. **Lehrer**   c. **Freund**
  2. **Peter hat einen Großonkel in**
     a. **Wien**   b. **München**   c. **Grünau**
  3. **Peter dirigiert lieber mit**
     a. **den Händen**   b. **den Füßen**   c. **dem Taktstock**
  4. **Das Studium eines Dirigenten dauert**
     a. **eine kurze Zeit**   b. **nicht sehr lang**   c. **sehr lang**

EXERCISE 9 Complete the following sentences.
  1. **Der Großonkel in Grünau ist ein pensionierter** _____.
  2. **Gretchen wird Karl später im Geschäft** _____.
  3. **Warum hat Peter ein Geheimnis daraus** _____?
  4. **Karl wird mit dem Klassenlehrer darüber** _____.
  5. **Kannst du dir Peter auf dem Podium** _____?

EXERCISE 10 Fill in the missing words.
  1. _____ **kostet es Geld,** _____
     On the one hand   on the other hand
     ist es eine Kapitalanlage.

  2. _____ **ist es eine sehr gute Idee.**
     Besides
  3. _____ **werde ich mit Noras Onkel sprechen.**
     Nevertheless
  4. _____ **wird es viel Geld kosten.**
     However
  5. _____ **muß er jeden Tag viel üben.**
     Also

Der Sopran

    Vater nahm den kleinen Jungen zu seinem ersten Orchesterkonzert mit einem berühmten Sopran° mit. Der Dirigent faszinierte° Johnny ganz besonders.
    „**Vater, warum droht° der Mann der netten Dame mit seinem kleinen Stock°?**''
      „**Sei still.° Er droht ihr nicht.**''
      „**Aber warum schreit° sie dann?**''

soprano
fascinated
threatens
stick
be quiet
screams

Ein Dirigent

GRETCHEN	Weißt du, was ein Dirigent ist?
PETER	Eine Person, die ein Orchester leitet.
GRETCHEN	Ja, aber einmal sagte bösartig ein Orchestermitglied: „Ein Dirigent ist einer, der von hinten über- und von vorne unterschätzt wird."

Schätzen means *to estimate. Überschätzen* is *to overestimate;* **unterschätzen,** *to underestimate.* Did you notice the German use of the hyphen to avoid saying *estimated* twice?

A Conductor

Do you know what a conductor is?

A person who directs an orchestra.

Yes, but once an orchestra member maliciously said, "A conductor is someone who is overestimated from the rear and underestimated from the front."

Sein musikalisches Talent

More Coordinating Conjunctions and Conjunctive Adverbs

entweder—oder, dazu, sowohl—als auch, daher, hingegen, weder—noch, trotzdem

Vocabulary

angesehen	respected
Anzahl (f)	number
ausübend	practicing
Chor (m) (pronounce **kōr**)	choir
daher	therefore
entweder—oder	either—or
Ehrgeiz (m)	ambition
Geiger (m)	violinist
hingegen	on the other hand
Kirche (f)	church
Klavierlehrerin	piano teacher
Mädchenname (m)	maiden name
Mezzosopran (m)	mezzo soprano
musikliebend	music-loving
Opernkarriere (f)	operatic career
regelmäßig	regularly
schwierig	difficult
sowohl—als (wie) auch	as well as
stolz	proud
Streichquartett (n)	string quartet
träumen (w)	to dream
trotzdem	in spite of it
übermäßig	overmuch
verbergen (verbirgt, verbarg, verborgen)	to hide
verdanken	to thank
vortrefflich	superior
weder—noch	neither—nor

Peter wird man wahrscheinlich nie sagen müssen: „*Entweder* du übst *oder* wir verkaufen das Cello." *Dazu* hat er es zu gern.

Das musikalische Talent verdankt er wahrscheinlich seiner Mutter. Nora kommt aus einer musikliebenden Familie. *Sowohl* ihr Vater *als auch* ihre Mutter sind ausübende Musiker. Herr Bachmann (Noras Mädchenname) ist ein vortrefflicher Geiger, der regelmäßig jede Woche in einem Streichquartett spielt; und Noras Mutter ist eine sehr populäre Klavierlehrerin, die eine große Anzahl Schüler hat.

Onkel Leopold—der jetzt in Grünau wohnt—war ein angesehener Kapellmeister, der dreißig Jahre lang das Orchester des Stadttheaters dirigierte. *Daher* ist es kein Wunder, daß Nora den Ehrgeiz ihres Sohnes versteht. Sie selbst hat eine sehr schöne Stimme gehabt (Mezzosopran), hat vor vielen Jahren von einer Opernkarriere geträumt, und singt jetzt gelegentlich im Chor ihrer Kirche.

Hingegen sind Karls Eltern, *weder* sein Vater *noch* seine Mutter, an Musik übermäßig interessiert. Karl selbst hat Musik gern, wenn sie nicht zu schwierig ist. *Trotzdem* ist er stolz auf das Talent seines Sohnes, auch wenn er diesen Stolz meistens verbirgt.

Practice Makes Perfect
(Übung macht den Meister)

Entweder du übst *oder* wir verkaufen das Cello: Here we have the ever-recurring threat of the either—or.

Dazu hat er es zu gern (for that to happen . . .).

Sowohl ihr Vater *als auch* ihre Mutter: You could also say: . . . **wie auch ihre Mutter.**

Daher ist es kein Wunder . . . You could substitute **daher** by *darum* or *deshalb*.

Hingegen sind Karls Eltern . . . : *Dagegen* oder *indessen* sind Karls Eltern . . .

Weder sein Vater *noch* seine Mutter sind interessiert.

Trotzdem ist er stolz auf das Talent seines Sohnes.

Please note: **Noras Mutter hat** *eine große Anzahl Schüler.* Translated this would be "a large number *of* pupils." In German we do without the "of."

Eine ganz kurze Kritik° erschien in der Zeitung: "Ein Amateurstreichquartett spielte Beethoven gestern abend. Beethoven verlor."°	criticism; *here*: music review lost

EXERCISE 11 Choose the correct words.
1. **Peter verdankt das musikalische Talent**
   a. **seinem Onkel**   b. **seiner Mutter**   c. **seinem Vater**
2. **Noras Mädchenname ist**
   a. **Bachmann**   b. **Gruber**   c. **Brown**
3. **Herr Bachmann spielt**
   a. **die Geige**   b. **die Flöte**   c. **das Cello**
4. **Was Nora werden wollte, war**
   a. **Hausfrau**   b. **Lehrerin**   c. **Opernsängerin**
5. **Karls Eltern interessieren sich für Musik**
   a. **nicht übermäßig**   b. **gar nicht**   c. **ein bißchen**

EXERCISE 12 True or false?   T / F
1. **Man wird Peters Cello verkaufen.**   _____
2. **Noras Mutter ist eine populäre Klavierlehrerin.**   _____
3. **Nora versteht den Ehrgeiz ihres Sohnes.**   _____
4. **Karl hat Musik nur gern, wenn sie schwierig ist.**   _____
5. **Karl verbirgt meistens seinen Stolz auf Peter.**   _____

EXERCISE 13 Translate the following into German.
1. They are practicing musicians.
2. Uncle Leopold conducted an orchestra.
3. Nora dreamed of an operatic career.
4. He hides his pride.
5. On the other hand, he is not too much interested.

EXERCISE 14 Answer in complete German sentences.
1. **Wo singt Nora noch gelegentlich?**
2. **Wo wohnt Onkel Leopold jetzt?**
3. **Wem verdankt Peter sein musikalisches Talent?**
4. **Was für ein Instrument spielt Herr Bachmann?**
5. **Warum versteht Nora den Ehrgeiz ihres Sohnes?**

EXERCISE 15 Fill in the missing German words.
1. _____ **du übst,** _____ **wir verkaufen es.** (either—or)
2. _____ **werde ich ihn besuchen.** (in spite of it)
3. **Ich werde** _____ **ihn,** _____ **seine Tante sehen.** (neither—nor)
4. _____ **komme ich heute um fünf Uhr.** (therefore)
5. _____ **er** _____ **seine Mutter sind begabt.** (as well as)

„Haben Sie Musik gern?"°	Do you like music?
fragte eine Dame den berühmten Mann.	
„Nein," antwortete er. „Aber	
von allen Geräuschen° stört° mich	noise / bothers
die Musik noch am wenigsten."	

Gretchen und die Welt des Geschäfts

Subordinating Conjunctions

während, obzwar, daß, sooft, obwohl, solange, seitdem

Vocabulary

anscheinend	apparently, obviously
Auffassungsvermögen (n)	perception, ability to comprehend, grasp things
Aushilfe (f)	temporary or extra help
aushilfsweise	as extra help
bereit sein	to be ready
beweisen (bewies, bewiesen)	to prove
Buchhandel (m)	book trade
definitiv	definite(ly)
dringend	urgent(ly)
enttäuscht	disappointed
erstaunlich	amazing(ly)
ersuchen (w)	to call upon, to request
fortführen (w)	to continue, to carry on
Geschäftsleben (n)	business life
künstlerisch	artistic
Laden (m)	store
mithelfen (hilft mit, half mit, mitgeholfen)	to help
Neigung (f)	inclination

obzwar, obwohl, obgleich, obschon	although
seitdem, seit	since
solange	as long as
sooft (pronounce *both* o's)	as often as
tätig	active
ungleich	unlike
vorhergehend	preceding
vor kurzem	a short while ago
vorziehen (zog vor, vorgezogen)	to prefer
(sich) wohlfühlen (w)	*here*: to be at home

Während sich Peter wenig für das Geschäft seines Vaters interessiert, ist Gretchen trotz ihrer romantischen Neigungen eine erstaunlich praktische kleine Person.

Obzwar sie bis vor kurzem nur als Babysitter gearbeitet hat, war sie an den zwei vorhergehenden Wochenenden im Geschäft aushilfsweise tätig und hat ihrem Vater bewiesen, *daß* sie eine gute Verkäuferin ist.

Sooft Karl sie braucht, sagt sie, wird sie bereit sein, im Laden mitzuhelfen. Es macht ihr anscheinend großen Spaß und es tut ihr leid, *daß* sie nicht mehr Zeit dazu hat. *Obwohl* sie, ungleich ihrem Bruder, kein künstlerisches Talent besitzt, ist sie ein intelligentes Mädchen mit einem schnellen Auffassungsvermögen. Man kann sehen, daß sie sich in der Welt des Geschäfts sehr wohlfühlt.

Karl weiß jetzt, *daß* Peter die Musik dem Geschäftsleben definitiv vorzieht. Vielleicht ist er ein bißchen enttäuscht darüber, aber *solange* er Gretchen hat (und *seitdem* er ihren Enthusiasmus für das Geschäft entdeckt hat), weiß er, *daß* eines seiner Kinder die stolze Tradition des Buchhandels in der Familie Bauer fortführen wird. Wenn er diesmal auf der Höhe der Weihnachtssaison dringend Aushilfe braucht, wird er seine Tochter darum ersuchen.

Watch Your Conjunctions

Please note that subordinating conjunctions *do* affect word order; they all introduce dependent clauses, which are separated from the main clause by a comma.

Während as a subordinating conjunction means "while"; it is, as we know, also used as a preposition: *während des Sommers* (during the summer).

Obzwar can be replaced by *obwohl, obgleich,* or *obschon* (although, even though).

Daß should present no difficulty since it is used in exactly the same way as in English. But watch the **"scharfes s (ß)."** It is now acceptable to write it *dass*. *Das,* with one ordinary *s,* is the neuter definite article (the) or a relative pronoun standing for it, as in *das* Haus, *das* ich gekauft habe (the house that I bought). Be sure not to confuse it with the conjunction *daß (dass),* despite the same pronunciation.

Sooft means "as often as, every time that."

Solange means "as long as" referring to the length of time.

Seitdem or *seit* can be used in various ways:

Seitdem **er ihren Enthusiasmus entdeckt hat,. . .** (ever since)

Seitdem raucht sie nicht mehr. (An adverb meaning "since then")

Seit letztem Winter . . . (A preposition: "since last winter")

Seit **sie nicht mehr kommt, spielen wir mit Frau Braun.** (Here the conjunction *seit* means "because" or "as long as.") The conjunction *da* (of which more in the following section) emphasizes the causality even more: *Da* **sie nicht mehr kommt, . . .**

EXERCISE 16 True or false?   T / F
    1. **Gretchen hat romantische Neigungen.**   _____
    2. **Sie ist eine schlechte Verkäuferin.**   _____
    3. **Peter zieht die Musik dem Geschäftsleben vor.**   _____
    4. **Gretchen fühlt Enthusiasmus fürs Geschäft.**   _____
    5. **Für Weihnachten braucht Karl keine Aushilfe.**   _____

EXERCISE 17 Complete the following sentences.
    1. **Gretchen arbeitete im Geschäft an zwei** _____.
    2. **Sie ist bereit, im Geschäft** _____.
    3. **Karl ist stolz auf die große Tradition des** _____.
    4. **Peter besitzt ein künstlerisches** _____.
    5. **Das Verkaufen macht Gretchen anscheinend großen** _____.

EXERCISE 18 Combine the two sentences, using the conjunction indicated.
    1. (while) **Peter interessiert sich wenig dafür. Gretchen interessiert sich sehr.**
    2. (although) **Sie hat nur als Babysitter gearbeitet. Sie beweist ihrem Vater, daß sie als** (as a) **Verkäuferin gut ist.**
    3. (as often as) **Er geht weg. Er sagt: „Servus!"**
    4. (since) **Voriges Wochenende arbeitete sie im Laden. Karl ist stolz auf sie.**
    5. **Karl ist froh.** (that) **Sie interessiert sich fürs Geschäft.**

EXERCISE 19 Translate into German.
    1. She is an amazingly practical little person.
    2. She is ready as often as Karl needs her.
    3. Obviously, she is sorry that she does not have more time.
    4. At the height of the Christmas season he needs extra help.
    5. As long as he has her, he is satisfied.

EXERCISE 20 Answer the following in complete German sentences.
    1. **Wann hat Gretchen zuerst im Laden gearbeitet?**
    2. **Was hat sie ihrem Vater bewiesen?**
    3. **Wer zieht die Musik dem Geschäftsleben vor?**
    4. **Wann braucht Karl dringend Aushilfe?**
    5. **Als was hat Gretchen bis vor kurzem gearbeitet?**

    In reference to exercise 18, please remember: A dependent clause always has dependent word order (verb at end of clause), no matter where in the sentence that clause occurs; and the word order in the main clause *is* affected by the location of the dependent clause.

Karl der Buchhändler

Subordinating Conjunctions (continued)

wenn, weil, da, indem, falls, sofern (insofern)

Vocabulary

abhalten (hält ab, hielt ab, abgehalten)	*here*: to hold
Abteilung (f)	department, section
Antiquariat (n)	used books department
Ausverkauf (m)	clearance sale
bedienen (w)	to serve

berechtigt	justified
Betriebskapital (n)	working capital
Branche (f)	line of business
Buchhändler (m)	bookseller
da	*here:* since, because
d.h. = das heißt	i.e., that is to say
etwa	at about
falls	in case of, if
gewissenhaft	conscientious(ly)
gut erhalten	well preserved
indem er abhält	by holding . . .
(auf) Kommission (f)	on consignment
Ladenhüter (m)	slow seller, white elephant
loswerden	to get rid of
nämlich	namely, that is to say
Prozent = % (n)	per cent
sofern	inasmuch as, provided
Umsatz (m)	volume of sales
unverkäuflich	unsalable
(eine) Unzahl (f)	a lot of
verlassen, sich darauf	to depend on
(verläßt, verließ, verlassen)	
Verleger (m)	publisher
veröffentlichen (w)	to publish
vollauf	perfectly
vorsichtig	cautious(ly)
zurückschicken (w)	to send back
zurückverkaufen (w)	to sell back

Wenn Karl von der stolzen Tradition des Buchhandels spricht, so ist er dazu vollauf berechtigt. Der Buchladen ist in seiner Familie seit beinahe 100 Jahren und immer noch unter demselben Namen.

Karls Umsatz ist nicht sehr groß, einfach *weil* er nicht genug Platz hat für die vielen neuen Bücher, die jedes Jahr veröffentlicht werden. *Da* sein Betriebskapital nicht sehr groß ist, muß er vorsichtig einkaufen. Sehr wenige Verleger verkaufen auf Kommission, d.h. so, daß man die unverkäuflichen Bücher zurückschicken kann. *Indem* er gelegentlich einen Ausverkauf abhält, wird er viele von den Ladenhütern los. Es gibt eine Unzahl Buchhändler in der Stadt, die natürlich alle miteinander konkurrieren.

Wie die meisten in der Branche, so hat auch er ein Antiquariat, *nämlich* eine Abteilung für gebrauchte Bücher. *Falls* ein Buch gut erhalten ist, kann man es dem Buchhändler—*sofern* er daran interessiert ist—um etwa 20% bis 25% des ursprünglichen Preises zurückverkaufen. *Indem* Karl seine Kunden freundlich und gewissenhaft bedient, kann er sich darauf verlassen, daß sie nächstes Mal zu ihm zurückkommen werden.

Conjunctions, conjunctions . . .

Wenn is used here in the meaning of "when" or "whenever." But it is also used for the English "if."

. . ., *weil* (**der Umsatz**) **nicht groß genug ist:** "because, due to the fact that . . ."

Indem **er einen Ausverkauf abhält,** . . . "By holding a clearance sale . . ." This is the only way to translate an *indem* clause into idiomatic English.

Falls **ein Buch gut erhalten ist,** . . . "in case the book is well preserved." A *Fall* (m) is a "case," and *falls* means *in case, in the event that.*

Sofern **er daran interessiert ist,** . . . "insofar as, provided that" would be the best English equivalents.

Eine Drohung°

Den dritten Mahnbrief,° den
Karl einem Mann schickte, der ihm
schon vier Monate lang DM 20 für
ein Buch schuldete,° beantwortete
der Kunde wie folgt:°
    Ihr garstiger° Brief vom
23. September hat mir überhaupt
nicht gefallen.°
    Einmal im Monat werfe° ich
alle unbezahlten Rechnungen° in
einen alten Papierkorb.° Dann zieht
meine Frau mit verbundenen° Augen
eine von ihnen heraus.° Wenn Sie
Glück haben,° wird das Ihre Rechnung
sein. Aber wenn Sie nicht aufhören,°
mir Ihre unverschämten° Mahnbriefe
zu schicken, werde ich Ihre Rechnung
nächsten Monat nicht mehr in den
Papierkorb werfen.

° a threat
° request for payment
° owed
° as follows
° nasty
° I did not like one bit
° throw
° unpaid bills
° wastepaper basket
° blindfolded
° draws
° if you are lucky
° stop
° impudent

EXERCISE 21 True or false?   T / F
1. Karl hat sein Geschäft vor drei Jahren gekauft.   _____
2. Sein Umsatz ist nicht sehr groß.   _____
3. Er kauft die meisten Bücher auf Kommission.   _____
4. Im Antiquariat verkauft er nur neue Bücher.   _____
5. Karl ist ein gewissenhafter Mensch.   _____

EXERCISE 22 Answer the following questions in complete German sentences.
1. Wie lange ist der Buchladen in seiner Familie?
2. Warum ist sein Umsatz nicht größer?
3. Warum muß er vorsichtig einkaufen?
4. Wie wird er die Ladenhüter los?
5. Wie nennt man die Abteilung für gebrauchte Bücher?

EXERCISE 23 Fill in the German conjunctions as indicated.
1. Er ist dazu berechtigt, _____ er davon spricht. (whenever)
2. Sein Umsatz ist nicht sehr groß, _____ er keinen Platz hat.
   (because)
3. _____ ein Buch gut erhalten ist, bekommt man mehr dafür.
   (in case)
4. Gretchen arbeitet für ihn, _____ sie Zeit hat. (inasmuch as)
5. _____ Karl die Kunden gut bedient, kommen sie zurück.
   (if)

EXERCISE 24 Choose the correct words.
1. Ladenhüter
   a. behält man gern   b. benutzt man
   c. will man loswerden
2. Konkurrenten im Buchhandel?
   a. viele   b. wenige   c. keine
3. Ein Antiquariat ist
   a. ein Bildergeschäft   b. eine Schule
   c. eine Abteilung für gebrauchte Bücher
4. Karl hat nicht viel
   a. Geschmack   b. Betriebskapital   c. Zeit
5. Manchmal kann man Bücher an Karl zurückverkaufen.
   a. um 20%-25% des ursprünglichen Preises
   b. 40%   c. 50%

Gretchens Ehrgeiz°   ambition

Subordinating Conjunctions (continued)

sobald, so daß, nachdem, als, ob, je—desto

Vocabulary

Ausgabe (f)	*here*: expense
ausgeben (gibt aus, gab aus, ausgegeben)	to spend
ausständige Rechnungen (f. pl.)	bills in arrears
Buchhaltung (f)	bookkeeping
Computerprogrammierung (f)	computer programming
das ist keine Kunst	there is nothing to it
einnehmen (nimmt ein, nahm ein, eingenommen)	to take in
Fachhochschule (f)	specialized college
fehlerlos	without an error
garantieren (w)	to guarantee
Geschäftsbrief (m)	business letter
geschickt	skilled
Hauswirtschaft (f)	household
installieren (w)	to install
Inventur (f)	inventory
je mehr—desto besser	the more—the better
Kurzschrift (f)	shorthand
Maschinenschreiben (n)	typing
Mathe (f)	"math," i.e., mathematics
Mittlere Reife (f)	a secondary school diploma
nachdem	after
ob	if, whether
richtig	*here*: regular
schlagen (schlägt, schlug, geschlagen)	to beat
Schularbeit (f)	*here*: assignment
sobald	as soon as
Sparkonto (n)	savings account
so daß	so that
tippen (w)	to type
Studium (n)	study
wegräumen (w)	to put away
wie ihre finanzielle Situation beschaffen ist	how her finances stand
wie Peter . . .	*here*: like Peter . . .
wird fortgesetzt	is being continued

Sobald Gretchen etwas Geld beisammen hat, trägt sie es auf die Bank. Sie hat dort bereits ein Sparkonto unter ihrem eigenen und dem Namen ihres Vaters. Das kleine Taschengeld von Karl ist anscheinend genug für ihre privaten Ausgaben.

Wenn sie etwas einnimmt oder ausgibt, trägt sie es in ein kleines Buch ein, *so daß* sie immer weiß, wie ihre finanzielle Situation beschaffen ist. Für die Hauswirtschaft zeigt sie wenig Interesse. Aber wie Peter, so hat auch sie ihre eigenen Pläne. Heute abend, *nachdem* man das Geschirr weggeräumt und gewaschen hat, wird die Familienkonferenz fortgesetzt.

KARL Also, Gretchen, wie stellst *du* dir die Zukunft vor?

GRETCHEN Ich möchte sehr gern geschäftlich tätig sein.

KARL Gut. Ich glaube, du hast ein natürliches Talent dafür.

GRETCHEN Wie du weißt, Vati, nehme ich jetzt Buchhaltung, Maschinenschreiben und Kurzschrift in der Schule. Wir schreiben schon richtige Geschäftsbriefe. *Als* ich die letzte Schularbeit ablieferte, machte mir die Lehrerin ein Kompliment.

KARL Ja?

GRETCHEN Ich hatte drei Mahnbriefe fehlerlos getippt.

KARL Vielleicht kannst du mir dann auch einige an meine Kunden tippen.

GRETCHEN Gern, Vati. Aber *ob* du dann wirklich das Geld kriegst, kann ich dir nicht garantieren.

NORA Was willst du nach der Mittleren Reife machen?

GRETCHEN Computerprogrammierung studieren.

PETER Sie schlägt mich jedesmal beim „Teufelsbalg.''

GRETCHEN Das ist keine Kunst.

PETER Aber sie ist wirklich sehr geschickt. Und in Mathe ist sie auch sehr gut. Vielleicht kann sie dann einen Computer in deinem Geschäft installieren, Vati.

KARL Keine schlechte Idee. Besonders für Inventur und die ausständigen Rechnungen.

NORA Wie lange dauert dieses Studium?

GRETCHEN Das kann man schon in zwei Jahren gut lernen.

KARL Willst du nicht auf eine Fachhochschule gehen? *Je* mehr du lernst, *desto* besser ist es für dich.

. . . And More Conjunctions

Sobald Gretchen etwas Geld beisammen hat, . . . This refers to a specific time: *as soon as* . . .

Sie trägt es in ein Buch ein, **so daß** sie weiß, . . . (or: **damit** sie weiß . . .): *so that* . . .

Nachdem man das Geschirr weggeräumt hat, . . . *After* one has put away the dishes . . . (or, more idiomatically: *After* the dishes were put away . . .)

Als ich die letzte Schularbeit ablieferte, . . . *When* I handed in my last assignment . . .

Ob du dann das Geld kriegst, . . . *If* (or *whether*) you then get the money . . .

Je mehr du lernst, *desto besser* ist es für dich. *The more* you learn, *the better* it is for you.

EXERCISE 25 True or false?   T / F
1. **Gretchen hat ihr eigenes Sparkonto.**   _____
2. **An der Hauswirtschaft ist sie sehr interessiert.**   _____
3. **Sie hat ihre eigenen Pläne.**   _____
4. **Sie will Medizin studieren.**   _____
5. **In Mathe ist sie sehr schlecht.**   _____

EXERCISE 26 Choose the correct words.
1. **Sobald Gretchen genug Geld beisammen hat,**
   a. **kauft sie Süßigkeiten**   b. **trägt sie es auf die Bank**
   c. **gibt sie es Peter**
2. **Das kleine Taschengeld von Karl**
   a. **ist genug für sie**   b. **spart sie**
   c. **gibt sie Mutter**

3. **Sie tippte drei Mahnbriefe**
   a. **mit zehn Fehlern**   b. **mit zwei Fehlern**
   c. **fehlerlos**
4. **Was sie studieren will, ist**
   a. **Computerprogrammierung**   b. **Mathe**   c. **English**
5. **Wofür sie wenig Interesse zeigt, ist**
   a. **Kurzschrift**   b. **Buchhaltung**   c. **Hauswirtschaft**

EXERCISE 27   Write the following in German.
1. She has her own savings account.
2. She wants to know how her finances stand.
3. After they put away the dishes, they talk.
4. When she handed in her paper, the teacher paid her a compliment.
5. "The more, the better," her father told her.

EXERCISE 28   Answer in complete German sentences.
1. **Was ist genug für ihre privaten Ausgaben?**
2. **Wann wird die Familienkonferenz fortgesetzt?**
3. **Was möchte Gretchen in der Zukunft gerne tun?**
4. **Welche Fächer nimmt sie jetzt in der Schule?**
5. **Wo, sagt Peter, soll sie einen Computer installieren?**

EXERCISE 29   Translate into English.
1. **Ihre finanzielle Situation ist sehr gut.**
2. **Sie lernt Kurzschrift, Buchhaltung und Maschinenschreiben.**
3. **Karl braucht einen Computer für Inventur und ausständige Rechnungen.**
4. **Sie kann Geschäftsbriefe fehlerlos tippen.**
5. **Das ist keine Kunst.**

CHAPTER 13

Kristy besucht ihre Wiener Verwandten
Kristy Visits Her Viennese Relatives

Conjunctions (concluded)

Kristy in Wien
Ferdinand und Maria Sacher

More Subordinating Conjunctions

bevor, ehe, bis

Vocabulary

ablehnen (w)	to reject
Also abgemacht!	OK, it's a deal.
andernfalls	otherwise
beherbergen (w)	to accommodate
bevor, ehe	before
bis (conjunction)	*here*: until
bis auf (preposition)	except for
dankbar	grateful
Ehre (f)	honor
erfinden (erfindet, erfand, erfunden)	to invent
erkennen (erkannte, erkannt)	to recognize
erstens, zweitens, drittens etc.	in the first place, second place, third place etc.
faktisch	for all practical purposes
fesch	dashing
Flugplatz (m)	airport
Fürst (m)	prince
Geschichte (f)	history
Hausgehilfin (f)	maid, domestic
hinauswerfen (wirft hinaus, warf hinaus, hinausgeworfen)	to throw out
hübsch	pretty
irgendeinmal	some time
Junggeselle (m)	bachelor
kein Anlaß	don't mention it

kosten	*here*: to taste
Kristy ist sicher	*here*: Kristy is certain
Leckerbissen (m)	delicacy
Nachkomme (m)	descendant
Österreich	Austria
Persönlichkeit (f)	personality
Ritter (m)	knight, chevalier
Romanschriftsteller (m)	novelist
rückgängig machen	to cancel
Scherz beiseite	joking aside
(sich) Sorgen machen	to worry
Torte (f)	torte, tart, cake
vorher	before
wäre interessant gewesen	would have been interesting
widerstehen (widerstand, widerstanden)	to resist
Zuckerbäcker, Konditor (m)	pastry cook
Zusammensetzung (f)	composition, ingredients

Kristy hat beschlossen, ihre Verwandten in Wien zu besuchen, bevor sie nach Amerika zurückkehrt.

Kristy weiß, daß ihre Familie mit dem Romanschriftsteller Leopold Ritter von Sacher-Masoch nicht verwandt ist. Das wäre interessant gewesen, glaubt sie, obwohl sie sowohl den Masochismus als auch den Sadismus ablehnt. Ferdinand Sacher ist ein Vetter ihrer Mutter, dessen Familie in Wien schon seit 1700 ansässig ist. Er ist ein Nachkomme von Franz Sacher, der Zuckerbäcker (oder Konditor) des Fürsten Metternich war—einer berühmten Persönlichkeit in der Geschichte Österreichs—und der im Jahre 1832 eine Torte erfand, die seinen Namen trägt. Sacher war damals nur 16 Jahre alt! In Wien haben so viele junge Genies gelebt, unter ihnen Mozart und Schubert. Sie starben jung, aber Franz Sacher wurde sehr alt. Es gibt wahrscheinlich keinen Besucher Wiens, der diesen Leckerbissen, die Sachertorte, nicht irgendeinmal gekostet hat. Die genaue Zusammensetzung dieser köstlichen Torte bleibt bis heute ein „süßes Geheimnis."

Kristy ist sicher, daß sie während ihres Aufenthaltes in Wien keine Kalorien zählen wird. Leider nimmt sie sehr leicht zu, aber darüber wird sie sich später Sorgen machen. Ferdinand (oder Ferdl, wie ihn seine Freunde nennen) holt sie vom Flugplatz ab. Er hat sie nie vorher gesehen, aber sie haben miteinander korrespondiert, und er erkennt sie von einem Bild, das sie ihm geschickt hat.

FERDL Servus, Kristy. Gib mir einen Kuß. Du bist noch viel hübscher als auf dem Bild.

KRISTY Servus. Also du bist der fesche Ferdl, von dem mir mein Vater erzählt hat. Noch immer nicht verheiratet?

FERDL Nein, und ich werde wahrscheinlich Junggeselle bleiben. Es gibt zu viele schöne Frauen in Wien. Ich hoffe, du hast keine Hotelreservierung gemacht, Kristy. Andernfalls mußt du sie rückgängig machen. Meine Mutter hat eine Villa in Sievering, du kannst bei ihr wohnen, solange du willst.

KRISTY Du meinst, *bis* sie mich hinauswirft? Scherz beiseite, ich bin euch beiden sehr dankbar.

FERDL Kein Anlaß. Erstens ist die Villa bis auf meine Mutter und eine Hausgehilfin faktisch leer; zweitens sind Hotels in Wien sehr teuer; und drittens haben wir sehr selten die Ehre, einen attraktiven Gast aus Amerika zu beherbergen.

KRISTY Vetter Ferdl, es ist schwer, deinem Wiener Charme zu widerstehen.

FERDL Also abgemacht!

Note: Napoleon's uncle, Cardinal Fesch, son of Swiss soldier Franz Fesch, was no doubt a dashing ecclesiastic. But believe it or not, *fesch* (a word Austrians are particularly fond of) derives not from him, but from the mispronunciation of the first *a* in *fashionable.* Germans sometimes call the banking metropolis Frankfurt am Main, "**Menhetten am Main.**" They mean *Manhattan,* of course. Even though they'd probably write it correctly, they usually mispronounce it **Menhetten.**

. . . And Some More Conjunctions

Bevor **Kristy nach Amerika zurückkehrt. . .**

Instead of *bevor* we can also say:

Ehe **sie zurückkehrt**

Before she returns. . .

Du meinst, *bis* **sie mich hinauswirft?**

You mean until she throws me out?

Shortly after this, Ferdl tells Kristy that the house is practically empty:

bis auf meine Mutter und eine Hausgehilfin

except for my mother and a maid

The first *bis* is a conjunction, the second *bis* a preposition.

EXERCISE 1 True or false?   T / F
1. **Ferdinand Sacher ist Kristys Onkel.**   _____
2. **Franz Sacher erfand die Sachertorte.**   _____
3. **Kristy wird in Wien nicht viel essen.**   _____
4. **Ferdl ist verheiratet.**   _____
5. **Kristy wird bei Ferdls Mutter wohnen.**   _____

EXERCISE 2 Answer the following in complete German sentences.
1. **Was war Franz Sacher?**
2. **Von wo holt Ferdl Kristy ab?**
3. **Warum muß Ferdl ein Junggeselle bleiben?**
4. **Was wird Kristy wahrscheinlich rückgängig machen?**
5. **Wie lange, sagt sie, wird sie bei Ferdls Mutter bleiben?**

EXERCISE 3 Complete each sentence with the German equivalent of the words listed here: delicacy, descendant, calories, empty, married
1. **Ferdl ist ein** _____ **von Franz Sacher.**
2. **Kristy wird in Wien keine** _____ **zählen.**
3. **Ferdl ist noch immer nicht** _____.
4. **Die Sachertorte ist ein** _____.
5. **Die Wohnung seiner Mutter ist faktisch** _____.

EXERCISE 4 Choose the correct words.
1. **Bevor Kristy nach Amerika zurückkehrt, will sie**
   a. **England sehen**   b. **nach Berlin fliegen**
   c. **Wien besuchen**
2. **Fürst Metternich war eine berühmte Persönlichkeit in der Geschichte**
   a. **Österreichs**   b. **Amerikas**   c. **Italiens**
3. **Ferdl nennt Kristy**
   a. **schön**   b. **attraktiv**   c. **nett**
4. **In Sievering hat Frau Sacher**
   a. **eine Wohnung**   b. **ein Haus**   c. **eine Villa**
5. **Sie wohnt dort mit ihrer**
   a. **Hausgehilfin**   b. **Tochter**   c. **Kusine**

EXERCISE 5 Translate into German.
  1. Franz Sacher was a pastry cook.
  2. In 1832 he invented a famous torte.
  3. Kristy calls Ferdl "dashing."
  4. "Cancel your hotel reservation!" he tells her.
  5. Joking aside, she will stay with his mother.

Essen° und Kultur   food

Vocabulary

aufrechterhalten (erhält aufrecht, erhielt aufrecht, aufrechterhalten)	to maintain
Beziehungen (f. pl.)	relations
circa = ca. (pronounce "tsirka")	circa, about
eindringlich	emphatic(ally)
endlich	finally
Figur (f)	figure
gebildet	educated, cultured
Gesandtschaftsattaché (m)	attaché at the embassy
Gesichtszüge (m. pl.)	features
jugendlich	youthful
na, ja. . .	well. . .
nahezu	almost
Sprache (f)	language
schlohweiß	snow-white
(eine) Unmenge Kultur	loads of culture
willkommen	welcome
Witwe (f)	widow

FERDL Also das ist dein erster Besuch in Wien, nicht wahr?

KRISTY Ja; und du kannst dir nicht vorstellen, wie ich mich darauf gefreut habe. Wien, Wien, nur du allein. . .

FERDL Na ja, wir leben hier ganz schön. Gutes Essen und eine Unmenge Kultur, das kann man schon sagen. Ich hoffe, daß es so bleibt. Siehst du, wir sind ein kleines Land und versuchen, zu allen Ländern gute Beziehungen aufrechtzuerhalten. Also hier ist mein kleiner Volkswagen. Es dauert ca. 30 Minuten bis nach Hause, wenn der Verkehr nicht zu arg ist.

Endlich sind sie in Sievering angekommen. Frau Sacher ist die Witwe eines österreichischen Diplomaten, der Gesandtschaftsattaché in Rom, London und Madrid war. Nahezu sechzig Jahre alt ist sie noch immer eine schöne Frau, mit regelmäßigen Gesichtszügen, schlohweißem Haar und einer jugendlichen Figur. Sie ist eine sehr gebildete Dame, die vier Sprachen fließend spricht.

FRAU SACHER Willkommen, Kristy. Als ich dich das letzte Mal sah, warst du ein süßes Baby, das kaum reden konnte. Heute bist du eine elegante junge Dame. Ich hoffe, Ferdl hat dir eindringlich genug gesagt, du kannst hier bleiben, solange du willst.

KRISTY Ich weiß nicht, wie ich dir danken soll. Darf ich dich Tante nennen?

FRAU SACHER Nein. Nenn mich Maria.

EXERCISE 6   True or false?   T / F
1. **Das ist Kristys erster Besuch in Wien.**   _____
2. **Österreich ist ein sehr großes Land.**   _____
3. **Frau Sacher spricht nur Deutsch.**   _____
4. **Sie ist dick und hat dunkles Haar.**   _____
5. **Kristy soll sie Maria nennen.**   _____

EXERCISE 7   Choose the correct words.
1. **Ferdl hat einen**
   a. **Ford**   b. **Volkswagen**   c. **Mercedes**
2. **Ferdls Vater war**
   a. **Diplomat**   b. **Buchhändler**   c. **Lehrer**
3. **Kristy soll**
   a. **im Hotel wohnen**   b. **gleich zurückkehren**
   c. **bei Maria wohnen**
4. **Als Frau Sacher Kristy zuletzt sah, war diese**
   a. **ein junges Mädchen**   b. **noch nicht geboren**
   c. **ein süßes Baby**
5. **Maria hat eine Villa in**
   a. **Sievering**   b. **Grinzing**   c. **Währing**

EXERCISE 8   Answer in complete German sentences.
1. **Was für ein Auto hat Ferdl?**
2. **Wie alt ist Maria?**
3. **Was spricht sie fließend?**
4. **Wie sind ihre Gesichtszüge?**
5. **Was war Kristy, als Maria sie zuletzt sah?**

EXERCISE 9   Match the following sentences:
1. **Maria hat eine jugendliche**   _____ It took about 30
   Figur.   minutes.
2. **Österreich hat gute**   _____ She speaks four
   Beziehungen.   languages fluently.
3. **Gutes Essen und eine Unmenge**   _____ She has a maid.
   Kultur.   _____ Austria has good
4. **Sie spricht vier Sprachen**   relations.
   fließend.   _____ Maria has a
5. **Sie hat eine Hausgehilfin.**   youthful figure.
6. **Es dauerte ca. 30 Minuten.**   _____ Good food and loads
                                                 of culture.

EXERCISE 10   Translate into English.
1. **Ich hoffe, daß es so bleibt.**
2. **Endlich sind sie zu Hause angekommen.**
3. **Heute ist Kristy eine elegante junge Dame.**
4. **Sie kann hier bleiben, solange sie will.**
5. **Man will gute Beziehungen aufrechterhalten.**

Der Heurige und das Café

People drink coffee and wine everywhere. Yet drinking them in Vienna is special. Of course you can get basic black coffee in Vienna's coffee houses. But they're famous for offering a great variety of coffees, in various concentrations and combinations, with or without alcohol, and often crowned with **Schlagsahne** (whipped cream), or **Schlagobers** as the Viennese often call it. These coffees sport names like **Einspänner, Konsul, Mélange,** and **Piccolo.**

In all wine-growing regions, the new wine is awaited eagerly. In Vienna, **der Heurige** continues to be celebrated in song and folklore. Instead of saying **dieses Jahr,** Austrians often use **heuer** (this year). **Heurig** is an adjective used in Austria and other southern areas for *this year's.* It could be this year's harvest, or this year's anything. But **der Heurige** is something special. It means both *this year's wine* and an establishment where the new wine is served, often in charming Vienna suburbs like Grinzing, or the one in which Kristy is staying, Sievering. In other German-speaking wine-growing regions, the new wine is known variously as **Federweiße, Most, Sturm** and **Sauser.**

Vocabulary

ausschenken (w)	to pour out, to dispense
(sich) befinden	to be located
beobachten (w)	to watch
Billard (n) (pronounce ''bílyart'')	billiards
erledigen (w)	to take care of
(im) Freien	in the open, outdoors
Freizeit (f)	leisure time
Gaststätte (f)	restaurant
genießen (genoß, genossen)	to enjoy
in der Gesellschaft von . . .	in the company of . . .
Heimatstadt(f)	home town
Holzbank, -bänke (f)	wooden bench
kennenlernen (w)	to get to know
Krug (m)	jug, pitcher
Mahlzeit (f)	meal
Passant (m)	passer-by
plaudern (w)	to chat
Sänger (m)	singer
Schach (n)	chess
Schrammelquartett (n)	quartet for popular Viennese music: two violins, guitar, bandoneon (or accordion)
stören (w)	to disturb, bother
Weise (f)	*here:* tune

Ungefähr zwei Kilometer von der Villa, in der Maria wohnt, findet man eine Anzahl von ﴾﴿Heurigen'', kleine Gaststätten, wo der junge Wein ausgeschenkt wird. Man sitzt da auf Holzbänken im Freien mit einem Krug Wein auf dem Tisch vor sich in der Gesellschaft von Freunden. Ein Schrammelquartett spielt die alten, populären Weisen und manchmal ist auch ein Sänger dabei. Man sitzt, plaudert, genießt den Wein, und weiß am Ende nicht, wie viel man getrunken hat. Eines weiß man: man fühlt sich sehr wohl.

Eine andere Institution, die Wien berühmt gemacht hat, ist das Wiener Cafe. Wir haben in einem früheren Kapitel die Cafe-Konditorei in Karls Heimatstadt kennengelernt. In Wien ist es das Cafe oder Kaffeehaus, wo man einen Teil seiner Freizeit verbringen kann, seine Mahlzeiten einnimmt, Zeitungen und Zeitschriften aus der ganzen Welt liest, Schach, Karten oder Billard spielt, seine Korrespondenz erledigt, Geschäftskonferenzen abhält oder einfach sitzt und die Passanten auf der Straße beobachtet. Kein Kellner wird einen stören, auch wenn man während eines ganzen Nachmittags nur eine Tasse Kaffee konsumiert hat.

EXERCISE 11 True or false T / F

1. **Man sitzt auf Holzbänken im Freien.** _____
2. **Man fühlt sich überhaupt nicht wohl.** _____
3. **Im Cafe spielt man Schach und Billard.** _____
4. **Der Kellner stört einen alle 20 Minuten.** _____
5. **Manchmal konsumiert man nur eine Tasse Kaffee.** _____

EXERCISE 12 Construct sentences using the cue words.

1. **sitzt / Holzbänke / Freien**
2. **Teil / Freizeit / Cafe**
3. **Passanten / Straße / beobachten**
4. **Schach / Karten / Korrespondenz**
5. **Zeitungen / Zeitschriften / Welt**

EXERCISE 13 Choose the correct words.

1. **Nicht weit von Marias Villa befinden sich**
   a. **die ,,Heurigen''** b. **große Hotels** c. **zwei Kinos**
2. **Auf dem Tisch beim ,,Heurigen'' steht**
   a. **eine Tasse Kaffee** b. **ein Glas Tee**
   c. **ein Krug Wein**
3. **In einem Wiener Cafe kann man**
   a. **keine Zeitungen lesen** b. **stundenlang sitzenbleiben**
   c. **nie Karten spielen**
4. **Ein Schrammelquartett spielt**
   a. **die alten, populären Weisen** b. **Beethoven** c. **Bach**
5. **Am Ende fühlt man sich dort**
   a. **ganz miserabel** b. **sehr wohl** c. **belästigt**

EXERCISE 14 Complete each sentence with a word listed here: **erster, Unmenge, versuchen, gebildete, Tante**

1. **Wir _____ , gute Beziehungen aufrechtzuerhalten.**
2. **Sie ist eine sehr _____ Dame.**
3. **Das ist ihr _____ Besuch in Wien.**
4. **Darf ich dich _____ nennen?**
5. **Gutes Essen und eine _____ Kultur.**

EXERCISE 15 Answer each question with a complete German sentence.

1. **Was versucht Österreich als kleines Land?**
2. **Wo sind Ferdl und Kristy endlich angekommen?**
3. **Wie sind Marias Gesichtszüge?**
4. **Was, sagt Maria, ist Kristy jetzt?**
5. **Was für ein Auto hat Ferdl?**

Die Brücke°

bridge

    **Ein Amerikaner kam nach Wien
und ersuchte einen Bekannten, ihm
einige der Sehenswürdigkeiten° zu**   sights
**zeigen. Der Wiener zeigte ihm die
Staatsoper. ,,Die hat man in zwei Jahren
wieder aufgebaut.°''***   to rebuild
    **,,In Amerika dauert das bloß
neun Monate.''**
    Dann **führte ihn der Wiener zum
neuen Westbahnhof.° ,,Das war in einem**   West Railroad Sta-
Jahr fertig.'' tion

*Actually, of course, it took much longer.

„In Amerika stellen wir so ein
Gebäude in drei Monaten hin.°"   we put up
    Schließlich kamen sie zu der
neuen Brücke über der Donau.°   Danube
    „Das ist eine sehr schöne
Brücke", sagte der Amerikaner. „Wie
lange hat das gedauert?"
    „Die Brücke, meinen Sie?"
erwiderte der Wiener. „*Als* ich heute
früh in die Stadt hineinfuhr,° war sie   entered the city
noch gar nicht° da."   was not there yet

CHAPTER 14

Susie will umschulen
Susie Wants to Learn Something New

Encouraged by Anton's example, Susie, too, wants to change jobs. And who can blame her after her description of a day at the office?

The Passive Voice

In German, the passive voice consists of the auxiliary verb **werden** and the past participle. The auxiliary verb expresses the time, and the past participle describes the action that is performed; example: **Zur Mahlzeıt** *wird* **von Susie Bier** *serviert*. (With the meal beer is being served by Susie).

Die rechte Hand ihres Chefs?

Vocabulary

Abendessen (n)	dinner
auftragen (trägt auf, trug auf, aufgetragen)	*here*: to dish up
aufwarten (w)	to serve
Brief (m)	letter
bunter Salat (m)	a salad consisting of potatoes, beets, celery, pickles, mayonnaise, etc.
Chef (m) (pronounce ''sheff'')	boss
den ihrigen	hers
erfolgreich	successful(ly)
(sich) ermutigt fühlen (w)	to feel encouraged
Fach(n)	line (of business)
glorreich	glorious
genügen	to be sufficient
es gibt nichts auszusetzen	there is nothing to criticize
Koch (m)	cook
langweilen (w)	to bore
Nachtisch (m)	dessert
Pause (f)	pause
Pause einschalten	to take a break
Pflicht (f)	duty
Pilz (m)	mushroom
Rotkraut (n)	red cabbage

Schweinebraten (m)	pork roast
Verantwortung (f)	responsibility
vorzüglich	excellent

Seitdem Anton seinen Job erfolgreich gewechselt hat, fühlt sich seine Freundin Susie mehr und mehr ermutigt, den ihrigen aufzugeben. Aber Anton arbeitet, wie wir wissen, immer noch in demselben Fach. Mit Susie ist das anders. Sie ist Sekretärin, aber die Pflichten einer Sekretärin langweilen sie. Man hat ihr oft versichert, daß sie die rechte Hand ihres Chefs ist, aber das genügt ihr nicht. Sie will vor allem mehr wirkliche Verantwortung haben und weniger Briefe schreiben.

Susies Mutter, Frau Braun, hat Anton für heute zum Abendessen eingeladen. Frau Braun ist eine vorzügliche Köchin. An ihren Mahlzeiten ist nichts auszusetzen außer einem: was immer sie serviert, ist zu viel und zu schwer. Nach einer glorreichen Kartoffelsuppe mit Pilzen (die allein schon ein komplettes Mahl darstellt) *wird ein Schweinebraten* mit Knödeln und Rotkraut *aufgetragen*, dazu ein bunter Salat, der Frau Brauns Spezialität ist. *Zur Mahlzeit wird von Susie Bier serviert.* Bevor man mit dem Nachtisch aufwartet, fragt Anton sehr höflich: „Gnädige Frau, haben Sie was dagegen, wenn *jetzt eine kleine Pause eingeschaltet wird?*"

Here Is Your Grammar

Compare the active with the passive voice:

Zur Mahlzeit serviert Susie Bier.

or turn it around:

Susie serviert Bier zur Mahlzeit.
Susie serves beer . . .

Susie is the subject, *Bier* is the object. Now we change this sentence to the passive voice:

Bier wird von Susie zur Mahlzeit serviert,
Beer is being served by Susie . . .

or the way we read it in the text:

Zur Mahlzeit wird von Susie Bier serviert.

The direct object in the active-voice sentence (**Bier**) becomes the subject of the passive-voice sentence. The previous subject (**Susie**) now becomes the agent that performs the action; if it is a person (as in this particular case), it is preceded by *von* and is in the dative:

Bier wird von Susie serviert.
Beer is being served by Susie.

If the agent is a blind force, it is preceded by *durch* and is in the accusative:

Ein Blitz tötet den Mann.
Lightning kills the man.

Der Mann wird *durch* einen Blitz getötet.
The man is being killed by lightning.

There are exceptions to this general rule that will come up later and will be explained then.

EXERCISE 1 True or false? T / F
1. Susie will ihren Job wechseln. _____
2. Die Pflichten einer Sekretärin faszinieren sie. _____
3. Sie will mehr Verantwortung haben. _____
4. Heute essen sie Krautsuppe. _____
5. Frau Braun serviert nicht genug. _____

EXERCISE 2 Answer the following in complete German sentences.
1. **Wer hat heute das Abendessen gekocht?**
2. **Wen hat man dazu eingeladen?**
3. **Wie ist die Kartoffelsuppe?**
4. **Was ist Frau Brauns Spezialität?**
5. **Was wird zur Mahlzeit getrunken?**

EXERCISE 3 Change from the active to the passive voice.
Example: **Anton wechselt seinen Job.**
              Der Job wird von Anton gewechselt.
1. **Susies Mutter lädt Anton ein.**
2. **Frau Braun serviert einen Schweinebraten.**
3. **Susie serviert Bier.**
4. **Wir schalten eine kleine Pause ein.**
5. **Susie gibt ihren Job auf.**

EXERCISE 4 Write the following sentences in German.
1. Anton still works in the same line.
2. She is her boss's right hand.
3. Mrs. Braun is an excellent cook.
4. They will have the dessert later.
5. There is nothing to criticize.

EXERCISE 5 Choose the correct words.
1. **Susie arbeitet als**
   a. **Tankwart** b. **Verkäuferin** c. **Sekretärin**
2. **Leute sagen, sie ist die rechte Hand ihres**
   a. **Chefs** b. **Vaters** c. **Antons**
3. **Frau Braun serviert**
   a. **zu wenig** b. **nicht genug** c. **zu viel**
4. **Die Kartoffelsuppe ist**
   a. **glorreich** b. **süß** c. **kalt**
5. **Anton nennt Susies Mutter**
   a. **Mutti** b. **gnädige Frau** c. **Paula**

Ein Wecker im Büro

Vocabulary

andrehen (w)	to turn on
Bissen (m)	bite
Bürovorstand (m)	office manager
fasten (w)	to fast
es geht mir auf die Nerven	it gets on my nerves
Gehalt (n)	salary
geizig	stingy
kontrollieren (w)	to check
(sich) langweilen (w)	to get bored
Mohnkuchen (m)	poppyseed cake
Oberbuchhalter (m)	head bookkeeper
platzen (w)	to burst
punkt acht	at eight sharp
schlau	shrewd
Stechuhr (f)	time clock
Tod (m)	death
wäre	would be
Wecker (m)	alarm clock

Mohnkuchen wird zum Nachtisch *serviert.* Dazu Kaffee; Anton trinkt ihn schwarz, Susie nimmt etwas Sahne; Frau Braun trinkt Tee.

FRAU BRAUN Wenn ich um diese Zeit Kaffee trinke, kann ich nicht schlafen.

ANTON Das war ein Mahl für Götter, Frau Braun.

FRAU BRAUN Sind Sie sicher, Herr Anton, daß ich Ihnen genug zu essen gegeben habe?

SUSIE *Wird jetzt wieder mit der Suppe angefangen?*

ANTON Noch einen Bissen und ich platze. *Morgen wird gefastet.*

SUSIE Mutter, warum setzt du dich nicht zu uns, ich helfe dir später mit dem Geschirr. (Mrs. Braun sits down.)

ANTON Also erzähl mir, Susie. Du bist mit deinem jetzigen Job unzufrieden, sagst du. Verdienst du nicht genug oder magst du die Arbeit nicht?

SUSIE Das Gehalt ist nicht schlecht, aber ich langweile mich zu Tode. Es ist die gleiche, alte Routine, die mir auf die Nerven geht.

ANTON Erklär mir das.

SUSIE Punkt acht *wird der Wecker angedreht.*

ANTON Ein Wecker? Im Büro?

SUSIE Die Idee unseres Oberbuchhalters, der zugleich der Bürovorstand ist. *Alle Türen sind geöffnet*; er weiß genau, wer zu spät kommt.

ANTON Eine Stechuhr wäre praktischer.

SUSIE Dazu ist er zu geizig. *Dann wird* fünfmal am Tag *jedes Büro von ihm kontrolliert.*

ANTON Immer um dieselbe Zeit?

SUSIE Nein; dazu ist er zu schlau.

More Important Grammar

Sometimes there is no apparent subject in a passive-voice sentence:

Wird jetzt wieder mit der Suppe angefangen?

To turn the question into a statement Susie would have to say:

Es **wird jetzt wieder mit der Suppe angefangen.**

Or look at Anton's reply:

Morgen wird gefastet.

To insert the *es* into this sentence would make it sound awkward.

What is called the false or the stative passive uses **sein**, not **werden**, and is illustrated by:

Alle Türen *sind geöffnet*.

Here a condition is described rather than an action. (The action, of course, would be: **Alle Türen werden geöffnet.**)

EXERCISE 6 True or false?   T / F

1. **Frau Braun trinkt Kaffee zum Abendessen.** _____
2. **Susie wird ihr später mit dem Geschirr helfen.** _____
3. **Sie langweilt sich in ihrem Büro.** _____
4. **Um acht sind alle Bürotüren geöffnet.** _____
5. **Sie werden von einer Stechuhr kontrolliert.** _____

EXERCISE 7 Translate into German.

1. Did I give you enough to eat?
2. I am bored to death.
3. It gets on my nerves.
4. The office manager is very shrewd.
5. I cannot eat anymore; I'm bursting already.

EXERCISE 8 Complete each sentence with a word listed here: **Gehalt, Götter, Punkt, geöffnet, Stechuhr**

   1. _____ acht wird der Wecker angedreht.

   2. Alle Türen sind _____.

   3. Das _____ ist nicht schlecht.

   4. Eine _____ wäre praktischer.

   5. Das war ein Mahl für _____.

EXERCISE 9 Choose the correct words.

   1. Susie trinkt ihren Kaffee
      a. mit Sahne b. schwarz c. nicht

   2. Morgen, sagt Anton, wird
      a. studiert b. gegessen c. gefastet

   3. Susies Mutter
      a. geht zurück in die Küche b. liest
      c. setzt sich zu ihnen

   4. Im Büro haben sie
      a. einen Wecker b. eine Stechuhr c. einen Fernseher

   5. Der Bürovorstand ist
      a. sehr nett b. freundlich c. schlau

Die Pflichten einer Sekretärin

Vocabulary

Allergie (f)	allergy
aufgeben	*here:* to mail
Ausschlag (m)	rash
diktieren (w)	to dictate
einschreiben (schrieb ein, eingeschrieben)	to register
Erhalt, (m)	receipt
Gericht (n)	*here:* court
liefern (w)	to deliver
Paket (n)	package
Post (f)	mail
Schokolade (f)	chocolate
überfahren (überfährt, überfuhr, überfahren)	to run over
unterbrechen (unterbricht, unterbrach, unterbrochen)	to interrupt
untersuchen (w)	to examine
verantwortlich	responsible
Ware (f)	merchandise

SUSIE Um neun *wird die Post geliefert. Sie wird geöffnet* und auf den Schreibtisch des Chefs *gelegt.* Um 9:30 *werde ich* telephonisch in sein Büro *bestellt.* Ich bin verantwortlich für die ausgehende Post. „Susie? *Wurde das Paket* an Pfister & Sohn gestern nach Zürich *aufgegeben? Wurde es eingeschrieben* und *versichert?* Gut. Schreiben Sie an Ulrich Möller A.G. in Hamburg, daß *die Ware,* die er bestellt hat, morgen *geliefert werden wird.* Bestätigen Sie den Erhalt des Briefes von Kurt Krone. Drohen Sie ihm, *es wurde lange genug gewartet.* Entweder er zahlt oder wir gehen vor Gericht. Dasselbe an M.A.T. in Köln und F.O.P.C. in Stuttgart."

Zehn weitere Briefe *werden von ihm diktiert,* unterbrochen von der Geschichte seiner Familie, seiner Allergien und den Problemen seiner Kinder. Vorgestern *ist sein Sohn Günther* wegen eines Ausschlags *untersucht worden.*

Er darf keine Schokolade mehr essen. Gestern *ist seine Tochter* **Ruth beinahe** *überfahren worden.* **Sie geht über die Straße, ohne zu schauen.**

„Bis jetzt *bin ich von Dr. Schwarz* **auf meine Allergien** *behandelt worden.* **Kennen Sie ihn, Susie? Glauben Sie, er ist gut? Wo war ich?'' Dann erzählt er mir von seinen Symptomen.** *Kein Brief wird zu Ende diktiert.*

Please compare the German with the English version and note the different *tenses* of the passive voice used in this text:

past

> **Das Paket** *wurde eingeschrieben.*
> The package was registered.

Past tense of *werden* plus past participle of main verb: *wurde + eingeschrieben*

future

> **Die Ware** *wird* **morgen** *geliefert werden.*
> The merchandise will be delivered tomorrow.

Present tense of *werden* plus past participle of main verb plus infinitive of *werden: wird + geliefert + werden*

present perfect

> **Sein Sohn** *ist untersucht worden.*
> His son was examined (literally: has been examined).

Present tense of *sein* plus past participle of main verb plus special past participle of *werden (worden)* used in combination with past participles of main verbs: *ist + untersucht + worden*

EXERCISE 10 True or false?   T / F
1. **Susie wird um 8:30 ins Büro des Chefs bestellt.**   _____
2. **Das Paket an Pfister & Sohn wurde versichert.**   _____
3. **Kurt Krone hat seine Rechnung noch nicht bezahlt.**   _____
4. **Günther wurde wegen eines Ausschlags untersucht.**   _____
5. **Jeder Brief wird zu Ende diktiert.**   _____

EXERCISE 11 Change the passive from the past tense to the present perfect.
Example: **Der Brief wurde eingeschrieben.**
            Der Brief ist eingeschrieben worden.
1. **Sie wurden geöffnet und auf den Schreibtisch gelegt.**
2. **Seine Tochter wurde beinahe überfahren.**
3. **Der Erhalt des Briefes wurde bestätigt.**
4. **Der Chef wurde von Dr. Schwarz behandelt.**
5. **Kein Brief wurde zu Ende diktiert.**

EXERCISE 12 Answer in complete German sentences.
1. **Wohin wird die geöffnete Post gelegt?**
2. **Wann wird die Ware nach Hamburg geliefert werden?**
3. **Worauf wurde lange genug gewartet?**
4. **Wieso ist Ruth beinahe überfahren worden?**
5. **Warum darf Günther keine Schokolade mehr essen?**

EXERCISE 13 Choose the correct words.
1. **Wohin wird Susie jeden Tag um 9:30 bestellt?**
   a. **in sein Haus**   b. **in sein Büro**   c. **ins Kino**
2. **Das Paket an Pfister & Sohn wurde**
   a. **eingeschrieben**   b. **verloren**   c. **vergessen**
3. **Susie ist verantwortlich für**
   a. **das Geld der Firma**   b. **die ausgehende Post**   c. **nichts**

4. **Sein Sohn Günther hatte**
   a. **hohes Fieber**   b. **einen Ausschlag**   c. **Zahnweh**
5. **Wann wird die Post geliefert?**
   a. **um 9**   b. **um 11**   c. **um 2**

Rauchen verboten

Vocabulary

Apfel (m)	apple
Apfelsaft (m)	apple juice
aufmachen (w)	to open
Ausnahme (f)	exception
blasen (bläst, blies, geblasen)	to blow
brennend	burning, lit
Buttersemmel (f)	buttered roll
feuern (w)	to fire
Geschichte (f)	story
Gesicht (n)	face
hinausschmeißen (schmeißt hinaus, schmiß hinaus, hinausgeschmissen)	to throw out
irgendein, -e, -es	some, any
Kaffeepause (f)	coffee break
Kraut, Unkraut, (n)	*here:* weed
mittelgroß	medium size
mittendrin	in the middle of it
Mund (m)	mouth
Papiertüte (f)	paper bag
Rauch (m)	smoke
Scheibe (f)	*here:* slice
Schild (n)	sign
schmatzen (w)	to eat noisily
schreien (schrie, geschrien)	to shout
Stenotypistin (f)	stenographer-typist
Thermosflasche (f)	thermos bottle
(sich) unterstehen (unterstand, unterstanden)	to dare, to have the impudence
verdammt	damned
vergiften (w)	to poison
verrückt	crazy
Vorhang (m)	curtain
ziehen (zog, gezogen)	to draw

SUSIE Mittendrin fragt er mich: „Kennen Sie Hauptmann? Ja, den Reisenden. Also der kommt gestern mit der brennenden Zigarre herein, erzählt mir irgendeine Geschichte und bläst mir dabei den dicken Rauch ins Gesicht. ‚Hier wird nicht geraucht', schrei ich. ‚Sind Sie verrückt geworden? Sehen Sie nicht die Schilder überall? Wollen Sie mich mit Ihrem verdammten Kraut vergiften?' Er ist der beste Reisende, den wir haben, aber bei uns wird keine Ausnahme gemacht. Die Vorhänge werden gezogen, die Fenster werden aufgemacht, der Kerl wird hinausgeschmissen, ‚Wenn Sie sich noch einmal unterstehen, mit dem brennenden Unkraut hier zu erscheinen, sind Sie gefeuert!' "

ANTON Bei euch darf überhaupt nicht geraucht werden?

SUSIE Nein. Hauptmann hatte das wahrscheinlich vergessen.

ANTON In unserer Firma kann ohne weiteres geraucht werden.

*Please note: **Sie sind gefeuert!** is another example of a so-called false passive (denoting a condition rather than an action).

Also, in the last couple of sentences the passive voice has been used with the modal auxiliaries *dürfen* and *können*:

Bei euch darf/kann geraucht werden.

A Simple Alternative

The passive construction is frequently replaced by the active voice and the pronoun *man*. Thus, instead of saying:

Hier wird nicht geraucht

one could say:

Hier raucht man nicht.

**Die Vorhänge werden gezogen;
man zieht die Vorhänge.**

**Die Fenster werden aufgemacht;
man macht die Fenster auf.**

**Der Kerl wird hinausgeschmissen;
man schmeißt den Kerl hinaus.**

**Der Kerl wurde hinausgeschmissen;
man schmiß den Kerl hinaus.**

**Der Kerl ist hinausgeschmissen worden;
man hat den Kerl hinausgeschmissen.**

Ein kleiner Witz

CHEF Sie sind wieder zehn Minuten zu spät gekommen. Wissen Sie denn nicht, wann wir hier zu arbeiten beginnen?

NEUER ANGESTELLTER° Nein; die anderen arbeiten schon alle, wenn ich herkomme. employee

Apfel mit Apfelsaft

SUSIE Punkt elf *wird die erste Kaffeepause eingeschaltet.* Um zwölf nimmt Marie Golz, die Buchhalterin in meinem Büro, eine Buttersemmel, belegt mit drei Scheiben Salami und einem kleinen Stück Limburger, aus einer braunen Papiertüte und beginnt zu schmatzen.

ANTON Schmatzen?

SUSIE Mit offenem Mund. Das dauert zwanzig Minuten. Emma Schröder, die Stenotypistin, nimmt sich ihre Thermosflasche mit Apfelsaft aufs Klo und raucht.

ANTON Die ganze Zeit?

SUSIE Dort ist die einzige Gelegenheit. Dazu ißt sie einen mittelgroßen Apfel.

ANTON Apfel mit Apfelsaft?

SUSIE Warum nicht? Emma ist eine sehr pedantische Dame. Aber nicht so pedantisch wie Herr Ignaz Fliegenschläger.

ANTON Wer ist das?

SUSIE Der Oberbuchhalter.

EXERCISE 14 True or false?   T / F
1. **Hauptmann kam ins Büro mit der brennenden Zigarre.**   _____
2. **Der Chef schrie: „Hier wird geraucht!"**   _____
3. **Die Fenster wurden nicht geöffnet.**   _____
4. **Die erste Kaffeepause ist um 11 Uhr.**   _____
5. **Ignaz ist pedantischer als Emma.**   _____

EXERCISE 15 Change from the passive to the active voice, using the impersonal pronoun *man* (as in the examples).
1. **Im Büro wird gearbeitet.**
2. **Dort wurde nie geraucht.**
3. **Bei Anton ist immer geraucht worden.**
4. **Die Vorhänge wurden gezogen.**
5. **Die Fenster sind aufgemacht worden.**

EXERCISE 16 Translate into German.
1. He blows the smoke into my face.
2. Do you want to poison me?
3. Hauptmann is being thrown out.
4. Don't you dare!
5. She eats noisily and with her mouth open.

EXERCISE 17 Answer in complete German sentences.
1. **Wer bläst wem den Rauch ins Gesicht?**
2. **Warum mag der Chef keinen Rauch?**
3. **Was passiert dem Reisenden?**
4. **Was ißt Marie Golz?**
5. **Was trinkt Emma?**

EXERCISE 18 Complete the following sentences.
1. **Wollen Sie mich mit dem verdammten Kraut** _____?
2. **Er bläst ihm den Rauch ins** _____.
3. **Wenn er das noch einmal tut, ist er** _____.
4. **Mit dem Apfelsaft ißt Emma einen mittelgroßen** _____.
5. **Der Chef sagt: „Bei uns wird keine Ausnahme** _____."

Ein Brief

A letter that another boss dictated to another secretary who was very accurate in taking down every word:

Sehr geehrter° Herr Steiner!	dear
Was soll ich dem alten Trottel°	idiot
sagen? In Beantwortung° Ihres Briefes	in response
vom 12. dieses Monats tut es mir leid,°	I am sorry
daß Sie mit der Ware unzufrieden sind.	
Wir mußten sie schnell loswerden, damit	
wir nicht noch mehr dabei verlieren. Die	
Qualität° der Hemden ist ausgezeichnet	quality
und Sie sind der einzige Kunde, der sich	
beklagt hat. Das ist eine schöne Bluse,°	blouse
die Sie anhaben.° Deshalb können wir sie	have on
leider nicht zurücknehmen.° Wieso	to take back
bemerkte ich nicht vorher,° daß Sie ein	before
Grübchen° in der linken Wange° haben?	dimple, cheek
Mit besten Grüßen,°	greetings
Haben Sie heute abend Zeit?	

Modezeichnen

Vocabulary

anbrechen (bricht an, brach an, angebrochen)	*here:* to open
aushalten (hält aus, hielt aus, ausgehalten)	to stand
Brosche (f)	brooch
Charakter (m)	character
entwerfen (entwirft, entwarf, entworfen)	to design
Entwurf (m)	design
Etikett (n)	label
etwas Bestimmtes	something definite
herausstellen (w)	*here:* to set off, to bring out
hingehen (ging hin, ist hingegangen)	to go there
Karikatur (f)	cartoon
Kunstwerk (n)	work of art
Kurs (m)	course
Liebhaberei (f)	hobby
Modezeichnen (n)	dress designing
nähen (w)	to sew
originell	original, amusing, ingenious
schick	chic, stylish
Silber (n)	silver
Strich (m)	stroke
verschieden (adjective)	various, different
verstehen (verstand, verstanden)	to understand
wenn du sie kaufen müßtest...	if you had to buy them. . .
(eine) Zeitlang	for a time
zu dieser Gelegenheit	for this occasion

SUSIE   Willst du mehr von meiner Firma hören?

ANTON   Bitte nein.

FRAU BRAUN   Wieso hast du mir nie davon erzählt? Ich verstehe nicht, wie du das aushalten kannst.

SUSIE   Ist es ein Wunder, daß ich etwas anderes tun will?

ANTON   Denkst du an etwas Bestimmtes? Du hast eine Anzahl verschiedener Talente. Eine Zeitlang hast du in Gold und Silber gearbeitet; der Ring, den du mir geschenkt hast, ist wirklich sehr schön, und so ein origineller Entwurf.

FRAU BRAUN   Hier, sehen Sie sich die Brosche an, die sie für mich gemacht hat.

ANTON   Ein kleines Kunstwerk.

SUSIE   Eine nette Liebhaberei. Ich hab eine Menge zu lernen.

ANTON   Aber es gibt doch Kurse...und deine Kleider, zum Beispiel; ich weiß, du nähst dir die meisten selbst. Und sie sind so schick. Kosten wahrscheinlich ein kleines Vermögen, wenn du sie im Geschäft kaufen müßtest.

FRAU BRAUN   Und ihre Karikaturen, Herr Anton. Wie da mit einigen Strichen der Charakter einer Figur herausgestellt wird. . .

SUSIE   Was mich wirklich interessiert, ist Modezeichnen.

ANTON   Wie lange dauert das, wenn du es mit deinen Kenntnissen gründlich lernen willst?

SUSIE Ungefähr zwei Jahre, vielleicht anderthalb (one and a half). **Und ich kann abends hingehen.**

ANTON **Großartig. Darf ich das Etikett für die neuen** *Susie Braun Originale* **entwerfen?**

SUSIE **Du bist der Werbefachmann.**

ANTON **Frau Braun, haben Sie was dagegen, wenn wir zu dieser Gelegenheit die Flasche Rheinwein, die ich Ihnen heute gebracht habe, anbrechen?**

EXERCISE 19 True or false?   T / F
1. **Susie hat eine Zeitlang in Gold und Silber gearbeitet.** _____
2. **Sie sagt, sie hat nichts mehr zu lernen.** _____
3. **Sie kann auch Karikaturen zeichnen.** _____
4. **Anton will ein Etikett für sie entwerfen.** _____
5. **Sie werden eine Flasche Whisky anbrechen.** _____

EXERCISE 20 Answer the following in complete German sentences.
1. **Was nennt Anton Susies originellen Entwurf?**
2. **Was hat Susie für ihre Mutter gemacht?**
3. **Was nennt Anton schick?**
4. **Was bewundert Frau Braun ganz besonders?**
5. **Was interessiert Susie am meisten?**

EXERCISE 21 Choose the correct words.
1. **Susie hat eine Anzahl verschiedener**
   a. **Talente** b. **Bücher** c. **Bilder**
2. **Wann kann sie den Kurs nehmen?**
   a. **tagsüber** b. **Dienstag nachmittags** c. **abends**
3. **Wie lange dauert er?**
   a. **zwei Jahre, vielleicht anderthalb** b. **3½ Jahre**
   c. **ein Jahr**
4. **Was hat Susie Anton geschenkt?**
   a. **einen Ring** b. **eine Krawatte** c. **ein Hemd**
5. **Was Susie wirklich interessiert, ist**
   a. **ihre Arbeit als Sekretärin** b. **Modezeichnen**
   c. **Kochen**

EXERCISE 22 Complete each sentence with a word listed here: **Liebhaberei, aushalten, Talente, näht, Etikett.**
1. **Ich verstehe nicht, wie du das _____ kannst.**
2. **Anton wird das _____ entwerfen.**
3. **Susie _____ sich die meisten ihrer Kleider selbst.**
4. **Sie nennt ihre Arbeit in Gold und Silber eine _____.**
5. **Sie hat eine Anzahl verschiedener _____.**

EXERCISE 23 Translate into English.
1. **Wie kannst du das aushalten?**
2. **Sie hat eine Anzahl verschiedener Talente.**
3. **Im Geschäft kostet das ein kleines Vermögen.**
4. **Eine Flasche Rheinwein wird angebrochen.**
5. **Frau Brauns Brosche wird von Anton bewundert.**

CHAPTER 15

Ringstrom und sein Orchester
Der jährliche Ball
Ringstrom and his Orchestra
The Annual Ball

Subjunctive; Conditional Sentences

Up to now we have been using verbs in the so-called indicative mood—verbs indicating facts or actions. We have been dealing with "real" situations.

Verbs in the subjunctive mood deal with "unreal" situations, with actions that have not taken place or may not take place. In a conditional sentence (If he were here, I would talk to him. *Wenn er hier wäre, würde ich mit ihm sprechen*), the subjunctive mood is used to make statements contrary to fact.

Das Orchester

Vocabulary

angeblich	allegedly
Aufführung (f)	performance
bekanntlich	as is well known
Bericht (m)	report
Blick (m)	*here:* glance; look
dauern (w)	to last
eintreten (tritt ein, trat ein, ist eingetreten)	*here:* to advocate
erdolchen (w)	to stab (with a dagger)
erwähnen (w)	to mention
es gab (es gibt, es hat gegeben)	there was
glänzend	splendid(ly)
häßlich	ugly
hineinschmuggeln (w)	to smuggle in
Klassiker (m)	classic
Kulturzentrum (n)	cultural center
kürzlich	a short time ago
Lärm (m)	noise
laut	loud
mitsummen (w)	to hum along
modern	modern
mögen (mag, mochte, gemocht)	to like
nennen (nannte, genannt)	to call, name
Philharmonie (f)	the philharmonic society

Publikum (n)	audience
Repertoire (n) (pronounce "repertoahr")	repertory
sinnlos	senseless
städtisch	municipal
streng	strict
Theaterstück (n)	play
töten (w)	to kill
unerwartet	unexpected(ly)
Werk (n)	work, piece, selection
zum Glück	fortunately
zum Leidwesen	to the regret
zweitrangig	second-rate

Please note: the name of the city **Ludwigsheim** is pronounced "Lōōdvix-heim." It is a fictitious place, although similarities to real places are entirely intentional.

Ludwigsheim—die Stadt, in der die Personen dieses Berichtes ansässig sind—hat immer schon den Ehrgeiz gehabt, ein Kulturzentrum zu sein. Die Saison des städtischen Theaters währt von September bis Juni, also zehn Monate jedes Jahr. Es werden hauptsächlich Theaterstücke gespielt, wenig Modernes, vor allem deutsche Klassiker und eine Menge Shakespeare. Die Deutschen bilden sich bekanntlich ein, *ihr* Shakespeare (vor über 150 Jahren glänzend übersetzt) *sei* besser als das Original. Auch Opern kann mann dort in zweitrangigen Aufführungen hören, meistens Verdi und Puccini, aber kürzlich gab es *Porgy and Bess;* die älteren Leute mochten das nicht sehr, aber der Kapellmeister ist ein großer Jazzfan. Das Orchester des Stadttheaters ist angeblich gut und nennt sich stolz die Ludwigsheimer Philharmonie. Jeden Sonntag um zwölf Uhr mittag (außer Juli und August) gibt es ein Konzert im Ameliensaal, hauptsächlich klassisches Repertoire, sehr zum Leidwesen des Dirigenten, des Herrn Klaus Ringstrom, der für moderne Musik eintritt. Da spielt er zum Beispiel ein schönes altes Werk. *Wenn er nicht so streng wäre, würde man gern mitsummen; wenn Blicke töten könnten, hätte er schon das halbe Publikum erdolcht.* Aber ganz unerwartet und immer öfter kommt dann ein miserables Stück sogenannter moderner Musik, auf dem Programm meistens gar nicht erwähnt, sinnloser Lärm, laut und häßlich. Ringstrom schmuggelt das einfach hinein. Manchmal ist es ein Stück von ihm. Zum Glück ist es meistens kurz.

The Subjunctive, the Mood of Wishful Thinking

> **Wenn er nicht so streng wäre,**
> **würde man gern mitsummen.**
> If he were not so strict,
> one would like to hum along.

Try to visualize a conductor who is less strict than the fellow we are talking about: **Er war gar nicht so streng, man summte gern mit.** This is a statement of fact, and we use the indicative mood.

But our **Klaus Ringstrom** is different. He is not Mr. Nice Guy; he can be very strict, *sehr streng.* Humming along while he conducts is strictly **verboten.** Therefore we use the other mood, the subjunctive, to express a situation contrary to fact: **wenn er nicht so streng wäre...** But there's the rub. We know that he *is* strict, but we wish that he were not. What we express by the subjunctive mood is wishful thinking.

> **Wenn Blicke töten könnten,**
> **hätte er schon das halbe Publikum erdolcht.**
> If glances could kill,
> he would have stabbed half the audience to death already.

This last quote makes the situation even clearer. Our unhappy artist feels misunderstood by a lowbrow audience, and dreams of doing them in. Thank God for the subjunctive. It lets him think murder without actually committing it. If glances could kill. . . . Fortunately they can't. This statement is contrary to fact.

Rules for the subjunctive are a little complicated. It's better to see and use the subjunctive forms and let proficiency come with practice.

EXERCISE 1 True or false?   T / F
1. **Die Theatersaison währt sechs Monate.**   _____
2. **Man spielt vor allem Tennessee Williams.**   _____
3. **Die Opern sind meistens von Verdi und Puccini.**   _____
4. **Der Kapellmeister ist ein Jazzfan.**   _____
5. **Er ist streng mit dem Publikum.**   _____

EXERCISE 2 Choose the correct words.
1. **Viele Theaterstücke in Ludwigsheim sind von**
   a. **Bernard Shaw** b. **Arthur Miller** c. **Shakespeare**
2. **Das Orchester nennt sich**
   a. **die Ludwigsheimer Philharmonie** b. **das Städtische Symphonieorchester** c. **die Ludwigsheimer Musiker**
3. **Die Saison ist von**
   a. **Juli bis Juni** b. **November bis Juni**
   c. **September bis Juni**
4. **Man hört die Konzerte**
   a. **im Stadttheater** b. **im Ameliensaal** c. **im Kino**
5. **Die modernen Werke, die Ringstrom spielt, sind meistens**
   a. **kurz** b. **schön** c. **lang**

EXERCISE 3 Fill in the correct German words.
1. **Wenn Blicke töten** _____ ,...
                              could
2. **Man** _____ **gern mitsummen...**
            would
3. **Er** _____ **schon das halbe Publikum erdolcht.**
        would have
4. **Wenn er nicht so streng** _____ ,...
                                 were

EXERCISE 4 Answer in complete German sentences.
1. **Was würde man tun, wenn er nicht so streng wäre?**
2. **Was würde passieren, wenn seine Blicke töten könnten?**
3. **Was bilden sich die Deutschen bekanntlich ein?**
4. **Wie nennt sich das Ludwigsheimer Orchester?**
5. **Welche amerikanische Oper konnte man dort hören?**

EXERCISE 5 Translate into German.
1. They play a lot of Shakespeare.
2. To the regret of Mr. Ringstrom they play mainly Beethoven.
3. Modern pieces are not mentioned on the program.
4. He prefers the classical repertory.
5. Fortunately, it is short most of the time.

EXERCISE 6 Complete each sentence with a word listed here: **übersetzt, Kulturzentrum, Jazzfan, unerwartet, Repertoire**
1. Klaus Ringstrom ist ein großer _____.
2. Manchmal kommt ein modernes Stück Musik ganz _____.
3. Shakespeare wurde vor mehr als 150 Jahren glänzend _____.
4. Sie spielen hauptsächlich klassisches _____.
5. Ludwigsheim hat den Ehrgeiz, ein _____ zu sein

Mehr über Ringstrom

Vocabulary

Abonnement (n)	subscription
bedauern (w)	to regret
eigensinnig	stubborn
eingeschüchtert	intimidated
erziehen (erzog, erzogen)	to educate
es ist nicht gefragt	there is no demand for it
(er) hält nicht viel von ihm	he does not think much of him
im geheimen	secretly
Mehrzahl (f)	majority
Nachfolger (m)	successor
pensioniert	retired
(ein) Risiko eingehen	to take a risk
übereinstimmen (w)	to agree
verbleiben (verblieb, ist verblieben)	to remain
Vertrag (m)	contract
wenn es nach ihr ginge (gehen, ging, ist gegangen)	if she had her way
Zuhörer (m)	listener

Ringstrom glaubt, er hat die Pflicht, das Publikum von Ludwigsheim musikalisch zu erziehen. Die meisten Zuhörer respektieren ihn, aber sind von ihm eingeschüchtert. *Wenn sie so tun könnten, wie sie wollten, würden sie ihn feuern.* Aber er hat einen Vertrag auf fünf Jahre und er ist sehr eigensinnig. Moderne Musik ist in Ludwigsheim nicht gefragt. Karl und Nora haben ein Abonnement für die Konzertsaison und nehmen die Kinder jedes Mal natürlich mit. Karl hält nicht viel von dem Dirigenten. Er bedauert, daß Onkel Leopold pensioniert ist; Nora ist nicht sicher; aber Peter (wie Sie sich vorstellen können) ist begeistert von dem Mann. Onkel Leopold mag seinen Nachfolger auch nicht. Was gute Musik ist, weiß man erst in 100 Jahren, meint er, also warum ein Risiko eingehen?

Wenn Leopold noch einige Monate auf seinem Posten verblieben wäre, würde Ringstrom nach Regensburg gegangen sein. Schade, denkt Karl im geheimen. Er stimmt mit der Mehrzahl der Ludwigsheimer überein. Gretchen ist das alles nicht so wichtig. Aber sie liebt Jazz und besonders Rock. *Wenn es nach ihr ginge, brauchte sie kein Orchester* in Ludwigsheim, bloß eine gute Rock-Gruppe.

Iffy Situations

Wenn Leopold. . .auf seinem Posten verblieben wäre, würde Ringstrom nach Regensburg gegangen sein. Instead of **würde gegangen sein,** we could say **wäre gegangen.**

> **Wenn es nach Gretchen ginge,**
> **brauchte sie kein Orchester.**
>
> If Gretchen had her way,
> she would not need an orchestra.

In English, as you see, we use what looks like the simple past tense after *if;* in German we use the subjunctive (subjunctive II):

ich ginge, du gingest, er ginge, ihr ginget

The subjunctive II differs from the past tense indicative only by the *-e* placed between the verb stem and its ending.

Instead of **"wenn es nach Gretchen ginge"**, we could say: **"wenn es nach Gretchen *gehen würde.*"** Some grammarians still insist that this is bad German. **"Wenn ist würdelos"** (*wenn* should not be followed by *würde*), they holler, but the bad German of today quite often becomes the good German of tomorrow.

. . .*brauchte* sie kein Orchester. This *brauchte,* too, is a subjunctive, though it looks like an indicative. And it, too, could be replaced by *würde* plus the infinitive: *würde* **sie kein Orchester** *brauchen.*

EXERCISE 7 True or false?   T / F
1. **Ringstrom will sein Publikum musikalisch erziehen.** _____
2. **Er ging nach Regensburg.** _____
3. **Moderne Musik ist in Ludwigsheim nicht gefragt.** _____
4. **Gretchen liebt klassische Musik.** _____
5. **Peter ist von Ringstrom begeistert.** _____

EXERCISE 8 Answer in complete German sentences.
1. **Mit wem stimmt Karl überein?**
2. **Was bedauert er?**
3. **Was würden die meisten Zuhörer tun, wenn sie es könnten?**
4. **Warum können sie Ringstrom nicht feuern?**
5. **Was für eine Musik liebt Gretchen?**

EXERCISE 9 Translate into English.
1. **Warum ein Risiko eingehen?**
2. **Wie Sie sich vorstellen können . . .**
3. **Sie sind von ihm eingeschüchtert.**
4. **Wenn sie so tun könnten, wie sie wollten . . .**
5. **Karl hält nicht viel von dem Dirigenten.**

Das Interview (1. Teil)

Vocabulary

Anfänger (m)	beginner
bekanntgeben (gibt bekannt, gab bekannt, bekanntgegeben)	to make known
bewilligen (w)	to grant
blutig	bloody
bruchstückweise abgedruckt	printed in excerpts

drucken (w)	to print
Ersatz (m)	substitution, replacement
ersetzen (w)	to replace
Fußballstadion (n)	soccer stadium
Geiz (m)	stinginess
geizig	stingy
gewähren (w)	to grant
Kräfte (f. pl.)	*here:* personnel
Leser (m)	reader
Mangel (m)	shortage
Mittel (n. pl.)	means; resources
persönlich	personal(ly)
Politik (f)	*here:* policy
Probe (f)	*here:* rehearsal
reduzieren (w)	to reduce
richten (w)	*here:* to direct
sterben (stirbt, starb, ist gestorben	to die
umstritten	controversial
unbeschränkt	unlimited
vergrößern (w)	to enlarge
Wirtschaftskrise (f)	economic crisis

   Gestern hat Ringstrom dem Reporter des *Ludwigsheimer Planeten* ein Interview gewährt, das hier bruchstückweise abgedruckt ist:

PLANET Herr Kapellmeister, *würden Sie bitte meinen Lesern Ihre Pläne* für die nächste Saison *bekanntgeben?*

RINGSTROM *Wenn Ludwigsheim weniger geizig ist, werde ich das Orchester vergrößern.*

PLANET Ist das Ihre erste Priorität?

RINGSTROM Eine der ersten. Wir brauchen sechs Violinisten, drei Cellisten, zwei Klarinettisten. . . . Soll ich Sie mit den Zahlen langweilen?

PLANET Wie erklären Sie diesen Mangel?

RINGSTROM Geiz. Wenn ein Orchestermitglied stirbt, wird kein Geld für seinen Ersatz bewilligt.

PLANET Ist das eine Politik, die gegen Sie persönlich gerichtet ist?

RINGSTROM Möglicherweise. Wie Sie wissen, bin ich eine umstrittene Figur.

PLANET Könnte es vielleicht die gegenwärtige Wirtschaftskrise sein?

RINGSTROM Man hat genug Geld für das neue Fußballstadion. *Wenn ich ein Zehntel davon hätte, würde ich der Stadt zeigen,* was gute Musik ist.

PLANET *Was würden Sie tun, wenn Sie unbeschränkte Mittel hätten?*

RINGSTROM Müssen Sie das drucken? Also gut. *Ich würde 20% des Orchesters feuern* und mit besseren Kräften ersetzen; das Orchester um 15 vergrößern; mehr Proben abhalten; und unsere Opernaufführungen reduzieren. Was man auf unserer Opernbühne sieht, ist ein Skandal.

PLANET Könnten wir amerikanische Sänger importieren?

RINGSTROM Blutige Anfänger? Auch die kosten Geld. Alles kostet Geld.

Conditional, Indicative, Subjunctive

Würden Sie bitte meinen Lesern Ihre Pläne bekanntgeben?
Would you please *make* your plans *known* to my readers?
This is the conditional form (**würden Sie?**) used as a polite form of request.

> **Wenn Ludwigsheim weniger geizig *ist*,**
> ***werde* ich das Orchester *vergrößern*.**
>
> If Ludwigsheim *is* less stingy,
> I *shall enlarge* the orchestra.

Here we have two statements of fact (or assumed fact). One follows on the other; there is not much doubt or uncertainty involved; hence, the subjunctive is not required, and the indicative is used. But:

> **Was *würden* Sie tun,**
> **wenn Sie unbeschränkte Mittel *hätten*?**
>
> What *would* you do
> *if* you *had* unlimited means?

As far as Ringstrom is concerned, Ludwigsheim has been and is stingy. He therefore uses the indicative. He could have expressed his sentiments as a contrary-to-fact condition and used, in either English or German, the subjunctive and the conditional *würde* (would):

> **Wenn Ludwigsheim weniger geizig *wäre*, *würde* ich das**
> **Orchester *vergrößern*.**
>
> If Ludwigsheim *were* less stingy, I *would enlarge* the orchestra.

EXERCISE 10 True or false?   T / F
1. **Ringstrom braucht keine Violinisten.** _____
2. **Er hat unbeschränkte Mittel.** _____
3. **Er würde 20% des Orchesters feuern.** _____
4. **Er sagt, daß die Opernaufführungen sehr gut sind.** _____
5. **Er ist eine umstrittene Figur.** _____

EXERCISE 11 Write the following in German.
1. Would you please tell me all about your plans.
2. This is a policy which is directed against him.
3. I shall enlarge the orchestra if they give me the money.
4. What would you do with unlimited means?
5. I would hold more rehearsals.

EXERCISE 12 Answer in complete German sentences.
1. **Was ist die erste Frage des Reporters?**
2. **Warum ist ein Mangel an Musikern im Orchester?**
3. **Womit würde er 20% des Orchesters ersetzen?**
4. **Wie denkt er über die Opernaufführungen?**
5. **Wie nennt sich Ringstrom selbst?**

EXERCISE 13 Construct questions using the cue words.
1. **Leser / Pläne / bekanntgeben**
2. **Geld / Ersatz / bewilligt**
3. **Opernbühne / sieht / Skandal**
4. **Orchester / 15 / vergrößern**
5. **Interview / Pläne / bekanntgeben**

EXERCISE 14 Match the following.
1. **Ringstrom ist eine umstrittene Figur.**   _____ Even beginners cost money.
2. **Er gibt die Pläne für die nächste Saison bekannt.**   _____ He needs more rehearsals.
3. **20% des Orchesters wird gefeuert.**   _____ Opera performances are being reduced.
4. **Opernaufführungen werden reduziert.**   _____ He makes known the plans for the next season.
5. **Auch Anfänger kosten Geld.**   _____ 20% of the orchestra will be fired.
6. **Er braucht mehr Proben.**   _____ Ringstrom is a controversial figure.

Das Interview (2. Teil)

Vocabulary

Automat (m)	automaton
denken (dachte, gedacht)	to think
eifersüchtig	jealous
Erfolg (m)	success
fliegen (flog, ist geflogen)	to fly
Faust, Fäuste (f)	fist
Frage (f)	question
Fuß, Füße (m)	foot
Gespräch (n)	conversation, interview
Konzertmeister (m)	concertmaster
Kritiker (m)	critic
kritisieren (w)	to criticize
Mätzchen (n)	antics
sabotieren	to sabotage
schließen (schloß, geschlossen)	to close
schütteln (w)	to shake
stampfen (w)	to stamp
Trommler (m)	drummer
ungebildet	uneducated
unglaublich	unbelievable
verhauen (w)	*here*: to muff, to louse up
Viertelton (m)	quarter tone
Vorgänger (m)	predecessor
Weltall (n)	outer space, cosmos
wissen (weiß, wußte, gewußt)	to know
zerreißen (zerriß, zerrissen)	to tear apart
zu früh einsetzen	to come in too soon
Zukunft (f)	future

PLANET Was denken Sie von Ihren Kritikern? Ihr Vorgänger auf dem Podium hat gesagt, *wenn Sie weniger Mätzchen machten, wären Sie ein besserer Dirigent.*

RINGSTROM Mätzchen? Sie meinen, weil ich manchmal den Kopf schüttle, daß das Haar nach allen Seiten fliegt, wenn der Konzertmeister um einen Viertelton zu hoch spielt? Weil ich mit den Füßen stampfe, wenn der Cellist sein Solo verhaut? Weil ich dem Trommler mit meinen Fäusten drohe, wenn er zu früh einsetzt? Weil ich auf dem Podium ein wenig tanze, wenn ich gelangweilt bin? Oder die Augen schließe und träume, wenn einmal alles gut geht?

PLANET Die Frage des Taktstocks, Maestro.

RINGSTROM Ah—der Taktstock. *Wenn ich den Taktstock benutzte und wie ein Automat dirigierte, wäre ich dann ein besserer Dirigent?* Was ist das mit dem Taktstock? Sind diese Hände nicht gut genug? *Wenn ich den Taktstock in der Hand hielte, wäre ich damit ein besserer Musiker? Hätte ich mehr Erfolg,* eine bessere Presse? *Würden die Ludwigsheimer mir dann mehr Geld bewilligen?* Ich habe eine Mission hier, Herr, Herr . . .

PLANET Bruck, Herr Kapellmeister, Robert Bruck.

RINGSTROM *Wenn ich ein Jazzkonzert mit dem Orchester geben würde, Herr Bruck, würden die Ludwigsheimer mich zerreißen?*

PLANET *Ich würde es nicht riskieren,* Maestro. Aber Sie haben nicht gesagt, was Sie nächste Saison spielen werden.

RINGSTROM Wenn ich es weiß, rufe ich Sie an.

PLANET   *Wenn Sie es wüßten, würden Sie es mir sagen?*

RINGSTROM   **Wahrscheinlich nicht.** *Sie würden es drucken und jeder würde das Programm*
             im voraus kritisieren.

PLANET   **Warum hat Ihre eigene Oper** *Ultraviolette Blumen im Weltall* **gar keinen**
             Erfolg gehabt?

RINGSTROM   **Weil das Publikum musikalisch ungebildet, zu dumm ist. Drucken Sie das**
             nicht! Und weil eifersüchtige Sänger und inkompetente Orchestermitglieder
             mich und mein Werk sabotiert haben. Ihr Egoismus ist unglaublich!
             Drucken Sie das auch nicht! Ach, auch Händel und Mozart haben ähnliche
             Probleme gehabt. Aber ich werde triumphieren. Mir und meiner Musik
             gehört die Zukunft. Das dürfen Sie drucken.

PLANET   **Herr Ringstrom, wir danken Ihnen für das Gespräch.**

Würde Or No *Würde?*

   Subjunctive II forms resemble the past indicative. Past indicative and
subjunctive II forms of weak or regular verbs are identical. Strong verbs add
subjunctive endings *-e, -est, -e, -en, -et, -en* to the past tense and take an umlaut,
if possible. These subjunctive II forms are sometimes used in place of *würde* +
infinitive. *Hätte, wäre,* and the subjunctive II forms of the modals (*könnte,
wollte, müßte,* etc.) are very common. Others, particularly umlauted forms like
hülfe, stünde, and *stürbe,* sound stilted. It's more conversational to say **ich
würde gehen** rather than **ich ginge** for *I would go.* In the preceding dialog
Ringstrom asks **Hätte ich mehr Erfolg. . . .** He could also have asked **Würde
ich mehr Erfolg haben?** The meaning (Would I have more success?) is the
same.

   Here is the reply to a bill that a mail-order company mailed out to one of its
customers:

Sehr geehrter Herr!	
Dieses verfluchte° Radio	cursed
habe ich nie bestellt.	
Wenn ich es bestellt hätte,	
hätten Sie es nie geschickt.	
Wenn Sie es nie geschickt hätten,	
hätte ich es nie bekommen.	
Wenn ich es bekommen hätte,	
hätte ich dafür bezahlt.°	paid
Wenn ich nicht dafür bezahlt habe,	
werde ich nicht dafür bezahlen.	
Hol' Sie der Teufel!°	Go to hell!
Ihr sehr ergebener°	Yours very truly

EXERCISE 15 True or false?   T / F
   1. **Ringstrom stampft manchmal mit den Füßen.**   _____
   2. **Der Name des Interviewers ist Robert Bruck.**   _____
   3. **Er will nicht wie ein Automat dirigieren.**   _____
   4. **Er hat eine Mission in Ludwigsheim.**   _____
   5. **Er macht überhaupt keine Mätzchen.**   _____

EXERCISE 16 Write the following in German.
   1. He threatens the drummer with his fists.
   2. Is he a better conductor with the baton?
   3. Would he have more success?
   4. Sometimes he closes his eyes and dreams.
   5. The reporter thanks him for the interview.

EXERCISE 17 Answer the following in complete German sentences.
1. **Warum stampft er mit den Füßen?**
2. **Warum schüttelt er den Kopf?**
3. **Warum droht er dem Trommler?**
4. **Warum mag er den Taktstock nicht?**
5. **Was wird er in der nächsten Saison spielen?**
6. **Wie heißt Ringstroms eigene Oper?**
7. **Was für Probleme hatten auch Händel und Mozart?**

EXERCISE 18 Fill in the missing letters in the German words.
1. **ER MA__HT ZU__IEL M__TZCHEN**
2. **SE__N VORG__N__ER AUF D__M P__DIUM**
3. **ER BENU__ZT K__NEN TAK__STO__K**
4. **SIE WÜ__DEN IH__ ZE__EISSEN**
5. **ER SP__LT N__CHSTE S__SON**

EXERCISE 19 Complete each sentence with a word listed here: **Fäusten, gut, Vorgänger, Musiker, Haar**
1. **Leopold war sein _____ auf dem Podium.**
2. **Er droht dem Trommler mit den _____ .**
3. **Wäre ich damit ein besserer _____ ?**
4. **Das _____ fliegt nach allen Seiten.**
5. **Sind diese Hände nicht _____ genug?**

Der Ball (1. Teil)

This is the night of the annual ball that is sponsored by Ludwigsheim's artists. Everyone will be there, including Maestro Ringstrom.

Vocabulary

Allgemeines Krankenhaus (n)	General Hospital
Assistenzarzt (m)	intern
abwechselnd	in turn
aufsuchen (w)	to go to see
Darauf können Sie sich verlassen!	You can depend on that.
erwidern (w)	to reply
geläufig	fluent(ly)
(die) letztere	the latter
Realgymnasium (n)	secondary school emphasizing scientific subjects
verlassen (verläßt, verließ, verlassen)	to leave
Zufall (m)	coincidence

Der Ball ist ein großer Erfolg. Alle unsere Freunde sind gekommen. Karl, Nora und Gretchen, Anton und Susie, auch Kristy; die letztere mit einem jungen Mann, Dr. Richard Glaser, den sie beim letzten Konzert kennengelernt hat. Dick, wie ihn seine Freunde nennen, ist ein Arzt, der zwei Jahre in den Vereinigten Staaten studiert hat und jetzt im Ludwigsheimer Allgemeinen Krankenhaus als Assistenzarzt arbeitet. Sie sprechen abwechselnd Deutsch und Englisch. *Kristy sagt ihm, er spräche Englisch sehr gut und geläufig.* Dick erwidert, *er hätte die Sprache schon vorher gelernt; er wäre in München aufs Realgymnasium gegangen,* wo man neben Latein auch Englisch lernen muß.

KRISTY	In welcher amerikanischen Stadt haben Sie studiert?
DICK	In Denver; an der Universität von Colorado.
KRISTY	Also das ist doch ein unglaublicher Zufall.
DICK	Was meinen Sie?
KRISTY	In Denver bin ich doch zu Hause.
DICK	Wirklich?
KRISTY	Und Sie haben im Universitätsspital gearbeitet?
DICK	Ja; zwei Jahre, als Student.
KRISTY	Da hab ich bloß drei Meilen von Ihnen gewohnt. Kommen Sie je zurück nach Denver?
DICK	Vielleicht. Ich hab dort sehr gute Freunde.
KRISTY	Wenn Sie kommen, müssen Sie mich aufsuchen.
DICK	Sure thing. Darauf können Sie sich verlassen!

Indirect Speech and Subjunctive I and II

Kristy sagt ihm,
er spräche Englisch sehr gut.

Dick erwidert,
er hätte die Sprache schon vorher gelernt;
er wäre in München aufs Realgymnasium gegangen.

Kristy tells him
he speaks English very well.
Dick replies
he learned the language before;
he attended a *Realgymnasium* in Munich.

Why do we use the subjunctive in German and the indicative in English when it comes to indirect speech? Perhaps the Germans are a little skeptical about information they report from other people's statements. Maybe Kristy was just flattering Dick when she said he speaks good German. At any rate, it is not an established, demonstrable fact that Dick speaks good English. So we report what Kristy says in the tentative, subjunctive mood: **Sie sagt ihm,** *er spräche* . . . Kristy said *spräche* (subjunctive II). She could also have used *spreche,* (subjunctive I). To form subjunctive I, add the subjunctive endings (*-e, -est, -e, -en, -et, -en*) to the stem of the infinitive, which, as you remember, is what's left after you take off the *-en.* For regular verbs subjunctive I forms look very much like the indicative, except for the third person singular, which ends in *-e* instead of the usual indicative *-t.* An exception is *sei,* subjunctive I of *sein.* Subjunctive I is used less often than subjunctive II, although reporters and newscasters frequently employ subjunctive I to report indirect speech, as in:

Der Präsident sagte, er *könne* (*wolle, müsse, solle,* etc.) **es tun.** The president said he could, (would, must, should) do it.

EXERCISE 20 True or false?   T / F

1. **Kristy hat Dick beim letzten Konzert kennengelernt.** _____
2. **Dick arbeitet in Ludwigsheim als Tankwart.** _____
3. **Er sagt, er hätte Deutsch schon vorher gelernt.** _____
4. **Er studierte an der Universität von Kansas.** _____
5. **Er hat gute Freunde in Amerika.** _____

EXERCISE 21 Answer in complete German sentences.
1. **Mit wem kommt Kristy zum Ball?**
2. **Was tut Dick in Ludwigsheim?**
3. **Auf welche Schule ist er in München gegangen?**
4. **Welche Sprache hat er dort neben Englisch gelernt?**
5. **Wo hat er in Denver gearbeitet?**

EXERCISE 22 Translate into German.
1. They speak in turn English and German.
2. That is an incredible coincidence.
3. Dick studied in America for two years.
4. Kristy lived only three miles from him.
5. You can depend on that.

EXERCISE 23 Choose the correct words.
1. **Kristy kommt zum Ball mit**
   a. **Ferdl**   b. **Tim**   c. **Dick**
2. **Dick arbeitet in**
   a. **einer Tankstelle**   b. **einem Spital**   c. **einem Buchladen**
3. **An welcher amerikanischen Universität hat er studiert?**
   a. **Colorado**   b. **New Mexico**   c. **Kentucky**
4. **Kristy sagt, er spräche English**
   a. **schlecht**   b. **geläufig**   c. **nicht sehr gut**
5. **Wenn Dick wieder nach Denver kommt, wird er sie**
   a. **vielleicht anrufen**   b. **bestimmt aufsuchen**
   c. **überhaupt nicht sehen**

EXERCISE 24 Complete each sentence with a word listed here: **Arzt, vorher, Konzert, Latein, Zufall**
1. **Neben _____ lernte er dort Englisch.**
2. **Das war ein unglaublicher _____ .**
3. **Dick Glaser ist ein junger _____ .**
4. **Er hat Englisch schon _____ gelernt.**
5. **Sie hat ihn beim letzten _____ kennengelernt.**

Der Ball (2. Teil)

Vocabulary

argentinisch	Argentinian
(sich) ausruhen	to rest, to take a rest
Bruderschaft trinken (trinkt, trank, getrunken)	to pledge close friendship
Cowboystiefel (m. pl.)	cowboy boots
es tut gut	it is good, feels good
gefällt's dir? (gefallen, gefiel, gefallen)	do you like it?
gerade	just
Gott sei Dank!	Thank God!
Irrenhaus (n)	insane asylum
kompliziert	complicated
lateinamerikanisch	Latin-American
Lieblingstanz (m)	favorite dance
mit Vergnügen!	with pleasure
mir ist heiß	I am warm
(sich) niedersetzen (w)	to sit down

probieren Sie mal! (w)	please try (it)
rhythmisch	rhythmic
Saal (m)	hall
Schritt (m)	step
sehen (sieht, sah, gesehen)	to see
siezen (w)	to use the polite form *(sie)*
Spätlese (f)	wine made from grapes gathered late in the fall
Sporthemd (n)	sport shirt
sperren = einsperren (w)	to lock up
Walzer (m)	waltz
weitertanzen (w)	to go on dancing
wo = irgendwo	*here*: somewhere

Anton tanzt mit Nora und Karl mit Susie. Im großen Saal spielen zehn Musiker der Ludwigsheimer Philharmonie einen Walzer nach dem anderen, auch Polkas und ab und zu Foxtrott und Swing; die letzteren dirigiert Maestro Ringstrom in Sporthemd, Jeans und Cowboystiefeln.

Im kleineren Saal spielt eine argentinische Gruppe, *Los Cinco Gauchos*, lateinamerikanische Musik. Anton tanzt gerade einen Samba mit Nora.

ANTON Der Cha-Cha ist mein Lieblingstanz. Der ist sehr rhythmisch und die Schritte sind nicht sehr kompliziert.

NORA Vielleicht kannst du ihn mir mal zeigen.

ANTON Gern. Du hast ein natürliches Talent. Hast du wo tanzen gelernt?

NORA Nein. Aber es hat mir schon immer Spaß gemacht.

ANTON Du bist sehr musikalisch.

NORA Ja, das ist in der Familie. O, hier ist Susie. Mir ist ein bißchen heiß; willst du mit ihr tanzen?

ANTON Mit Vergnügen. (He changes over to Susie)

SUSIE Gefällt's dir?

ANTON Sehr. Dir nicht? Die Kerle spielen wunderbar.

SUSIE Willst du weitertanzen oder dich niedersetzen? Schau, dort ist Kristy mit ihrem jungen Mann.
(At a small table)

KRISTY Es tut gut, sich ein wenig auszuruhen.

DICK Möchten Sie ein Glas Wein von der Bar? Bin gleich zurück.—Hier: Ludwigsheimer Spätlese. Nicht schlecht. Probieren Sie mal. Warten Sie. Ich glaub, wir haben uns schon lange genug gesiezt. Wir waren doch in Denver praktisch Nachbarn zwei Jahre lang. Also—Bruderschaft?
(They intertwine their arms, drink, and kiss)
Wie sagt unser Freund Anton?

KRISTY Servus.

DICK Servus.

EXERCISE 25 True or false?   T / F

    1. **Im kleineren Saal spielt die Philharmonie.**   _____

    2. **Maestro Ringstrom trägt einen Smoking.**   _____

    3. **Antons Lieblingstanz ist die Polka.**   _____

    4. **Er tanzt auch mit Nora.**   _____

    5. **Kristy und Dick trinken Bruderschaft.**   _____

EXERCISE 26 Answer in complete German sentences.
1. **Wer spielt im großen Saal?**
2. **Was für Musik dirigiert Ringstrom?**
3. **Was spielt die argentinische Gruppe?**
4. **Wo waren sie praktisch Nachbarn?**
5. **Was trinken Dick und Kristy?**

EXERCISE 27 Choose the correct words.
1. **Wieviele Musiker spielen von der Philharmonie?**
   a. **zehn**   b. **sieben**   c. **zwölf**
2. **Die Dekorationen gefallen ihnen**
   a. **überhaupt nicht**   b. **ganz gut**   c. **sehr**
3. **Der Name der argentinischen Gruppe ist**
   a. *Los Cinco Tontos*   b. *Los Cinco Caballeros*
   c. *Los Cinco Gauchos*
4. **Die Schritte im Cha-Cha, sagt Anton, sind**
   a. **ganz verrückt**   b. **leicht**   c. **nicht sehr kompliziert**
5. **Kristy und Dick trinken etwas**
   a. **Wein**   b. **Bier**   c. **Wasser**

EXERCISE 28 Write the following sentences in German.
1. Did you learn to dance somewhere?
2. I am a little warm.
3. Do you like the decorations?
4. It's good to rest a little.
5. Do you want to go on dancing?

EXERCISE 29 Match the following.
1. **Sie spielen viele Walzer.**
2. **Mir ist ein bißchen heiß.**
3. **Gott sei Dank, nicht!**
4. **Gefällt's dir?**
5. **Willst du weitertanzen?**
6. **Probieren Sie mal!**

_____ Please try.
_____ Do you want to go on dancing?
_____ They play many waltzes.
_____ I am a little warm.
_____ Thank God, no.
_____ Do you like it?

SIE **Abgesehen von zwei Sachen°**
       wärest du ein wunderbarer
       Tänzer.

°apart from two things

ER **Ja? Was sind die zwei Sachen?**

SIE **Deine Füße.**

CHAPTER 16

Nora im Supermarkt
Nora at the Supermarket

Word Order

Once a week Nora goes shopping for food.

Auf dem Weg zum Supermarkt

Normal and Inverted Word Order

Vocabulary

anbieten (bietet an, bot an, angeboten)	to offer
anziehen (zog an, angezogen)	*here*: to put on
Auflistung (f)	listing
Bauer (m)	peasant, farmer
bis jetzt	so far
brauchen (w)	to need
(schwarzes) Brett (n)	bulletin board
denken (dachte, gedacht)	to think
einkaufen = kaufen (w)	to buy
fahren (fährt, fuhr, ist gefahren)	to drive
fett	fat
Fremdwort (n)	foreign word
Gemüse (n)	vegetables
Genossenschaft (f)	co-op
Gott sei Dank	thank God
Hausfrau (f)	housewife
ihrer Ansicht nach	in her opinion
jederzeit	at any time, always
Knie (n)	knee
landwirtschaftlich	agricultural
Lebensmittel (n. pl.)	foodstuffs, groceries
Lebensmittelhändler (m)	grocer
Liste (f)	list
Milchprodukt (n)	dairy product
Minirock (m)	mini skirt
Nahrungsmittelbeilage (f)	food supplement
offerieren (w)	to offer
Ruf (m)	reputation
schlagen (schlägt, schlug, geschlagen)	to hit, beat
Schlagwort (n)	catch phrase
Schlagzeile (f)	headline
Sonderangebot (n)	special offer

(großen) Staat machen	to make a grand display, look one's best
treu	faithful
übrigens	besides
Umgebung (f)	environs
umtauschen (w)	to exchange
unmodern	out of fashion
unterbieten (unterbietet, unterbot, unterboten)	to undersell
verläßlich	dependable
vermerken (w)	to note down, to enter
verwenden (w)	to use
von Tag zu Tag	from day to day
wachsen (wächst, wuchs, ist gewachsen)	to grow
zurückbringen (brachte zurück, zurückgebracht)	to bring back
zurückgeben (gibt zurück, gab zurück, zurückgegeben)	to give back, to return
zurückkommen (kam zurück, ist zurückgekommen)	to come back

Nora hat ein schwarzes Brett in der Küche, auf dem sie vermerkt, welche Lebensmittel sie braucht. *Die Liste wächst und wird von Tag zu Tag weiter wachsen.* Heute ist der Tag, an dem sie einkaufen fährt. *Am liebsten geht sie zu Polzers Supermarkt.* Polzer ist zwar nicht der größte Lebensmittelhändler Ludwigsheims, aber er ist, Noras Ansicht nach, der verläßlichste. Gemüse und Obst sind jederzeit frisch, auch Fleisch, und die Milchprodukte und Eier, die er teils von der führenden landwirtschaftlichen Genossenschaft, teils von den Bauern der Umgebung direkt einkauft. Polzers Konkurrenz versucht, ihn zu unterbieten, *aber die meisten Kunden bleiben ihm treu.* Wenn jemand etwas zurückbringt, *hat er die Ware bis jetzt immer umgetauscht* oder das Geld zurückgegeben. Sein Ruf als "Freund der Hausfrau" ist ihm wichtiger als die paar Mark, die er vielleicht dabei verliert.

Übrigens ist das auch sein Werbeslogan, der jeden Donnerstag *als große Schlagzeile* in der Nahrungsmittelbeilage des *Ludwigsheimer Planeten* zu finden ist:

Polzer, der Freund der Hausfrau, offeriert.

Nach der Auflistung seiner Sonderangebote liest man das Schlagwort:
Seine Preise sind nicht zu schlagen. Das ist Polzers Stolz!

Gretchen hat einen Lehrer in ihrer Deutschklasse, der sich immer wieder darüber aufregt, daß man jetzt in der deutschen Sprache so viele Fremdwörter verwendet. Warum "offeriert" Polzer, warum bietet er nicht an oder dar, fragt er. Aber das ist eben der Trend, denkt Nora, während sie sich ihre Jeans anzieht (Gott sei Dank, der Minirock ist schon lange unmodern; hoffentlich kommt er nie zurück. Mit ihren Knien kann sie keinen großen Staat machen, die sind ihr zu fett.).

Note: A *Schlagwort* is a "catch phrase." It "hits" or "slugs" you, the same way a headline *(Schlagzeile)* or a slogan does. English *to slay, to slug,* and the *slaw* in "cole slaw" are related to German *schlagen.* Etymology is interesting. But we must return to our grammatical onions. Don't sigh. It's an easy topic. You've already seen and worked quite a bit with "normal" and "inverted" word order, as well as with word order in dependent clauses. The following will serve to review and reinforce.

Word Order Explained

SUBJECT	VERB	OBJECT	OTHER PARTS OF THE SENTENCE
Nora	**hat**	**ein schwarzes Brett**	**in der Küche.**
Nora	has	a bulletin board	in the kitchen.

COORDINATING CONJUNCTION	SUBJECT	VERB
Aber	**die meisten Kunden**	**bleiben ihm treu.**
But	most customers	remain faithful to him.

No problem here. The normal word order, as in English, is maintained: subject, conjugated verb, object, other parts of the sentence. The same normal word order applies in a sentence introduced by a coordinating conjunction, such as *aber, sondern, und, oder, denn.*

We called the German *hat* a conjugated verb form; it is, as we know, the third person singular of *haben* (to have). Other conjugated forms of *haben* are: ich *habe,* du *hast,* wir *haben,* etc.

Now let's look at a sentence in which the German word order differs from the English one:

Die Liste wächst und wird von Tag zu Tag wachsen.
The list grows and will grow from day to day.

Notice that the German infinitive *wachsen* is at the end of the sentence, whereas the English infinitive *grow* follows the *will.* Or in this sentence:

Polzer hat bis jetzt die Ware immer umgetauscht.
Polzer so far always has exchanged the merchandise.

Here the German past participle *umgetauscht* stands at the end of the sentence, whereas the English past participle *exchanged* follows the *has* in the middle of the sentence.

From this we can derive a rule: The infinitive and the past participle will ordinarily stand *at the end* of a German sentence.

Am liebsten geht sie zu Polzers Supermarkt.
She likes best going to Polzer's supermarket.
Übrigens ist das auch sein Werbeslogan.
Besides, this is also his advertising slogan.

In a main clause the position of the conjugated verb is item number 2, with the subject either in first or in third position; example:

SUBJECT, ITEM #1	VERB, ITEM #2	ITEM #3
Nora	**geht**	**zu Polzer. . .**

but:

ITEM #3	VERB, ITEM #2	SUBJECT, ITEM #1
Zu Polzer	**geht**	**Nora. . .**

EXERCISE 1 True or false?   T / F
1. **Nora hat ein schwarzes Brett im Schlafzimmer.**   _____
2. **Polzers Gemüse ist immer frisch.**   _____
3. **Er nennt sich *Freund der Hausfrau.***   _____
4. **Die meisten Kunden bleiben ihm treu.**   _____
5. **Er hat keine Konkurrenz.**   _____

EXERCISE 2 Answer the following in complete German sentences.
1. **Was wächst von Tag zu Tag?**
2. **Was ist Polzer wichtiger als ein paar Mark?**
3. **Was zieht sich Nora zum Einkaufen an?**
4. **Worüber regt sich Gretchens Lehrer auf?**
5. **Warum hat Nora ihre Knie nicht gern?**

EXERCISE 3 Choose the correct words.

1. **Wo vermerkt Nora, was sie braucht?**
   a. **in einem Buch**   b. **auf einem Tisch**   c. **auf einem schwarzen Brett**
2. **Warum zieht sie Polzers Supermarkt vor?**
   a. **er ist billiger**   b. **er bietet mehr an**   c. **er ist verläßlicher**
3. **Wer regt sich über die vielen Fremdwörter auf?**
   a. **Gretchens Deutschlehrer**   b. **Anton**   c. **Herr Polzer**
4. **Wo erscheint Polzers Inserat jede Woche?**
   a. **in den *Süddeutschen Nachrichten***   b. **in der *Zeit***
   c. **im *Ludwigsheimer Planeten***
5. **Wenn man Polzer etwas zurückbringen will,**
   a. **muß man das erklären**   b. **regt er sich auf**
   c. **tauscht er es immer um**

EXERCISE 4 Complete each sentence with a word listed here: **wachsen, Genossenschaft, Minirock, Umgebung, Konkurrenz.**

1. **Der _____ ist schon lange unmodern.**
2. **Polzer kauft auch von den Bauern der _____.**
3. **Seine _____ versucht, ihn zu unterbieten.**
4. **Die Liste wird von Tag zu Tag _____.**
5. **Polzer bezieht Milchprodukte von der führenden landwirtschaftlichen _____.**

Polzer, der Freund der Hausfrau

Inverted Word Order

Vocabulary

aufrechterhalten (erhält aufrecht, erhielt aufrecht, aufrechterhalten)	to maintain
beschränken (w)	to restrict
behilflich sein	to be of service
beinahe	almost
dadurch, daß . . .	due to the fact that . . .
einladen (lädt ein, lud ein, eingeladen)	to invite
einlangen (w)	to arrive
enger Kontakt (m)	close contact
entgehen (entging, entgangen)	to escape (a person's attention)
(etwas) ernstnehmen (nimmt ernst, nahm ernst, ernstgenommen)	to take (something) seriously
erwerben (erwirbt, erwarb, erworben)	to acquire, *here:* win
Festessen (n)	festive meal, feast
führen (w)	*here:* to carry (as in a store)
Gegenwart (f)	*here:* presence
Grundlage (f)	basis
Grüß Gott!	a greeting: "Hello!" used mainly in Southern Germany
Kalbsbeuschel (n)	veal lung
langjährig	of long duration
macht nichts	doesn't matter

mit schallender Stimme	at the top of his voice
Nierenbraten (m)	loin roast
Petersilie (f)	parsley
Pfefferkörner (n. pl.)	peppercorns
Rahm (m)	cream
Rede (f)	speech
(eine) Rede halten	to give a speech
Sardelle (f)	anchovy
schätzen (w)	to value
Schweinskotelett (n)	pork chop
(der) seinige	his
Spezialgeschäft (n)	specialty store
Tante-Emma-Laden (m)	Mom-and-Pop store
Thymian (m)	thyme
Unternehmen (n)	business, firm
Vertrauen (n)	confidence
verwechseln (w)	to mistake
wie eh und je	as always
Zwiebel (f)	onion

Dadurch, daß er engen Kontakt mit seinen Kunden aufrechterhält, von denen er die meisten persönlich kennt, hat Polzer sich das Vertrauen vieler Hausfrauen in Ludwigsheim erworben. Wie jeder andere Supermarkt ist auch der seinige auf einer Self-service Grundlage. Nora findet es praktischer, sich auf *ein* größeres Unternehmen zu beschränken, wo sie ihre Nahrungsmitteleinkäufe besorgt, als in drei oder vier verschiedene Tante-Emma-Läden zu gehen. Allerdings führt Polzer keinen Fisch, den sie in einem Spezialgeschäft kaufen muß.

Dem Herrn Polzer ist ihre Gegenwart auch heute *nicht entgangen.* Er schätzt sie als eine seiner treuesten Kundinnen und begrüßt sie schon von weitem mit schallender Stimme:

POLZER   Grüß Gott, Frau Bauer! Jung und schön wie eh und je. Beinahe hätte ich Sie mit Ihrer Tochter verwechselt. Erst gestern hab ich meiner Frau gesagt, also Resi, ich weiß nicht, wie die Frau Bauer das macht, die wird nicht älter.

Herrn Polzers Komplimente sind natürlich nicht ernstzunehmen, Nora weiß das. *Die gleiche Rede* (mit Variationen) *hält er wahrscheinlich 75% seiner Kundinnen.* Macht nichts, Nora hört sie trotzdem gern.

POLZER   Darf ich Ihnen behilflich sein? Die Schweinskoteletts sind besonders schön heute. Oder wenn Sie einen Nierenbraten machen wollen . . .

NORA   Haben Sie Kalbsbeuschel?

POLZER   Kalbslunge? Soeben eingelangt.

NORA   Sie kennen doch Herrn Anton Gruber aus Wien? Den haben wir morgen zum Essen eingeladen, und was der sich gewünscht hat, ist Beuschel.

POLZER   *Mit Knödeln ist das ein Festessen.* Pfefferkörner, Zwiebeln, Petersilie, Thymian, Sardellen, Kapern, Rahm . . .

NORA   Wieso wissen Sie das alles?

POLZER   Langjährige Erfahrung. Wenn ich zu Hause bin, bin ich der Koch.

Inverted Word Order (continued)

Dem Herrn Polzer ist ihre Gegenwart auch heute nicht entgangen.
Today, too, her presence has not escaped Mr. Polzer's attention.

Here we have a German sentence starting with an indirect object (**dem Herrn Polzer**) which causes inverted word order (the subject following the verb).

Die gleiche Rede hält er 75% seiner Kundinnen.
The same speech he gives 75% of his female customers.

Here is a sentence starting with a direct object (**die gleiche Rede**). Again the subject has to follow the verb.

Mit Knödeln ist das ein Festessen.
With dumplings this is a feast.

And here we have a sentence starting with a prepositional phrase (**mit Knödeln**) causing the inversion.

Ein Witz

HAUSFRAU **Es ist hart,° zehn Mark für ein Kilo Fleisch zu zahlen.**   tough

METZGER° **Aber wenn Sie nur fünf Mark zahlen, ist es noch härter.**   butcher

EXERCISE 5 True or false?   T / F
1. **Nora kauft Fisch in Polzers Supermarkt.** ____
2. **Polzer sagt, daß sie alt aussieht.** ____
3. **Er kennt die meisten seiner Kundinnen persönlich.** ____
4. **Er begrüßt sie mit „Guten Tag, Frau Bauer".** ____
5. **Nora will Kalbsbeuschel.** ____

EXERCISE 6 Answer in complete German sentences.
1. **Wodurch hat sich Polzer das Vertrauen seiner Kundinnen erworben?**
2. **Was findet Nora praktischer?**
3. **Mit wem hat Polzer gestern über Nora gesprochen?**
4. **Was empfiehlt er Nora besonders?**
5. **Wen hat Nora für morgen zum Essen eingeladen?**

EXERCISE 7 Translate into English.
1. **Sie ist eine seiner treuesten Kundinnen.**
2. **Darf ich Ihnen behilflich sein?**
3. **Ihre Gegenwart ist ihm nicht entgangen.**
4. **Er begrüßt sie mit schallender Stimme.**
5. **Macht nichts!**

EXERCISE 8 Choose the correct words.
1. **Die meisten seiner Kundinnen kennt Herr Polzer**
   a. **persönlich** b. **von weitem** c. **nicht**
2. **Mit wem hätte Herr Polzer sie beinahe verwechselt?**
   a. **mit Susie** b. **mit Kristy** c. **mit Gretchen**
3. **Der Name von Polzers Frau ist**
   a. **Resi** b. **Anna** c. **Maria**
4. **Was ist ein Festessen?**
   a. **gekochtes Rindfleisch** b. **Beuschel mit Knödeln**
   c. **Kalbsbraten**
5. **Um Beuschel richtig zu machen, braucht man**
   a. **Vanille** b. **Schokolade** c. **Zwiebeln**

EXERCISE 9 Complete the following sentences.
1. **Polzer hat sich das Vertrauen vieler Hausfrauen _____.**
2. **Fisch muß Nora allerdings in einem anderen Geschäft _____.**
3. **Was Anton sich gewünscht hat, ist _____.**
4. **Wenn Polzer zu Hause ist, ist er der _____.**
5. **Er hätte sie beinahe mit ihrer Tochter _____.**

Nora kauft ein.

Inverted Word Order (continued)

Vocabulary

Abendbrot (n)	supper
Birne (f)	pear
darum, deshalb	therefore
Deckel (m)	cover
diätbewußt	diet-conscious
empfehlen (empfiehlt, empfahl, empfohlen)	to recommend
entsetzlich	awful(ly)
es vergeht kaum ein Tag…	a day hardly passes…
gelb	yellow
Genuß (m)	enjoyment
Gestank (m)	stench
Glasgefäß (n)	glass jar
heimbringen (brachte heim, heimgebracht)	to bring home
hineinschneiden (schneidet hinein, schnitt hinein, hineingeschnitten)	to cut into
Jungfernkranz grün	an invented name for a cheese; literally translated: ''virgin's wreath green''
Kakao (m)	cocoa
knusprig	crisp
Kohl (m)	cabbage
Molkereiprodukt (n)	dairy product
Rat (m)	advice
Rezept (n)	*here:* recipe
Schinken (m)	ham
schmackhaft	tasty
Soße (f)	sauce, dressing
Spargel (m)	asparagus
stecken (w)	*here:* to put
stinken (stank, gestunken)	to stink
Tiefkühltruhe (f)	freezer
(sie ist) überzeugt	(she is) convinced
verderben (verdirbt, verdarb, verdorben)	to spoil
verpesten (w)	to pollute
verstauen (w)	to tuck away
was übrig bleibt	what remains
weg	*here:* away
zubereiten (w)	to prepare
zuschrauben (w)	to screw tight

„Also geben Sie mir das Beuschel und den Nierenbraten'', *sagt sie* zu Polzer. „Vielleicht auch einige von den Schweinskoteletts, da Sie sie so warm empfehlen. Die werde ich wahrscheinlich in die Tiefkühltruhe stecken, für nächste Woche.'' Und sie dankt ihm für seinen Rat.

Sie braucht vor allem Milch, darum geht sie zu den Molkereiprodukten.
Peter trinkt eine Menge davon, sie ist froh darüber. Gut für die Knochen.
Gretchen mag Milch überhaupt nicht; sie und Karl nehmen ein wenig für
den Morgenkaffee. Karl ist verrückt nach *Jungfernkranz grün*, ein komischer Name für einen Käse. Stinkt entsetzlich, den ißt nur er und muß, was
übrig bleibt, sofort in ein Glasgefäß verstauen, den Deckel fest zuschrauben
und weg in den Kühlschrank, sonst verpestet das die ganze Wohnung und
jeder regt sich darüber auf. *Schön ist es nicht,* daß man Karl seinen harm-
losen Genuß verdirbt, aber der Gestank . . .

Der nächste Stopp ist die Obst- und Gemüseabteilung, wo sie Äpfel,
Birnen, Karotten, Tomaten, Spinat, Kohl, Spargel und Salat einkauft.
Gemüse ist für Nora sehr wichtig. Da sie sehr diätbewußt und auch davon
überzeugt ist, daß man so oft wie möglich etwas Gelbes und etwas Grünes
essen soll, vergeht kaum ein Tag, an dem nicht irgendein Gemüse oder ein
Salat auf dem Tisch steht. Mit Spinat hat sie leider nicht viel Glück, aber
ihre Salate sind sehr populär. Sie bereitet sie hauptsächlich mit Essig und Öl
zu (ihr eigenes Rezept) und sie schmecken ausgezeichnet, besonders wenn
Nora auch Eier und Schinken hineinschneidet. Mit heißen, knusprigen Buttersemmeln, Tee oder Kaffee (für Peter Kakao) macht das ein sehr schmack-
haftes Abendbrot. *Als sie einmal eine Soße für den Salat vom Supermarkt
heimbrachte, gab es beinahe eine Revolution.*

Inverted Word Order (continued)

„Also geben Sie mir das Beuschel'', sagt sie.
''Well, I'll buy the lung,'' she says.

After a direct quotation, the word order is inverted (**sagt sie**).

Sie braucht vor allem Milch, darum geht sie zu den Molkereiprodukten.
Above all, she needs milk; therefore, she goes to the dairy products.

Darum (or *deshalb*) are what is called conjunctive adverbs like *therefore* or
thus; introducing a sentence, they cause inversion (**darum geht sie;** *not* **darum
sie geht**).

Schön ist es nicht...
It is not nice...

The normal word order would be: *Es ist nicht schön.* Since Nora starts her
sentence in a turned-around (inverted) fashion by using the predicate adjective
first, she has to put the subject (**es**) after the verb (**ist**).

And at the end of the previous section we have:

Als sie einmal eine Soße heimbrachte, gab es beinahe eine Revolution.
Once, when she brought home a (salad) dressing, there almost was a revolution.

If the dependent clause (**Als sie einmal...**) is followed by the main clause (**gab es
beinahe...**), the word order is inverted. You can restore normal word order to the
main clause by turning the two clauses around:

Es gab beinahe eine Revolution,
als sie einmal eine Soße heimbrachte.

EXERCISE 10 True or false?   T / F
1. **Nora kauft nur Rindfleisch.**   _____
2. **Milch ist gut für die Knochen.**   _____
3. **Karls Käse verpestet die Wohnung.**   _____
4. **Jeder mag Spinat.**   _____
5. **Noras Salate sind sehr populär.**   _____

EXERCISE 11 Choose the correct words.
1. **Was kauft Nora nicht?**
   a. **Beuschel**   b. **Ochsenschwanz**   c. **Schweinskoteletts**

2. **Wann wird man wahrscheinlich die Schweinskoteletts essen?**
   a. **heute** b. **nächste Woche** c. **morgen**
3. **Wohin wird der Jungfernkranz grün verstaut?**
   a. **in die Geschirrspülmaschine** b. **in die Tiefkühltruhe** c. **in ein Glasgefäß**
4. **Gemüse ist für Nora**
   a. **sehr wichtig** b. **zu teuer** c. **nicht sehr gut**
5. **Was soll man so oft wie möglich essen?**
   a. **etwas Gelbes und Rotes** b. **Gelbes und Grünes** c. **Grünes und Blaues**

EXERCISE 12 Complete each sentence with a word listed here: **zuschrauben, Rat, Glück, Stopp, Soße.**
1. **Sie dankt ihm für seinen _____.**
2. **Mit Spinat hat sie leider nicht viel _____.**
3. **Man muß den Deckel fest _____.**
4. **Keiner mag die _____ aus dem Supermarkt.**
5. **Der nächste _____ ist die Gemüseabteilung.**

EXERCISE 13 Answer the following in complete German sentences.
1. **Wer trinkt Milch besonders gern?**
2. **Was stinkt entsetzlich?**
3. **Wie bereitet Nora ihren Salat zu?**
4. **Was schneidet sie in den Salat?**
5. **Was ißt man mit dem Salat?**

Word Order in Dependent Clauses

A clause that is introduced by a subordinating conjunction, such as *als, bevor, bis, da, damit, daß, nachdem, ob, obwohl, seit, während, weil, wenn,* etc., by a relative or interrogative pronoun (*der, welcher, wer*), or by a preposition followed by a relative or interrogative pronoun (**Das ist der Tisch,** *an dem* **er sitzt.** —That is the table *at which* he sits. **Er fragte mich,** *von wem* **er es bekommen hat.** —He asked me *from whom* he has received it.) has the conjugated verb in the final position.

Most of this will be familiar to you from some of our previous chapters. In this chapter we will recapitulate and practice German word order again. *Please note:* In this section and in the following sections any subordinating element (conjunction, relative pronoun, etc.) that causes dependent word order will be italicized, as will the conjugated verb standing in last position.

Lillys vegetarische Küche

Vocabulary

ab und zu	now and then
achten (w)	to pay attention
ausgebackener Blumenkohl (m)	baked cauliflower
Berechtigung (f)	justification
besorgen (w)	to attend to
Brokkolibrei (m)	mashed broccoli
enttäuscht	disappointed
eröffnen (w)	to open
Gericht (n)	*here*: dish
Graupensuppe (f)	barley soup
Gurkensaft (m)	cucumber juice
Haferschleimsuppe (f)	oatmeal soup

Herz (n)	heart
hungrig	hungry
Imbiß (m)	snack
Kohlrabipüree (n)	kohlrabi (a kind of cabbage) purée
Kräutertee (m)	herb tea
Lokal (n)	restaurant; eating place
Lust haben auf	to be in the mood for, want
Magen (m)	stomach
mißtrauisch	suspicious
müde	tired
Olivenöl (n)	olive oil
ohne Mühe (f)	without any difficulty
Pflaume (f)	plum
Pilzbratling (m)	fried mushroom
Rettichlimonade (f)	radish lemonade
Stock (m)	stick
treffen (trifft, traf, getroffen)	to meet
vegetarisch	vegetarian (adj.)
Vegetarier (m)	vegetarian (noun)
Wahl (f)	choice
Zitrone (f)	lemon

Inzwischen ist es 12 Uhr geworden. Nora ist hungrig und möchte etwas essen. Sie hat alle ihre Einkäufe in Polzers Supermarkt besorgt. Da sieht sie Frau Agnes List, eine kleine, alte Dame (dünn wie ein Stock), *die* sie beim Einkaufen ab und zu *trifft.* Frau List ist eine fanatische Vegetarierin, während Nora eine eingefleischte Fleischesserin ist.

FRAU LIST Nett, Sie wiederzusehen, Nora. *Wenn* Sie mit Ihren Einkäufen *fertig sind*, können wir essen gehen.

NORA Ich bin müde und hungrig.

FRAU LIST Ich habe das Richtige für Sie. Drei Minuten von hier ist ein kleines Restaurant, erst vor kurzem eröffnet, *welches* die schmackhaftesten Gerichte *serviert.*

NORA *Da* ich nur an einen kleinen Imbiß *gedacht habe*, weiß ich nicht, ob ich . . .

FRAU LIST *Da* Sie keine Lust auf ein großes Mahl *haben*, werden Sie bestimmt nicht enttäuscht sein. Kommen Sie mit mir.

NORA Ich muß auf meine Diät achten.

FRAU LIST Das können Sie dort ohne Mühe.—Da, wir haben Glück, ein Tisch für zwei. Das Lokal ist voll. *Als* ich zuerst von Lillys vegetarischer Küche *hörte*, war ich mißtrauisch. Ganz ohne Berechtigung. Wir müssen wahrscheinlich etwas warten. Also hier ist die Speisekarte. Ah, Haferschleimsuppe oder Graupensuppe mit Pflaumen. Ausgebackener Blumenkohl. Pilzbratlinge, in Olivenöl natürlich; Brokkolibrei, Kohlrabipüree, herrlich. Was wollen Sie bestellen?

NORA Das Kohlrabipüree vielleicht . . .

FRAU LIST Meine eigene Wahl. Mit etwas Reis?

NORA Gut.

FRAU LIST Und zum Trinken? Gurkensaft mit Zitrone? Das ist sehr erfrischend. Oder Rettichlimonade?

NORA Eine Tasse Kaffee.

FRAU LIST Bekommen Sie hier nicht. Schlecht für Herz und Magen.

NORA Dann ein Glas Wasser.

FRAU LIST Kräutertee?

NORA Wie Sie wollen.

FRAU LIST Ich nehme das gleiche.

EXERCISE 14 True or false?   T / F

1. Frau Agnes List ist so dick wie Herr Polzer.   _____
2. Nora ist müde und hungrig.   _____
3. Sie muß auf ihre Diät achten.   _____
4. Frau List war zuerst mißtrauisch.   _____
5. Sie bestellt Kräutertee für sich und Nora.   _____

EXERCISE 15 Answer the following in complete German sentences.

1. Wen trifft Nora in Polzers Supermarkt?
2. Warum will Nora nicht sehr viel essen?
3. Wie sieht Frau List aus?
4. Welche Suppen sind auf der Speisekarte?
5. Wie weit ist Lillys vegetarische Küche vom Supermarkt?

EXERCISE 16 Complete the following sentences.

1. Agnes List ist eine fanatische _____.
2. Nora ist hungrig, aber sie hat keine Lust auf ein großes _____.
3. Sie muß auf ihre Diät _____.
4. Im Restaurant finden sie einen Tisch für _____.
5. Frau List sagt, Kaffee ist schlecht für Herz und _____.

EXERCISE 17 Translate into English.

1. Agnes ist dünn wie ein Stock.
2. Sie war mißtrauisch ohne Berechtigung.
3. Nora wird nicht enttäuscht sein.
4. Sie servieren die schmackhaftesten Gerichte.
5. Ich nehme das gleiche.

CHAPTER 17

Das Fußballspiel
The Soccer Game

Grammatical Odds and Ends
Idiomatic Expressions

Today the decisive soccer game takes place between the **Ludwigsheimer Kickers** and the **Haselburger Elf.** If the home team beats the **Haselburgers,** the **Ludwigsheimers** win the German championship. At half-time the score is 1:0 in favor of the **Haselburgers.**

Das Spiel (I)

Some Useful Expressions

es gefällt mir, es gibt, ich habe es gern, ich habe es lieber, ich habe es am liebsten

Vocabulary

Angriff (m)	offense
applaudieren (w)	to applaud
aufstehen (stand auf, ist aufgestanden)	to stand up
drohend	threatening(ly)
Elfmeter (m)	a penalty kick, made 11 meters from the midpoint of the goal line and directly in front of the goal
es gefällt mir (gefiel mir, hat mir gefallen)	I like it
fast	almost
Feld (n)	field
folgen (w)	to follow
führend	leading
gefährlich	dangerous
ich habe es gern	I like it
ich habe es lieber	I prefer it
ich habe es am liebsten	I like it best
johlen (w)	to yell
Knirps (m)	midget, "shrimp"
jemandem die Leviten lesen	to give someone a dressing-down
Mittelfeldspieler (m)	half-back
naß	wet

pfeifen (pfiff, gepfiffen)	to whistle
Publikum (n)	*here:* spectators, crowd
Regel (f)	rule
Riese (m)	giant
sie sind wie ausgewechselt	they are like changed men
Sportkritiker (m)	sports critic
Tor (n)	goal
Torhüter (m)	goalkeeper, goalie
sich verschlechtern (w)	to get worse
verstehen (verstand, verstanden)	to understand
Verteidiger (m)	full-back
Verteidigung (f)	defense

ANTON (to Tim) **Wie *gefällt dir* das Spiel?**

TIM **Sehr gut.**

ANTON **Verstehst du die Regeln?**

TIM **Peter hat sie mir erklärt. Aber *es gibt* so viele.**

ANTON **Was hast du *lieber*, amerikanischen Fußball oder Soccer?**

TIM **Hier rennen sie herum wie verrückt. Es ist schwer, dem Ball zu folgen. Aber bei uns ist es viel, viel . . .**

PETER **Gefährlicher, meinst du?**

TIM **Ja. Das meiste, was man in Amerika tut, ist hier ein Foul. Es ist alles so verschieden. Ich hab beide Spiele *gern. Am liebsten* hab ich Baseball.**

ANTON **Den kennt man hier überhaupt nicht.**

PETER ***Mir gefällt* unser Fußball besser. Die Spieler in Amerika schauen so komisch aus. Und jeder muß ein Riese sein.**

TIM **Unseren Fußball werde ich nie spielen.**

PETER **Wieso weißt du das?**

TIM **Ich hab keine Muskeln. Und ich eß nicht genug Spinat. Vielleicht spiele ich Soccer. Da kann man ein Knirps sein.**

ANTON **Gott sei Dank, es hat aufgehört zu regnen.**

TIM **Hier regnet es immer. Ich bin ziemlich naß.**

ANTON **Seien wir froh, daß es nicht ärger war.**

Die Spieler sind wieder auf dem Feld. Der Trainer muß ihnen die Leviten gelesen haben, denn sie sind plötzlich wie ausgewechselt. Das Publikum folgt nun dem Spiel mit großem Interesse, applaudiert, pfeift und johlt. Der *führende* Sportkritiker des *Planeten* ist aufgestanden; er sieht, die Kickers sind jetzt im Angriff. Das Wetter hat sich verschlechtert; *drohende* Wolken zeigen sich am Himmel.

Compare the German with the English version:

Wie *gefällt* dir das Spiel?
How do you like the game?
(How does the game please you?)

***Es gibt* so viele.**
There are so many.

In German, *es gibt* is used for both *there is* and *there are*.

Es gibt eine Regel; es gibt viele Regeln.
There is a rule; there are many rules.

Ich *habe* beide Spiele *gern*.
I like both games.

Ich *habe* Tennis *lieber* (als Fußball).
I prefer tennis (to football).

Ich *habe* Baseball *am liebsten*.
I like baseball best.

Subjunctive I (Present Subjunctive)

Gott *sei* Dank; *seien* wir froh.
God be praised; let's be glad.

The *sei* and *seien* are forms of what is called the subjunctive I. As we mentioned in Chapter 15, subjunctive I is used less than subjunctive II. Either subjunctive I or subjunctive II can be used to report what other people say (indirect speech). Subjunctive I is also used to express wishes and is often translated by "may" or "let," as in **seien wir froh** (let's be glad). Forms like *gehen wir* (let's go) and *trinken wir* (let's drink) will give you no trouble because they are the same as the indicative.

Present Participle

der *führende* Sportkritiker
the leading sports critic

drohende Wolken
threatening clouds

We form what is called the present participle simply by adding a -*d* to the infinitive. Don't confuse the present participle (used only as an adjective or adverb) with verbal nouns, like *das Rauchen* (smoking).

EXERCISE 1   True or false?   T / F
1. **Peter hat Tim die Regeln erklärt.**   _____
2. **Tim hat Soccer am liebsten.**   _____
3. **Tim ißt nicht genug Spinat.**   _____
4. **Die Kickers sind wieder in der Verteidigung.**   _____
5. **Für amerikanischen Fußball muß man groß sein.**   _____

EXERCISE 2   Answer the following in complete German sentences.
1. **Warum wird Tim in Amerika nie Fußball spielen?**
2. **Was wird er vielleicht spielen?**
3. **Wem hat der Trainer die Leviten gelesen?**
4. **Wer ist aufgestanden?**
5. **Wer ist jetzt im Angriff?**

EXERCISE 3   Choose the correct words:
1. **Wem gefällt das Spiel sehr gut?**
   a. **dem Jungen**   b. **der Mutter**   c. **Herrn Polzer**
2. **Was hat Tim am liebsten?**
   a. **Soccer**   b. **Tennis**   c. **Baseball**
3. **Die Spieler sind plötzlich**
   a. **ganz traurig**   b. **wie ausgewechselt**   c. **wie früher**
4. **Der führende Sportkritiker**
   a. **ist aufgestanden**   b. **geht weg**   c. **schläft**
5. **Wie ist jetzt das Wetter?**
   a. **die Sonne scheint**   b. **es regnet stark**   c. **es verschlechtert sich**

EXERCISE 4   Complete the following sentences.
1. **Peter hat ihm die Regeln** _____.
2. **Die Spieler rennen herum wie** _____.
3. **Die Kickers sind jetzt** _____.
4. **Das Publikum folgt dem Spiel mit großem** _____.
5. **Drohende Wolken zeigen sich am** _____.

EXERCISE 5   Translate the following.
1. **Ich habe Soccer am liebsten.**
2. **Er hat jedes Spiel gern.**
3. **In Amerika gibt es viele Fußballklubs.**
4. **Ich habe Tennis lieber als Soccer.**
5. **Gefällt dir das Spiel?**

Das Spiel (II)

Vocabulary

abwehren (w)	to beat back
Anhänger (m)	fan
(sich) auszureden versuchen	to try to talk oneself out of something
befördern (w)	*here:* to forward, pass (the ball)
das ist die Feuerprobe für ihn	that's his acid test
deutlich	clearly
(sich) entpuppen (w)	to turn out to be
er ist an die falsche Adresse gekommen	he has come to the wrong man
er hat ihm ein Bein gestellt	he tripped him
er läuft schnurstracks...	he makes a beeline...
er wird kein Glück haben	he won't have any luck
gerecht	just, fair
heißen (hieß, geheißen)	to be called
im siebten Himmel	in Seventh Heaven
Linksaußen (Außenstürmer) (m)	left forward
mächtig	powerful
nach hinten	to the rear
passen (w)	*here:* to pass (to a fellow-player)
Pfosten (m)	*here:* goalpost
Schiedsrichter (m)	referee
schießen (schoß, geschossen)	to shoot, score
sie gewinnen die Oberhand	they get the better (of the others)
sie setzen alles auf eine Karte	they are putting all their eggs in one basket
sie sind außer sich vor Freude	they are beside themselves with joy
soeben	just now
Strafraum (m)	penalty area
über alles Erwarten	beyond all expectations
vergeblich	in vain
(sich) verlassen (verläßt, verließ, verlassen)	to depend (on someone)
verstärken (w)	to strengthen
vor drei Monaten	three months ago
wie es sich gehört	as it should be
zum Angriff übergehen (ging über, ist übergegangen)	to take the offensive

ANTON *Also* schaut euch das *mal* an! Ihr könnt deutlich sehen, daß die Kickers jetzt *die Oberhand gewinnen.*

PETER Und der Linksaußen, wie heißt der?

ANTON Fritz Pfaff. Der ist erst *vor drei Monaten* zu den Kickers gekommen. *Das ist die Feuerprobe für ihn.* Er läuft *schnurstracks* aufs Tor zu.

PETER Die Zuschauer sind *außer sich vor Freude.*

ANTON Da! Der Verteidiger hat ihm *ein Bein gestellt.* Ein Foul! Das hat doch jeder gesehen! Da kommt der Schiedsrichter. Das war im Strafraum.

PETER Der Kerl *versucht gar, sich auszureden.*

ANTON *Da ist er wohl an die falsche Adresse gekommen.*

PETER Kennst du den Schiedsrichter?

ANTON Bei dem *wird er kein Glück haben.* Herr Pichler ist streng und gerecht.

TIM   **Ein Elfmeter!**

ANTON   *Wie es sich gehört.*

PETER   **Wer wird den schießen? Dietz, hoffe ich.**

TIM   **Da ist er schon.**

ANTON   **Tor! Ganz nah beim Pfosten. Auf den Dietz kann man sich verlassen!**

TIM   *Also* **jetzt steht es 1:1.**

ANTON   **Das ist** *aber* **erst der Anfang.**

Anton hat recht. *Über alles Erwarten* haben sich die Kickers wieder als ein großes Team *entpuppt*. Hannes Birgel hat soeben einen Angriff der Haselburger abgewehrt und mit einem mächtigen Kick den Ball zu Hubert Klaar, dem rechten Außenstürmer, befördert. Der paßt ihn sofort zu Braunsteiner und der zu Hacker und das Spiel steht 2:1. Die Anhänger der Kickers sind *im siebten Himmel*. Die Elf *setzen jetzt alles auf eine Karte*. Die Mittelfeldspieler gehen nach hinten, um die Verteidigung zu verstärken. Ihre Stürmer warten vergeblich auf eine Chance, *zum Angriff überzugehen*.

Idiomatic Expressions

Accentuating (or Flavoring) Particles

also, mal, doch, gar, wohl, aber

These are little words that add color and emphasis to your speech. Any attempt to find exact English equivalents to them is hopeless.

Put Your Best Foot Forward.
Zeigen Sie sich von Ihrer besten Seite!

As was pointed out before, the knowledge of idiomatic expressions is crucial. They are used a lot in everyday conversation at all levels of style and on any topic. You will find them used as often in newspapers as they are in personal letters. They enrich the language and give it its special flavor. You are going to enjoy learning and using them. Most of them have one thing in common: They cannot be translated literally or word for word. Sometimes a German idiom will be almost identical with the English idiom; for example: *Sie sind außer sich vor Freude* (They are beside themselves with joy). But now take *Da ist er an die falsche Adresse gekommen.* You could, of course, translate this idiom literally: "There he came to the wrong address"; but a translation of this kind leaves an English-speaking person totally mystified. You have to find an equivalent English expression, in this case: "He went to the wrong man that time."

Also schaut euch das *mal* an!

Here we have two of those accentuating particles, *also* and *mal*. Anton expresses both surprise and admiration about the comeback of the kickers.

Das hat *doch* jeder gesehen!

Anton could not be more emphatic about it.

Der Kerl versucht *gar*, sich auszureden.

The *gar* intensifies Tim's disgust.

Da ist er *wohl* an die falsche Adresse gekommen.

This is Anton's firm conviction hiding behind a pretense of uncertainty.

Das ist *aber* erst der Anfang.

This expresses admiration and joyful anticipation.

EXERCISE 6 True or false? T / F
1. **Fritz Pfaff spielt schon lange für die Kickers.** _____
2. **Die Zuschauer sind außer sich vor Freude.** _____
3. **Herr Pichler ist ein schlechter Schiedsrichter.** _____
4. **Birgel spielt genau so schlecht wie früher.** _____
5. **Die Haselburger können nicht zum Angriff übergehen.** _____

EXERCISE 7 Choose the correct answers.
1. **Die Kickers gewinnen jetzt**
   a. **2 000 Mark** b. **alles** c. **die Oberhand**
2. **Der Verteidiger der Elf hat ihm**
   a. **ein Bein gestellt** b. **geholfen** c. **gedankt**
3. **Wohin ist er da gekommen?**
   a. **nach Wien** b. **an den richtigen Ort**
   c. **an die falsche Adresse**
4. **Nach dem zweiten Tor sind die Kickers**
   a. **im siebten Himmel** b. **ganz zufrieden**
   c. **unglücklich**
5. **Die Elf setzen jetzt alles auf**
   a. **ihr Glück** b. **das Wetter** c. **eine Karte**

EXERCISE 8 Complete each sentence with a word listed here: **übergehen, Glück, Erwarten, Monaten, entpuppt.**
1. **Die Kickers haben sich als ein großes Team** _____.
2. **Die Haselburger möchten gern zum Angriff** _____.
3. **Beim Pichler wird er kein** _____ **haben.**
4. **Pfaff ist erst seit drei** _____ **bei den Kickers.**
5. **Über alles** _____ **spielen sie sehr gut.**

EXERCISE 9 Answer the following in complete German sentences.
1. **Was hat Birgel soeben abgewehrt?**
2. **Wohin hat er den Ball befördert?**
3. **Wohin gehen die Mittelfeldspieler der Haselburger?**
4. **Wer ist streng und gerecht?**
5. **Für wen war das die Feuerprobe?**

EXERCISE 10 Translate into English:
1. **Er läuft schnurstracks auf ihn zu.**
2. **Sie versucht, sich auszureden.**
3. **Über alles Erwarten spielt er sehr gut.**
4. **Auf den Kerl kann man sich verlassen.**
5. **Wie es sich gehört.**

Sieg!° victory

Vocabulary

abnehmen (nimmt ab, nahm ab, abgenommen)	to take away
(sie) amüsieren sich königlich	they enjoy themselves immensely
auf der Hut sein	to be on one's guard
belagern (w)	to lay siege (to)
durchbrechen (bricht durch, brach durch, ist durchgebrochen)	to break through
erleben (w)	to witness
Enttäuschung (f)	disappointment
es geht uns schlecht	we are in a bad way
es paßt mir ausgezeichnet	it suits me to a T

(sich) freidribbeln	to dribble oneself free
Gegner (m)	opponent
(aus dem) Gleichgewicht bringen	to throw off balance
heiser	hoarse
in der Klemme sein	to be in a fix
in eine Sackgasse geraten	to be up against a brick wall
je nach der Situation	depending on the situation
(sie) kommen auf ihre Kosten	they are getting their money's worth
(sich) konzentrieren	to concentrate
köpfen (w)	to hit the ball with one's head; to head
mit halsbrecherischer Geschwindigkeit	with breakneck speed
Mütze (f)	cap
obendrein	on top of that, *here:* to boot
(die) Rechnung ohne den Wirt machen	to overlook one vital factor
Rückendeckung (f)	rear guard
Schluß machen (mit jemandem)	to knock off (someone)
schreien (schrie, geschrien)	to shout
Sieg (m)	victory
(einander) umarmen (w)	to embrace one another
unbeschreiblich	indescribable
vergessen (vergißt, vergaß, vergessen)	to forget
verzeihen (verzieh, verziehen)	to forgive
werfen (wirft, warf, geworfen)	to throw
wie ein geölter Blitz	like greased lightning
zu Ende	at an end; over
zurückbleiben (blieb zurück, ist zurückgeblieben)	to stay behind

ANTON Die Elf sind *in eine Sackgasse geraten.* Wenn sie sich zu sehr auf die Verteidigung konzentrieren, können sie das Spiel nie gewinnen.

PETER Den Kickers *paßt das ja ausgezeichnet.*

ANTON Ja, die Elf sind nun *in der Klemme.* Obendrein kommt jetzt noch Arnold Dietz, der Libero. . .

TIM Warum heißt er eigentlich Libero, Anton?

ANTON Das ist der Spieler, der *je nach der Situation* in der Verteidigung oder im Angriff spielen kann. Libero bedeutet „frei" auf italienisch, weißt du?

TIM Er kann also spielen, wo er will?

ANTON *Das ist es eben.* Ich glaube, er will mit den Haselburgern *Schluß machen.* Da! Was ist *denn* das? Ein hoher Ball von Schumacher und Dietz köpft ihn direkt ins Tor: 3:1.

Die Zuschauer *amüsieren sich königlich.* Die erste Halbzeit war eine Enttäuschung. Aber jetzt *kommen sie auf ihre Kosten.* Die Kickers haben die Elf *aus dem Gleichgewicht gebracht.* Die Verteidigung der Kickers ist jetzt im Mittelfeld und die Mittelfeldspieler belagern das Tor des Gegners zusammen mit den Stürmern. Der einzige, der *zurückgeblieben ist,* ist Birgel, der Vorstopper.

ANTON Wenn die Elf durchbrechen, *geht es uns schlecht.* Das kann gefährlich werden. Keine Rückendeckung. Die sollten *halt* mehr *auf der Hut sein.* Da, der Libero von den Elf hat sich freigedribbelt und kommt *mit halsbrecherischer Geschwindigkeit* auf unser Tor zu.

PETER *Wie ein geölter Blitz!*

ANTON Gott helf uns!

PETER Hat er *etwa die Rechnung ohne den Wirt gemacht*?

ANTON Du meinst Birgel?

PETER Natürlich. Der nimmt ihm den Ball prompt ab und schießt ihn in der Richtung von Hacker . . .

TIM Und Hacker schießt den Ball ins Tor: 4:1.

Der Beifall des Publikums ist unbeschreiblich. Mützen werden in die Luft geworfen, Leute umarmen einander, man schreit sich heiser. Das Fiasko der ersten Halbzeit ist vergessen. Ein solches Comeback hat man noch nie erlebt. Das Spiel ist zu Ende.

More Idiomatic Expressions

More Accentuating Particles

ja, eigentlich, eben, denn, halt, etwa

Take another of those colorful idioms, and try to translate it literally: ***die Rechnung ohne den Wirt machen***. Just look at what you get: to add up the bill without the innkeeper.

Den Kickers paßt das *ja* ausgezeichnet.

The particle gives added emphasis to Anton's conviction.

Warum heißt er *eigentlich* Libero?

There is genuine interest on the part of Tim.

Das ist es *eben*.

Anton expresses his agreement with Tim's interpretation.

Was ist *denn* das?

The ***denn*** is part of an idiomatic expression and impossible to translate. Compare this with the English *why* in:

"Why, this is incredible."

Die sollten *halt* mehr auf der Hut sein.

This is fear mixed with resignation. There's an expression, allegedly typical for Austrians:

Da kann man halt nix (nichts) machen.

There's nothing one can do about it.

Hat er *etwa* die Rechnung ohne den Wirt gemacht?

Peter speculating: a mixture of fear, caution and confidence.

EXERCISE 11 True or false?   T / F
  1. **Die Elf sind in der Klemme.**   ———
  2. **Die erste Halbzeit war eine Enttäuschung.**   ———
  3. **Die Kickers haben immer Rückendeckung.**   ———
  4. **Die Elf konzentrieren sich nur auf den Angriff.**   ———
  5. **Dietz köpft den Ball ins Tor.**   ———

EXERCISE 12 Choose the correct words.
  1. **Der Libero spielt *nicht***
       a. **im Angriff** b. **im Tor** c. **in der Verteidigung**
  2. **Den Kickers paßt das ja**
       a. **ausgezeichnet** b. **gar nicht** c. **nicht sehr gut**

3. **Gegen Ende des Spieles ist die Verteidigung der Kickers**
   a. **im Mittelfeld**   b. **bei den Stürmern**
   c. **wo sie früher war**
4. **Der Beifall des Publikums ist**
   a. **nicht sehr laut**   b. **ziemlich laut**
   c. **unbeschreiblich**
5. **Die Geschwindigkeit des Libero der Elf ist**
   a. **halsbrecherisch**   b. **sehr gut**   c. **nichts Besonderes**

EXERCISE 13 Answer the following in complete German sentences.
1. **Was heißt „Libero'' auf Deutsch?**
2. **Womit will Arnold Dietz Schluß machen?**
3. **Was geschieht, wenn die Elf durchbrechen?**
4. **Was hat man in Ludwigsheim noch nie erlebt?**
5. **Was wird am Ende des Spieles in die Luft geworfen?**

EXERCISE 14 Translate into English.
1. **Er ist in eine Sackgasse geraten.**
2. **Obendrein kommt jetzt noch Dietz.**
3. **Ich hoffe, ich komme auf meine Kosten.**
4. **Der Mann rennt wie ein geölter Blitz.**
5. **Er hat die Rechnung ohne den Wirt gemacht.**

EXERCISE 15 Complete each sentence with a word listed here: **königlich, Gleichgewicht, Kosten, Klemme, Hut**.
1. **Die Zuschauer kommen jetzt auf ihre _____.**
2. **Die Elf sind jetzt in der _____.**
3. **Die Leute amüsieren sich _____.**
4. **Ohne Rückendeckung sollten die Kickers auf der _____ sein.**
5. **Er hat ihn aus dem _____ gebracht.**

Weihnachten
Christmas

Mainly Conversation with an Occasional Idiom Thrown In

Christmas at the Bauers'. Everybody is invited. There's carp and roast goose tonight.

Dicks Pläne

Vocabulary

ähnlich	similar
ausschicken (w)	to send out
brechen (bricht, brach, gebrochen)	to break
Chirurg (m)	surgeon
Chirurgie (f)	surgery
es wird mir schlecht	I get sick
es tut weh	it hurts
Gatte, Gattin	spouse
geschwollen	swollen
mitnehmen (nimmt mit, nahm mit, mitgenommen)	to take along
(sich) niederlassen	to settle
Reiz (m)	charm
Schlinge (f)	sling
sehen (sieht, sah, gesehen)	to see
(sich) spezialisieren (w)	to specialize
sprechen (spricht, sprach, gesprochen)	to speak
verstauchen (w)	to sprain
vorziehen (zieht vor, zog vor, vorgezogen)	to prefer
Weihnachten (f. pl.)	Christmas
weit voraus	far ahead
wochenlang	for weeks

DICK (to Nora) **Das war eine originelle Karte, die Sie ausgeschickt haben.**

NORA **Gretchens Idee. Und Peter hat ihr dabei geholfen. Die Kinder freuen sich immer sehr auf Weihnachten und sprechen wochenlang von nichts anderem.**

DICK **Das kann ich mir vorstellen.**

KRISTY **Bei uns in Amerika ist es auch ein ganz großes Fest. Aber leider ist es jetzt schon sehr kommerzialisiert.**

NORA Wir haben ein ähnliches Problem hier. Aber Weihnachten hat noch immer seinen eigenen Reiz. (to Dick) Ich bin froh, daß Sie kommen konnten.

DICK Ich hab Glück gehabt, daß ich heute abend nicht im Spital bleiben mußte.

NORA Wie lange arbeiten Sie noch dort?

DICK Vielleicht noch zwei Jahre.

NORA Wollen Sie sich auf etwas spezialisieren?

DICK Ich möchte gern Chirurg sein. Als Junge ist mir schlecht geworden, wenn ich Blut gesehen habe. Aber das hat sich geändert. Vielleicht kann ich wieder nach Amerika gehen. Dort sind sie jetzt in der Chirurgie weit voraus.—O, hier ist Tim. Wie geht's, junger Mann?

TIM Danke, sehr gut. Das ist sehr nett von Ihnen, Frau Bauer, daß Sie mich eingeladen haben.

NORA Peters Freund ist mein Freund. Tims Eltern, Major Kelley und seine Gattin, sind nach Berchtesgaden skilaufen gefahren. Aber sie haben Tim nicht mitnehmen können, weil er sich vor einer Woche den Arm verstaucht hat.

DICK Laß sehen!

TIM Man sieht fast nichts mehr.

DICK Er ist noch immer etwas geschwollen. Tut er noch weh?

TIM Nur ein bißchen. Bis gestern mußte ich ihn noch in einer Schlinge tragen.

DICK Sei froh, daß du dir ihn nicht gebrochen hast.

NORA Wollen Sie sich dann in Ludwigsheim niederlassen?

DICK Weiß ich noch nicht. Sie haben sehr viele Ärzte hier. Das Krankenhaus ist sehr gut, aber ich würde wahrscheinlich eine größere Stadt vorziehen.

Note: You may have wondered why **Weihnachten** (Christmas) is plural. As you know, the plural of *Nacht* is *Nächte.* The old form in *-nachten* derives from pre-Christian times when the holy nights around the winter solstice (**die Wintersonnenwende**) were revered as Yule "Girth," or "Circle," a part of the **Julfest** (Yuletide celebrations), lasting from December 18 to January 7. *Weihen* means to consecrate. Many peoples have, or had, festivals celebrating the light at this time of the year. For Romans in classical antiquity for instance, December 25 was the "Day of the Invincible Sun."

    Apropos of Yuletide girth, after putting on many pounds in Vienna consuming **Sachertorte** and numerous whipped-cream-laden pastries, Kristy is back in Germany now. She plans to be careful and not overdo on German **Weihnachtsgebäck** (Christmas baked goodies), like **Weihnachtsstollen** and **Pfeffernüsse** (small round gingerbread cookies) or the many sweets named for the cities that specialize in producing them, including **Nürnberger Lebkuchen** (gingerbread), **Aachener Printen** (oblong spice biscuits), and **Lübecker Marzipan** (almond paste, often chocolate covered).

EXERCISE 1 True or false?   T / F
1. **Die Kinder mögen Weihnachten nicht.** ——
2. **Dick muß heute abend im Spital sein.** ——
3. **Er möchte sich gern spezialisieren.** ——
4. **Major Kelley und seine Frau sind skilaufen gefahren.** ——
5. **In Ludwigsheim gibt es sehr wenige Ärzte.** ——

EXERCISE 2 Answer the following in complete German sentences.
1. **Wann ist es Dick als Jungem schlecht geworden?**
2. **Wie lange wird er vielleicht noch in Ludwigsheim arbeiten?**
3. **Wo sind sie in der Chirurgie weit voraus?**
4. **Wo sind Tims Eltern heute?**
5. **Was ist los mit seinem Arm?**

EXERCISE 3 Complete each sentence with a word listed here: **Idee, Fest, Schlinge, mitnehmen, geschwollen.**

1. Tim hat bis gestern den Arm in einer _____ getragen.
2. Deshalb konnten die Eltern Tim nicht _____.
3. Sein Arm ist noch immer etwas _____.
4. Die Karte war Gretchens _____.
5. In Amerika ist Weihnachten auch ein großes _____.

EXERCISE 4 Translate into English.

1. Er freut sich auf Weihnachten.
2. Es hat seinen eigenen Reiz.
3. Dort sind sie weit voraus.
4. Er hat sich den Arm verstaucht.
5. Er hat sich ihn nicht gebrochen.

EXERCISE 5 Write the following in German.

1. I was lucky.
2. She talks of nothing else.
3. He would like to be a surgeon.
4. That happened a week ago.
5. He wants to settle in a larger city.

Der Fluch des Rauchens

Vocabulary

(sie) ablösen (w)	to take her place
anrühren (w)	to touch
anzünden (w)	to light
Brei (m)	pap, broth
Fluch (m)	curse
für eine Prüfung büffeln	to cram for an exam
Halsweh (n)	sore throat
Husten (m)	cough
ich bin dort überflüssig	they can do without me there
ich hab mir das Rauchen abgewöhnt	I gave up smoking
ich habe Pech	I have bad luck
keine Gefahr	no danger
Kettenraucher (m)	chainsmoker
Rate (f)	installment
Sargnagel (m)	"coffin nail," i.e., cigarette
sezieren (w)	to dissect (a corpse)
Vorsicht!	look out!
wacker (in an ironical sense)	brave(ly), stout(ly), like a trooper
willensstark	having willpower
(sich) zeigen (w)	to show oneself
zu viele Köche verderben den Brei	too many cooks spoil the broth

NORA Entschuldigen Sie bitte. Ich muß sehen, was in der Küche los ist. *Ich bin dort wahrscheinlich überflüssig*, mit Frau Braun und Gretchen . . .

DICK Vorsicht, Frau Nora: *Viele Köche verderben den Brei.*

NORA Keine Gefahr. Trotzdem glaube ich, ich sollte mich zeigen. Anton, wo ist Susie?

ANTON Arbeitet wacker in der Küche.

NORA Die auch? Ich glaube, ich werde sie ablösen.

ANTON Wie geht's, Dick? Nett, Sie wiederzusehen. Zigarette?

DICK Nein, danke. Ich bin froh, *ich hab' mir das Rauchen abgewöhnt.* Ich war ein Kettenraucher. Habe mir förmlich eine an der anderen angezündet. Besonders in meinen Studententagen, wenn ich *für eine Prüfung büffeln* mußte.

ANTON Wie haben Sie sich das abgewöhnt?

DICK Wann immer ich zu viel rauchte, bekam ich Halsweh. Aber ich hab' trotzdem weiter geraucht. Eines Tages war es so schlimm, ich konnte kaum reden. Und der fürchterliche Husten am Morgen! Da hab' ich mir gedacht, Schluß damit, und ich hab' die Sargnägel seither nicht angerührt.

KRISTY Ich glaube, du bist sehr willensstark.

DICK Ich habe beim Sezieren einige Lungen gesehen, ich sage euch . . .

KRISTY Bitte, nicht heute. Zum Glück essen wir kein Beuschel.

DICK Man muß total damit aufhören. Auf Raten geht das nicht.

ANTON Sie haben recht. Ich habe schon fünfmal aufgehört. Aber *ich habe Pech.*

DICK Was meinen Sie?

ANTON Ich kriege nie Halsweh.

Despite his tongue-in-cheek essay *The Awful German Language,* Mark Twain was fond of Germany and Austria, and spent considerable time in both countries. Therefore, he might have had occasion to translate into German his famous quip about giving up smoking: **Man sagt, es sei schwer, mit dem Rauchen aufzuhören. Nichts dergleichen! Das hab ich schon vielmals gemacht!** (People say it's difficult to stop smoking. Nothing of the sort! I've done it many times!)

EXERCISE 6 True or false?

T / F

1. Susie ist auch in der Küche. _____
2. Dick raucht jetzt 30 Zigaretten täglich. _____
3. Anton hat sich das Rauchen abgewöhnt. _____
4. Dick hustete am Morgen. _____
5. Anton bekommt nie Halsweh. _____

EXERCISE 7 Answer the following in complete German sentences.

1. Wer verdirbt den Brei?
2. Was bietet Anton Dick an?
3. Wann hat Dick besonders viel geraucht?

EXERCISE 8 Choose the correct words.

1. Wie oft hat Anton zu rauchen aufgehört?
   a. nie b. zweimal c. fünfmal
2. Was bekam Dick, wenn er zu viel rauchte?
   a. Halsweh b. Zahnweh c. Kopfweh
3. Wann rauchte er am meisten?
   a. wenn er auf Ferien war b. beim Autofahren
   c. vor einer Prüfung
4. Wobei hat er die Lungen gesehen?
   a. bei einem Besuch im Museum b. beim Essen
   c. beim Sezieren
5. Kristy glaubt, Dick ist sehr
   a. willensstark b. stolz c. eigensinnig

EXERCISE 9 Translate into English.

1. Sie ist dort überflüssig.
2. Nora wird sie ablösen.
3. Er mußte für die Prüfung büffeln.
4. Auf Raten geht das nicht.
5. Er hat Pech.

EXERCISE 10 Complete the following sentences.
1. Susie arbeitet wacker in der _____.
2. Dick hat sich eine Zigarette an der anderen _____.
3. Es war so schlimm, er konnte kaum _____.
4. Er meint, man muß total damit _____.
5. Anton kriegt nie _____.

Wie war das Weihnachtsgeschäft?

Vocabulary

anno dazumal	way back
Außenstände (m. pl.)	outstanding debts
das ist Geschmacksache	that's a matter of taste
das ist keine Kunst	that's easy
Einband (m)	binding (of a book)
gegen bar verkaufen	to sell for cash
Geschenk (n)	present, gift
(eine) gewinnende Art	a winning way
hineintun (tut hinein, tat hinein, hineingetan)	to put into
Kalkulationsaufschlag (m)	markup
Klassiker (m)	classic
(es) läuft wie am Schnürchen	it goes like clockwork, smoothly
mit Kunden umgehen	to deal with customers
pünktlich	*here:* promptly
Schuld (f)	*here:* debt
Schund (m)	trash
überhandnehmen (nimmt überhand, nahm überhand, überhandgenommen)	to spread, *here:* to take over (the market)
üblich	usual
umtauschen (w)	to exchange
unter uns gesagt	between you and me
zahlen (w)	to pay

KARL   Bitte nehmt euch doch etwas zu trinken. Der Punsch ist wirklich nicht schlecht. Ich habe sogar etwas Alkohol hineingetan.

DICK   Vielen Dank. Und die Hors d'oeuvres sind ausgezeichnet.

ANTON   Nora ist eine erstklassige Köchin.—Wie war das Weihnachtsgeschäft?

KARL   Nicht schlecht.

ANTON   Was verkaufst du am meisten?

KARL   Die üblichen Bestsellers. *Unter uns gesagt,* die meisten sind Schund. Aber *das ist* natürlich *Geschmacksache.* Klassiker gehen noch immer ganz gut; besonders mit schönen Einbänden, als Weihnachtsgeschenke. Nach Weihnachten versuchen die Leute, sie dann umzutauschen, weil die Kinder drei Schiller oder zwei Goethe bekommen haben.

DICK   Tauschen Sie sie um?

KARL   Ja, das muß man wohl tun.

DICK   Die meisten Bücher, die ich kaufe, sind Paperbacks. Die haben sehr überhandgenommen, nicht?

KARL   Sehr. Leider sind sie auch nicht mehr so billig wie *anno dazumal.* Und man muß eine Menge davon verkaufen, denn der Kalkulationsaufschlag ist sehr klein.

ANTON   Ich höre, daß Gretchen eine sehr gute Verkäuferin ist.

KARL   Ich glaube, Gretchen könnte alles verkaufen. Sie hat eine sehr gewinnende Art, mit den Kunden umzugehen. Wenn sie im Laden ist, *läuft alles wie am Schnürchen.*

ANTON   Verkaufst du *gegen bar?*

KARL   Ich würde gern; aber heutzutage will jeder auf Kredit kaufen, und die Außenstände wachsen von Jahr zu Jahr.

ANTON   Du solltest mehr Chinesen als Kunden haben.

KARL   Wie meinst du das?

ANTON   Die Chinesen zahlen alle ihre Schulden pünktlich am 1. Januar.

KARL   *Das ist keine Kunst.* Die haben ja keine Weihnachten die Woche vorher.

EXERCISE 11 True or false?   T / F
1. **Das Weihnachtsgeschäft war nicht schlecht.**   _____
2. **Nach Weihnachten werden viele Bücher umgetauscht.**   _____
3. **Karl verkauft nur gegen bar.**   _____
4. **Die meisten Bestsellers sind Schund.**   _____
5. **Chinesen zahlen ihre Schulden nie.**   _____

EXERCISE 12 Complete each sentence with a word listed here: **Schnürchen, Einbänden, Paperbacks, schlecht, Schund.**
1. **Die meisten Bücher, die Karl verkauft, sind _____.**
2. **Klassiker gehen ganz gut, besonders die mit schönen _____.**
3. **Die meisten Bestsellers sind _____.**
4. **Mit Gretchen im Geschäft läuft alles wie am _____.**
5. **Der Punsch ist wirklich nicht _____.**

EXERCISE 13 Choose the correct words.
1. **Karl sagt, Nora ist eine ausgezeichnete**
   a. **Angestellte** b. **Köchin** c. **Lehrerin**
2. **Das Weihnachtsgeschäft war**
   a. **nicht schlecht** b. **miserabel** c. **wunderbar**
3. **Karl verkauft am meisten**
   a. **Schulbücher** b. **Witzbücher** c. **Bestsellers**
4. **Tauscht Karl Bücher um?**
   a. **immer** b. **manchmal** c. **nie**
5. **Karl nennt Gretchens Art, mit den Kunden umzugehen**
   a. **gewinnend** b. **freundlich** c. **nett**

EXERCISE 14 Translate into English:
1. **Unter uns gesagt**
2. **Alles läuft wie am Schnürchen.**
3. **Sie weiß, mit den Kunden umzugehen.**
4. **Das ist Geschmacksache.**
5. **Karl kann nicht nur gegen bar verkaufen.**

EXERCISE 15 Answer the following in complete German sentences.
1. **Was ißt man zum Punsch?**
2. **Was nennt Karl die meisten Bestsellers?**
3. **Warum muß Karl eine Menge Paperbacks verkaufen?**
4. **Wieso können die Chinesen ihre Schulden pünktlich am 1. Januar bezahlen?**
5. **Was wächst bei Karl von Jahr zu Jahr?**

Mehr über Ludwigsheim

Vocabulary

abzählen = zählen (w)	to count
alle Hebel in Bewegung setzen	to do all one can
Armut (f)	poverty
Bedeutung (f)	importance
bewahren (w)	to preserve
Bürger (m)	citizen
darstellen (w)	to represent
eingestellt	*here:* inclined
Einkommensquelle (f)	source of income
einsehen (sieht ein, sah ein, eingesehen)	to realize
entdecken (w)	to discover
fallen lassen	to drop
Fremdenverkehr (m)	tourism
geschniegelt und gebügelt	spick and span
Großstädter (m)	big-city dweller
gründen (w)	to found
Handels- und Industriezentrum (n)	commercial and industrial center
Kaiser (m)	emperor
langweilig	boring, dull
lieblich	*here:* smooth
Mauer (f)	wall
Mehrheit (f)	majority
mit einem lachenden und einem weinenden Auge	with mixed emotions
Nachtlokal (n)	nightclub
nichtsahnend	unsuspecting
öffentliche Anlagen (f. pl.)	public grounds
Rathaus (n)	city hall
Rotwein (m)	red wine
Seeweg (m)	maritime route
Siedlung (f)	settlement
Stadtväter (m. pl.)	city fathers
sternhagelvoll	dead drunk
Stil (m)	style
süffig	very drinkable
Tor (n)	gate
Turm (m)	tower
uralt	ancient
verpflanzen (w)	to transplant
(es) wimmelt von Touristen	it is crawling with tourists
Wohlstand (m)	wealth
(sie) zeigen sich von ihrer besten Seite	they put their best foot forward
Zigarettenstummel (m)	cigarette butt

Ludwigsheim ist eine der ältesten Städte Deutschlands. Sie wurde von Kaiser Ludwig II. im Jahre 856 gegründet und ist ein schönes Beispiel für eine mittelalterliche Siedlung, flankiert von uralten Mauern, Türmen and Toren.

Das interessanteste Gebäude ist das Rathaus, das seinen gotischen Stil am reinsten bewahrt hat. Zwischen den Jahren 1200 und 1500 wurde Ludwigsheim ein berühmtes Handels- und Industriezentrum Süddeutschlands, welches seine kommerzielle Bedeutung erst nach dem Jahre 1500 verlor, als der Seeweg nach Indien entdeckt wurde.

Heute ist Ludwigsheim eine Stadt solider Bürger von relativem Wohlstand, die Mehrheit konservativ eingestellt, kulturell interessiert und stolz auf ihr Fußballteam. Von Armut ist wenig zu sehen, die Straßen und öffentlichen Anlagen sind *geschniegelt und gebügelt.* Wenn man einen Zigarettenstummel auf der Straße fallen läßt, kostet das 20 Mark. Die Nachtlokale in Ludwigsheim kann man an den Fingern einer Hand abzählen. Die moralischen Standards sind hier angeblich sehr hoch. Ein Großstädter, der nach Ludwigsheim verpflanzt ist, wird die Stadt wahrscheinlich langweilig finden.

Aber heute *wimmelt es* dort von Touristen. Die Stadtväter haben schon seit langem eingesehen, daß der Fremdenverkehr die einzige solide Einkommensquelle für Ludwigsheim darstellt, und haben *alle Hebel in Bewegung gesetzt*—wahrscheinlich *mit einem lachenden und einem weinenden Auge*—um *sich von ihrer besten Seite zu zeigen.*

Der Ludwigsheimer Rotwein ist berühmt in ganz Deutschland, er ist süffig, lieblich und leicht, und wird daher von den nichtsahnenden Besuchern in großen Mengen konsumiert; aber man wird sehr schnell *sternhagelvoll* davon.

Note: As we mentioned, Ludwigsheim is a fictitious place. But the above could apply to various places. Two later Ludwigs, Kings Ludwig I and II of Bavaria, embarked on ambitious building programs and left behind architectural monuments much visited by tourists, among them a "Valhalla" and, as the brochures put it, the "dream castle" Neuschwanstein, which inspired Walt Disney's "Sleeping Beauty" castle in Anaheim, California.

EXERCISE 16 True or false?   T / F
1. **Ludwigsheim ist über 1000 Jahre alt.** _____
2. **Das interessanteste Gebäude ist das Rathaus.** _____
3. **Heute ist Ludwigsheim ein großes kommerzielles Zentrum.** _____
4. **Von Touristen wimmelt es dort.** _____
5. **Der Wein in dieser Stadt ist miserabel.** _____

EXERCISE 17 Answer the following in complete German sentences.
1. **Wofür ist die Stadt ein schönes Beispiel?**
2. **Was geschieht, wenn man einen Zigarettenstummel fallen läßt?**
3. **Wovon ist wenig zu sehen?**
4. **Wovon wimmelt es heute?**
5. **Wie ist der Ludwigsheimer Rotwein?**

EXERCISE 18 Translate into English:
1. **Geschniegelt und gebügelt.**
2. **Er hat alle Hebel in Bewegung gesetzt.**
3. **Er ist sternhagelvoll.**
4. **Sie zeigt sich von ihrer besten Seite.**
5. **Die Stadtväter haben das schon lange eingesehen.**

EXERCISE 19 Choose the correct words:
1. **Die Straßen Ludwigsheims sind**
   a. **schmutzig** b. **sehr rein** c. **ziemlich rein**
2. **Der Wein von Ludwigsheim ist**
   a. **süffig** b. **bitter** c. **schlecht**
3. **Wie findet ein Großstädter Ludwigsheim?**
   a. **interessant** b. **traurig** c. **langweilig**
4. **Von wem wurde die Stadt gegründet?**
   a. **Napoleon** b. **Ludwig II.** c. **Rudolf I.**

5. **Die einzige solide Einkommensquelle für Ludwigsheim ist**
   a. **der Fremdenverkehr**   b. **der Buchhandel**
   c. **das Fußballteam**

EXERCISE 20 Complete each sentence with a word listed here: **Siedlung, Bewegung, Wohlstand, süffig, Nachtlokale**
1. **Ludwigsheim ist eine Stadt von relativem** _____.
2. **Der Ludwigsheimer Rotwein ist** _____.
3. **Die Stadt ist ein schönes Beispiel für eine mittelalterliche** _____.
4. **Was man an den Fingern einer Hand abzählen kann, sind** _____.
5. **Sie haben alle Hebel in** _____ **gesetzt.**

Zurück zu den Bauers
In der Küche

Vocabulary

ach!	ah!
Angst (f)	fear, anguish
Äpfel im Schlafrock	apple dumplings
auswaschen (wäscht aus, wusch aus, ausgewaschen)	to wash out, cleanse
duften (w)	to smell pleasant
da fällt mir die Wahl schwer	this is a hard choice for me to make
emsig	busy
engagieren (w)	to hire
Haselnußtorte (f)	hazelnut torte
im Wege stehen (stand im Wege, ist im Wege gestanden)	to be in the way
Ingwergebäck (n)	ginger cookies
Karpfen (m)	carp
kosten (w)	*here*: to taste
Kunst (f)	art
Lebkuchen (m)	gingerbread
Meisterwerk (n)	masterpiece
panieren (w)	to bread
Preiselbeeren (f. pl.)	cranberries
(eine) Riesengans (f)	a giant goose
Spargel (m)	asparagus
stadtbekannt	known city-wide
sülzen (w)	to put in aspic
Topf, Töpfe (m)	pot
verhungern (w)	to starve
Vorbereitungen treffen (trifft, traf, getroffen)	to make preparations
zweierlei	two kinds of

   In Noras Küche war man während der letzten Woche sehr emsig. Jetzt werden die letzten Vorbereitungen für das große Weihnachtsessen getroffen, alles sieht wunderbar aus und duftet herrlich.

KRISTY **Bitte verzeiht mir, daß ich euch nicht geholfen habe. Leider hab' ich nie richtig kochen gelernt.**

NORA   Ach, du wärest uns doch nur im Wege gestanden. Vier von uns sind mehr als genug.

KRISTY   Vielleicht kann ich die Töpfe auswaschen.

NORA   Gut. Ich engagiere dich für später.

KRISTY   Ich sehe, du hast zweierlei Karpfen.

GRETCHEN Ja, ein Teil ist paniert und der andere gesülzt.

KRISTY   *Da fällt mir die Wahl schwer.*

SUSIE   Du mußt von beiden kosten. Sie sind Meisterwerke kulinarischer Kunst.

KRISTY   Ich hab Karpfen sehr gern. Leider bekommt man den in Denver nicht oder nur sehr selten.

GRETCHEN Die wissen nicht, was gut ist.

FRAU BRAUN Da, kost ein Stück.

KRISTY   Mmm! Herrlich!

FRAU BRAUN Und schau dir die Riesengans an! Nichts für deine Freundin, Frau List, die Vegetarierin. Und die Knödel! Mit Spargel und Preiselbeeren.

SUSIE   Glaubst du, wir werden genug haben?

KRISTY   Ich bin nicht sicher.

SUSIE   Nora hat immer große Angst, daß die Gäste in ihrem Haus verhungern werden.

NORA   O, hör auf damit!

SUSIE   Ich muß dir den Nachtisch zeigen. Hier. Äpfel im Schlafrock, Haselnußtorte und, weil's Weihnachten ist, Ingwergebäck und Lebkuchen.

KRISTY   Ist das alles?

SUSIE   Hier ist die Suppe—Blumenkohlsuppe. Riech mal!

KRISTY   Ich werde eine Woche lang nichts essen können . . .

SUSIE   Wart! Und hier ist Noras stadtbekannte Spezialität: ihr berühmter bunter Salat!

EXERCISE 21 True or false?   T / F
1. **In Noras Küche riecht es schlecht.**   _____
2. **Karpfen ist in Denver nicht sehr populär.**   _____
3. **Noras Gans ist leider zu klein.**   _____
4. **Aber sie wird zweierlei Karpfen servieren.**   _____
5. **Kristy hat Nora nicht geholfen.**   _____

EXERCISE 22 Answer the following in complete German sentences.
1. **Was wird Kristy vielleicht später tun?**
2. **Was muß Kristy kosten?**
3. **Wie nennt Susie Noras Karpfen?**
4. **Was wird mit der Gans serviert?**
5. **Was hat man noch, weil's Weihnachten ist?**

EXERCISE 23 Choose the correct words.
1. **Kristy kann nicht richtig**
   a. **skilaufen** b. **schwimmen** c. **kochen**
2. **Welche Art Nachtisch wird Nora nicht servieren?**
   a. **Liebesknochen** b. **Lebkuchen** c. **Haselnußtorte**
3. **Was wird Kristy später auswaschen?**
   a. **Teller** b. **Tassen** c. **Töpfe**
4. **Was bekommt man in Denver nur selten?**
   a. **Forelle** b. **Karpfen** c. **Weißfisch**
5. **Die Gans, die Nora serviert, ist**
   a. **sehr groß** b. **nicht sehr groß** c. **klein**

EXERCISE 24 Match the following.

1. **Vier von uns sind mehr als genug.**
2. **Ich engagiere dich für später.**
3. **Sie hat zweierlei Karpfen.**
4. **Glaubst du, haben wir genug?**
5. **Der Salat ist Noras Spezialität.**
6. **Ich bin nicht sicher.**

_____ I am not certain.
_____ Do you think we have enough?
_____ The salad is Nora's specialty.
_____ She has two kinds of carp.
_____ Four of us are more than enough.
_____ I'll hire you for later.

EXERCISE 25 Translate into English.

1. **Du wärest uns nur im Wege gestanden.**
2. **Die wissen nicht, was gut ist.**
3. **Kristy kostet ein Stück.**
4. **Werden sie in Noras Haus verhungern?**
5. **Alles duftet herrlich.**

Das Weihnachtsessen

Vocabulary

beleidigen (w)	to offend
beschwípst	tipsy
entkorken (w)	to uncork
erzählen (w)	to tell
essen (ißt, aß, gegessen)	to eat
füllen (w)	to fill
Gastgeberin (f)	hostess
Katzentisch (m)	small, separate table
Kost (f)	food
Leben (n)	life
satt	full
schmecken (w)	to taste
sitzen (saß, gesessen)	to sit
Truthahn (m)	turkey
widerstehen (widerstand, widerstanden)	to resist

Die Mahlzeit ist ein großer Erfolg. Jeder ißt viel mehr als er (oder sie) sollte. Da der Tisch im Speisezimmer nicht groß genug ist, sitzen die Kinder an einem ,,Katzentisch'' in der Ecke. Karl hat ein paar Flaschen Rheinwein entkorkt und füllt immer wieder die Gläser der Gäste. Kristy ist ein bißchen beschwipst.

DICK Ein Toast auf unsere liebenswürdige Gastgeberin. Ich muß sagen, das war die beste Mahlzeit meines Lebens. (All applaud.)

KRISTY (to him) Besonders nach der Kost im Krankenhaus.

NORA Vielen Dank, Dick. Aber Sie essen so wenig. Nehmen Sie doch mehr Gans.

DICK Frau Nora, manchmal esse ich mehr als gewöhnlich, aber niemals weniger. Danke. Wie kann ich widerstehen.

ANTON Das ist schrecklich. Der schöne Hunger ist ganz weg.

SUSIE Laßt euch noch etwas Raum für den Nachtisch. Oder ihr beleidigt meine Mutter. Die Haselnußtorte ist ihre Spezialität. (All applaud.)

NORA Kinder, habt ihr genug?

TIM Kann ich noch eine Portion Preiselbeeren haben, Frau Bauer? Sie sind sooo gut.

NORA Gretchen hat sie gemacht. Hier.

TIM Ich werde meiner Mutter davon erzählen, vielleicht kannst du ihr das Rezept geben.

GRETCHEN O, sie kennt das bestimmt. Habt ihr die nicht mit Truthahn in Amerika?

TIM Ja, aber hier schmecken sie viel besser.

PETER Ich glaube, ich bin satt.

GRETCHEN Keine Torte?

PETER Vielleicht später.

EXERCISE 26 True or false?   T / F
1. Alle Gäste sitzen an *einem* Tisch.   ——
2. Die Haselnußtorte ist Susies Spezialität.   ——
3. Antons Hunger ist ganz weg.   ——
4. Die Mahlzeit ist ein großer Erfolg.   ——
5. Die Kost im Krankenhaus ist sehr gut.   ——

EXERCISE 27 Answer the following in complete German sentences.
1. Wo sitzen die Kinder?
2. Womit füllt Karl die Gläser der Gäste?
3. Wer ist die „liebenswürdige Gastgeberin"?
4. Wofür sollen sich die Gäste Raum lassen?
5. Was essen sie mit Truthahn in Amerika?

EXERCISE 28 Complete each sentence with a word listed here: **genug, Krankenhaus, wenig, beschwipst, Rezept**
1. Nora sagt, „Dick, Sie essen so _____."
2. Kristy ist ein bißchen _____.
3. Der Tisch im Speisezimmer ist nicht groß _____.
4. Vielleicht sollst du ihr das _____ geben.
5. Die Mahlzeit ist ausgezeichnet, besonders nach der Kost im _____.

EXERCISE 29 Translate into English.
1. Die Kost im Krankenhaus ist miserabel.
2. Manchmal ißt Dick mehr als gewöhnlich.
3. Tim bekommt noch eine Portion Preiselbeeren.
4. In Amerika ist Truthahn sehr populär.
5. Wie kann er widerstehen?

EXERCISE 30 Choose the correct words.
1. Nora sagt zu Dick, „Nehmen Sie doch etwas mehr
   a. Fisch   b. Gans   c. Wein
2. Tim will noch eine Portion
   a. Preiselbeeren   b. Spargel   c. Knödel
3. Was hat Frau Braun gemacht?
   a. den Karpfen   b. die Haselnußtorte
   c. den Lebkuchen
4. Was ist für Anton ganz weg?
   a. der Hunger   b. die Torte   c. das Ingwergebäck
5. Was sagt Peter am Ende des Mahles?
   a. Ich bin hungrig.   b. Ich bin satt.
   c. Ich bin müde.

O, Tannenbaum (fir tree, Christmas tree)

Vocabulary

behangen	decked out
bewundern (w)	to admire
einziehen (zog ein, ist eingezogen)	to move (into)
Flügel (m)	*here:* grand piano
Gitarre (f)	guitar
glitzern (w)	to glitter
herumfuchteln (w)	to saw the air
ich kann's nicht ausstehen	I cannot stand it
jetzt kommst *du* dran	now it's your turn
Klavier (n)	piano
Kümmel (m)	caraway liqueur
mitbringen (brachte mit, mitgebracht)	to bring along
Nuß (f)	nut
Slivovitz (m)	plum brandy
stören (w)	to disturb
Verdauung (f)	digestion
Weihnachtsbaum (m)	Christmas tree
Weihnachtslieder (n. pl.)	Christmas carols*
wild	wild

*Strictly speaking, "Christmas carol" is a misnomer for songs like *"O Tannenbaum"* and *"Am Weihnachtsbaum die Lichter brennen"* (On the Christmas Tree the Lights are Burning), which are "rooted" in pre-Christian tree and nature worship. Santa and his reindeers, including *"Rudolph the Red-Nosed Reindeer,"* relate ultimately to the Germanic god Odin (Woden, Wotan), for whom Wednesday is named. In December, he rides Sleipnir, his eight-legged horse, faster than the wind, and brings gifts to deserving children. Kristy believes not only in equal rights for women in all fields, but also in equal time for world religions. Although she enjoys the music, she doesn't much like the words to some Christmas carols. Those texts that are less seasonal-solstice and more theologically oriented she finds difficult to take. But she doesn't want to rain on Peter's and Tim's parade, so she sings along, most of the time at least, just to be sociable (**gesellig, gemütlich**).

Die Gäste machen es sich im Wohnzimmer bequem und bewundern den schönen Weihnachtsbaum, der mit glitzernden Dekorationen, aber auch mit Nüssen, Bonbons und Gebäck behangen ist. Die Kinder öffnen ihre Geschenke und sind im siebenten Himmel. Karl bietet den Gästen Kümmel oder Slivovitz an. Angeblich ist Kümmel gut für die Verdauung.

SUSIE Jetzt sollten wir Weihnachtslieder singen.

NORA Leider haben wir kein Klavier. Karl wollte mir eins kaufen, da habe ich ihm gesagt, wart, bis wir ins neue Haus einziehen. Dort haben wir mehr Platz für einen Flügel. Aber ich habe eine Überraschung für euch.

KRISTY Was ist es, Nora?

NORA Ihr wißt doch, daß Peter Musiker ist. Ein sehr guter Cellist. Im letzten Schulorchesterkonzert spielte er ein Solo. Ausgezeichnet. Aber er will Dirigent werden.

GRETCHEN Manchmal steht er im Zimmer und dirigiert mit den Schallplatten. Fuchtelt ganz wild mit den Händen herum; aber dabei darf man ihn nicht stören. Onkel Leopold sagt, er macht das sehr gut.

NORA   *Mein* Onkel, der pensionierte Kapellmeister. Sag's ihnen, Peter.

PETER   Nach dem Cello wollte ich gern Flöte lernen. Aber mit meinen Zähnen ist etwas nicht in Ordnung. Und Klavier haben wir noch keins. Ein Kapellmeister soll mehrere Instrumente spielen. Paganini und Berlioz waren auch ausgezeichnete Gitarristen. Da hat mir Vati vor zwei Monaten eine Gitarre gekauft.

DICK   Kannst du sie bereits spielen?

PETER   Das ist ziemlich leicht. Aber ich war nicht der einzige, der eine Gitarre bekommen hat. Tim, *jetzt kommst du dran.*

TIM   Ich spiel die Violine schon seit vier Jahren. Und *ich kann's nicht ausstehen.* Dann kriegt Peter seine Gitarre, ich hör ihm zu und es ist super. Da sag ich meinem Dad, „Dad, kannst du mir auch eine Gitarre kaufen?"

KRISTY   Und hast du sie bekommen?

TIM   Ja. Hier, ich hab sie mitgebracht.

EXERCISE 31   True or false?   T / F

1. Die Gäste sitzen jetzt im Wohnzimmer.   ————
2. Karl bietet ihnen Wasser an.   ————
3. Nora hat kein Klavier in ihrem Haus.   ————
4. Peter spielt jetzt auch die Flöte.   ————
5. Tim hat auch eine Gitarre bekommen.   ————

EXERCISE 32   Answer the following in complete German sentences.

1. Was hängt am Weihnachtsbaum?
2. Wann wird Nora ein Klavier haben?
3. Wo dirigiert Peter?
4. Was hat ihm sein Vater geschenkt?
5. Was kann Tim nicht ausstehen?

EXERCISE 33   Choose the correct words.

1. Die Gäste sitzen im Wohnzimmer und bewundern
   a. die Geschenke   b. Kristys Kleid
   c. den Weihnachtsbaum
2. Was wird den Gästen *nicht* angeboten?
   a. Coca-Cola   b. Slivovitz   c. Kümmel
3. Noras Onkel ist ein pensionierter
   a. Kapellmeister   b. Offizier   c. Angestellter
4. Wieviele Instrumente soll ein Kapellmeister spielen?
   a. alle   b. mehrere   c. eines
5. Was hat Tim auch bekommen?
   a. eine Gitarre   b. ein Cello   c. eine Flöte

EXERCISE 34   Translate into English.

1. Kümmel ist angeblich gut für die Verdauung.
2. Nora zieht einen Flügel vor.
3. Peter fuchtelt mit den Händen herum.
4. Was, sagt er, ist ziemlich leicht?
5. Jetzt kommst du dran.

EXERCISE 35   Complete each sentence with a word listed here: **Flöte, Solo, Violine, Ordnung, Klavier**

1. Tim kann die _____ nicht ausstehen.
2. Mit Peters Zähnen ist etwas nicht in _____.
3. Nora wird im neuen Haus ein _____ haben.
4. Nach dem Cello wollte Peter gern die _____ lernen.
5. Im letzten Schulorchesterkonzert spielte er ein _____.

"Stille Nacht, heilige Nacht"

Vocabulary

annagen (w)	to gnaw at
begleiten (w)	to accompany
Chor (m)	choir
Dorf (n)	village
Getriebe (n)	works, *here:* of an organ
heilig	holy
in der Nähe von	near
klingen (klang, geklungen)	to sound
komponieren (w)	to compose
künstlerisch	artistic
lehren (w)	to teach
Maus, Mäuse (f)	mouse
Mitternachtsmesse (f)	midnight mass
Orgel (f)	organ
singen (sang, gesungen)	to sing
(jemanden) spielen lehren (w)	to teach (someone) to play
Urgroßvater (m)	great-grandfather
ursprünglich	originally
Weihnachtsabend (m)	Christmas Eve
Wiedergabe (f)	rendition

KRISTY Was ist die Überraschung, Nora? Wir können kaum warten.

NORA Peter hat Tim die Gitarre spielen gelehrt. Und sie haben die letzten zwei Wochen Weihnachtslieder geübt. Aber das ist nicht alles.

ANTON Eigentlich sollte *ich* die Gitarre spielen.

DICK Wieso?

ANTON Ihr wißt doch, mein Name ist Gruber.

DICK Und?

ANTON Am 24. Dezember 1818 hat Franz Gruber *"Stille Nacht, heilige Nacht"* komponiert, nach einem Text des Priesters Joseph Mohr. Es wurde zum ersten Mal zur Mitternachtsmesse gesungen. Das war in einem Dorf in der Nähe von Salzburg.

DICK Sind Sie ein Nachkomme von Franz Gruber?

ANTON Sehr leicht möglich. Mein Urgroßvater ist von Salzburg nach Wien übersiedelt.

KRISTY Was hat das mit der Gitarre zu tun?

ANTON Franz Gruber war Schullehrer und Organist in Oberndorf. Aber am Weihnachtsabend, als er die Orgel spielen sollte, war sie kaputt. Mäuse hatten das Getriebe angenagt und kein Ton kam heraus. Also mußte er den Chor auf der Gitarre begleiten. Aber wir haben Glück. Wir haben nicht nur eine, sondern zwei Gitarren hier. Heute hört ihr die künstlerische Wiedergabe von *"Stille Nacht, heilige Nacht,"* nicht auf der Orgel, sondern so, wie sie ursprünglich geklungen hat. Meine Damen und Herren, ich präsentiere hier zwei authentische Interpreten von Grubers Musik: Peter und Tim.

EXERCISE 36 True or false?   T / F

1. Grubers Familie kommt aus Salzburg. ——
2. Nora und Peter werden *"Stille Nacht"* präsentieren. ——
3. Eigentlich sollte Anton die Gitarre spielen. ——
4. Nora hat Tim die Gitarre spielen gelehrt. ——
5. Mäuse hatten das Getriebe angenagt. ——

EXERCISE 37   Answer the following in complete German sentences.
1. **Was hat Peter Tim gelehrt?**
2. **Wann wurde „Stille Nacht" zuerst gesungen?**
3. **Wer ist von Salzburg nach Wien übersiedelt?**
4. **Was war am Weihnachtsabend kaputt?**
5. **Wer sind heute die Interpreten von Grubers Musik?**

EXERCISE 38   Complete each sentence with a word listed here: **Getriebe, Organist, Weihnachtslieder, Dorf, Wiedergabe**
1. **Die Jungen haben _____ geübt.**
2. **Das war in einem _____ in der Nähe von Salzburg.**
3. **Heute hören sie die künstlerische _____ von „Stille Nacht."**
4. **Franz Gruber war _____ und Schullehrer.**
5. **Mäuse hatten das _____ angenagt.**

EXERCISE 39   Translate into English.
1. **Er hat ihn die Gitarre spielen gelehrt.**
2. **Ist Anton ein Nachkomme von Franz Gruber?**
3. **Die Jungen sind authentische Interpreten von „Stille Nacht."**
4. **Die Orgel war kaputt.**
5. **Kein Ton kam heraus.**

EXERCISE 40   Choose the correct word.
1. **Tim lernte die Gitarre spielen von**
   a. **Anton**   b. **Peter**   c. **Nora**
2. **Wer hatte das Getriebe der Orgel angenagt?**
   a. **Mäuse**   b. **Katzen**   c. **Hunde**
3. **Wann wurde „Stille Nacht, heilige Nacht" zuerst gespielt?**
   a. **am 1. Januar 1818**   b. **am 1. März 1819**
   c. **am 24. Dezember 1818**
4. **Was war Franz Gruber *nicht*?**
   a. **Werbefachmann**   b. **Organist**   c. **Schullehrer**
5. **Wer ist *nicht* einer der authentischen Interpreten?**
   a. **Tim**   b. **Dick**   c. **Peter**

ANSWER KEY

Chapter 1, **p. 1,** On the Way to the Pool
p. 7, Exercises
1. **b** 2. **c** 3. **a** 4. **b** 5. **a** 6. **b** 7. **a** 8. **c**
9. **b** 10. **a** 11. **b** 12. **c** 13. **a** 14. **a** 15. **c**
16. **a** 17. **c** 18. **a** 19. **b** 20. **c**

Chapter 2, **p. 8,** Anton and His Nice Neighbor, Mrs. Müller
pp. 11-12, Exercise 1
1. **den** 2. **der** 3. **das** 4. **dem** 5. **die** 6. **des**
7. **der** 8. **der** 9. **den, die** 10. **das** 11. **einen**
12. **einem** 13. **eines** 14. **einer** 15. **ein**

p. 12, Exercise 2
1. **der** 2. **die** 3. **der** 4. **die** 5. **das** 6. **der**
7. **das** 8. **das** 9. **die** 10. **der** 11. **das**
12. **der**

p. 12, Exercise 3
1. **eine** 2. **eine** 3. **ein** 4. **eine** 5. **ein** 6. **eine**
7. **ein** 8. **ein**

p. 12, Exercise 4
1. **Der Eisschrank ist in der Küche.**
2. **In dem großen Kasten im Wohnzimmer sind viele Bücher.**
3. **Das Fenster in der Küche ist immer offen.**
4. **Er zahlt den Besitzern die Miete.**
5. **Die Nachbarin heißt Frau Müller.**
6. **Anton hat einen guten Sinn für Humor.**

p. 12, Exercise 5
1. **In dem Kasten sind viele Bücher.**
2. **Er bekam die Geschirrspülmaschine von der Mutter.**
3. **Der Eisschrank ist in der Küche.**
4. **Anton zahlt die Miete.**
5. **Die Preise sind hoch.**
6. **Frau Müller ist eine hilfsbereite Nachbarin.**
7. **Er öffnet die Hauseingangstür.**
8. **Das Fenster ist immer offen.**
9. **Er betritt das Wohnzimmer.**
10. **Er bietet ihr ein Glas Tee an.**

p.12, Exercise 6
1. **Bücher**
2. **nett**
3. **Flur**
4. **Rechnungen**
5. **Hauseingangstür**
6. **ziemlich hoch**
7. **Geschirrspülmaschine**
8. **Schlafzimmer**
9. **offen**
10. **voll**

pp. 12-13, Exercise 7
1. **a** 2. **b** 3. **c** 4. **b** 5. **a** 6. **b**

p. 13, Exercise 8
1. **f** 2. **t** 3. **f** 4. **f** 5. **t** 6. **f** 7. **t** 8. **t**
9. **f** 10. **f**

p. 14, Exercise 9
1. **Morgen** 2. **Wetter** 3. **letzten paar** 4. **sehr froh** 5. **Samstag (Sonnabend)** 6. **Himmel**
7. **vielen Dank** 8. **traurig**

p. 14, Exercise 10
1. **ist** 2. **keine** 3. **Tage** 4. **bitte** 5. **Rede**
6. **zuviel** 7. **sehr** 8. **Sonne**

p. 14, Exercise 11
1. **Ich schlafe immer gut.**
2. **Die Sonne scheint.**
3. **Vielen Dank für die Zeitung.**
4. **Keine Ursache**
5. **Trinken Sie bitte den Tee.**
6. **Kein Büro?**
7. **Nicht der Rede wert**
8. **Weil es Samstag ist?**
9. **Genau**
10. **Ich bin sehr froh.**

pp. 14-15, Exercise 12
1. excellent
2. especially today
3. Please, drink the tea.
4. Anything new in it?
5. No cloud in the sky
6. Very well, thank you
7. wonderful
8. Good morning, Herr Anton

p. 15, Exercise 13
1. **Z/H** 2. **E/W** 3. **S** 4. **I/Ü** 5. **U/A** 6. **T/H**
7. **Z/G** 8. **N/E** 9. **W/E** 10. **C/D/R**

p. 15, Exercise 14
1. **die** 2. **der** 3. **das** 4. **das** 5. **die** 6. **die**

p. 15, Exercise 15
1. **Das Wetter ist sehr schön.**
2. **Am Himmel ist keine Wolke.**
3. **Anton trinkt Tee.**
4. **Die Nachbarin heißt Frau Müller.**
5. **Die Sonne scheint am Himmel.**
6. **Frau Müller bringt die Zeitung.**

p. 15, Exercise 16
1. **Haben Sie gut geschlafen?**
2. **Die Sonne scheint und keine Wolke ist am Himmel.**
3. **Danke für die Zeitung.**
4. **Die letzten paar Tage hat es geregnet.**
5. **Ich bin froh.**
6. **Weil es Samstag ist.**

p. 15, Exercise 17
1. **b** 2. **c** 3. **b** 4. **b**

p. 15, Exercise 18
1. **f** 2. **f** 3. **f** 4. **t** 5. **f** 6. **f** 7. **t** 8. **f** 9. **t**

Chapter 3, p. 17, The Cousin from Denver

p. 18, Exercise 1
1. **die Messer und die Löffel**   2. **die Fenster**
3. **die Teller**   4. **einen Wagen**   5. **Brauns Tochter**
6. **die Mädchen**   7. **Fräulein**

p. 18, Exercise 2
1. **Kristy verbringt einen Monat in Deutschland.**
2. **Wo sind die Teller und die Löffel?**
3. **Susie hat einen Freund.**
4. **Sie ist Frau Brauns Tochter.**
5. **Kristy hat zwei Brüder.**
6. **Das ist komisch.**
7. **Das Wetter ist sehr schön.**
8. **Man hört einen Wagen.**
9. **Frau Braun ist die Mutter eines Mädchens.**

p. 18, Exercise 3
1. **Kristy verbringt ihre Ferien in Deutschland.**
2. **Susie ist Frau Brauns Tochter.**
3. **Susies Freund heißt Anton.**
4. **Susies Mutter stellt die Teller auf den Tisch.**
5. **Man hört einen Wagen vorfahren.**
6. **Die Mädchen helfen Frau Braun.**
7. **Kristy erzählt einen Witz.**

p. 19, Exercise 4
1. **a**   2. **c**   3. **a**   4. **b**   5. **c**

p. 20, Exercise 5
1. **Nora und Karl sind Susies Freunde.**
2. **Noras Pudel sind tot.**
3. **Sie hießen Pipsi und Putzi.**
4. **Sie war vor dreizehn Jahren zuletzt in Deutschland.**
5. **Die Hunde waren herzig.**

p. 20, Exercise 6
1. **angekommen**   2. **Tisch**   3. **anbieten**   4. **tot**
5. **Akzent**   6. **nett**   7. **wiederzusehen**

p. 20, Exercise 7
1. *-en*   2. *-e*   3. *-en*   4. *-e*   5. *-en*   6. *-e*

pp. 20-21, Exercise 8
1. **I/H/H**   2. **C/T**   3. **R/E**   4. **A/K**   5. **U**
6. **E/H**   7. **K**

p. 21, Exercise 9
1. **vor dreizehn Jahren**   2. **Glauben Sie?**   3. **Sie waren so herzig.**   4. **Nett, Sie wiederzusehen.**
5. **Das ist schade.**   6. **Behalt ihn!**   7. **Anton ist gerade angekommen.**

p. 22, Exercise 10
1. **c**   2. **b**   3. **c**   4. **a**   5. **b**

p. 22, Exercise 11
1. **3**   2. **1**   3. **5**   4. **2**   5. **4**

p. 22, Exercise 12
1. **Ä**   2. **Ü**   3. **I**   4. **N**   5. **C**

p. 22, Exercise 13
1. **Die Gäste machen es sich bequem.**
2. **Vorige Woche habe ich zwei Bücher gekauft.**
3. **Die Männer rauchen.**
4. **Ich glaube schon.**
5. **Ich weiß noch nicht.**

p. 23, Exercise 14
1. **f**   2. **t**   3. **t**   4. **f**   5. **f**

p. 24, Exercise 15
1. *-en*   2. *-en -en*   3. *-en*   4. *-en*   5. *-en*

p. 24, Exercise 16
1. **f**   2. **t**   3. **f**   4. **f**   5. **t**

p. 24, Exercise 17
1. **Amerika**   2. **höflicher**   3. **amerikanischen**
4. **Universitäten**   5. **Herren**

p. 24, Exercise 18
1. After the card game
2. Please compare.
3. The students (male) at the universities
4. The schools in Germany
5. They talk about various topics.

pp. 24-25, Exercise 19
1. **Sie verbeugen sich.**
2. **Wir haben Schwestern.**
3. **Sie hat zwei Katzen.**
4. **Sie bringen oft Blumen.**
5. **Die Schulen in Amerika**

p. 26, Exercise 20
1. **Kristy wohnt mit einer Freundin.**
2. **Sofas, Radios und Fernseher sind in jedem Zimmer.**
3. **Kristy ist eine Lehrerin.**
4. **In der Garage sind zwei Autos.**
5. **Die Freundinnen teilen die Kosten.**

p. 26, Exercise 21
1. **Die Namen sind Kristy und Susie.**
2. **Eine herrliche Aussicht**
3. **Eine Garage für zwei Autos**
4. **Ich habe Glück.**
5. **Ich bin sehr zufrieden.**

p. 26, Exercise 22
1. **bequem**   2. **klingt**   3. **Themen**   4. **Firmen**
5. **Namen**

p. 26, Exercise 23
1. **N/H**   2. **E/D**   3. **W/A/E**   4. **B/U**   5. **E/H**

Chapter 4, p. 29, An Evening with the Bauer Family: Word Games and TV

pp. 30-31, Exercise 1
1. *-en*   2. *-es*   3. *-e*   4. *-e*   5. *-en*   6. *-e*
7. *-en*   8. *-er*   9. *-es*   10. *-e*   11. *-en*   12. *-em*

p. 31, Exercise 2
1. des jungen   2. in dem neuen   3. der kleinen
4. dem alten   5. des guten   6. das kleine

p. 31, Exercise 3
1. c   2. b   3. b   4. a

p. 31, Exercise 4
1. Sie sind nette Leute.
2. Die Eltern haben gute Manieren.
3. Sie sind überall beliebt.
4. Die Kinder sind brav.
5. Wer hat eine glänzende Erziehungsmethode?

p. 33, Exercise 5
1. Nora und Anton haben ein kleines, nettes Haus.
2. Es besteht aus Wohnzimmer, Eßzimmer, Diele, zwei Schlafzimmern, Küche, Badezimmer und Toilette.
3. Kristy findet das Haus sehr gemütlich.
4. Erika spricht mit Gretchen am Telephon.
5. Jürgen Kaiser ist schöner als Hans Hinnemann.

p. 33, Exercise 6
1. Die Bauers haben ein kleines Haus in einem Vorort.
2. Kann ich mit Erika sprechen?
3. Hast du den Film mit Kaiser gesehen?
4. Ist dein Telephon kaputt?
5. War in eurer Gegend ein Gewitter?
6. Grüße an deinen Bruder Paul

p. 33, Exercise 7
1. -er -e   2. -e   3. -en -en   4. -e   5. -e -e
6. -e -e

p. 33, Exercise 8
1. The house also has a den.
2. Erika talks to her girlfriend.
3. The telephone is out of order.
4. That is an excellent film.
5. The thunderstorm was in my area.
6. I have to hang up now.

pp. 33-34, Exercise 9
1. c   2. a   3. b   4. a

p. 34, Exercise 10
1. Mein Haus ist neu.
2. Seine Töchter sind schön.
3. Diese nette Frau ist meine Mutter.
4. Welches Mädchen hat blondes Haar?
5. Ich sah viele gute Filme.
6. Wir hatten einige große Präsidenten.

p. 38, Exercise 11
1. größer   2. der stärkste   3. besser   4. die beste   5. älter

p. 38, Exercise 12
1. schön   2. wütend   3. leicht   4. wirklich
5. hoffentlich   6. nie   7. damals   8. mehr

p. 38, Exercise 13
1. Freundin   2. zerstritten   3. Büchern
4. Schlafzimmer   5. unzufrieden   6. fest

p. 38, Exercise 14
1. t   2. f   3. f   4. f   5. t   6. t

p. 38, Exercise 15
1. I love you.
2. That's a matter of taste.
3. I am talking to my bosom friend.
4. What is going on here?
5. You bet.
6. There he comes.
7. There is no such thing.
8. No decent program

Chapter 5, **p. 40,** Anton Looks for Another Job

p. 41   Anton in Germany
Anton was born in Vienna. He came to Germany nine years ago and still speaks with a Viennese accent. To his friends he says "Servus" when coming or going. Most members of the female sex he honors with "Kiss your hand, gracious lady (madam)." Susie has often teased him about this. "That's just the way I talk," he always says. "You won't change me." People like him. They respect his courtesy and admire his charm.

p. 42, Exercise 1
1. Er   2. ihn   3. mich   4. mir   5. dir

p. 42, Exercise 2
1. Anton ist in Wien geboren.
2. Er wohnt jetzt in Deutschland.
3. Er sagt „Servus!" zu seinen Freunden.
4. Sie bewundern seinen Charme.
5. Er sagt „Küss die Hand, gnädige Frau (oder Fräulein)" zu manchen Damen.

p. 42, Exercise 3
1. They admire him.
2. He comes from Vienna.
3. Susie has teased him about it.
4. He speaks with a Viennese accent.
5. Bring me coffee, please.

p. 42, Exercise 4
1. C/H   2. E/E/E   3. V   4. U/N   5. H/Ä

p. 43   In the Café-Pastry Shop
Today we find him in the café-pastry shop Walser.
"Do you have the *Münchener Neuesten?*" he asks the waitress.
"Unfortunately not (I'm sorry, we don't)," she answers. "Shall I bring you the *Süddeutsche Zeitung?*"
"Good. Give it to me, please."
Here comes Susie. "Servus," he says, gets up, and offers her a seat. "Nice of you to come. — Herr

Ober!'' ''Please bring us two cups of coffee with whipped cream and some of your delicious croissants.'' And to Susie he says: ''The pastry cook here is Austrian. Everything is homemade.''

p. 43   A Litle Joke
''How do you do,'' Fritz says at the newsstand. ''Do you still have yesterday's newspaper?''
''I'm sorry, we don't, but do come tomorrow and get today's paper.''

p. 43, Exercise 5
1. **b**   2. **a**   3. **b**   4. **a**   5. **c**

p. 44, Exercise 6
1. **Platz an**   2. **Österreicher**   3. **Schlag**
4. **Kellnerin**   5. **Café-Konditorei**

p. 44, Exercise 7
1. **f**   2. **t**   3. **t**   4. **f**   5. **t**

p. 44, Exercise 8
1. **ihr**   2. **Ihnen**   3. **uns**   4. **dir**   5. **sie**

p. 44, Exercise 9
1. **Er fragt die Kellnerin.**
2. **Schön von dir zu kommen**
3. **Zwei Tassen Kaffee mit Schlag**
4. **Der Mehlspeiskoch ist ausgezeichnet.**
5. **Alles hausgemacht**

p. 44   Another Job?
SUSIE Well, you have hinted that you want to give up your job.
ANTON Yes, Susie. I don't earn enough there, and I also do not have any chances for the future. But it is difficult to find something nowadays. Lots of ads but nothing in particular for me.—Ah, the coffee! My father advises me not to change jobs. ''Watch out,'' he says. ''Look at the unemployment.'' Many people are of the same opinion, and they are probably right. On the other hand, if you don't take a chance, you can't win.
SUSIE That you must decide for yourself.

p. 45, Exercise 10
1. **ich**   2. **es**   3. **sie**   4. **du**   5. **sie**

p. 45, Exercise 11
1. **Ich verdiene dort nicht genug.**
2. **Keine Aussichten für die Zukunft**
3. **Eine Menge von deliziösen Kipfeln**
4. **Es ist schwer heutzutage.**
5. **Anderseits ist mein Job gut.**

p. 45, Exercise 12
1. **wunderbar**   2. **derselben Ansicht**   3. **aufgeben**
4. **davon ab**   5. **acht**

p. 45, Exercise 13
1. **genug**   2. **wahrscheinlich**   3. **Arbeitslosigkeit**
4. **wagt**   5. **entscheiden**

p. 46, Exercise 14
1. **Ich habe keine Aussichten.**
2. **Nimm dich in acht!**
3. **Wir sind derselben Ansicht.**
4. **Du hast angedeutet.**
5. **Ich habe Kaffee mit Schlag (Sahne) gern.**

p. 46, Exercise 15
1. **er**   2. **sie**   3. **ihr**   4. **sie**   5. **es**

p. 46   Ads
pp. 46-47
ANTON Did you not say recently that you want a cat? Listen to this: Beautiful black cat, a neutered, friendly, cuddly, snuggle cat, to give away only to an affectionate animal lover.
SUSIE Look, here is a dog that can talk. He says: Am looking for new home. Am a sweet little St. Bernard, two months old and housebroken. I don't cost much.
ANTON Just wait until he is one year old. He will eat you bankrupt.—But look here. Maybe that's a job for me:
Wanted: Advertising Executive (direct mail advertising). Very good salary, excellent opportunity. Minimum of six years experience. AWC 52-34-81. What do you think, Susie?
SUSIE Sounds good.
ANTON If I don't deceive myself (unless I am mistaken), this is the biggest advertising firm here.
SUSIE I think you see yourself as an executive already.
ANTON We'll see.

p. 47, Exercise 16
1. **Erfahrung**   2. **reden**   3. **Tierfreund**   4. **Katze**
5. **gut**

p. 47, Exercise 17
1. **Der Hund will ein neues Heim.**
2. **Er ist zwei Monate alt.**
3. **Ein führender Werbefachmann wird für Postwurfsendungen gesucht.**
4. **Er frißt Anton bankrott.**
5. **Die beiden sehen sich Inserate in der Zeitung an.**

p. 47, Exercise 18
1. **f**   2. **t**   3. **f**   4. **f**   5. **f**

p. 47, Exercise 19
1. **Er täuscht sich.**
2. **Das wird sich zeigen.**
3. **Wir rasieren uns.**
4. **Sie waschen sich.**
5. **Sie sieht sich.**

p. 47, Exercise 20
1. **sich**   2. **sich**   3. **mich**   4. **dich**   5. **euch**

p. 48   Anton's Acquaintance

ANTON Do you know the man who is standing there? That is an acquaintance whose wife works at our place. He also is the man to whom I owe my present job, the job I don't want anymore.

SUSIE Is that the woman who is so beautiful and whose daughter goes to school with Gretchen, the lady to whom I once lent a jacket that she never returned to me?

ANTON Right. The daughter is the girl who is Gretchen's schoolmate, whose green eyes she envies, and with whom she likes to play tennis. Vicky is a girl that everyone likes.

SUSIE The firms that need advertising executives are mainly in Munich, aren't they?

ANTON You mean the firms whose home offices are in Munich?

SUSIE Yes, the big firms in which one can be promoted quickly.

ANTON Yes, unfortunately. This is true for the organizations that I know.

p. 49   Three Jokes

HERR SCHMIDT (on the phone) Are you going to pay our bill today?

HERR KRAUSE Not yet.

HERR SCHMIDT If you do not pay it now, I'll tell all your creditors that you have paid us.

p. 49

''No, I don't need the job. It has no future for me. The boss's daughter is already married.''

p. 49

''Mr. Schulz, my wife told me to ask you for a raise in salary.''
''Good. I'll ask my wife whether I should give you one.''

p. 49, Exercise 21
1. **der** 2. **deren** 3. **das** 4. **dessen** 5. **dem**
6. **der** 7. **die** 8. **die** 9. **denen** 10. **deren**

p. 50, Exercise 22
1. **Sie lieh ihr eine Jacke.**
2. **Gretchen spielt Tennis mit ihrer Schulkollegin.**
3. **Die Hauptsitze der Werbefirmen sind in München.**
4. **Anton verdankt seine jetzige Stellung einem Bekannten.**
5. **Kristy ist Lehrerin.**

p. 50, Exercise 23
1. **diesen** 2. **dieser** 3. **das** 4. **diese** 5. **dieser**

p. 50, Exercise 24
1. The firm that has its home office in Munich is big.
2. The man whom I know is small.
3. The green eyes that she has are beautiful.
4. The woman who is so beautiful is my friend.
5. The friend to whom I owe my job is Konrad.

p. 50, Exercise 25
1. **Stellung** 2. **Augen** 3. **liebt** 4. **Jacke**
5. **machen kann**

Chapter 6, **p. 51,** Tonight We Are Going to a Restaurant and Then to the Movies

p. 51   One of Us Is Telepathic
pp. 51-52
NORA Nice outside?

KARL A wonderful day.

NORA How was the walk?

KARL Very agreeable. As I walk (was walking) along the street around the corner, I am (was) thinking it would be nice to invite Kristy.

NORA You mean to the restaurant?

KARL Exactly. And then to the movies.

NORA Do you know what? I just called her.

KARL And invited her?

NORA Yes.

KARL But it went through my head only ten minutes ago. One of us must be telepathic.

NORA She is (will be) here at about five. But we (will) have to go without the boy, unfortunately.

KARL Does he still have a fever?

NORA Not much. 37.5 (thirty-seven, five). Mrs. Schulze stays (will stay) with him for the evening.

KARL Too bad. Peter likes to eat out.

NORA To which restaurant shall we go?

KARL Obermayer's, maybe? Or something better (fancier)?

NORA No. Obermayer's is nice and cozy.

p. 52, Exercise 1
1. **durch** 2. **gegen** 3. **ohne** 4. **entlang** 5. **gegen**

p. 52, Exercise 2
1. **Er kann nicht mitkommen, weil er Fieber hat.**
2. **Sie ist gegen fünf Uhr hier.**
3. **Frau Schulze bleibt bei Peter für den Abend.**
4. **Das ist ihm erst vor zehn Minuten durch den Kopf gegangen.**
5. **Sie gehen zu Obermayers Gasthaus.**

p. 52, Exercise 3
1. **angerufen** 2. **telepathisch sein** 3. **essen**
4. **Ecke** 5. **gehen**

p. 53, Exercise 4
1. **Er geht die Straße entlang.**
2. **Ich habe sie gerade angerufen.**
3. **Er muß ohne den Jungen gehen.**
4. **Es ist gegen 7 Uhr.**
5. **Ich kaufe es für ihn.**
6. **Sie kommt um die Ecke.**
7. **Ich bekomme es durch ihn.**

p. 53, Exercise 5
1. Nice outside?
2. It would be nice to invite her.

3. Maybe something better (fancier)?
4. It went through my head.
5. I walk along the street.

p. 53   Obermayer's Restaurant
pp. 53-54
Mr. Obermayer's restaurant is about twenty minutes
away from Mr. Bauer's house. By car this probably
takes only four minutes. But they go on foot. It is in
an old building opposite the Central Cinema. Aside
from this one there are ten other movie theaters in
town, also a municipal theater and a concert hall.
After the meal they want to see the latest Jürgen
Kaiser movie, which has been running at the Central
Cinema for five days. Kristy, the young lady from
America who lives with her cousin Susie, has come
along. They enter the restaurant. Nora and Karl are
regular guests. Herr Obermayer comes toward them
and greets them with a friendly handshake. They sit
down, and he shows them the menu, a large
blackboard on which one can see today's menu.

p. 54, Exercise 6
1. **dem** 2. **dem** 3. **aus einem** 4. **mit der** 5. **der**
6. **dem zum** 7. **einem** 8. **dem**

p. 54, Exercise 7
1. Aside from the Central Cinema there are ten
   others.
2. Mr. Obermayer comes with the menu.
3. They have been regular guests for many years.
4. They go to the restaurant on foot.
5. Opposite the concert hall is the theater.

p. 54, Exercise 8
1. **c** 2. **c** 3. **c** 4. **b** 5. **a**

p. 54, Exercise 9
1. **Sie gehen zu Fuß.**
2. **außer Herrn Obermayers Restaurant**
3. **Das heutige Menu ist auf einer großen Tafel.**
4. **Mit dem Wagen dauert es vier Minuten.**
5. **Sie sind Stammgäste.**

p. 55   The Naughty Cat
pp. 55-56
The waitress comes with a large soup tureen and puts
it on the table at which the guests are sitting. Next to
the tureen she puts a big basket with freshly baked
bread. Mr. Obermayer's beautiful black cat is sitting
under the table. Suddenly she jumps over the chair that
stands between the American girl and Gretchen and
back again under the table. The guests are laughing.
Mr. Obermayer shows up with a frown.

OBERMAYER Excuse me, please. Come here. You
   are very naughty today. (He takes the cat on his
   arm.) Don't you know that you must lie quietly on
   the floor under the table?
KARL Please, it doesn't matter.
GRETCHEN She is so cute.

OBERMAYER She won't bother you anymore. Is the
   soup OK?
ALL Excellent.

Today many tourists are in town. They have come to
   the city to admire the medieval architecture and also
   the statues in front of and behind the church. Over
   the city hangs a wonderful full moon.

pp. 56-57, Exercise 10
1. **die** 2. **der** 3. **den** 4. **der** 5. **die** 6. **dem**
7. **dem** 8. **dem** 9. **das** 10. **das**

p. 57, Exercise 11
1. **Bitte entschuldigen Sie mich.**
2. **Das spielt (doch) keine Rolle.**
3. **Du bist heute sehr schlimm.**
4. **Wir essen frischgebackenes Brot.**
5. **Die Katze sitzt auf dem Boden.**

p. 57, Exercise 12
1. She will not bother you anymore.
2. She walks behind the church.
3. The waitress brings a big basket.
4. The soup is OK.
5. We admire the medieval architecture.

p. 57, Exercise 13
1. **Viele Touristen sind in die Stadt gekommen.**
2. **Die Katze sitzt unter dem Tisch.**
3. **Die Suppe ist auf dem Tisch.**
4. **Die Kellnerin stellt den Korb auf den Tisch.**
5. **Die Statuen sind vor und hinter der Kirche.**

p. 57   A Joke (?)
GUEST Waiter, this soup is cold.
WAITER What do you want me to do? Should I burn
   my fingers?

p. 57   Beef and Eclairs
pp. 57-58
   The guests have ordered boiled beef and, for
dessert, eclairs, and everything tastes very good to
them all. Nora eats spinach instead of boiled potatoes.
Potatoes, she says, make her too fat. In spite of the
large portions they eat up everything. During the
dessert Karl looks at his watch. Because of the movie
they must hurry up, for it starts in ten minutes.

p. 58   Gretchen and Jürgen Kaiser
pp. 58-59
NORA Look at the line!
KRISTY Terrific!
NORA No wonder. Kaiser is the most popular film
   star in Germany.
GRETCHEN He is gorgeous!
KARL Did you take along enough handkerchiefs?
NORA Please, stop it!
KRISTY But it (the line) is moving pretty fast. We
   are (will be) at the ticket window right away.

KARL Four tickets, please; three adults, one for a girl under fourteen. How much is it?

CASHIER Twenty marks, please.
(They enter the theater.)

KRISTY (to Karl) Would you please give me the tickets? For (as) a souvenir of our movie visit?

KARL (He does.) You collect movie tickets? Gretchen collects programs. Especially of films with Jürgen. But you must relinquish the stubs to the usher.

NORA The sweets!

KARL Forgot (them) totally. Nora, be so kind and give Gretchen the money for them. I have only a 100 mark bill with me.

GRETCHEN What shall I buy? Ice cream?

NORA No, that drips. Maybe anise cookies and stuffed dates.
Half an hour later one hears much sighing and blowing of noses in the audience. Nora gives Gretchen a handkerchief.

KARL (to Kristy) Did you like the picture?

KRISTY So-so. And you?

KARL A tearjerker. (to Gretchen) Gretchen?

GRETCHEN He is wonderful!

pp. 59-60, Exercise 14
1. **statt des**   2. **Während der**   3. **Trotz des**
4. **wegen des**

p. 60, Exercise 15
1. **c** 2. **a** 3. **b** 4. **a** 5. **b**

p. 60, Exercise 16
1. **Rindfleisch** 2. **Uhr** 3. **Kinobesuches**
4. **Platzanweiser** 5. **Schmachtfetzen**

p. 60, Exercise 17
1. **Kartoffeln machen Nora dick.**
2. **Hast du genug Taschentücher mitgenommen?**
3. **Karl sagt, der Film ist ein Schmachtfetzen.**
4. **Hör auf damit!**
5. **Unerhört!**
6. **Kein Wunder.**
7. **Wieviel kostet das?**

p. 60, Exercise 18
1. **t** 2. **f** 3. **f** 4. **f** 5. **t**

p. 60, Exercise 19
1. **dem Platzanweiser** 2. **das Programm** 3. **den Touristen** 4. **der Mutter das Brot** 5. **der Schwester die Uhr**

p. 60, Exercise 20
1. **sie ihm** 2. **es ihm** 3. **sie ihnen** 4. **es ihr**
5. **sie ihr**

Chapter 7, **p. 61,** Susie, Nora, and Kristy Go Shopping

p. 61   Family Matters
pp. 61-62
NORA I am in a bad mood . . .

SUSIE What happened?

NORA You are still unmarried, Susie. Family matters . . . he is a nice boy . . .

KRISTY You mean Peter?

NORA Yes. He is a good boy and Gretchen—well, she is a good girl, isn't she? How shall I explain that? Karl and I, we are very happy with the children. You are not bored with my problems? They are basically . . .

SUSIE The best children in the world. You should go out more. Like today. Too much togetherness within the family is bad for the nerves.

p. 62   A New Fur Coat?
SUSIE I have the intention—well, today I'm not going to skimp.

NORA I suppose you have enough money with you, or on your credit card.

KRISTY She received her salary yesterday.

NORA A new fur coat would not be bad.

SALESLADY Today we have a final bargain sale in furs.

KRISTY I hope you have sufficient credit here for the purchase of mink coats. Do they carry mink?

SUSIE Mink, silver fox, beaver—they have everything.

KRISTY But oh, the poor animals! We should protect them, not kill them. We should really wear only fake furs. They're just as beautiful. Don't you think?

NORA That's a bit of an inner conflict for you. But I have very different problems.

p. 63, Exercise 1
1. **ist** 2. **haben** 3. **Bist** 4. **sind** 5. **hat**
6. **habt** 7. **wirst** 8. **wird** 9. **werdet**

p. 63, Exercise 2
1. **Das Warenhaus heißt Brandstätter.**
2. **Nora sollte mehr ausgehen.**
3. **Zu viel Beisammensein ist schlecht für die Nerven.**
4. **Susie hat gestern ihr Gehalt bekommen.**
5. **Brandstätter führt alle Pelze.**

p. 63, Exercise 3
1. **Ich bin mit deinen Problemen nicht gelangweilt.**
2. **Für mich ist das schwer zu verstehen.**
3. **Was ist passiert?**
4. **Ein Nerzmantel wäre nicht schlecht.**
5. **Ich bin schlechter Laune.**

p. 64, Exercise 4
1. **Ihr habt neue Autos.**
2. **Sie werden Ärzte.**
3. **Sie sind schlechter Laune.**
4. **Wir werden böse.**
5. **Werdet ihr es kaufen?**

p. 65   Susie and Her Boss
p. 65

NORA Do you sometimes work on Saturdays, too, Susie?

SUSIE Only when we are very busy and my boss asks me for it (asks me to). Unfortunately he is very talkative. You speak to him, but he doesn't listen; he talks and talks without interruption. But enough of business.

NORA Do you like to dance?

SUSIE Yes, very (much). And Anton dances very well, as you know.

NORA Maybe we can go out together again.

SUSIE That would be nice.—Where is Kristy?

NORA In the leather goods department.

SUSIE I'd like to go there, too. So we'll meet later.

p. 66   Kristy and Susie Do Their Shopping.

Susie meets Kristy who wants to bring something back to her mother in America.

KRISTY Mom still carries her old pocketbook. I believe she needs a new one. Maybe this one here, made of imitation leather.

SUSIE Do you talk with her on the telephone? That is much cheaper now.

KRISTY No, but I write her every week.—Will you go with me to the cosmetics department? I need a bottle of cologne.

SUSIE I must buy myself a new (tailored) suit. Don't you think that a suit suits me better than a dress?

KRISTY Exactly. Do you mind if I come along?

p. 66, Exercise 5
1. **a.**   2. **c.**   3. **a.**   4. **b.**   5. **c.**

p. 66, Exercise 6
1. **tanzt**   2. **badet**   3. **Arbeitest**   4. **Gib**
5. **trägt**

p. 66, Exercise 7
1. **Du triffst ihn später.**
2. **Du schläfst während des Tages.**
3. **Das Mädchen läuft schnell.**
4. **Der Junge hilft mir.**
5. **Sprich mit ihm!**

p. 66, Exercise 8
1. **Wir sind sehr beschäftigt.**
2. **Sie gehen zusammen aus.**
3. **Er spricht ohne Unterbrechung.**
4. **Er hört mir nicht zu.**
5. **Hast du (Haben Sie) was dagegen?**

p. 66   "Devil's Brat"
p. 67
KRISTY Does Peter collect stamps? Most boys do.

NORA Of course. We all collect something. Karl collects old beer bottles. I collect coins. Especially silver coins. That is supposedly a good investment.

KRISTY What do you advise me to buy for my friend in America?

NORA Something typically German? Maybe leather shorts?

KRISTY Good idea.

NORA Meantime I (I'll) go to Computer World. What is the latest in software for computer games?

SALESLADY "Devil's Brat" is by far the biggest seller of the season. It gave short shrift to the competition. "Do you think I am stupid enough to still be playing Pac-Man?" my boy scolds me. " 'Devil's Brat,' he deals with his enemies one after the other and burns them up with flame throwers. How come you don't know that?"

NORA Your son must be a great joy to you.

SALESLADY He does his utmost (best).

NORA Does he also read something sometimes?

SALESLADY Very rarely. But he knows that he has to do his homework first; then he can play war.

NORA Give me one "Devil's Brat."

p. 68, Exercise 9
1. **Er sammelt Briefmarken.**
2. **Er schilt Nora.**
3. **Er weiß alles.**
4. **Was tut er heute?**
5. **Er nimmt das Buch.**
6. **Was hält er in der Hand?**
7. **Was rät er mir?**
8. **Er liest viel.**

p. 68, Exercise 10
1. **L/Ü**   2. **H/Ö**   3. **E/P/L**   4. **W/Y/E**   5. **N/E/I**

p. 68, Exercise 11
1. **Das ist eine gute Kapitalanlage.**
2. **Lederhosen sind typisch deutsch.**
3. **Das ist der größte Verkaufsschlager der Saison.**
4. **Die Konkurrenz ist sehr stark.**
5. **Er tut sein möglichstes.**

p. 68, Exercise 12
1. **c**   2. **a**   3. **b**   4. **a**   5. **c**

p. 69   Nora's Plans

NORA Did you make all your purchases?

KRISTY Pretty much.

SUSIE I ran short of money in doing so. No mink, but a charm for Anton.

NORA Let me see.

SUSIE I don't have it yet. Because of the initials. A golden magical pyramid to wear around the neck.

KRISTY That sounds super.

NORA He'll be very glad (pleased). Birthday?

SUSIE Yes. Are you going to buy new furniture?

NORA Possibly. I have had mine for thirteen years.

KRISTY How long have you been living here?

NORA I was born here.

KRISTY My parents have been living in America for thirty years and have moved five times.

NORA I need new furniture when we move. The present house is too small. Peter has been sleeping in the living room for two years already. And who knows?

SUSIE Is that an announcement?

NORA Maybe we'll get an addition to the family.

SUSIE, KRISTY We congratulate (you).

p. 70, Exercise 13
1. **Wir leben seit zwanzig Jahren in Deutschland.**
2. **Er ist seit zwei Stunden hier.**
3. **Sie arbeitet seit drei Monaten.**
4. **Ich bin in New York geboren.**
5. **Wer weiß?**

p. 70, Exercise 14
1. **b**   2. **a**   3. **b**   4. **a**   5. **c**

p. 70, Exercise 15
1. I have been living here for ten years.
2. Is that an announcement?
3. That is unthinkable.
4. Possibly.
5. Pretty much.

p. 70, Exercise 16
1. **f**   2. **t**   3. **f**   4. **f**   5. **t**

p. 70, Exercise 17
1. **Nora ist in Deutschland geboren.**
2. **Kristys Eltern leben in Amerika.**
3. **Nora wohnt in ihrem Haus seit dreizehn Jahren.**
4. **Peter schläft seit zwei Jahren im Wohnzimmer.**
5. **Anton trägt bald ein Amulett um den Hals.**

Chapter 8, **p. 71,** Anton Finds a New Job

p. 71   The Interview
pp. 71-72

ANTON Susie, how are you?—Were you at the movies yesterday? Was it nice?—Do you have a few minutes? Good. Well, as you know, I didn't get the job about which we talked in the café. I was (got) there too late. But I have another one. It happened like this . . .

SCHELLING Please take a seat, Mr. Gruber. You sent us an application ten days ago. I showed the letter to my partner, and he said, "Let him come."

ANTON I appreciate that, Mr. Schelling.

SCHELLING How long did you work for your previous firm?

ANTON Seven years. I still work there. But I gave notice and assured my boss at the same time that I (would) remain until he finds someone else.

SCHELLING Very decent. Why did you give notice?

ANTON I didn't have any opportunity there to be creatively active.

SCHELLING What do you mean by that?

ANTON You know the firm.

SCHELLING Ballyhoo for worthless products.

ANTON I did this ballyhoo.

SCHELLING I think you are an idealist.

ANTON I became a hack writer. But I can do better.

SCHELLING I think you are right.

pp. 72-73, Exercise 1
1. **gewesen**   2. **bekommen**   3. **geschickt**
4. **gemacht**   5. **geworden**   6. **gearbeitet**
7. **gekündigt**

p. 73, Exercise 2
1. **b**   2. **a**   3. **b**   4. **c**   5. **a**

p. 73, Exercise 3
1. **Hast du ein paar Minuten gehabt?**
2. **Ich habe einen Job gekriegt.**
3. **Ich habe ihm gekündigt.**
4. **Er hat sehr viel gearbeitet.**
5. **Er hat ihm das Schreiben gezeigt.**

p. 73, Exercise 4
1. **Anton hat sieben Jahre für seine frühere Firma gearbeitet.**
2. **Er kündigt, weil er dort keine Aussichten hat.**
3. **Herr Schelling nennt ihn einen Idealisten.**
4. **Susie ist gestern im Kino gewesen.**
5. **Anton hat das Schreiben vor zehn Tagen geschickt.**

p. 73, Exercise 5
1. **Marktschreierische Reklame**
2. **Laß (Lassen Sie) ihn kommen.**
3. **Was meinen Sie damit?**
4. **Sie sind ein Idealist.**
5. **Susie, wie geht's?**

p. 73   The Catchy First Line
p. 74

It was just after his final high school exam when Anton left Vienna in order to look for a job in Germany. He went to Munich University and studied economics. Then he decided to move to a smaller town. There he found a job with an advertising agency. He always had a talent for writing, and that, of course, helped him. First they asked him to compose commercials for radio, texts for jingles, and newspaper ads. "At that time I wrote more ads than you find in ten Sunday editions," he once confessed to Susie. He knew that a catchy first line is everything. Often he stayed in the office until midnight, ate, drank and slept in the office, lost weight, studied the first lines and jingles of the competition, then tried and sang his own.

p. 76, Exercise 6
1. **Anton fand einen neuen Job.**
2. **Damals schrieb er viele Briefe.**
3. **Er blieb bis Mitternacht im Büro.**
4. **Er arbeitete dort lange.**

5. **Dann verließ er Wien.**
6. **Das Talent fürs Schreiben half ihm.**
7. **Er bat Susie darum.**
8. **Manchmal aß er im Büro.**
9. **Er trank meistens Wasser.**
10. **Das Kind sang gern.**

p. 76, Exercise 7
1. **empfohlen**   2. **zerrissen**   3. **verloren**
4. **verfaßt**   5. **probiert**

p. 76, Exercise 8
1. **Anton verließ Wien (München).**
2. **In Deutschland suchte er einen Job.**
3. **Er studierte Volkswirtschaftslehre in München.**
4. **Er verfaßte Werbespots und musikalisches Reimgeklingel (Jingles) mehr als alles andere.**
5. **Sein Talent fürs Schreiben half ihm dabei.**

p. 76, Exercise 9
1. **Büro**   2. **übersiedeln**   3. **Werbeagentur**
4. **Schreiben**   5. **geschrieben (verfaßt)**

p. 76   I have flown (I flew), I have counted
(I counted).

pp. 76-77
Last week Anton flew to Bonn to a friend who has a sleeping problem.
"Yesterday I slept very badly again; I don't know what to do."
"Why don't you count sheep?" Anton suggests.
"That, too, I tried. I imagined that I raised sheep. In the end there were 6,000; they grew very fast, more and more of them came, ran back and forth, and jumped around, and I counted them all. Then I sheared them all. Finally I made 6,000 coats from the wool and counted them again. But then I had a horrible problem. It occurred to me that I needed linings for the 6,000 coats. It went around in my head so that I could not fall asleep.

p. 77, Exercise 10
1. **haben**   2. **ist**   3. **sind**   4. **habt**   5. **sind**

p. 78, Exercise 11
1. **Vorige Woche ist Anton nach Bonn geflogen.**
2. **Er hat 6 000 Schafe gezählt.**
3. **Er hat Mäntel aus der Wolle gemacht.**
4. **Das Problem war, daß er kein Futter hatte.**

p. 78, Exercise 12
1. **4**   2. **6**   3. **5**   4. **1**   5. **2**   6. **3**

p. 78, Exercise 13
1. **Die Schafe sind sehr schnell gewachsen.**
2. **Es ist mir eingefallen (es fiel mir ein).**
3. **Sie sind hin und her gelaufen.**
4. **Ich machte 6 000 Mäntel.**
5. **Ich hatte ein gräßliches Problem.**

p. 78   Big Shot Anton

ANTON Whether I am satisfied with my present job? Very. I will probably stay here several years. Schelling will give me a raise in salary in six months. In one or two years I (will) get a partnership perhaps. What do you say? A big shot? You bet. Are you then going to treat me with more respect? Seriously, it looks good. — What are you doing today? I (will) pick you up. Dinner and dancing. Will you put on your red evening gown? — You must get up early tomorrow? — We are (will be) home before twelve. That's probably the new client. Servus.

p. 79, Exercise 14
1. **f**   2. **t**   3. **f**   4. **f**   5. **t**

p. 79, Exercise 15
1. **c**   2. **b**   3. **a**   4. **c**

p. 79, Exercise 16
1. **Schelling wird ihm eine Gehaltsaufbesserung geben.**
2. **Bald bekommt er vielleicht eine Teilhaberschaft.**
3. **Susie wird sich ihr Abendkleid anziehen.**
4. **Abends gehen sie essen und tanzen.**
5. **Anton ist mit seinem Job sehr zufrieden.**

p. 79, Exercise 17
1. **Anton ist mit seinem jetzigen Job zufrieden.**
2. **Sie wird ihn mit mehr Respekt behandeln.**
3. **Er wird eine Gehaltserhöhung bekommen.**
4. **Im Ernst, es sieht gut aus.**
5. **Das wird der neue Klient sein.**

p. 79, Exercise 18
1. **Anton wird wahrscheinlich einige Jahre bei Schelling & Holz bleiben.**
2. **Susie wird sich abends ihr rotes Abendkleid anziehen.**
3. **In zwei Jahren bekommt Anton vielleicht eine Teilhaberschaft.**
4. **In sechs Monaten bekommt er vielleicht eine Gehaltsaufbesserung.**
5. **Sie werden vor zwölf wieder zu Hause sein.**

Chapter 9. **p. 80,** Starting the Day at the Bauers
A Flat Tire on the Way Home

p. 80   Nora and the Scales
p. 81
Karl's day starts very early. He gets up, washes, shaves himself, and is dressed (in no time), and it is not even seven o'clock. Then he sits down at the breakfast table. Nora has prepared breakfast and sits down with him.

NORA I'm surprised that you need so little sleep.
KARL Some people have enough with six hours.
NORA But you eat so little. Spread some honey on the bread.
KARL No, thanks. Too many calories.

NORA Last year, I remember, you caught a cold at this time. Are you taking your vitamins?

KARL Don't worry, darling. I feel strong and healthy. But if I lose control of myself, I gain weight right away.

NORA I admire your self-discipline. I just stepped on the scales. . .

KARL And you have a few pounds too many?

NORA No, my weight is normal. But according to the table (chart) I should be ten centimeters taller.

p. 81, Exercise 1
1. **erinnert sich**   2. **erkältet sich**   3. **Fühlst du dich**   4. **Entschuldige mich**   5. **unterhalten uns**

p. 81, Exercise 2
1. **Nora bereitet das Frühstück.**
2. **Nora wundert sich, daß Karl so wenig Schlaf braucht.**
3. **Karl streicht sich wegen der Kalorien keinen Honig aufs Brot.**
4. **Nora bewundert seine Selbstdisziplin.**
5. **Karl fragt seine Frau, „Hast du ein paar Pfund zu viel?"**

p. 82, Exercise 3
1. **f** 2. **f** 3. **t** 4. **t** 5. **f**

p. 82, Exercise 4
1. It is not even seven.
2. Nora sits down with him.
3. At this time (of year) you catch cold.
4. I just stepped on the scales.
5. According to the table (chart) my weight is normal.

p. 82, Exercise 5
1. **Schlaf** 2. **Vitamine** 3. **ihm** 4. **Frühstück**
5. **gestiegen** 6. **normal**

p. 82   Peter and the Dentist

The children are awake now and want their breakfast. Nora asks them the same (thing) each morning: (to Peter) "Did you brush your teeth?" (to Gretchen) "Did you brush your hair?"
Yesterday Peter complained about a toothache.
"Does the tooth still hurt you, Peter?"
"Yes, a little."
"But not enough to stay home?"
"Unfortunately not."
"Karl," says Nora, "please get me the aspirin bottle. I (will) make a note to myself that I call the dentist (to call the dentist). No protest, Peter? Imagine, Karl; Peter will go to the dentist without wailing (complaining)."

p. 83, Exercise 6
1. **b** 2. **a** 3. **c** 4. **a** 5. **b**

p. 83, Exercise 7
1. **b** 2. **b** 3. **a** 4. **b** 5. **b**

p. 83, Exercise 8
1. **Nora fragt jedes Kind dasselbe.**
2. **Hast du dir das Haar gebürstet?**
3. **Hast du Zahnweh?**
4. **Peter will nicht zu Hause bleiben.**
5. **Geh, wasch dir die Hände.**

p. 83, Exercise 9
1. **wach** 2. **Aspirinbüchse** 3. **bleiben**
4. **Zahnweh** 5. **Notiz**

p. 83, Exercise 10
1. **Hast du dir das Haar gebürstet?**
2. **Karl holt die Aspirinbüchse.**
3. **Peter hat sich über Zahnweh beklagt.**
4. **Der Zahn tut ihm nur ein bißchen weh.**
5. **Sie macht sich eine Notiz.**

p. 84   The Flat Tire
p. 84-85

KARL (is driving to the service station on the way home) Will you please look at the right front tire? I think I have a flat tire.

SERVICE STATION ATTENDANT Looks that way. We have to change it. You can take a seat inside meanwhile. There is coffee and cookies.

KARL (inside)

MANAGER How are you, Mr. Bauer?

KARL Except for the flat tire, not bad. And you?

MANAGER Cannot complain. May I offer you a cigar?

KARL No, thanks. I am not supposed to smoke. Stomach ulcers.

MANAGER No wonder, nowadays. Is you car otherwise OK? Shall we check it? Shock absorbers? He now has it on the hydraulic platform (lift).

KARL Please.

MANAGER (inspecting them) Shock absorbers are OK. But we have to fasten the exhaust pipe; it wobbles. Wouldn't you like more coffee?

KARL I am not supposed to drink coffee either. When your man has finished, he can check the battery, also the oil and the water in the radiator.

MANAGER Very good.

p. 85, Exercise 11
1. **kann** 2. **darfst** 3. **mag** 4. **will** 5. **soll (sollen)** 6. **müßt**

p. 85, Exercise 12
1. **Stoßdämpfer** 2. **Kühler** 3. **Hebebühne**
4. **Panne** 5. **Auspuffrohr**

p. 85, Exercise 13
1. **Karl will keine Zigarre, weil er Magengeschwüre hat.**
2. **Der rechte Vorderreifen hat die Panne.**
3. **Der Tankwart soll die Stoßdämpfer überprüfen.**
4. **Das Wasser in einem Auto ist im Kühler.**
5. **Er inspiziert die Stoßdämpfer auf der Hebebühne.**

p. 85, Exercise 14
1. Karl has a flat tire.
2. He must fasten the exhaust pipe.
3. May I offer you a cigarette?
4. Please check the water in the radiator.
5. Isn't he supposed to look at the shock absorbers?
6. Cannot complain.
7. Except for the stomach ulcers, not bad
8. Looks like it.

p. 86, Exercise 15
1. **f** 2. **f** 3. **f** 4. **t** 5. **t**

p. 86   Everything's OK.
pp. 86-87
ATTENDANT Everything's OK, Mr. Bauer. Anything else?

KARL Did you have to replace the exhaust valve?

ATTENDANT No, that was not necessary.

KARL Did you want to lubricate the car?

ATTENDANT Today I was not able to work on it. But I recommend lubrication and an oil change for next week. I'll wash the windshield. Do you need gas?

KARL I had the tank filled up only the day before yesterday. Shall I leave the car here for the oil change next week?

ATTENDANT As you wish, Mr. Bauer. The whole thing takes half an hour if nobody is here before you.—I see a customer coming. Excuse me, please.

KARL May I use your phone?

MANAGER By all means.

KARL Nora? How are you feeling? I had a flat tire.—I hear Gretchen singing; yes, with the radio. Are you helping Peter to write the (his) English essay? Do you need anything? Cold cuts, butter, and cheese? Then I won't be able to come home before six. See you.

p. 87, Exercise 16
1. **Mußten Sie das Auspuffrohr ersetzen?**
2. **Wollte er den Wagen schmieren?**
3. **Ließest du den Tank anfüllen?**
4. **Hörte sie Gretchen sprechen?**
5. **Konnte er nach Hause kommen?**

p. 87, Exercise 17
1. **a** 2. **c** 3. **b** 4. **a** 5. **c**

p. 88, Exercise 18
1. **4** 2. **5** 3. **6** 4. **3** 5. **1** 6. **2**

p. 88, Exercise 19
1. **Der Tankwart wird den Wagen nächste Woche schmieren.**
2. **Karl hat den Tank anfüllen lassen, weil er Benzin gebraucht hat.**
3. **Der Tankwart entschuldigt sich, weil er einen Kunden kommen sieht.**

4. **Peter muß einen englischen Aufsatz schreiben.**
5. **Nora braucht kalten Aufschnitt, Butter und Käse fürs Abendessen.**

p. 88   A Surprise?
pp. 88-89
Karl has taken care of his purchases and is at home again. Nora is in the kitchen and is busy with the preparation of dinner. Karl has made himself comfortable and wants to read the evening paper.

KARL Peter, where is the paper?

PETER I believe it still lies (is) outside.

KARL Go and get it, please. Where is Gretchen?

PETER In her room.

KARL Tell her to come here.

PETER Right away.—Gretchen! Come here.—She doesn't hear me.

KARL Call her once more. Or look (find out) what she is doing. Tell her I want to speak with her.

PETER (into Gretchen's room; they both come out)

KARL Come here, children. I have to ask you something.

GRETCHEN A surprise?

KARL Maybe. Get your mother and ask her to come here.

GRETCHEN Mom! A surprise! Come quickly!

NORA What happened?

KARL Sit down, all of you. As you know, I have just come from the service station. A flat tire, nothing special. But lately there is always something the matter with the car. It is pretty old already. Say, Nora, shall we not buy a new one?

NORA Wait a minute. How long actually do we have it (have we actually had it)?

KARL About ten years.

NORA But basically it is still OK?

KARL Yes—it rattles a little . . .

NORA Is that all?

KARL And sometimes it doesn't start right away. . .

PETER Hooray! A new car!

NORA Peter, don't be childish. (to both children) Go and wash your hands. The meal is (will be) ready right away. And open the windows, it is very warm in here. (to Karl) Let's drive into the foothills on Sunday, and let's see if the old coach is still of any use. How much is a new one?

KARL More than we can afford at the present time. Give me the newspaper. Let's look at the ads. Aha! Well, a used one. . .

NORA No, don't. Better to save longer and then buy a new one.

KARL You are right.

p. 90, Exercise 20
1. **hol** 2. **bitte sie** 3. **öffne** 4. **Sag mir** 5. **sei nicht**

p. 90, Exercise 21
1. **Bitte gib mir die Zeitung!**
2. **Wascht euch die Hände!**
3. **Wart einmal!**
4. **Sag ihr herzukommen.**
5. **Gretchen, öffne die Tür!**

p. 90, Exercise 22
1. **Karl will die Zeitung lesen, wenn er nach Hause kommt.**
2. **Gretchen ist in ihrem Zimmer.**
3. **Karl will einen neuen Wagen kaufen.**
4. **Es ist immer etwas anderes los mit dem Wagen.**
5. **Nora nennt ihn die alte Karosse.**

p. 90, Exercise 23
1. **b** 2. **a** 3. **b** 4. **b** 5. **a**

p. 90, Exercise 24
1. **f** 2. **f** 3. **t** 4. **f** 5. **t**

p. 90   The Driver's Test
pp. 90-91

NEIGHBOR I am still all excited. Just passed my exam (test).

KARL I congratulate you. Please, take a seat.

NEIGHBOR You know, that much ordering-about I haven't experienced in a long time.

KARL What are you talking about?

NEIGHBOR About my driver's test. Please, excuse me, I didn't want to bother you with my affairs.

KARL No, tell me.

NEIGHBOR Well. It starts with: Fasten the (your) seat belt, please. Drive to the left, drive to the right. Look into the rearview mirror. Wait for the streetcar; it always has the right of way. Turn around here. Not so fast. Step on the brakes. Don't let the clutch slip. Toward the end he became quite curt: Slow down. Stop. Park. Get out.

p. 92, Exercise 25
1. **Ein Nachbar kommt zur Tür.**
2. **Der Nachbar hat seine Führerscheinprüfung gerade bestanden.**
3. **Es fängt an mit "Bitte anschnallen"!**
4. **Die Straßenbahn hat immer das Vorrecht.**
5. **Das letzte Kommando (Der letzte Befehl) des Prüfers war „Aussteigen!"**

p. 92, Exercise 26
1. I just passed the driver's test.
2. That I have not experienced in a long time.
3. I don't want to bother you with my affairs.
4. Look into the rearview mirror.
5. Don't let the clutch slip.

p. 92, Exercise 27
1. **f** 2. **t** 3. **f** 4. **t** 5. **f**

p. 92, Exercise 28
1. **4** 2. **6** 3. **1** 4. **2** 5. **3** 6. **5**

p. 92, Exercise 29
1. **aufgeregt** 2. **erlebt** 3. **belästigen**
4. **Kupplung** 5. **Bremse**

Chapter 10, **p. 93,** The Bauer Family Wants to Take a Vacation

p. 93   The Sunny South
pp. 93-94

Until now the Bauer family has spent its vacations mostly at the North Sea or in Scandinavia, mainly because they had to leave at the beginning of August at a time when it is very hot in the south of Europe. This time Karl had to stay in town for business reasons during the summer, and they (the Bauers) have vacation plans for the fall.

Today Nora goes out and comes home with a bunch of travel folders that describe the scenic wonders of southern Europe. The weather at home is gloomy, rainy, and cold, and the pictures with the shining sun and the blue sky of the Riviera are irresistible.

Does she sometimes also think back to the unavoidable accompanying circumstances of a stay in the sunny South? She walks back and forth in the room and remembers the sunburn in Crete and the water in Spain. "I advise you against drinking from the faucet," a friend had warned her. "And wash off the fruit before you eat it." But the children paid no attention, and the consequences were catastrophic. "Take along your sunglasses; the light is very bright." The sunglasses did not come off their noses, she saw to that.

p. 95, Exercise 1
1. **Er kommt zurück.**
2. **Sie geht weg.**
3. **Wir gehen auf und ab.**
4. **Er ißt es auf.**
5. **Sie gibt viel Geld aus.**

p. 95, Exercise 2
1. **Kommst du mit? (Kommen Sie mit?)**
2. **Wann holt er uns ab?**
3. **Wann fängt es an?**
4. **Gehst du zurück? (Gehen Sie zurück?)**
5. **Rätst du ihr davon ab? (Raten Sie ihr davon ab?)**

p. 95, Exercise 3
1. **Die Familie Bauer hat bisher ihre Ferien an der Nordsee oder in Skandinavien verbracht.**
2. **Sie ging nicht nach Südeuropa, weil es dort zu heiß war.**
3. **Karl mußte während des Sommers geschäftshalber in der Stadt bleiben.**
4. **Nora bringt heute Reisebroschüren mit.**
5. **Das Herbstwetter in Deutschland ist meistens trüb, regnerisch und kalt.**
6. **Eine Freundin hat sie vor dem Wasser gewarnt.**
7. **Die Folgen waren katastrophal für die Kinder.**
8. **Man soll Sonnenbrillen mitnehmen, weil das Licht sehr grell ist.**

p. 95, Exercise 4
1. **a**   2. **c**   3. **a**   4. **b**   5. **a**

p. 95, Exercise 5
1. **t**   2. **f**   3. **t**   4. **t**   5. **f**

p. 96   Hotel with Bedbugs
Nora remembers the splendid Greek island with the fabulous sunset and the greedy bedbugs that drew a liter of blood from her. She arrives; everything looks wonderful. She says, ''Karl, it is marvelous here; I won't leave for a month.'' Then she falls asleep, wakes up, and everything is different.

Has she forgotten that already? What does she have in mind?

On the other hand, that is (was) long ago. Today Karl earns much more. They can afford a first-class hotel where things like that do not happen. They have two cars in the garage. One of them Karl will finish paying for this year; the other he will pay off within a year. Maybe they fly away (will fly somewhere) in November when the weather is miserable. Maybe they (will) hold a family conference about it today.

p. 97, Exercise 6
1. **Nora erinnert sich an den schönen Sonnenuntergang.**
2. **Die Wanzen zapfen ihr Blut ab.**
3. **Sie schläft glücklich ein.**
4. **Vielleicht fliegen sie im November fort.**
5. **Karl bezahlt den anderen Wagen innerhalb eines Jahres ab.**
6. **In einem erstklassigen Hotel passiert das nicht.**
7. **Was hat sie vor?**

p. 97, Exercise 7
1. They can afford a first-class hotel.
2. The greedy bedbugs draw blood from her.
3. She wakes up and everything is different.
4. I won't leave for a month.
5. Today we hold a family conference.

p. 97, Exercise 8
1. **f**   2. **t**   3. **t**   4. **t**   5. **f**

p. 97, Exercise 9
1. **c**   2. **a**   3. **b**   4. **a**   5. **b**

p. 97, Exercise 10
1. **Heuer**   2. **Insel**   3. **anders**   4. **ausbezahlen**
5. **Wanzen**

p. 97   Where to?
pp. 97-99

KARL Well, you have visited the travel agency and have practically ransacked it. All these brochures!

NORA Look at the pictures of Mallorca. A dream!

GRETCHEN And this one, Mom: "Come back to Sorrento!"

KARL I don't want to go back there. Mosquitoes as big as grasshoppers.

GRETCHEN But it is so romantic.

PETER Look, Dad, here is a picture of a stewardess

who says: "Come along to Va-raz-din." Where is that, Daddy?

KARL In Croatia; we've never been there.

NORA But there's a war going on there. I'm afraid.

KARL There have already been so many wars in the Balkans, the "powder keg of Europe." The murder in Sarajevo of the heir to the Austrian throne, Archduke Franz Ferdinand, and his wife set off World War I. But in some parts of Croatia there is no war now. We could live dangerously and maybe risk it.

NORA Oh, no! Do think of the children!

GRETCHEN Why don't we go to Japan, Australia, or California?

KARL Too expensive! Too far!

PETER How about Egypt, Israel, or Turkey?

NORA Too much unrest!

GRETCHEN Here are beautiful pictures of Lake Balaton in Hungary.

KARL We don't know Hungary yet.

NORA I totally forgot to tell you, Karl, the Ribars like Hungary very much. They've already been there three times.

KARL I confess, it tempts me more than Italy, Greece, or Spain, which we already know. I'm already thinking of Lake Balaton, of the puszta (plain) and paprika, of Tokay wine and gypsy songs. Varazdin isn't far from Hungary. "Come along to Varazdin" is a beautiful song from the operetta *Countess Maritza*. If there's no war, maybe we could take a side trip there.

NORA We pity the victims of the war, especially the children, and the many refugees and expellees. Germany has taken in many of them. Let us hope that there will soon be peace in the Balkans.

KARL Well then, let's go to Hungary. I'll order the plane tickets. We can easily cancel them if we change our minds. Or we can sell them to somebody else. Maybe we'll travel with the Ribars.

NORA She is a very nice person.

KARL And he is a funny guy. I always have a good time with him. Why don't we get together with them?

NORA Good idea!

KARL His family is originally from Hungary. If we don't understand something, he'll translate it for us.

NORA Excellent.

KARL Good. Then I'll phone him tomorrow.

GRETCHEN Look at the beautiful pictures, Daddy. Lake Balaton and the mountains.

KARL Yes, and the crazy people who climb around in the burning sun with their backpacks. I prefer to lie down and go out in the evening when it's cool.

p. 100, Exercise 11
1. **Ich raube das Reisebüro aus.**
2. **Schauen Sie sich diese schönen Bilder an.**
3. **Ich gestehe, es reizt mich nicht.**
4. **Warum bestellen Sie nicht die Flugkarten?**
5. **Er kann es für uns übersetzen.**
6. **Ich lege mich lieber jetzt nieder.**

7. **Ich unterhalte mich oft mit ihm.**
8. **Er hat es sich anders überlegt.**
9. **Hast du seinen Geburtstag vergessen?**
10. **Ich übersetze es für ihn.**

p. 100, Exercise 12
1. **In Sorrent waren die Stechmücken so groß wie Heuschrecken.**
2. **Die Ribars waren schon dreimal in Ungarn.**
3. **Eine Stewardeß sagt, «Komm mit nach Warasdin.»**
4. **Sie können die Flugkarten ohne weiteres annulieren.**
5. **Die verrückten Leute klettern mit ihren Rucksäcken in der glühenden Sonne herum.**
6. **Karl denkt an Tokaierwein, wenn er an Ungarn denkt.**
7. **Die Ermordung des österreichischen Thronfolgers hat den ersten Weltkrieg ausgelöst.**

p. 100, Exercise 13
1. **Ungarn**   2. **Heuschrecken**   3. **annulieren**
4. **traumhaft** 5. **Stewardeß**

p. 100, Exercise 14
1. **c** 2. **b** 3. **c** 4. **a** 5. **a**

p. 101, Exercise 15
1. I confess that tempts me.
2. Why don't you order them?
3. I forgot to tell it to you.
4. Did you change your mind?
5. He climbs around there like crazy.

Chapter 11, **p. 102** Peter Has a Pupil

p. 102   Introduction: Little Tim
pp. 102-103

Gretchen and Peter have been receiving pocket money from their parents from an early age—amounts with which they are to make do until the end of each week. Also, they started early on to earn some money themselves. Gretchen works as a babysitter and occasionally helps her father in the business. Peter works as a tutor for the children of American officers who are stationed at the neighboring military base.

Tim, nine years old, is one of the children that Peter tutors. The little boy has been in Germany now for two years and is generally a good student even though weak in arithmetic. His German is fluent, and he speaks almost without an accent.

His father takes him to Peter's house twice a week, and the children have become friends. Everybody likes Tim; he is a very nice little guy.

He is very good-natured and well-behaved. Unfortunately, he has one big shortcoming; he eats too much and everything pell-mell and awfully fast. Chocolate is his great passion, also sugar candy of which he always carries a supply in his pocket which gets all sticky from it.

p. 103, Exercise 1
1. **Kandiszucker** 2. **Taschengeld** 3. **Babysitter**
4. **Zögling** 5. **Offiziere**

p. 103, Exercise 2
1. **f** 2. **t** 3. **t** 4. **t** 5. **f**

p. 103, Exercise 3
1. **Peter hilft Tim zweimal wöchentlich nach.**
2. **Tim ist etwas schwach im Rechnen.**
3. **Tims Vater ist in dem benachbarten militärischen Standort wohnhaft.**
4. **Tim ist ein netter, kleiner Kerl.**
5. **Er trägt einen Vorrat Kandiszucker in der Tasche.**

p. 103, Exercise 4
1. **b** 2. **c** 3. **a** 4. **b** 5. **a**

p. 103, Exercise 5
1. **Peter arbeitet als Hauslehrer.**
2. **Er hilft Tim nach.**
3. **Tim spricht Deutsch beinahe akzentfrei.**
4. **Tims große Leidenschaft ist Schokolade.**
5. **Er trägt den Kandiszucker in der Tasche.**

p. 104   Tim Counts in German
pp. 104-105

The so-called cardinal numbers have never posed any difficulties for Tim. He knew them very well two weeks after his arrival in Germany.

Even a number like 987,654 is, he knows, written in *one* word:

With this he had a lot of fun.

He has never quite understood why one doesn't read the number 53 as fifty-three—as it is in English—instead of three and fifty. Also the way in which one writes certain numbers, as 1, not 1, and 7, not 7, was foreign to him.

Then, of course, there are the really big numbers like

1,000,000	a million
1,000,000,000	a "milliard," and
1,000,000,000,000	a "billion"

The American billion is the same as the German "milliard"; the American trillion equals the German billion. Why is that different from one language to the other?

If Tim doesn't have a watch with him, he'll perhaps ask someone: What time is it? The answer usually is: It is eight o'clock, or eleven o'clock, or one o'clock, or whatever. But one can also skip the o'clock: It is eight, or eleven, or one.

In his German textbook in America Tim (has) learned that 9:15 means quarter or one quarter past nine, and 9:45 quarter before ten. But he now lives in Southern Germany, and there one rather says (is more likely to say) "quarter ten" and "three quarter ten." At 9:30 it is always "half ten," to be sure. Of course, one can also say 9:15 or 9:45, or also: It is fifteen (minutes) past nine, or fifteen (minutes) before ten. When it is 9:37, it also means (you can also say) seven minutes past half ten, and at 9:25, five minutes before half ten.

He knows that people are using the twenty-four-hour system (train time) more and more now; for example:

The airplane arrives at 21:50, i.e., at 9:50 P.M.

The train departs at 5:10, i.e., at 5:10 A.M.

p. 105, Exercise 6
1. **acht Uhr dreißig**   2. **neunzehn Uhr vierzig**
3. **vierzehn Uhr zehn**   4. **neunzehn Uhr fünfzehn**
5. **neun Uhr dreißig**   6. **fünfzehn Uhr fünf**
7. **siebzehn Uhr achtundvierzig**
8. **zehn Uhr fünfzehn**
9. **dreiundzwanzig Uhr**

p. 105, Exercise 7
1. **dreihundertsiebenundachtzig**
2. **neunhundertfünfundzwanzig**   3. **eintausendelf**
4. **zwölfhundertachtundvierzig**
5. **siebzehntausendvierhundertneununddreißig**

p. 106   More about Tim
p. 107 (Joke)   The Good Luck of the Cat
"Father," he said, "come quickly! In the dining room there is a big black cat."

"Don't worry," replied his father. "A black cat means luck."

"She has it, Daddy," replied Tim. "She just finished your meal."

pp. 107-108 Tim Likes Peter Very Much
Wednesdays Tim comes to Peter at three P.M., and Sundays at nine A.M. Last time he came at ten; his mother forgot to wake him. Otherwise he is very much on time. Peter does not like to work on Saturdays. In the morning he is in school, like his pupil, and in the afternoon he does his assignments. One Wednesday Tim came home from school and heard that Peter was ill. "This afternoon you don't have a lesson," his mother told him. "Maybe again the day after tomorrow. Peter didn't feel well the day before yesterday. During the day he is OK, but in the evening he has some fever. That can continue this way for days." Tim was very sad about it, for he likes Peter very much.

p. 108, Exercise 8
1. **Der andere Name für Samstag ist Sonnabend.**
2. **1989 fiel die Berliner Mauer.**
3. **Tim kommt zu Peter gewöhnlich um drei Uhr nachmittags.**
4. **Letztes Mal ist er erst um zehn gekommen, weil seine Mutter vergessen hat, ihn aufzuwecken.**
5. **Peter und Tim machen nachmittags ihre Aufgaben.**
6. **Peter hat sich wegen des Fiebers vorgestern nicht wohlgefühlt.**
7. **Das Fieber kann tagelang so weitergehen.**
8. **Tim ist traurig darüber, weil er Peter sehr gern hat.**

p. 108, Exercise 9
1. **f** 2. **f** 3. **t** 4. **f** 5. **t**

p. 108, Exercise 10
1. **vorigen Sonntag** 2. **morgen abend** 3. **gestern nachmittag** 4. **jeden Tag** 5. **heute morgen**

p. 108, Exercise 11
1. **b** 2. **c** 3. **a** 4. **b**

p. 108, Exercise 12
1. **gekommen** 2. **Fieber** 3. **weitergehen**
4. **gefühlt** 5. **gern**

p. 108 (Joke)   Five Pairs of Horns
The teacher asks his pupils: "Six cows walk on a narrow country lane, one behind the other. Which one can turn around and say: 'I see five pairs of horns.'?"
Tim replies: "The first cow."
The teacher: "Wrong, Tim. Cows cannot talk."
Maybe we can't understand the language of the cows, Tim thought to himself. But he said nothing.

p. 109   Jokes and Puns
pp. 109-110
Sometimes Peter tries to make the lesson with Tim somewhat more amusing. Then he tells him jokes, fo instance this one:
1. The teacher in school: "What is farther away from us, Germany or the moon?"
One pupil answers: "Germany."
"How come?" asks the teacher.
The pupil: "Because we can see the moon but not Germany."
Or this one:
2. The teacher tells her pupils: "Write an essay: What I would do if I had ten million marks."
Every pupil started writing right away except for Michael. He played with his ballpoint pen and his ruler the whole time. After half an hour the teacher collected the essays. Michael gave her an empty sheet.
"What is that, Michael?" the teacher asked him. "Is that your essay? Every other pupil wrote two pages or more."
"Teacher," replied Michael. "That's what I would do if I were a millionaire."
3. Tim knows, of course, how one pronounces the letters of the German alphabet. Therefore, Peter can ask him the following:
"Tim, how do you write *Kuhhaare* (cow hairs) with only four letters, *Katze* with two, and *Zettel* (slip of paper) with two?"
Tim, of course, does not know that. So Peter gives him the solution: (which evidently cannot be translated). (See the chart for the German alphabet and its pronunciation in Chapter 1.)
4. At the very beginning Peter taught his pupil a funny little poem.
One, two, three, four, five, six, seven,
an old woman cooks turnips;
an old woman cooks bacon,
cuts herself the (her) finger off.

p. 110, Exercise 13
1. **Michael spielte die ganze Zeit mit Kugelschreiber und Lineal.**
2. **Er sagt, das würde er tun, wenn er Millionär wäre** (in other words, he would do nothing).
3. **Jeder andere Schüler hat zwei Seiten oder mehr geschrieben.**
4. **Michael hatte nichts geschrieben.**
5. **Die alte Frau in dem Gedicht kocht Rüben und Speck.**

p. 110, Exercise 14
1. **f** 2. **t** 3. **t** 4. **f** 5. **t**

p. 110, Exercise 15
1. **Lineal** 2. **Seiten** 3. **Mond** 4. **Schule**
5. **Aufsatz** 6. **Gedicht**

p. 110, Exercise 16
1. **Was ist weiter von uns entfernt, Deutschland oder der Mond?**
2. **Was würde ich tun, wenn ich zehn Millionen hätte?**
3. **Die Lehrerin sammelte die Aufsätze ein.**
4. **Tim wußte, wie man die Buchstaben ausspricht.**
5. **Eine alte Frau kocht Rüben.**

p. 110, Exercise 17
1. **C/EI/I/U/T** 2. **U/CH/EI/EA** 3. **E/MM/E/Ä**
4. **H/E/T** 5. **N/L/Ä/Ä**

Chapter 12, **p. 111,**   The Future of the Children

p. 111   What Peter Would Really Like To Be
pp. 111-112

Yesterday Nora and Karl talked about the future of their children. The whole thing had started with Peter telling them of his pupil Tim who does not like to play the violin. Peter cannot understand that, for music is the most beautiful thing in the world for him. But somebody to whom it does not mean anything will, on his part, not understand this.

KARL How long have you been taking cello lessons?

PETER For seven years.

KARL That's a long time.

NORA I recently talked to his teacher, and he said that Peter is unusually talented.

KARL But is he good enough to become a professional musician?

PETER I am the first cellist in our school orchestra.

NORA I think he is good, Karl. On Saturday he did not go to the movies with his friends but instead practiced the cello almost all day.

PETER We have a concert in one week and it is a very difficult piece. But I really enjoy practicing it. My friends tease me and say I am weird.

NORA Let them talk. You do what *you* want.

GRETCHEN Peter plays very beautifully. He hardly scratches at all.

PETER Thank you, Gretchen. Coming from you, that is a big compliment.

GRETCHEN Siblings have to stick together.

KARL That is all well and good. But do you know, Peter, what the professional outlook is for musicians?

PETER I'd like to learn yet another instrument. Maybe the flute or the oboe. But what I really would like to be I haven't revealed to anyone.

KARL That is?

PETER A conductor.

p. 112, Exercise 1
1. **Gestern sprach man über die Zukunft der Kinder.**
2. **Peter erzählte von Tim, daß er ungern Violine spielt.**
3. **Für Peter ist die Musik das Schönste auf der Welt.**
4. **Er nimmt Cellostunden seit sieben Jahren.**
5. **Sein Lehrer hat Nora gesagt, daß er unerhört begabt ist.**

pp. 112-113, Exercise 2
1. **f** 2. **t** 3. **t** 4. **f** 5. **t**

p. 113, Exercise 3
1. **4** 2. **1** 3. **5** 4. **6** 5. **2** 6. **3**

p. 113, Exercise 4
1. He doesn't like to play the violin.
2. The most beautiful thing in the world
3. Peter practiced almost all day.
4. I have a concert in one week.
5. He does not go out but stays at home.

p. 113, Exercise 5
1. **Zukunft** 2. **seinerseits** 3. **Violine**
4. **Instrument** 5. **kratzt** 6. **Berufsaussichten**

p. 113   A General in Tails
pp. 113-114

KARL A conductor, you say? That really is a surprise.

GRETCHEN Wonderful, Peter. And very romantic. A conductor reminds me of a general but without uniform.

NORA A general in tails.

PETER That's what I'd like to be.

KARL Do you know how long you have to study?

PETER I don't mind.

KARL On the one hand this costs (will cost) a lot of money; on the other hand it is perhaps a good investment. Some of them (conductors) earn a fortune. Besides, one can also teach.

NORA The main thing is our son is happy. Moreover, conductors supposedly live very long.

GRETCHEN Can you imagine, Daddy, Peter on the podium. . . Are you going to conduct with or without baton, Peter?

PETER It depends. First with, I think. Of course, it must be nicer with hands alone.

GRETCHEN But then you cannot break the baton when you get angry.

KARL Nevertheless I'll first have a thorough talk with your teacher about it. With him, and with your great-uncle in Grünau, who, as you know, is a retired conductor. It will also be necessary to speak about it with your class teacher.

PETER He'll support me.

KARL Why have you been making a secret of it for so long? None of us knew anything of it. Of course, we want the best for you. To be sure, I thought you would be able later on to help me in the business; however, I'll be glad to. . .

GRETCHEN Daddy, *I* will help you in the business; you know I am looking forward to it.

KARL All right, Peter. When the time comes, I won't stand in your way.

p. 115, Exercise 6
1. **t** 2. **f** 3. **t** 4. **t** 5. **f**

p. 115, Exercise 7
1. You will be able to help me in the business.
2. He made a secret of it.
3. We want the best for you.
4. Some of them earn very much.
5. It depends.

p. 115, Exercise 8
1. **a** 2. **c** 3. **a** 4. **c**

p. 115, Exercise 9
1. **Kapellmeister** 2. **helfen** 3. **gemacht**
4. **sprechen** 5. **vorstellen**

p. 115, Exercise 10
1. **Einerseits—anderseits** 2. **Überdies**
3. **Nichtsdestoweniger** 4. **Jedoch** 5. **Auch**

p. 115   The Soprano

Father took the little boy to his first orchestra concert with (to hear) a famous soprano. The conductor fascinated Johnny particularly.

"Father, why does the man threaten the nice lady with his little stick?"

"Be quiet. He isn't threatening her."

"But why then does she scream?"

p. 116   His Musical Talent
pp. 116-117

To Peter one probably never will have to say: "Either you practice or we sell the cello." (For that) he likes it too much.

He probably owes his musical talent to his mother. Nora comes from a music-loving family. Her father as well as her mother are practicing musicians. Mr. Bachmann (Nora's maiden name) is a superior violinist who plays regularly each week in a string quartet; and Nora's mother is a very popular piano teacher who has a great number of pupils.

Uncle Leopold, who is now living in Grünau, was a respected conductor who conducted the orchestra of the city theater for thirty years. It is, therefore, not surprising that Nora understands her son's ambition. She herself had a very beautiful voice (mezzo-soprano), many years ago dreamed of an operatic career, and now sings in the choir of her church occasionally.

(Neither of) Karl's parents, on the other hand— neither his father nor his mother—is overly interested in music. Karl himself likes music if it is not too difficult. But despite this he is proud of his son's talent, even though he hides his pride most of the time.

p. 117

A very short criticism (music review) appeared in the newspaper: "An amateur string quartet played Beethoven last night. Beethoven lost."

p. 117, Exercise 11
1. **b** 2. **a** 3. **a** 4. **c** 5. **a**

p. 117, Exercise 12
1. **f** 2. **t** 3. **t** 4. **f** 5. **t**

p. 118, Exercise 13
1. **Sie sind ausübende Musiker.**
2. **Onkel Leopold dirigierte ein Orchester.**
3. **Nora träumte von einer Opernkarriere.**
4. **Er verbirgt seinen Stolz.**
5. **Anderseits ist er nicht übermäßig interessiert.**

p. 118, Exercise 14
1. **Nora singt gelegentlich im Chor ihrer Kirche.**
2. **Onkel Leopold wohnt jetzt in Grünau.**
3. **Peter verdankt seiner Mutter das musikalische Talent.**
4. **Herr Bachmann spielt Violine.**
5. **Nora versteht den Ehrgeiz ihres Sohnes, weil sie aus einer musikalischen Familie kommt.**

p. 118, Exercise 15
1. **entweder—oder** 2. **trotzdem** 3. **weder—noch**
4. **deshalb** 5. **sowohl—als auch**

p. 118

"Do you like music?" a lady asked the famous man.
"No," he replied, 'but of all noises music bothers me the least."

p. 118   Gretchen and the World of Business
pp. 118-119

While Peter is little interested in his father's business, Gretchen, in spite of her romantic inclinations, is an amazingly practical little person.

Although she worked only as a babysitter until a short time ago, she was, on the two preceding weekends, active in the business as extra help and has proved to her father that she is a good saleslady.

As often as Karl needs her, she says, she will be ready to help in the store. Apparently she gets a big kick out of it, and she is sorry that she does not have more time for it. Although she, unlike her brother, does not have any artistic talent, she is an intelligent girl and grasps things quickly. One can see that she is very much at home in the world of business.

Karl now knows that Peter definitely prefers music to business life. Maybe he is a little disappointed about this, but as long as he has Gretchen (and since he has discovered her enthusiasm for the business) he knows that one of his children will continue the proud tradition of the book trade in the Bauer family. If he urgently needs extra help at the height of the Christmas season this time, he will ask his daughter for it.

p. 120, Exercise 16
1. **t** 2. **f** 3. **t** 4. **t** 5. **f**

p. 120, Exercise 17
1. **vorhergehenden Wochenenden** 2. **mitzuhelfen**
3. **Buchhandels in der Familie** 4. **Talent**
5. **Spaß**

p. 120, Exercise 18
1. **Während Peter sich wenig dafür interessiert, interessiert sich Gretchen sehr.**
2. **Obwohl sie nur als Babysitter gearbeitet hat, beweist sie ihrem Vater, daß sie als Verkäuferin gut ist.**
3. **Sooft er weggeht, sagt er, "Servus!"**
4. **Seitdem sie voriges Wochenende im Laden gearbeitet hat, ist Karl stolz auf sie.**
5. **Karl ist froh, daß sie sich fürs Geschäft interessiert.**

p. 120, Exercise 19
1. **Sie ist eine erstaunlich praktische kleine Person.**
2. **Sie ist bereit, sooft Karl sie braucht.**
3. **Offenbar tut es ihr leid, daß sie nicht mehr Zeit hat.**
4. **Auf der Höhe der Weihnachtssaison braucht er Aushilfe.**
5. **Solange er sie hat, ist er zufrieden.**

p. 120, Exercise 20
1. **Gretchen hat an den beiden vorhergehenden Wochenenden zuerst im Laden gearbeitet.**
2. **Sie hat ihrem Vater bewiesen, daß sie eine gute Verkäuferin ist.**
3. **Peter zieht die Musik dem Geschäftsleben vor.**
4. **Während der Weihnachtssaison braucht Karl dringend Aushilfe.**
5. **Gretchen hat bis vor kurzem als Babysitter gearbeitet.**

p. 120 Karl the Bookseller
pp. 120-121

When Karl speaks of the proud tradition of the book trade, he is perfectly justified (to do so). The bookstore has been in his family for almost 100 years, still under the same name.

Karl's volume of sales is not very big, simply because he does not have enough space for the many new books that are being published every year. Since his working capital is not very large, he has to purchase carefully. Very few publishers sell on consignment, that is, so that one can return the unsalable books. By occasionally holding a sale, he gets rid of many of the white elephants. There are a lot of booksellers in the city who all, of course, compete with one another.

Like most in his line of business, he, too, has an *Antiquariat,* that is, a section for used books. If a book is well preserved, one can sell it back to the bookseller—insofar as he is interested in it—at about 20-25% of the original price. By serving his customers in a friendly and conscientious way, he can depend on their coming back to him the next time.

p. 122 A Threat
The third request for payment that Karl sent to a man who had been owing him DM 20.-- for a book

for four months was answered by the customer as follows:

Your nasty letter of September 23 I did not like at all.

Once a month I throw all unpaid bills into an old wastepaper basket. Then my wife draws one of them blindfolded. If you are lucky, this will be your bill. But if you don't stop sending me your impudent requests for payment, I won't throw your bill into the wastepaper basket next month.

p. 122, Exercise 21
1. **f** 2. **t** 3. **f** 4. **f** 5. **t**

p. 122, Exercise 22
1. **Der Buchladen ist in seiner Familie seit beinahe 100 Jahren.**
2. **Sein Umsatz ist nicht größer, weil er nicht genug Platz hat.**
3. **Er muß vorsichtig einkaufen, da sein Betriebskapital nicht sehr groß ist.**
4. **Er wird die Ladenhüter los, indem er gelegentlich einen Ausverkauf abhält.**
5. **Die Abteilung für gebrauchte Bücher nennt man ein Antiquariat.**

p. 122, Exercise 23
1. **wann immer** 2. **weil** 3. **Falls** 4. **insofern als**
5. **wenn**

p. 122, Exercise 24
1. **c** 2. **a** 3. **c** 4. **b** 5. **a**

p. 123 Gretchen's Ambition
pp. 123-124

As soon as Gretchen has some money together, she takes (carries) it to the bank. There she already has a savings account in both her own and her father's name. The small allowance from Karl apparently is sufficient for her private expenses.

Whenever she takes in or spends something, she enters it into a little book so that she always knows how she is doing financially. For the household she shows little interest. But like Peter, she, too, has her own plans. Tonight, after the table has been cleared and the dishes washed, the family conference continues.

KARL Well, Gretchen, how do *you* picture your future?
GRETCHEN I would very much like to be active in business.
KARL Good. I believe you have a natural talent for it.
GRETCHEN As you know, Daddy, I now take bookkeeping, typing, and shorthand in school. We already write real business letters. When I handed in the latest assignment, the teacher paid me a compliment.
KARL Yes?
GRETCHEN I had typed three requests for payment without an error.
KARL Maybe you can also type some to my customers.
GRETCHEN Gladly, Daddy. But whether you really get the money then, I cannot guarantee.

NORA What do you want to do after you finish secondary school?

GRETCHEN Study computer programming.

PETER She beats me every time playing "Devil's Brat."

GRETCHEN There is nothing to it.

PETER But she really is very skilled (at it). And in math she is also very good. Maybe she can then install a computer in your store, Daddy.

KARL Not a bad idea. Especially for inventory and the bills in arrears.

NORA How long does this study take?

GRETCHEN One can learn (the field) well in two years.

KARL Don't you want to attend a professional school (specialized college)? The more you learn, the better it is for you.

p. 124, Exercise 25
1. **t.** 2. **f** 3. **t** 4. **f** 5. **f**

pp. 124-125, Exercise 26
1. **b** 2. **a** 3. **c** 4. **a** 5. **c**

p. 125, Exercise 27
1. **Sie hat ihr eigenes Sparkonto.**
2. **Sie will wissen, wie ihre finanzielle Situation beschaffen ist.**
3. **Nachdem sie das Geschirr weggeräumt haben, reden sie.**
4. **Als sie ihren Aufsatz ablieferte, machte ihr die Lehrerin ein Kompliment.**
5. **„Je mehr, desto besser", sagte ihr ihr Vater.**

p. 125, Exercise 28
1. **Das Taschengeld ist genug für ihre privaten Ausgaben.**
2. **Die Familienkonferenz wird nach dem Essen fortgesetzt.**
3. **Gretchen möchte gern Computerprogrammiererin werden.**
4. **In der Schule nimmt sie jetzt Buchhaltung, Maschinenschreiben und Kurzschrift.**
5. **Sie soll einen Computer in Karls Geschäft installieren.**

p. 125, Exercise 29
1. Her financial situation is very good.
2. She learns shorthand, bookkeeping, and typing.
3. Karl needs a computer for inventory and bills in arrears.
4. She can type business letters without an error.
5. There is nothing to it.

Chapter 13, **p. 126**   Kristy Visits Her Viennese Relatives

p. 126   Kristy in Vienna; Ferdinand and Maria Sacher
pp. 126-128
Kristy has decided to visit her relatives in Vienna before she returns to America.

Kristy knows that her family isn't related to the novelist Leopold Ritter (Knight) von Sacher-Masoch. That would have been interesting, she thinks, although she rejects masochism as well as sadism.

Ferdinand Sacher is a cousin of her mother. His family has been residing in Vienna since 1700. He is a descendant of Franz Sacher, who was the pastry cook of Prince Metternich—a famous personality in the history of Austria—and who in 1832 invented a torte that bears his name. At that time Sacher was only 16 years old! So many young geniuses have lived in Vienna, among them Mozart and Schubert. They died young, but Franz Sacher grew very old. There probably is no visitor to Vienna who hasn't tasted this delicacy, the Sachertorte. The exact composition of this delicious torte is still a "sweet mystery" today.

Kristy is certain that she won't count calories during her stay in Vienna. Unfortunately, she gains weight very easily, but she will worry about that later. Ferdinand (or Ferdl, as his friends call him) picks her up from the airport. He has never seen her before, but they have corresponded with each other, and he recognizes her from a picture that she sent him.

FERDL Servus, Kristy. Give me a kiss. You are much prettier than (you are) in the picture.

KRISTY Servus. So you are the dashing Ferdl of whom my father told me. Still not married?

FERDL No, and I'll probably stay a bachelor. There are too many beautiful women in Vienna. I hope you didn't make a hotel reservation, Kristy. Otherwise you (will) have to cancel it. My mother has a villa in Sievering; you can live with her as long as you want.

KRISTY You mean until she throws me out? Joking aside, I am very grateful to both of you.

FERDL Don't mention it. In the first place, the villa is practically empty except for my mother and a maid; in the second place, hotels are very expensive in Vienna; and thirdly, we very rarely have the honor to accommodate an attractive guest from America.

KRISTY Cousin Ferdl, it is difficult to resist your Viennese charm.

FERDL Fine! That's settled.

p. 128, Exercise 1
1. **f** 2. **t** 3. **f** 4. **f** 5. **t**

p. 128, Exercise 2
1. **Franz Sacher war ein Zuckerbäcker.**
2. **Ferdl holt Kristy vom Flugplatz ab.**
3. **Ferdl muß ein Junggeselle bleiben, weil es in Wien zu viele schöne Frauen gibt.**
4. **Kristy wird wahrscheinlich ihre Hotelreservierung rückgängig machen.**
5. **Sie wird bei Ferdls Mutter bleiben, bis man sie hinauswirft.**

p. 128, Exercise 3
1. **Nachkomme**   2. **Kalorien**   3. **verheiratet**
4. **Leckerbissen**   5. **leer**

p. 128, Exercise 4
1. **c**   2. **a**   3. **b**   4. **c**   5. **a**

p. 129, Exercise 5
1. **Franz Sacher war ein Zuckerbäcker.**
2. **Im Jahre 1832 erfand er eine berühmte Torte.**
3. **Kristy nennt Ferdl fesch.**
4. **„Mach deine Hotelreservierung rückgängig",
   sagt er ihr.**
5. **Scherz beiseite, sie wird bei seiner Mutter
   wohnen.**

p. 129   Food and Culture
p. 129

FERDL So this is your first visit to Vienna, isn't it?

KRISTY Yes, and you cannot imagine how much I
have looked forward to it. Vienna, Vienna, you
alone. . .

FERDL Well, we live quite well here. Good food and
loads of culture, that's for sure. I hope it stays that
way. You see, we are a small country, and we try
to maintain good relations with both the West and
the East. Well, here is my little Volkswagen. It
takes about thirty minutes to get home if the traffic
isn't too bad.

Finally they arrive in Sievering. Mrs. Sacher is the
widow of an Austrian diplomat who was an attaché in
Rome, London, and Madrid. Almost sixty years old,
she is still a beautiful woman with regular features,
snow-white hair, and a youthful figure. She is a very
cultured lady who speaks four languages fluently.

FRAU SACHER Welcome, Kristy. When I saw you
last, you were a sweet baby who could hardly talk.
Today you are an elegant young lady. I hope Ferdl
told you emphatically enough that you can stay here
as long as you want.

KRISTY I don't know how to thank you. May I call
you aunt?

FRAU SACHER No, call me Maria.

p. 130, Exercise 6
1. **t**   2. **f**   3. **f**   4. **f**   5. **t**

p. 130, Exercise 7
1. **b**   2. **a**   3. **c**   4. **c**   5. **a**

p. 130, Exercise 8
1. **Ferdl hat einen Volkswagen.**
2. **Maria ist beinahe sechzig Jahre alt.**
3. **Sie spricht vier Sprachen fließend.**
4. **Ihre Gesichtszüge sind regelmäßig.**
5. **Als Maria sie zuletzt sah, war Kristy ein süßes
   kleines Baby.**

p. 130, Exercise 9
1. **5**   2. **4**   3. **6**   4. **2**   5. **3**   6. **1**

p. 130, Exercise 10
1. I hope that it stays that way.
2. Finally they arrived at home.

3. Today Kristy is an elegant young lady.
4. She can stay here as long as she wants.
5. One wants to maintain good relations.

p. 130   The *Heurige* and the Café
pp. 130-131
About two kilometers from the villa in which Maria
lives one finds a number of "Heurigen," small
restaurants where new wine is dispensed. There you
sit on wooden benches in the open with a jug of wine
on the table before you in the company of friends. A
Schrammelquartett plays old, popular tunes, and
sometimes there is a singer there, also. One sits,
chats, enjoys the wine, and in the end does not know
how much one has been drinking. One thing one
knows: One feels very good.

Another institution that made Vienna famous is the
Viennese café. In a previous chapter we got to know
the *Café-Konditorei* in Karl's home town. In Vienna it
is the café or coffee house where you can spend a part
of your spare time, can take your meals, can read
newspapers and magazines from all over the world,
can play chess, cards, or billiards, can take care of
your correspondence, can hold business meetings, or
can simply sit and watch the passers-by in the street.
No waiter will disturb you even if you have consumed
but one cup of coffee during a whole afternoon.

p. 132, Exercise 11
1. **t**   2. **f**   3. **t**   4. **f**   5. **t**

p. 132, Exercise 12
1. **Man sitzt auf Holzbänken im Freien.**
2. **Man verbringt einen Teil seiner Freizeit im
   Café.**
3. **Man beobachtet die Passanten auf der Straße.**
4. **Man spielt Schach oder Karten und erledigt
   seine Korrespondenz.**
5. **Man kann Zeitungen und Zeitschriften aus der
   ganzen Welt lesen.**

p. 132, Exercise 13
1. **a**   2. **c**   3. **b**   4. **a**   5. **b**

p. 132, Exercise 14
1. **versuchen**   2. **gebildete**   3. **erster**   4. **Tante**
5. **Unmenge**

p. 132, Exercise 15
1. **Österreich versucht, gute Beziehungen zu allen
   Staaten aufrechtzuerhalten.**
2. **Ferdl und Kristy sind endlich in Sievering
   angekommen.**
3. **Marias Gesichtszüge sind regelmäßig.**
4. **Kristy ist jetzt eine elegante, junge Dame.**
5. **Ferdl hat einen Volkswagen.**

pp. 132-133   The Bridge
An American came to Vienna and asked an
acquaintance to show him some of the sights. The
Viennese showed him the State Opera.
   "They rebuilt it in two years."
   "In America this takes (would take) only nine
months."

Then the Viennese led him to the West Railroad Station.

"That was finished in one year."

"In America we put up a building like that in three months."

Finally they came to the new bridge across the Danube.

"That is a very beautiful bridge," said the American.

"How long did that take?"

"The bridge, you mean?" replied the Viennese.

"When I entered the city this morning, it was not there yet at all."

Chapter 14, **p. 134** Susie Wants to Learn Something New

p. 134 The Boss's Right Hand?
pp. 134-135

Since Anton successfully changed his job, his friend Susie feels more and more encouraged to give up hers. But Anton still works in the same field, as we know. With Susie this is different. She is a secretary, but the duties of a secretary bore her. She has often been assured that she is her boss's right hand, but that is not sufficient for her. Above all, she wants to have more real responsibility and fewer letters to write.

Susie's mother, Mrs. Braun, invited Anton for dinner tonight. Mrs. Braun is an excellent cook. There is nothing to criticize concerning her meals except one thing: Whatever she serves is too much and too heavy. After a glorious potato soup with mushrooms (which in itself represents a complete meal) a pork roast with dumplings and red cabbage is (being) dished up, with it a mixed salad, which is Mrs. Braun's specialty. Beer is (being) served with the meal by Susie. Before one serves the dessert (before dessert is served), Anton asks very politely: "Madam, do you mind if now a little break is taken (if we take a little break)?"

p. 135, Exercise 1
1. **t** 2. **f** 3. **t** 4. **f** 5. **f**

p. 136, Exercise 2
1. **Frau Braun hat heute das Abendessen gekocht.**
2. **Man hat Anton dazu eingeladen.**
3. **Die Kartoffelsuppe ist glorreich.**
4. **Frau Brauns Spezialität ist ihr bunter Salat.**
5. **Zur Mahlzeit wird Bier getrunken.**

p. 136, Exercise 3
1. **Anton wird von Susies Mutter eingeladen.**
2. **Ein Schweinebraten wird von Frau Braun serviert.**
3. **Bier wird von Susie serviert.**
4. **Eine kleine Pause wird eingeschaltet.**
5. **Der Job wird von Susie aufgegeben.**

p. 136, Exercise 4
1. **Anton arbeitet noch immer im gleichen Fach.**
2. **Sie ist die rechte Hand ihres Chefs.**
3. **Frau Braun ist eine ausgezeichnete Köchin.**

4. **Sie werden den Nachtisch später haben.**
5. **Es gibt nichts zu kritisieren.**

p. 136, Exercise 5
1. **c** 2. **a** 3. **c** 4. **a** 5. **b**

p. 136 An Alarm Clock in the Office
pp. 136-137

Poppyseed cake is being served for dessert. With it coffee. Anton drinks it black, Susie takes some whipped cream, Mrs. Braun drinks tea.

FRAU BRAUN When I drink coffee at this time, I cannot sleep.

ANTON That was a meal for the gods, Mrs. Braun.

FRAU BRAUN Are you sure, Mr. Anton, that I gave you enough to eat?

SUSIE Does one (shall we) start over again with the soup?

ANTON Another bite and I (will) burst. Tomorrow I'll fast.

SUSIE Mother, why don't you sit down with us? I'll help you with the dishes later. (Mrs. Braun sits down.)

ANTON Well, tell me, Susie. You say you are dissatisfied with your present job. Don't you earn enough, or don't you like the work?

SUSIE The salary is not bad, but I get bored to death. It is the same old routine that gets on my nerves.

ANTON Explain that to me.

SUSIE At eight sharp the alarm clock is turned on.

ANTON An alarm clock? In the office?

SUSIE The idea of our head bookkeeper who, at the same time, is the office manager. All the doors are open; he knows exactly who is late.

ANTON A time clock would be more practical.

SUSIE For that he is too stingy. Then every office is (being) checked by him five times a day.

ANTON Always at the same time?

SUSIE No; for that he is too shrewd.

p. 137, Exercise 6
1. **f** 2. **t** 3. **t** 4. **t** 5. **f**

p. 137, Exercise 7
1. **Habe ich Ihnen genug zu essen gegeben?**
2. **Ich langweile mich zu Tode.**
3. **Es geht mir auf die Nerven.**
4. **Der Bürovorstand ist sehr schlau.**
5. **Ich kann nicht mehr essen, ich platze bereits.**

p. 138, Exercise 8
1. **Punkt** 2. **geöffnet** 3. **Gehalt** 4. **Stechuhr**
5. **Götter**

p. 138, Exercise 9
1. **a** 2. **c** 3. **c** 4. **a** 5. **c**

p. 138 The Duties of a Secretary
pp. 138-139

SUSIE At nine the mail is (being) delivered. It is opened and put on the desk of the boss. At 9:30 I am (being) ordered to his office by phone. I am responsible for the outgoing mail.

"Susie? Was the package to Pfister & Son mailed to Zürich yesterday? Was it registered and insured? Good. Write to Ulrich Möller A.G. in Hamburg that the merchandise that he ordered will be delivered tomorrow. Confirm the receipt of the letter from Kurt Krone. Threaten him that we (have) waited long enough. Either he pays or we go to court. The same to M.A.T. in Cologne and F.O.P.C. in Stuttgart."

Ten more letters are (being) dictated by him, interrupted by the history of his family, his allergies, and the problems of his children. Day before yesterday his son Günther was examined because of a rash. He mustn't eat chocolate any more. Yesterday his daughter Ruth was almost run over. She crosses the street without looking. "Until now I have been treated for my allergies by Dr. Schwarz. Do you know him, Susie? Do you think he is good? Where was I?" Then he tells me about his symptoms. No letter is dictated to the end.

p. 139, Exercise 10
1. f 2. t 3. t 4. t 5. f

p. 139, Exercise 11
1. **Sie sind geöffnet und auf den Schreibtisch gelegt worden.**
2. **Seine Tochter ist beinahe überfahren worden.**
3. **Der Erhalt des Briefes ist bestätigt worden.**
4. **Der Chef ist von Dr. Schwarz behandelt worden.**
5. **Kein Brief ist zu Ende diktiert worden.**

p. 139, Exercise 12
1. **Die geöffnete Post wird auf den Schreibtisch des Chefs gelegt.**
2. **Die Ware nach Hamburg wird morgen geliefert werden.**
3. **Auf die Zahlung wurde lange genug gewartet.**
4. **Sie ging über die Straße, ohne zu schauen.**
5. **Günther darf keine Schokolade mehr essen, weil er einen Ausschlag davon bekommt.**

pp. 139-140, Exercise 13
1. **b** 2. **a** 3. **b** 4. **b** 5. **a**

p. 140   No Smoking
pp. 140-141
SUSIE In the middle of it he asks me: "Do you know Hauptmann? Yes, the traveling salesman. Well, yesterday he comes in with the burning (a lit) cigar, tells me some story while blowing the thick smoke into my face. 'Here one doesn't smoke,' I shout. 'Have you gone crazy? Don't you see the signs everywhere? Do you want to poison me with your damned weed?' He is the best traveling salesman we have, but here no exception is made. The curtains are drawn, the windows opened, and the guy is thrown out. 'You are fired if you have the impu-

dence to show up here again with the (your) burning weed.' "

ANTON At your place one mustn't smoke at all?

SUSIE No. Hauptmann probably had forgotten about that.

ANTON At our firm one can (readily) smoke.

p. 141   A Little Joke
BOSS You are ten minutes late again. Don't you know when we start working here?

NEW EMPLOYEE No. The others are always at work already whenever I come here (arrive).

p. 141   Apple With Apple Juice
SUSIE At eleven sharp the first coffee break takes place (literally: is being taken). At twelve Marie Golz, the bookkeeper in my office, takes a buttered roll with three slices of salami and a small piece of Limburger out of a brown paper bag and starts eating noisily.

ANTON Eating noisily?

SUSIE With her mouth open. That takes twenty minutes. Emma Schröder, the stenographer-typist, takes her thermos bottle with apple juice to the john and smokes.

ANTON All the time?

SUSIE That is the only chance (to smoke) she has. She eats a medium-size apple at the same time.

ANTON Apple with apple juice?

SUSIE Why not? Emma is a very pedantic lady. But not so pedantic as Herr Ignaz Fliegenschläger.

ANTON Who is that?

SUSIE The head bookkeeper.

p. 142, Exercise 14
1. t 2. f 3. f 4. t 5. t

p. 142, Exercise 15
1. **Man arbeitet im Büro.**
2. **Man rauchte dort nie.**
3. **Bei Anton hat man immer geraucht.**
4. **Man zog die Vorhänge.**
5. **Man hat die Fenster aufgemacht.**

p. 142, Exercise 16
1. **Er bläst mir den Rauch ins Gesicht.**
2. **Wollen Sie mich vergiften?**
3. **Hauptmann wird hinausgeschmissen.**
4. **Unterstehen Sie sich nicht!**
5. **Sie schmatzt, und mit offenem Mund.**

p. 142, Exercise 17
1. **Hauptmann bläst dem Chef den Rauch ins Gesicht.**
2. **Der Chef mag keinen Rauch, weil er eine Allergie hat.**
3. **Der Reisende wird hinausgeschmissen.**
4. **Marie Golz ißt eine Buttersemmel.**
5. **Emma trinkt Apfelsaft.**

p. 142, Exercise 18
1. **vergiften** 2. **Gesicht** 3. **gefeuert** 4. **Apfel**
5. **gemacht**

p. 142 A Letter
Dear Mr. Steiner!
 What shall I tell the old idiot? In response to your letter of the twelfth of this month, I am sorry that you are dissatisfied with the merchandise. We had to get rid of it fast so as not to lose more on it yet. The quality of the shirts is excellent, and you are the only customer who has complained. That's a beautiful blouse that you have on. Therefore, we cannot take them back, I am sorry to say. How come I didn't notice (it) before that you have a dimple in the (your) left cheek?
 With best greetings (sincerely yours),
 Do you have time tonight (are you free tonight)?

p. 143 Dress Designing
pp. 143-144

SUSIE Do you want to hear more about my firm?

ANTON No, please.

FRAU BRAUN Why did you never tell me about it? I don't understand how you can stand that.

SUSIE Is it a wonder (are you surprised) that I want to do something else?

ANTON Do you have something definite in mind? You have a number of different talents. For a time you worked with gold and silver; the ring that you gave me is really very beautiful and such an original design.

FRAU BRAUN Here, look at the brooch that she made for me.

ANTON A little work of art.

SUSIE A nice hobby. I have a lot to learn.

ANTON But there are classes (courses) . . . and your dresses, for instance; I know you sew most of them yourself. And they are so stylish. They probably (would) cost a small fortune if you had to buy them in the store.

FRAU BRAUN And her cartoons, Mr. Anton. The way the character of a figure is brought out with a few strokes . . .

SUSIE What I am really interested in is dress designing.

ANTON How long does it take if you, with your expertise, want to learn it thoroughly?

SUSIE About two years, maybe a year and a half. And I can go there in the evening.

ANTON Great. May I design the label for the new Susie Braun originals?

SUSIE You are the advertising expert.

ANTON Mrs. Braun, do you mind if, for this occasion, we open a bottle of Rhine wine that I brought you today?

p. 144, Exercise 19
1. **t** 2. **f** 3. **t** 4. **t** 5. **f**

p. 144, Exercise 20
1. **Anton meint damit den Ring.**
2. **Susie hat eine Brosche für ihre Mutter gemacht.**
3. **Anton nennt Susies Kleider schick.**
4. **Frau Braun bewundert Susies Karikaturen ganz besonders.**
5. **Modezeichnen interessiert Susie am meisten.**

p. 144, Exercise 21
1. **a** 2. **c** 3. **a** 4. **a** 5. **b**

p. 144, Exercise 22
1. **aushalten** 2. **Etikett** 3. **näht** 4. **Liebhaberei**
5. **Talente**

p. 144, Exercise 23
1. How can you stand that?
2. She has a number of different talents.
3. That costs a small fortune in the store.
4. A bottle of Rhine wine is (being) opened.
5. Mrs. Braun's brooch is (being) admired by Anton.

Chapter 15, **p. 145** Ringstrom and His Orchestra

p. 145 The Orchestra
pp. 145-146
 Ludwigsheim—the city in which the persons of this report are settled—always has had the ambition to be a cultural center. The season of the municipal theater lasts from September to June, that is, ten months each year. Mainly plays are (being) presented, few modern ones, above all German classics and a lot of Shakespeare. The Germans, as everybody knows, imagine *their* Shakespeare (splendidly translated more than 150 years ago) to be better than the original. Operas, too, can be heard there in second-rate performances, mostly Verdi and Puccini, but a short time ago there was *Porgy and Bess.* The older people didn't like that very much, but the conductor is a great jazz fan. The orchestra of the city theater is good, allegedly, and proudly calls itself the Ludwigsheim Philharmonic. Every Sunday at twelve noon (except in July and August) there is a concert in (the) *Ameliensaal* (Amelien Hall), mainly classical repertory, very much to the regret of the conductor, Mr. Klaus Ringstrom, who advocates modern music. Sometimes, for instance, he plays a beautiful, old piece. If he were not so strict, one would like to hum along. If looks could kill, he would have stabbed half of the audience to death long since. But quite unexpectedly and more and more often there comes a miserable piece of so-called modern music, not even mentioned on the program most of the time, senseless noise, loud and ugly. Sometimes it's a piece by him. Ringstrom simply smuggles this in. Fortunately, it is usually short.

p. 147, Exercise 1
1. **f** 2. **f** 3. **t** 4. **t** 5. **t**

p. 147, Exercise 2
1. **c** 2. **a** 3. **c** 4. **b** 5. **a**

p. 147, Exercise 3
1. **könnten** 2. **würde** 3. **hätte** 4. **wäre**

p. 147, Exercise 4
1. **Man würde gern mitsummen.**
2. **Wenn Blicke töten könnten, hätte er schon das halbe Publikum erdolcht.**
3. **Die Deutschen bilden sich bekanntlich ein, daß** *ihr* **Shakespeare besser sei als das Original.**
4. **Das Ludwigsheimer Orchester nennt sich die Ludwigsheimer Philharmonie.**
5. **Man konnte** *Porgy und Bess* **dort hören.**

p. 147, Exercise 5
1. **Sie spielen eine Menge Shakespeare.**
2. **Zu Herrn Ringstroms Leidwesen spielen sie hauptsächlich Beethoven.**
3. **Moderne Stücke sind auf dem Programm nicht erwähnt.**
4. **Er zieht das klassische Repertoire vor.**
5. **Zum Glück ist es meistens kurz.**

p. 148, Exercise 6
1. **Jazzfan** 2. **unerwartet** 3. **übersetzt**
4. **Repertoire** 5. **Kulturzentrum**

p. 148   More about Ringstrom
p. 148
Ringstrom believes he has the duty to educate the Ludwigsheim audience musically. Most of the listeners respect him but are intimidated by him. If they could do (act) the way they wanted to, they would fire him. But he has a contract for five years, and he is very stubborn. There is no demand for modern music in Ludwigsheim. Karl and Nora have a subscription to the concert season and, of course, take the children along every time. Karl does not think much of the conductor. He regrets that Uncle Leopold has retired. Nora is not certain, but Peter (as you can imagine) is enthusiastic about the man. Uncle Leopold does not like his successor either. You can't tell what is good music until 100 years later, he thinks, so why take a risk?

If Leopold had remained in his job for another few months, Ringstrom would have gone to Regensburg. Pity, Karl thinks secretly. He agrees with the majority of the Ludwigsheimers. To Gretchen all this is not all that important. But she loves jazz and especially rock. If she had her way, she would not need an orchestra in Ludwigsheim, just a good rock group.

p. 149, Exercise 7
1. **t** 2. **f** 3. **t** 4. **f** 5. **t**

p. 149, Exercise 8
1. **Karl stimmt mit der Mehrzahl der Ludwigsheimer überein.**
2. **Er bedauert, daß Onkel Leopold nicht noch einige Monate auf seinem Posten verblieben ist.**
3. **Die meisten Zuhörer würden ihn feuern.**
4. **Sie können Ringstrom nicht feuern, weil er einen Vertrag hat.**
5. **Gretchen liebt Jazz.**

p. 149, Exercise 9
1. Why take a risk?
2. As you can imagine . . .

3. They are intimidated by him.
4. If they could do (act) the way they wanted to, . . .
5. Karl does not think much of the conductor.

p. 149   The Interview (Part I)
pp. 149-150
Yesterday Ringstrom granted an interview to the reporter of the *Ludwigsheim Planet* that is printed here in excerpts:

PLANET Maestro, would you please make known to my readers your plans for the next season?

RINGSTROM If Ludwigsheim is less stingy, I shall enlarge the orchestra.

PLANET Is that your first priority?

RINGSTROM One of the first. We need six violinists, three cellists, two clarinetists. . . . Shall I bore you with the numbers?

PLANET How do you explain this shortage?

RINGSTROM Stinginess. When a member of the orchestra dies, no money is granted for his replacement.

PLANET Is that a policy that is directed against you personally?

RINGSTROM Possibly. As you know, I am a controversial figure.

PLANET Could it perhaps be the present economic crisis?

RINGSTROM One has money enough for the new football (soccer) stadium. If I had one-tenth of it (that money) I would show the city what good music is.

PLANET What would you do if you had unlimited means?

RINGSTROM Do you have to print that? All right. I would fire 20% of the orchestra and replace them with better employees (musicians); enlarge the orchestra by fifteen; hold more rehearsals; and reduce our operatic performances. What you see on our operatic stage is a scandal.

PLANET Could we import American singers?

RINGSTROM Bloody beginners? They, too, cost money. Everything costs money.

p. 151, Exercise 10
1. **f** 2. **f** 3. **t** 4. **f** 5. **t**

p. 151, Exercise 11
1. **Würden Sie mir bitte alles über Ihre Pläne mitteilen?**
2. **Das ist eine Politik, die gegen ihn gerichtet ist.**
3. **Ich werde das Orchester vergrößern, wenn sie mir das Geld geben.**
4. **Was würden Sie mit unbegrenzten Mitteln tun?**
5. **Ich würde mehr Proben abhalten.**

p. 151, Exercise 12
1. **Der Reporter fragt ihn zuerst nach seinen Plänen für die nächste Saison.**
2. **Ringstrom meint, es ist der Geiz der Ludwigsheimer.**

3. **Er würde 20% des Orchesters mit besseren Kräften ersetzen.**
4. **Die Opernaufführungen, denkt er, sind ein Skandal.**
5. **Ringstrom nennt sich eine umstrittene Figur.**

p. 151, Exercise 13
1. **Würden Sie den Lesern Ihre Pläne bekanntgeben?**
2. **Kein Geld wird für seinen Ersatz bewilligt.**
3. **Was man auf der Opernbühne sieht, ist ein Skandal.**
4. **Er würde das Orchester um 15 vergrößern.**
5. **Könnten Sie in dem Interview Ihre Pläne bekanntgeben?**

p. 151, Exercise 14
1. **6** 2. **4** 3. **5** 4. **3** 5. **1** 6. **2**

p. 152   The Interview (Part II)
pp. 152-153
PLANET What do you think of your critics? Your predecessor on the podium has said that if you made fewer antics, you would be a better conductor.

RINGSTROM Antics? You mean because I shake my head so that the (my) hair flies to all sides when the concertmaster is a quarter tone high? Because I stamp my feet when the cellist louses up his solo? Because I threaten the drummer with my fists when he comes in too soon? Because I dance on the podium when I am bored? Or close my eyes and dream when everything for once goes well?

PLANET The question of the baton, maestro.

RINGSTROM Ah—the baton. If I used the baton and conducted like an automaton, would I then be a better conductor? What is this with the baton? Are these hands not good enough? If I held the baton in my hand, would I then be a better musician? Would I have more success, a better press? Would the Ludwigsheimers then grant me more money? I have a mission here, Mr., Mr. . . .

PLANET Bruck, Maestro, Robert Bruck.

RINGSTROM If I were to give a jazz concert with the orchestra, Mr. Bruck, would the Ludwigsheimers tear me to pieces?

PLANET I would not risk it, Maestro. But you haven't said what you are going to play next season.

RINGSTROM When I know (it), I'll call you.

PLANET If you knew (it), would you tell me?

RINGSTROM Probably not. You would print it, and everybody would criticize the program beforehand.

PLANET Why did your own opera *Ultraviolet Flowers in Outer Space* have no success?

RINGSTROM Because the public is musically uneducated, too stupid. Don't print that. And because jealous singers and incompetent orchestra members sabotaged me and my work. Their egoism is unbelievable. Don't print that either. Oh, Händel and Mozart too had similar problems. But I will triumph. The future belongs to me and my music. You may print that.

PLANET Mr. Ringstrom, we thank you for the interview.

p. 153   *Würde* or No *würde?*
Dear Sir:
   I never ordered this cursed radio. If I had ordered it, you never would have sent it. If you had never sent it, I never would have received it. If I had received it, I would have paid for it. If I haven't paid for it, I won't pay for it.
   Go to hell!
   Yours very truly,

p. 153, Exercise 15
1. **t** 2. **t** 3. **t** 4. **t** 5. **f**

p. 153, Exercise 16
1. **Er droht dem Trommler mit seinen Fäusten.**
2. **Ist er mit dem Taktstock ein besserer Dirigent?**
3. **Würde er mehr Erfolg haben?**
4. **Manchmal schließt er seine Augen und träumt.**
5. **Der Reporter dankt ihm für das Interview.**

p. 154, Exercise 17
1. **Er stampft mit den Füßen, weil der Cellist sein Solo verhaut.**
2. **Er schüttelt den Kopf, weil der Konzertmeister um einen Viertelton zu hoch spielt.**
3. **Er droht dem Trommler, weil er zu früh einsetzt.**
4. **Er mag den Taktstock nicht, weil er nicht wie ein Automat dirigieren möchte.**
5. **Er weiß noch nicht, was er in der nächsten Saison spielen wird.**
6. **Seine eigene Oper heißt *Ultraviolette Blumen im Weltall.***
7. **Mozart und Händel hatten auch Probleme mit inkompetenten Orchestermitgliedern und eifersüchtigen Sängern.**

p. 154, Exercise 18
1. **C/V/Ä** 2. **I/Ä/G/E/O** 3. **T/EI/T/C**
4. **R/N/RR** 5. **IE/Ä/AI**

p. 154, Exercise 19
1. **Vorgänger** 2. **Fäusten** 3. **Musiker** 4. **Haar**
5. **gut**

p. 154   The Ball (Part I)
pp. 154-155
   The ball is a big success. All our friends have come. Karl, Nora and Gretchen, Anton and Susie, also Kristy, the latter with a young man, Dr. Richard Glaser, whom she met at the last concert. Dick, as his friends call him, is a physician who studied in the United States for two years and is now working as an intern in the Ludwigsheim General Hospital. They speak German and English in turn. Kristy tells him he speaks English very well and fluently. Dick replies he had learned the language before; he had attended *Realgymnasium* in Munich where one has to learn English as well as Latin.

KRISTY In which American city did you study?
DICK In Denver, at the University of Colorado.

KRISTY Well, this is an incredible coincidence.

DICK What do you mean?

KRISTY Denver is my home.

DICK Really?

KRISTY And you worked at the University Hospital?

DICK Yes; for two years, as a student.

KRISTY I lived just three miles from you. Will you ever go back to Denver?

DICK Maybe. I have very good friends there.

KRISTY If you come, you must look me up.

DICK Sure thing. You can depend on that.

p. 155, Exercise 20

1. **t** 2. **f** 3. **t** 4. **f** 5. **t**

p. 156, Exercise 21

1. **Kristy kommt zum Ball mit Dick.**
2. **Dick arbeitet als Assistenzarzt im Ludwigsheimer Allgemeinen Krankenhaus.**
3. **In München ist er aufs Realgymnasium gegangen.**
4. **Neben Englisch hat er dort auch Latein gelernt.**
5. **In Denver hat er im Universitätsspital gearbeitet.**

p. 156, Exercise 22

1. **Sie sprechen abwechselnd Englisch und Deutsch.**
2. **Das ist ein unglaublicher Zufall.**
3. **Dick studierte zwei Jahre in Amerika.**
4. **Kristy wohnte bloß drei Meilen von ihm.**
5. **Darauf können Sie sich verlassen.**

p. 156, Exercise 23

1. **c** 2. **b** 3. **a** 4. **b** 5. **b**

p. 156, Exercise 24

1. **Latein** 2. **Zufall** 3. **Arzt** 4. **vorher**
5. **Konzert**

p. 156   The Ball (Part II)
pp. 156-157

Anton dances with Nora, and Karl with Susie. In the big hall ten musicians of the Ludwigsheim Philharmonic play one waltz after another, also polkas and once in a while a foxtrot and swing, the latter conducted by Maestro Ringstrom in sport shirt, jeans, and cowboy boots.

In the smaller hall an Argentinian group, *Los Cinco Gauchos,* plays Latin-American music. Anton is just now dancing a samba with Nora.

ANTON The cha-cha is my favorite dance. It is very rhythmic, and the steps are not very complicated.

NORA Maybe you can show it to me.

ANTON Gladly. You have a natural talent. Did you learn dancing somewhere?

NORA No. But I always liked it. (I always got a kick out of it.)

ANTON You are very musical.

NORA Yes, that's in the family. Oh, here is Susie. I am a little warm. Would you like to dance with her?

ANTON With pleasure. (He changes over to Susie.)

SUSIE Do you like it?

ANTON Very (much). And you? The guys play marvelously.

SUSIE Do you want to go on dancing or sit down? Look, there is Kristy with her young man. (At a small table)

KRISTY It is good to rest a little.

DICK Would you like a glass of wine from the bar? Be back right away.—Here: Ludwigsheim *Spätlese.* Not bad. Please try (it)! Wait. I think we have been formal long enough. In Denver we were practically neighbors for two years. Well—***Bruderschaft?*** (They intertwine their arms, drink, and kiss.) How does our friend Anton say it?

KRISTY Servus.

DICK Servus.

p. 157, Exercise 25

1. **f** 2. **f** 3. **f** 4. **t** 5. **t**

p. 158, Exercise 26

1. **Im großen Saal spielen zehn Musiker der Philharmonie.**
2. **Ringstrom dirigiert Foxtrotts und Swings.**
3. **Die argentinische Gruppe spielt lateinamerikanische Musik.**
4. **In Denver waren sie praktisch Nachbarn.**
5. **Dick und Kristy trinken Wein.**

p. 158, Exercise 27

1. **a** 2. **a** 3. **c** 4. **c** 5. **a**

p. 158, Exercise 28

1. **Haben Sie (irgend)wo tanzen gelernt?**
2. **Mir ist ein bißchen heiß.**
3. **Gefallen dir die Dekorationen?**
4. **Es tut gut, sich ein wenig auszuruhen.**
5. **Willst du weitertanzen?**

p. 158, Exercise 29

1. **3** 2. **4** 3. **5** 4. **6** 5. **2** 6. **1**

p. 158

SHE Apart from two things you would be a marvelous dancer.

HE Yes? What are the two things?

SHE Your feet.

Chapter 16, **p. 159**   Nora at the Supermarket

p. 159   On the Way to the Supermarket
pp. 159-160

Nora has a bulletin board in the kitchen on which she notes down which groceries she needs. The list is growing and will continue growing from day to day. Today is the day on which she goes shopping. She

likes going to Polzer's Supermarket best. Polzer is not the biggest grocer in Ludwigsheim, to be sure, but he is, in Nora's opinion, the most dependable.
Vegetables and fruit are always fresh, also the meat and the milk products and eggs which he buys direct, partly from the leading co-op, partly from the farmers of the environs. Polzer's competition tries to undersell him, but most customers remain faithful to him. If someone returns something, he has so far always exchanged the merchandise or returned the money. His reputation as the "housewife's friend" is more important to him than the few marks that he perhaps loses thereby.

Besides, that's also his advertising slogan, which is to be found every Thursday as a large headline in the food supplement of the *Ludwigsheim Planet*: "Polzer, the Housewife's Friend, offers:" After the listing of his special offers one reads the catch phrase: "His prices can't be beat. That's Polzer's pride!"

Gretchen has a teacher in her German class who always gets excited about (the fact) that in the German language now so many foreign words are (being) used. Why does Polzer use the foreign word *offeriert?* Why not its German equivalent *anbieten* or *darbieten,* he asks. But this is the trend, thinks Nora while putting on her jeans. (Thank God the miniskirt has been out of fashion for a long time; she hopes it never comes back. With her knees she cannot make a grand display (look her best). They are too **fat.**)

p. 161, Exercise 1
1. f 2. t 3. t 4. t 5. f

p. 161, Exercise 2
1. **Die Liste wächst von Tag zu Tag.**
2. **Sein Ruf ist ihm wichtiger als ein paar Mark.**
3. **Nora zieht sich Jeans zum Einkaufen an.**
4. **Gretchens Lehrer regt sich über die vielen Fremdwörter auf.**
5. **Nora hat ihre Knie nicht gern, weil sie zu dick sind.**

p. 162, Exercise 3
1. c 2. c 3. a 4. c 5. c

p. 162, Exercise 4
1. **Minirock** 2. **Umgebung** 3. **Konkurrenz**
4. **wachsen** 5. **Genossenschaft**

p. 162   Polzer, the Housewife's Friend
pp. 162-163
Due to the fact that he maintains close contact with his customers, most of whom he knows personally, Polzer has won the confidence of many housewives in Ludwigsheim. Like every other supermarket, his, too, is on a self-service basis. Nora finds it more practical to restrict herself to one major store where she takes care of her grocery purchases rather than going to three or four different mom-and-pop stores. It is true, Polzer doesn't carry fish, which she has to buy in a specialty shop.

Today, too, her presence has not escaped Mr. Polzer's attention. He values her as one of his most

faithful customers and greets her from afar at the top of his voice:

POLZER Good morning, Mrs. Bauer. Young and beautiful as always. I almost mistook you for your daughter. Only yesterday I said to my wife, "Well, Resi, I don't know how Mrs. Bauer does it. She doesn't grow older."

Mr. Polzer's compliments are not to be taken seriously, of course. Nora knows that. He probably gives the same speech (with variations) to about 75% of his customers. It doesn't matter. Nora likes it anyway.

POLZER May I help you? The pork chops are particularly nice today. Or, if you want to make a loin roast . . .

NORA Do you have veal lung?

POLZER Veal lung? Just arrived.

NORA You know Mr. Anton Gruber from Vienna? We invited him for dinner tomorrow, and what he wanted is veal lung.

POLZER With dumplings this is a feast. Peppercorns, onions, parsley, thyme, anchovies, capers, cream . . .

NORA How come you know all that?

POLZER Long experience. When I'm at home, I am the cook.

p. 164   A Joke
HOUSEWIFE It is tough (hard) to pay ten marks for one kilo of meat.
BUTCHER But if you pay only five marks, it is tougher yet.

p. 164, Exercise 5
1. f 2. f 3. t 4. f 5. t

p. 164, Exercise 6
1. **Polzer hat sich das Vertrauen seiner Kundinnen dadurch erworben, daß er sehr verläßlich ist.**
2. **Nora findet es praktischer, in *einem* größeren Geschäft einzukaufen.**
3. **Er hat mit seiner Frau über Nora gesprochen.**
4. **Er empfiehlt Nora Schweinskoteletts und Nierenbraten.**
5. **Für morgen hat Nora Anton zum Essen eingeladen.**

p. 164, Exercise 7
1. She is one of his most faithful customers.
2. May I help you?
3. Her presence has not escaped his attention.
4. He greets her at the top of his voice.
5. Doesn't matter.

p. 164, Exercise 8
1. a 2. c 3. a 4. b 5. c

p. 164, Exercise 9
1. **erworben** 2. **einkaufen** 3. **Kalbsbeuschel**
4. **Koch** 5. **verwechselt**

p. 165   Nora Is Shopping
pp. 165-166

"Well, give me the veal lung and the roast loin,"
she says to Polzer. "Maybe also some of the pork
chops since you recommend them so highly. Those
I'll probably put into the freezer for next week." And
she thanks him for his advice.

Above all she needs milk; therefore, she goes to the
dairy products. Peter drinks a lot of it; she is glad.
Good for the bones. Gretchen doesn't like milk at all;
she and Karl take a little with the (their) morning
coffee. Karl is crazy about *Jungfernkranz grün,* a
funny name for a cheese. Stinks horribly, only he eats
it, and he has to tuck away into a glass jar whatever
remains, screw the cover tight, and stick it into the
refrigerator; otherwise it pollutes the whole house, and
everybody gets excited about it. It isn't nice that we
are spoiling Karl's harmless enjoyment, but the
stench . . .

The next stop is the fruit and vegetables
department, where she buys apples, pears, carrots,
tomatoes, spinach, cabbage, asparagus and lettuce.
Vegetables are very important for Nora. Since she is
very diet conscious and also convinced that one should
eat something yellow and something green as often as
possible, hardly a day passes on which there is not
some vegetable or a salad on the table. With spinach,
unfortunately, she is not very lucky, but her salads are
very popular. She prepares them mainly with vinegar
and oil (her own recipe), and they taste delicious,
especially if she cuts eggs and ham into them, too.
With hot, crisp, buttered rolls, tea or coffee (cocoa for
Peter) that makes for a very tasty supper. Once, when
she brought home a sauce (dressing) for the salad
from the supermarket, there was almost a revolution.

p. 166, Exercise 10
1. **f**   2. **t**   3. **t**   4. **f**   5. **t**

pp. 166-167, Exercise 11
1. **b**   2. **b**   3. **c**   4. **a**   5. **b**

p. 167, Exercise 12
1. **Rat**   2. **Glück**   3. **zuschrauben**   4. **Soße**
5. **Stopp**

p. 167, Exercise 13
1. **Peter trinkt Milch besonders gern.**
2. *Jungfernkranz grün* **stinkt entsetzlich.**
3. **Nora bereitet ihren Salat mit Essig und Öl zu.**
4. **Sie schneidet Eier und Schinken in den Salat.**
5. **Man ißt heiße Buttersemmeln mit dem Salat.**

p. 167   Lilly's Vegetarian Kitchen
pp. 167-169

In the meantime it (has) turned twelve o'clock.
Nora is hungry and would like to eat something. She
has taken care of all her purchases at Polzer's
Supermarket. Then she sees Mrs. Agnes List, a little
old lady (thin as a stick), whom she meets now and
then while shopping. Mrs. List is a fanatical vegetarian,

while Nora is a confirmed meat eater.

MRS. LIST Nice to see you again, Nora. If you are
done with your shopping, we can go eat.

NORA I am tired and hungry.

MRS. LIST I have the right thing for you. There's a
small restaurant three minutes from here, opened
only recently, which serves the most delicious
dishes.

NORA Since I was thinking of a little snack only, I
don't know whether I. . .

MRS. LIST As you are not in the mood for a big
meal, I'm sure you won't be disappointed. Come
with me.

NORA I have to pay attention to my diet.

MRS. LIST That you can do there without difficulty.
Here, we are lucky, a table for two. The place is
full. When I first heard of Lilly's Vegetarian Kitchen
I was suspicious. Quite without justification. We
(will) probably have to wait a little. Well, here is
the menu. Ah—oatmeal soup or barley soup with
plums. Baked cauliflower. Fried mushrooms—in
olive oil, of course; mashed broccoli, kohlrabi purée,
splendid. What do you want to order?

NORA The kohlrabi purée maybe—

MRS. LIST My own choice. With some rice?

NORA Good.

MRS. LIST And to drink? Cucumber juice with lemon? That's very refreshing. Or radish lemonade?

NORA A cup of coffee.

MRS. LIST We don't get that here. Bad for heart and
stomach.

NORA Then a glass of water.

MRS. LIST Herb tea?

NORA As you wish.

MRS. LIST I (will) take the same.

p. 169, Exercise 14
1. **f**   2. **t**   3. **t**   4. **t**   5. **t**

p. 169, Exercise 15
1. **Nora trifft Frau Agnes List.**
2. **Sie muß auf ihre Diät achten.**
3. **Frau List ist dünn wie ein Stock.**
4. **Auf der Speisekarte sind Haferschleimsuppe
   und Graupensuppe mit Pflaumen.**
5. **Lillys vegetarische Küche ist bloß drei Minuten
   vom Supermarkt.**

p. 169, Exercise 16
1. **Vegetarierin**   2. **Mahl**   3. **achten**   4. **zwei**
5. **Magen**

p. 169, Exercise 17
1. Agnes is as thin as a stick.
2. She was suspicious without justification.
3. Nora won't be disappointed.
4. They serve the tastiest dishes.
5. I (will) take the same.

Chapter 17, **p. 170**   The Soccer Game

p. 170   The Game (I)
pp. 170-171
ANTON (to Tim) How do you like the game?
TIM Very well (much).
ANTON Do you understand the rules?
TIM Peter explained them to me. But there are so many.
ANTON Which do you prefer, American football or soccer?
TIM Here they run around like crazy. It is difficult to follow the ball. But our kind is much, much. . .
PETER More dangerous, you mean?
TIM Yes. Most of what they do in America is (would be) a foul here. It is all so different. I like both games. I like baseball best.
ANTON That game nobody knows here at all.
PETER I like our football better. The players in America look so funny. And everybody has to be a giant.
TIM I'll never play our football.
PETER How do you know that?
TIM I have no muscles. And I don't eat enough spinach. Maybe I'll play soccer. Here **(in soccer)** one can be a shrimp.
ANTON Thank God, it stopped raining.
TIM Here it always rains. I am pretty wet.
ANTON Let's be glad that it wasn't worse.

The players are on the field again. The trainer (coach) must have given them a dressing-down, for they are suddenly like new. Now the crowd (audience) follows the game with great interest, applause, whistles and yells. The leading sports critic of the *Planet* has stood up. He sees that the Kickers are now on the offensive. The weather has gotten worse; threatening clouds show themselves (appear) in the sky.

p. 172, Exercise 1
1. **t** 2. **f** 3. **t** 4. **f** 5. **t**

p. 172, Exercise 2
1. **Tim wird in Amerika nie Fußball spielen, weil er keine Muskeln hat.**
2. **Er wird vielleicht Soccer spielen.**
3. **Der Trainer hat den Spielern die Leviten gelesen.**
4. **Der führende Sportkritiker ist aufgestanden.**
5. **Die Kickers sind jetzt im Angriff.**

p. 172, Exercise 3
1. **a** 2. **c** 3. **b** 4. **a** 5. **c**

p. 172, Exercise 4
1. **erklärt** 2. **Verrückt** 3. **im Angriff**
4. **Interesse** 5. **Himmel**

p. 172, Exercise 5
1. I like soccer best.

2. He likes every game.
3. In America there are many football clubs.
4. I like tennis more than soccer.
5. Do you like the game?

p. 173   The Game (II)
pp. 173-174
ANTON Well, look at this! You can clearly see that the Kickers are getting the better of them now.
PETER And the left wingforward, what's his name?
ANTON Fritz Pfaff. He came to the Kickers only three months ago. That's his acid test. He makes a beeline for the goal (runs in a straight line . . .).
PETER The spectators are beside themselves with joy.
ANTON There! The fullback tripped him. A foul! Everybody saw it. Here comes the referee. That was in the penalty area.
PETER The guy is trying to talk himself out of it.
ANTON He has come to the wrong man.
PETER Do you know the referee?
ANTON With him he'll be out of luck. Mr. Pichler is strict and fair.
TIM An eleven meter!
ANTON As it should be.
PETER Who's going to kick? Dietz, I hope.
TIM There he is.
ANTON Goal! Very close to the goal post. You can depend on Dietz!
TIM Now it is 1:1.
ANTON That's only the beginning.

Anton is right. The Kickers have again turned out to be a great team. Hannes Birgel just now beat back an attack of the Haselburgers and with a powerful kick forwarded the ball to Hubert Klaar, the right wing-forward. He passes it to Braunsteiner right away, and the latter (passes) to Hacker, and the score is 2:1. The fans of the Kickers are on cloud nine. The *Elf* now put all their eggs in one basket. The midfield players go to the rear in order to strengthen the defense. Their forwards wait in vain for a chance to take the offensive.

p. 175, Exercise 6
1. **f** 2. **t** 3. **f** 4. **f** 5. **t**

p. 175, Exercise 7
1. **c** 2. **a** 3. **c** 4. **a** 5. **c**

p. 175, Exercise 8
1. **entpuppt** 2. **übergehen** 3. **Glück**
4. **Monaten** 5. **Erwarten**

p. 175, Exercise 9
1. **Birgel hat soeben einen Angriff der Haselburger abgewehrt.**
2. **Er hat den Ball zu Hubert Klaar befördert.**
3. **Die Mittelfeldspieler der Haselburger gehen nach hinten.**

4. **Der Schiedsrichter ist streng und gerecht.**
5. **Für Fritz Pfaff war das die Feuerprobe.**

p. 175, Exercise 10
1. He runs toward him in a straight line.
2. She tries to talk herself out of it.
3. Surpassing all expectations, he plays very well.
4. One can depend on the guy.
5. As it should be.

p. 175   Victory!
pp. 175-177
ANTON The *Elf* are up against a brick wall. If they concentrate too much on defense, they can never win the game.

PETER This, of course, suits the Kickers to a T.

ANTON Yes, the *Elf* are now in a fix. Now, on top of that, here comes Arnold Dietz, the libero.

TIM Why, actually, is he called "libero," Anton?

ANTON That's the player who, depending on the situation, can play either defense or offense. Libero means *free* in Italian, do you know?

TIM Then he can play wherever he wants to?

ANTON Yes (that's it). I believe he wants to knock off the Haselburgers. There! What is this? A high ball from Schumacher, and Dietz heads it directly into the goal: 3:1.

The spectators enjoy themselves immensely. The first half was a disappointment. But now they get (are getting) their money's worth. The Kickers have thrown the *Elf* off balance. The defense of the Kickers is now in midfield, and the midfield players, together with the forwards, lay siege to the goal of the opponent. The only one who has remained behind is Birgel, the center half.

ANTON If the *Elf* break through, we are in a bad way. That can become (could get) dangerous. No rear guard. They should be more on their guard. There, the libero of the *Elf* has dribbled (himself) free and is coming toward our goal with breakneck speed.

PETER Like greased lightning!

ANTON God help us!

PETER But has he overlooked one vital factor?

ANTON You mean Birgel?

PETER Of course. He (Birgel) promptly takes the ball away from him and kicks it in the direction of Hacker.

TIM And Hacker kicks the ball into the goal: 4:1.

The applause of the audience is indescribable. Hats are thrown into the air; people embrace one another; they shout themselves hoarse. The fiasco of the first half is forgotten. One has never witnessed a comeback like this. The game is over.

p. 177, Exercise 11
1. t 2. t 3. f 4. f 5. t

pp. 177-178, Exercise 12
1. **b** 2. **a** 3. **a** 4. **c** 5. **a**

p. 178, Exercise 13
1. **„Libero" heißt frei auf deutsch.**
2. **Arnold Dietz will mit den Haselburgern Schluß machen.**
3. **Wenn die Elf durchbrechen, geht es den Kickers schlecht.**
4. **So ein Comeback hat man in Ludwigsheim noch nie erlebt.**
5. **Hüte werden am Ende des Spieles in die Luft geworfen.**

p. 178, Exercise 14
1. He is up against a brick wall.
2. Now, on top of that, here comes Dietz.
3. I hope I get my money's worth.
4. The man runs like greased lightning.
5. He overlooked one vital factor.

p. 178, Exercise 15
1. **Kosten** 2. **Klemme** 3. **königlich** 4. **Hut**
5. **Gleichgewicht**

Chapter 18, **p. 179**   Christmas

p. 179   Dick's Plans
pp. 179-180
DICK (to Nora) That was an amusing card that you sent out.

NORA Gretchen's idea. And Peter helped her with it. The children always look forward to Christmas very much and speak of nothing else for weeks.

DICK I can imagine.

KRISTY With us in America it is also a very great festival. Unfortunately, however, it has become overcommercialized.

NORA We have a similar problem here. But Christmas still has its own charm. (to Dick) I am glad that you could come.

DICK I was lucky that I didn't have to stay in the hospital tonight.

NORA How long are you going to work there (yet)?

DICK Maybe another two years.

NORA Do you want to specialize in something?

DICK I'd like to be a surgeon. As a boy I got sick when I saw blood. But that has changed. Maybe I can go to America again. There they are now far ahead in surgery.—Oh, here is Tim. How are you, young man?

TIM Thanks, very well. That is very nice of you, Mrs. Bauer, that you invited me.

NORA Peter's friend is my friend. Tim's parents, Major Kelley and his wife, went to Berchtesgaden for skiing. But they couldn't take Tim along because he sprained his arm a week ago.

DICK Let me see.

TIM One can see hardly anything anymore.

DICK It is still a little swollen. Does it hurt?

TIM Only a little. Until yesterday I still had to have it in a sling.

DICK Be glad that you did not break it.

NORA Do you want to settle down in Ludwigsheim?

DICK I don't know yet. You have a lot of physicians here. The hospital is very good, but I probably would prefer a larger city.

p. 180, Exercise 1
1. **f** 2. **f** 3. **t** 4. **t** 5. **f**

p. 180, Exercise 2
1. **Dick ist es als Jungem schlecht geworden, wenn er Blut sah.**
2. **Er wird vielleicht noch zwei Jahre in Ludwigsheim arbeiten.**
3. **In Amerika sind sie in der Chirurgie weit voraus.**
4. **Tims Eltern sind heute in Berchtesgaden.**
5. **Er hat sich seinen Arm verstaucht.**

p. 181, Exercise 3
1. **Schlinge**   2. **mitnehmen**   3. **geschwollen**
4. **Idee**   5. **Fest**

p. 181, Exercise 4
1. He looks forward to Christmas.
2. It has its own charm.
3. There they are far ahead.
4. He has sprained his arm.
5. He did not break it.

p. 181, Exercise 5
1. **Ich habe Glück gehabt.**
2. **Sie spricht von nichts anderem.**
3. **Er möchte gern Chirurg sein.**
4. **Das passierte vor einer Woche.**
5. **Er möchte sich in einer grösseren Stadt niederlassen.**

p. 181   The Curse of Smoking
pp. 181-182

NORA Excuse me, please. I have to see what's going on in the kitchen. They can probably do without me there with Mrs. Braun and Gretchen.

DICK Look out, Frau Nora: Too many cooks spoil the broth.

NORA No danger. Yet I think I should show myself (put in an appearance). Anton, where is Susie?

ANTON (She) is working like a trooper in the kitchen.

NORA She, too? I think I'll take her place.

ANTON How are you, Dick? Nice to see you again. Cigarette?

DICK No, thanks. I am glad I gave up smoking. I was a chain smoker. Practically lit up one on the other. Especially in my student days, when I had to cram for an exam.

ANTON How did you break the habit?

DICK Whenever I was smoking too much, I got a sore throat. But I continued smoking in spite of it.

One day it was so bad I could hardly talk. And the terrible cough in the morning! It was then that I told myself, knock it off, and I haven't touched a coffin nail since.

KRISTY I think you have a lot of willpower.

DICK While dissecting, I saw some lungs, let me tell you . . .

KRISTY Please, not today. Fortunately, we're not eating lung.

DICK You have to stop totally. In installments it does not work.

ANTON You are right. I have stopped five times already. But I have bad luck.

DICK What do you mean?

ANTON I never get a sore throat.

p. 182, Exercise 6
1. **t** 2. **f** 3. **f** 4. **t** 5. **t**

p. 182, Exercise 7
1. **Zu viele Köche verderben den Brei.**
2. **Anton bietet Dick eine Zigarette an.**
3. **Vor einer Prüfung hat Dick besonders viel geraucht.**

p. 182, Exercise 8
1. **c** 2. **a** 3. **c** 4. **c** 5. **a**

p. 182, Exercise 9
1. They can do without her there.
2. Nora will take her place.
3. He had to cram for the exam.
4. It does not work in installments.
5. He has bad luck.

p. 183, Exercise 10
1. **Küche**   2. **angezündet**   3. **reden**   4. **aufhören**
5. **Halsweh**

p. 183   How Was Christmas Business?
pp. 183-184

KARL Please take something to drink. The punch really is not bad. I even put some alcohol into it.

DICK Many thanks. And the hors d'oeuvres are really excellent.

ANTON Nora is a first-rate cook. — How was your Christmas business?

KARL Not bad.

ANTON What do you sell the most?

KARL The usual best-sellers. Between you and me, most of them are trash. But, of course, that is a matter of taste. Classics still sell pretty well as Christmas gifts, especially those with nice covers. After Christmas people try to exchange them because the children have received three Schillers or two Goethes.

DICK Do you exchange them?

KARL Yes, that you have to do.

DICK Most of the books that I buy are paperbacks. They have taken over the market, haven't they?

Answer Key   227

KARL Very much so. Unfortunately, they are not as cheap as they used to be. And one has to sell a lot of them, for the markup is very small.

ANTON I hear that Gretchen is a very good saleslady.

KARL I believe Gretchen could sell anything. She has a winning way of dealing with customers. When she is in the store, everything goes smoothly.

ANTON Do you sell for cash?

KARL I would like to, but nowadays everybody wants to buy on credit, and the bills in arrears grow from year to year.

ANTON You should have more Chinese for customers.

KARL What do you mean?

ANTON The Chinese pay all their debts punctually on January 1.

KARL That's easy for them. They don't have any Christmas the week before.

p. 184, Exercise 11
1. **t** 2. **t** 3. **f** 4. **t** 5. **f**

p. 184, Exercise 12
1. **Paperbacks** 2. **Einbänden** 3. **Schund**
4. **Schnürchen** 5. **schlecht**

p. 184, Exercise 13
1. **b** 2. **a** 3. **c** 4. **a** 5. **a**

p. 184, Exercise 14
1. Between you and me
2. Everything goes smoothly.
3. She knows how to deal with customers.
4. That is a matter of taste.
5. Karl cannot sell for cash only.

p. 184, Exercise 15
1. **Zum Punsch ißt man Hors d'oeuvres (Vorspeisen).**
2. **Karl nennt die meisten Bestsellers Schund.**
3. **Karl muß eine Menge Paperbacks verkaufen, weil der Kalkulationsaufschlag sehr klein ist.**
4. **Die Chinesen haben keine Weihnachten die Woche vorher.**
5. **Bei Karl wachsen die Außenstände von Jahr zu Jahr.**

p. 185   More About Ludwigsheim
pp. 185-186

Ludwigsheim is one of the oldest cities in Germany. It was founded by the emperor Ludwig II in 856, and is a beautiful example of a medieval settlement, flanked by ancient walls, towers, and gates.

The most interesting building is the city hall, in which the Gothic style is most purely preserved. Between 1200 and 1500 Ludwigsheim became a famous commercial and industrial center of southern Germany and did not lose its commercial importance until after the year 1500 when the maritime route to India was discovered.

Today Ludwigsheim is a city of solid citizens of relative wealth, the majority conservatively inclined, culturally interested, and proud of their soccer team. There is little poverty there, the streets and public grounds are spick and span. There is a fine of twenty marks for dropping a cigarette butt on the street. The night spots in Ludwigsheim you can count on the fingers of one hand. The moral standards are very high here, allegedly. A big-city dweller who is transplanted to Ludwigsheim will probably find the city boring.

But today it is crawling with tourists. The city fathers realized a long time ago that tourism is the only solid source of income for Ludwigsheim, and have done all they could—probably with mixed emotions—to put their best foot forward. The red wine of Ludwigsheim is famous in all of Germany: it is tasty, smooth, and light, and is consumed, therefore, in great quantities by the unsuspecting visitors; but you can get dead drunk on it very quickly.

p. 186, Exercise 16
1. **t** 2. **t** 3. **f** 4. **t** 5. **f**

p. 186, Exercise 17
1. **Die Stadt ist ein schönes Beispiel einer mittelalterlichen Siedlung.**
2. **Das kostet 20 Mark.**
3. **Von Armut ist wenig zu sehen.**
4. **Heute wimmelt es von Touristen.**
5. **Der Ludwigsheimer Rotwein ist süffig, lieblich, und leicht.**

p. 186, Exercise 18
1. spick and span
2. He did all he could.
3. He is dead drunk.
4. She puts her best foot forward.
5. The city fathers realized that a long time ago.

p. 186, Exercise 19
1. **b** 2. **a** 3. **c** 4. **b** 5. **a**

p. 187, Exercise 20
1. **Wohlstand** 2. **süffig** 3. **Siedlung**
4. **Nachtlokale** 5. **Bewegung**

p. 187   Back to the Bauers: In the Kitchen
pp. 187-188

During the last week one was very busy (there was a lot of activity) in Nora's kitchen. Now the last preparations for the big Christmas meal are being made; everything looks wonderful and smells marvelous.

KRISTY Please forgive me for not helping you. Unfortunately, I never really learned how to cook.

NORA Ah, you would only have been in the way. Four of us are more than enough.

KRISTY Maybe I can wash out the pots.

NORA Good. I hire you (you're hired) for later.

KRISTY I see you have two kinds of carp.

GRETCHEN Yes. One part is breaded, and the other is in aspic.

KRISTY It is hard to choose.

SUSIE You must taste both. They are masterpieces of culinary art.

KRISTY I like carp very much. Unfortunately, one doesn't get it in Denver, or very rarely.

GRETCHEN They don't know what's good.

MRS. BRAUN Here, taste a piece.

KRISTY Mmm—marvelous!

MRS. BRAUN And look at the giant goose. Nothing for your friend Mrs. List, the vegetarian. And the dumplings. With asparagus and cranberries.

SUSIE Do you think we'll have enough?

KRISTY I'm not sure.

SUSIE Nora is always very much afraid that the guests in her house are going to starve.

NORA Oh, stop it!

SUSIE I have to show you the dessert. Here. Apple dumplings, hazelnut torte, and, because it's Christmas, ginger cookies and gingerbread.

KRISTY Is that all?

SUSIE Here is the soup—cauliflower soup—smell it.

KRISTY I won't be able to eat anything for a week.

SUSIE Wait! And here is Nora's specialty, known city-wide: her famous mixed salad.

p. 188, Exercise 21
1. **f** 2. **t** 3. **f** 4. **t** 5. **t**

p. 188, Exercise 22
1. **Kristy wird später vielleicht die Töpfe auswaschen.**
2. **Kristy muß den Karpfen kosten.**
3. **Susie nennt Noras Karpfen ein Meisterwerk kulinarischer Kunst.**
4. **Mit der Gans serviert man Spargel und Preiselbeeren.**
5. **Dann hat man noch Ingwergebäck und Lebkuchen.**

p. 188, Exercise 23
1. **c** 2. **a** 3. **c** 4. **b** 5. **a**

p. 189, Exercise 24
1. **5** 2. **6** 3. **4** 4. **2** 5. **3** 6. **1**

p. 189, Exercise 25
1. You would only have been in our way.
2. They don't know what's good.
3. Kristy tastes a piece.
4. Are they going to starve in Nora's house?
5. Everything smells marvelous.

p. 189   The Christmas Meal
pp. 189-190

The meal is a great success. Everybody eats more than he (or she) should. Since the table in the dining room is not large enough, the children sit at a small, separate table in the corner. Karl has uncorked a few bottles of Rhine wine and fills the glasses of the guests again and again. Kristy is a little tipsy.

DICK A toast to our kind hostess. I must say that was the best meal of my life. (All applaud.)

KRISTY (to him) Especially after the food in the hospital.

NORA Many thanks, Dick. But you eat so little. Take more of the goose.

DICK Frau Nora, sometimes I eat more than usual, but never less. Thank you. How can I resist.

ANTON That's terrible. The nice hunger is all gone (I'm not hungry anymore).

SUSIE Leave some room for the dessert. Or you (will) offend my mother. The hazelnut torte is her specialty. (All applaud.)

NORA Children, have you had enough?

TIM May I have another portion of cranberries, Mrs. Bauer? They are sooo good.

NORA Gretchen made them. Here.

TIM I'll tell my mother about it. Maybe you can give her the recipe.

GRETCHEN Oh, she knows it I am sure. Don't you have them (cranberries) with turkey in America?

TIM Yes, but here they taste much better.

PETER I think I'm full.

GRETCHEN No torte?

PETER Maybe later.

p. 190, Exercise 26
1. **f** 2. **f** 3. **t** 4. **t** 5. **f**

p. 190, Exercise 27
1. **Die Kinder sitzen an einem Katzentisch.**
2. **Karl füllt die Gläser der Gäste mit Wein.**
3. **Nora ist die liebenswürdige Gastgeberin.**
4. **Die Gäste sollen sich für den Nachtisch Raum lassen.**
5. **In Amerika essen sie Preiselbeeren mit dem Truthahn.**

p. 190, Exercise 28
1. **wenig** 2. **beschwipst** 3. **genug** 4. **Rezept** 5. **Krankenhaus.**

p. 190, Exercise 29
1. The food in the hospital is miserable.
2. Sometimes Dick eats more than usual.
3. Tim gets another portion of cranberries.
4. In America turkey is very popular.
5. How can he resist?

p. 190, Exercise 30
1. **b** 2. **a** 3. **b** 4. **a** 5. **b**

p. 191   0 Tannenbaum
pp. 191-192

The guests make themselves comfortable in the living room and admire the beautiful Christmas tree that is decked out with glittering decorations but also with nuts, candy, and cookies. The children open their gifts and are on cloud nine. Karl offers **Kümmel** or **Slivovitz** to the guests. **Kümmel** is supposedly good for the digestion.

SUSIE Now we should sing carols.

NORA Unfortunately, we don't have a piano. Karl wanted to buy me one, but I told him: Wait until we move into the new house. There we'll have more room for a grand piano. But I have a surprise for you.

KRISTY What is it, Nora?

NORA You know that Peter is a musician. A very good cellist. He played a solo in the latest school orchestra concert. Excellently. But he wants to be a conductor.

GRETCHEN Sometimes he stands in the room and conducts with the records, sawing wildly in the air. But in this nobody must disturb him. Uncle Leopold says he does it very well.

NORA *My* uncle, the retired conductor. Tell them, Peter.

PETER After the cello I wanted to learn to play the flute. But there is something wrong with my teeth. And we don't have a piano yet. A conductor is supposed to play several instruments. Paganini and Berlioz were also excellent guitarists. Then Dad bought me a guitar two months ago.

DICK Can you play it already?

PETER That is pretty easy. But I wasn't the only one who got a guitar. Tim, now it's your turn.

TIM I've been playing the violin for four years. And I cannot stand it. Then Peter gets his guitar, I listen to him, and it is super. So I say to my Dad, "Dad, can you buy me a guitar, too?"

KRISTY And did you get it?

TIM Yes. here, I've brought it along.

p. 192, Exercise 31
1. t 2. f 3. t 4. f 5. t

p. 192, Exercise 32
1. **Am Weihnachtsbaum hängen Dekorationen.**
2. **Nora wird im neuen Haus ein Klavier haben.**
3. **Peter dirigiert im Zimmer.**
4. **Sein Vater hat ihm eine Gitarre geschenkt.**
5. **Tim kann das Violinspielen nicht ausstehen.**

p. 192, Exercise 33
1. c 2. a 3. a 4. b 5. a

p. 192, Exercise 34
1. Kümmel is supposedly good for the digestion.
2. Nora prefers a grand piano.
3. Peter saws the air.
4. What, says he, is pretty easy?
5. Now it's your turn.

p. 192, Exercise 35
1. **Violine** 2. **Ordnung** 3. **Klavier** 4. **Flöte**
5. **Solo**

p. 193   "Silent Night, Holy Night"
p. 193-

KRISTY What is the surprise, Nora? We can hardly wait.

NORA Peter taught Tim how to play the guitar. And they have been practicing carols for the last two weeks. But that isn't all.

ANTON It is I, actually, who should play the guitar.

DICK Why?

ANTON You know my name is Gruber.

DICK And?

ANTON On December 24, 1818, Franz Gruber composed "Silent Night, Holy Night," to a text by the priest Joseph Mohr. It was sung at midnight mass for the first time. That was in a village near Salzburg.

DICK Are you a descendant of Franz Gruber?

ANTON Quite possibly. My great-grandfather moved from Salzburg to Vienna.

KRISTY What does that have to do with the guitar?

ANTON Franz Gruber was a school teacher and organist in Oberndorf. But the organ that he should have played on Christmas Eve was ruined. Mice had gnawed at its works, and no sound came out. He, therefore, had to accompany the choir on the guitar. But we are lucky. We have not only one but two guitars here. Today you'll hear an artistic rendition of *"Silent Night, Holy Night"* not on the organ but the way it sounded originally. Ladies and gentlemen, I am presenting here two authentic interpreters of Gruber's music: Peter and Tim.

p. 193, Exercise 36
1. t 2. f 3. t 4. f 5. t

p. 194, Exercise 37
1. **Peter hat Tim die Gitarre spielen gelehrt.**
2. **„Stille Nacht" wurde 1818 zuerst gesungen.**
3. **Antons Urgroßvater ist von Salzburg nach Wien übersiedelt.**
4. **Die Orgel war am Weihnachtsabend kaputt.**
5. **Peter und Tim sind heute die Interpreten von Grubers Musik.**

p. 194, Exercise 38
1. **Weihnachtslieder** 2. **Dorf** 3. **Wiedergabe**
4. **Organist** 5. **Getriebe**

p. 194, Exercise 39
1. He taught him (how) to play the guitar.
2. Is Anton a descendant of Franz Gruber?
3. The boys are authentic interpreters of *"Silent Night."*
4. The organ was ruined.
5. No sound came out.

p. 194, Exercise 40
1. b 2. a 3. c 4. a 5. b

German-English Vocabulary

Definitions are limited to the contexts in which the words appear in the text.

Nouns are listed with their plural forms: *Tag, -e; Messer, -; Student, -en.* Plurals that take umlaut are shown as: *Fall, ⁻e; Mann, ⁻er; Mutter, ⁻.*

Nouns that are never (or rarely) used in a plural form are shown in the singular only: *Honig* **(m).** Similarly, nouns never or rarely used in the singular are shown in the plural form only: *Eltern* **(pl.).**

Strong and irregular verbs show their infinitive, simple past, and past participle forms. Any vowel change in the present tense is also shown: *geben, gibt, gab, gegeben.* Verbs taking the auxiliary *sein* are shown like this: *gehen, ging, ist gegangen.*

A

Aal, -e (m) eel
ab off, down, away
ab und zu once in a while, now and then
abbezahlen to pay off
abdrucken to print
Abend, -e (m) evening
Abendbrot (n) supper
Abendessen (n) dinner
Abendkleid, -er (n) evening gown
abends evenings
Abenteuer, - (n) adventure
aber but
abgemacht! it's a deal!
abgesehen davon apart from this
abgewöhnen (sich das Rauchen) to give up (smoking)
Abgott, ⁻er (m) idol
abhalten, hält ab, hielt ab, abgehalten to hold
abhängen to hang up
abholen to pick up
Abitur (n) final secondary school exam (college preparatory)
ablenken to divert
abliefern to deliver
ablösen to take the place of, relieve
abnehmen, nimmt ab, nahm ab, abgenommen to lose weight; to take away
abraten, rät ab, riet ab, abgeraten to advise against
Abonnement, -s (n) subscription
abrücken to move away, depart
Absicht, -en (f) intention
absolut absolute
Abteilung, -en (f) department
abwaschen, wäscht ab, wusch ab, abgewaschen to wash off
abwechselnd in turn
abwehren to beat back
abzapfen to draw off
abzählen to count off
ach! ah
achten to pay attention
sich in Acht nehmen to watch out
adelig titled

Adeliger, -en nobleman
Adresse, -n (f) address
ähnlich similar to
Akzent, -e (m) accent
akzentfrei accent-free
Album, Alben (n) album
allerdings to be sure
Allergie, -n (f) allergy
alles everything
allgemein general
Allgemeines Krankenhaus General Hospital
im allgemeinen in general
alliiert allied
Alphabet, -e (n) alphabet
als when, than, as
als ob, als wenn as if
also therefore, thus
alt old
altmodisch old-fashioned
Amateurstreichquartett, -e (n) amateur string quartet
Ameliensaal (m) Amelien Hall
Amerika (n) America
Amerikaner, - (m) American
amerikanisiert americanized
Amulett, -e (n) amulet, charm
sich amüsieren to amuse oneself
an to, at, on
anbieten, bot an, angeboten to offer
anbrechen, bricht an, brach an, angebrochen to open (as a bottle)
Andenken, - (n) souvenir
ander other
andernfalls otherwise
anders different
anderswo elsewhere
anderthalb one and a half
andeuten to hint
andrehen to turn on
Anfang, ⁻e, (m) start, beginning
anfangen, fängt an, fing an, angefangen to begin
Anfänger, - (m) beginner
anfüllen to fill
angeblich allegedly

Angelegenheit, -en (f) matter
angenehm agreeable
angesehen respected
Angestellter, -n (m) employee
Angriff, -e (m) offensive
zum Angriff übergehen to take the offensive
Angst, ⁻e (f) fear
ängstlich fearful
anhaben, hat an, hatte an, angehabt to have on, to be dressed in
anhalten, hält an, hielt an, angehalten to hold (one's breath)
Anhänger, - (m) fan (as of a team)
anhören to listen
Anisplätzchen, - (n) anise cookie
Ankauf, ⁻e, (m) purchase
anklopfen to knock at the door
ankommen, kam an, ist angekommen to arrive
Ankündigung, -en (f) announcement
Ankunft, ⁻e (f) arrival
Anlage, -n (f) investment
öffentliche Anlagen (f. pl.) public grounds
annagen to gnaw at
annehmen, nimmt an, nahm an, angenommen to suppose
anno dazumal way back
Annonce, -n (f) advertisement
annulieren to cancel
anrufen, rief an, angerufen to telephone
anrühren to touch
anschauen to look at
ansässig residing
sich ansässig machen to take up residence
sich anschnallen to buckle up
anscheinend apparently
sich (etwas) ansehen, sieht sich etwas an, sah sich etwas an, hat sich etwas angesehen to look (at something)
Ansicht, -en (f) opinion

ansonsten otherwise
anständig decent
anstreichen, strich an,
    angestrichen to paint
Antiquariat, -e (n) second-hand
    bookshop
(jemandem etwas) antun, tut an,
    tat an, angetan to do (a
    person) harm
Antwort, -en (f) answer
antworten to answer
Anzahl (f) number, amount
sich anziehen, zog sich an, sich
    angezogen to get dressed
Anzug, ¨e (m) suit
anzünden to light
Apfel, ¨ (m) apple
Äpfel im Schlafrock apple
    dumplings
Apfelsaft (m) apple juice
applaudieren to applaud
Applaus (m) applause
April, (m) April
Arbeit, -en (f) work
arbeiten to work
Architektur, -en (f) architecture
arg bad
Ärger (m) annoyance
Arie, -n (f) aria
Arm, -e (m) arm
Armut (f) poverty
Art, -en (f) kind, sort
auf diese Art in this way
Arzt, ¨e physician
Aspirinbüchse, -n (f) aspirin box
Assistenzarzt, ¨e (m) intern
astronomisch astronomical
Atelier, -s (n) studio
atlantisch Atlantic (adj.)
der atlantische Ozean the Atlantic
    Ocean
Attraktion, -en (f) attraction
attraktiv attractive
auch also
auf on, upon
aufbauen to build up, to construct
Aufenthalt, -e (m) stay
Auffassungsvermögen, - (n)
    perception; ability to
    comprehend, grasp things
aufgeben, gibt auf, gab auf,
    aufgegeben to give up, to send
aufhören to stop
aufgeregt excited
sich aufregen to get excited
Aufsatz, ¨e (m) essay
Aufschnitt, -e (m) cold cuts
aufstehen, stand auf, ist
    aufgestanden to get up
aufsuchen to go to see
auftragen, trägt auf, trug auf,
    aufgetragen to dish up
aufwecken to wake (someone)
Auge, -n (n) eye
mit einem lachenden und einem
    weinenden Auge with mixed
    emotions
mit verbundenen Augen
    blindfolded

August (m) August

aus out of, from
ausbezahlen to pay in full; here: to
    finish paying for
Ausblick, -e (m) outlook
Ausgabe, -n (f) expense
ausgebacken baked through, fully
    baked
ausgeben, gibt aus, gab aus,
    ausgegeben to spend
ausgehen, ging aus, ist
    ausgegangen to go out
er ist wie ausgewechselt he is like a
    new man
ausgezeichnet excellent
aushalten, hält aus, hielt aus,
    ausgehalten to stand
Aushilfe, -n (f) extra help
aushilfsweise as extra help
auskommen, kam aus, ist
    ausgekommen to make do
Ausnahme, -n (f) exception
ausnützen to take advantage of
Auspuffklappe, -n (f) exhaust valve
Auspuffrohr, -e (n) exhaust pipe
ausrauben to ransack
sich ausreden to excuse oneself
ausreichend sufficient
sich ausruhen to rest
ausschenken to pour out, to
    dispense
ausschicken to send out
Ausschlag, ¨e (m) rash
aussehen, sieht aus, sah aus,
    ausgesehen to look, appear
Außenstürmer, - (m) forward (on a
    soccer team)
außer except
außerdem besides
außerhalb outside of
aussetzen: was ist daran
    auszusetzen? what's wrong
    with that?
Aussicht, -en (f) chance
aussprechen, spricht aus, sprach
    aus, ausgesprochen to
    pronounce
ausständige Rechnungen (f. pl.)
    bills in arrears
ich kann ihn nicht ausstehen I
    cannot stand him
aussteigen, stieg aus, ist
    ausgestiegen to get off
Australien (n) Australia
ausübend practicing
Ausverkauf, ¨e (m) final sale
ausverkauft sold out
authentisch authentic
Automat, -en (m) automaton

B

Backwerk (n) pastries
baden to bathe
Badezimmer, - (n) bathroom
Bahnzeit, -en (f) railroad time
Ball, ¨e (m) ball
Ballorchester, - (n) ball orchestra
Bank, -en (f) bank
bankrott bankrupt
gegen bar verkaufen to sell for
    cash

Batterie, -n (f) battery
Bauer, -n (m) peasant, farmer
Baum, ¨e (m) tree
bayerisch Bavarian (adj.)
beantworten to reply
Beantwortung, -en (f) reply
bedauern to regret
bedeuten to mean
bedeutend important
es bedeutet ihm nichts it doesn't
    mean anything to him, is of no
    importance to him
Bedeutung, -en (f) importance
bedienen to serve
Beefsteak, -s (n) beefsteak
beehren to honor
befördern to forward
begabt talented
Beginn, - (m) beginning
beginnen, begann, begonnen to
    begin
begleiten to accompany
Begleitumstände (m. pl.)
    accompanying circumstances
begreifen, begriff, begriffen to
    grasp, comprehend
begrüßen to greet
behandeln to treat
behalten to keep
behängen to deck out
beherbergen to accommodate
behilflich sein to be of service
bei near, with, at the home of
bei weitem by far
beide both
Beifall (m) applause
Bein, -e (m) leg
(jemandem) ein Bein stellen to trip
    (someone)
beinahe almost
beichten to confess
sich beeilen to hurry
beisammen together
Beisammensein (n) togetherness
Beispiel, -e (n) example
zum Beispiel for example
ein Bekannter, -n (m) acquaintance
bekanntgeben to make known
bekanntlich as everybody knows
bekommen, bekam, bekommen to
    receive
belagern to lay siege to
belästigen to bother
belegen to cover
beleidigen to offend
beliebt popular
bellen to bark
bemerken to notice
benachbart neighboring
Benehmen (n) behavior
benennen to name
benutzen to use
Benzin, - (n) gasoline
beobachten to observe
bequem comfortable
berechtigt justified
Berechtigung, -en (f) justification
Berg, -e (m) mountain
bereiten to prepare
bereits already

Bericht, -e (f) report
Bernhardiner, - (m) St. Bernard dog
Berufsaussichten (f. pl.) professional outlook, prospects
berufsmäßig professional
berühmt famous
berühren to touch
wie ihre finanzielle Situation beschaffen ist how she is doing financially
beschäftigt busy
beschließen, beschloß, beschlossen to decide
beschränken to restrict
beschreiben, beschrieb, beschrieben to describe
beschwipst tipsy
besitzen, besaß, besessen to own
Besitzer, - (m) owner
besonders especially
besorgen to attend to
besser better
best- best
bestehen, bestand, bestanden to exist; to pass (an exam)
bestätigen to confirm
bestellen to order
bestimmt certain(ly)
bestürzt dismayed
besuchen to visit
Betrag, -e (m) amount
betreten to enter
Betriebskapital, -ien (n) working capital
Bett, -en (n) bed
bevor before
bevorzugen to prefer
bewahren to preserve
sich bewegen to move
beweisen, bewies, bewiesen to prove
bewilligen to grant
bewundern to admire
bezahlen to pay
sich beziehen auf, bezog sich, hat sich bezogen to refer to
Beziehung, -en (f) relation
Bezirk, -e (m) district
Biber, - (m) beaver
Bier, -e (n) beer
Bierflasche, -en (f) beer bottle
Bild, -er (n) picture
Bildhauer, - (m) sculptor
bildhauern to sculpt
Billard, -s (n) billiards
billig cheap
ich bin I am
Birne, -n (f) pear
bis until
bis auf except for
bisher, bis jetzt so far, until now
Biskuitschnitte, -n (f) slice of pound cake
ein bißchen a little
Bissen, - (m) bite (noun)
bitte please
Bitte, -n (f) request
bitten, bat, gebeten to request
blasen, bläst, blies, geblasen to blow

blasiert blasé
Blatt, -er (n) leaf, sheet
blau blue
bleiben, blieb, ist geblieben to stay
Blick, -e (m) glance
Blitz, -e (m) lightning
blöd(e) stupid
blond blonde
bloß only
Blume, -n (f) flower
Blumenkohl, -e (m) cauliflower
Bluse, -n (f) blouse
Blut, - (n) blood
blutig bloody
Boden, - (m) floor
Bonbon, -s (n) candy
Boot, -e (n) boat
böse angry
Branche, -n (f) line of business
brauchen to need
braun brown
brav well-behaved
Brei, - (m) pap, porridge, mush
Bremse, -n (f) brake
brennen, brannte, gebrannt to burn
schwarzes Brett, -er (n) bulletin board
Briefmarke, -n (f) stamp
bringen, brachte, gebracht to bring
Brosche, -n (f) brooch
Broschüre, -n (f) brochure
Brot, -e (n) bread
bruchstückweise in excerpts
Brücke, -n (f) bridge
Bruder, - (m) brother
Bruderschaft trinken to pledge close friendship
Bube, -n (m) boy
Buch, -er (n) book
Buchhalter, - (m) bookkeeper
Buchhandel (m) book trade
Buchhändler, - (m) bookseller
Buchladen, - (m) bookstore
Buchstabe, -n (m) letter
büffeln to cram (for an exam)
Bühne, -n (f) stage
Bündel, - (n) bunch
bunt many-colored
Bürger, - (m) citizen
Büro, -s (n) office
Bürovorstand, -e (m) office manager
bürsten to brush
Busenfreund, -e (m); (-in) (f) bosom friend
Butterkremtorte, -n (f) buttercream torte
Buttersemmel, -n (f) buttered roll

C

Café-Konditorei, -en (f) café-pastry shop
Cellist, -en (m) cello player
Cello, -s (n) cello
Cellostunde, -en (f) cello lesson
Charakter, -e (m) character
Charme (m) charm
Chef, -s (m) boss

Chinese, -n (m) Chinese
Chirurg, -en (m) surgeon
Chirurgie (f) surgery
Chor, -e (m) choir
Computer, - (m) computer
Computerprogrammierung, -en (f) computer programming
Couchtisch, -e (m) endtable
Cowboystiefel, - (m) cowboy boot

D

da there, then, since, because
dabei for all that
Dachstube, -n (f) attic
dadurch, daß due to the fact that
dafür for it
hast du etwas dagegen? do you mind?
daher therefore
damals at that time
Dame, -n (f) lady
damit with it; so that
dank due to
dankbar grateful
danke! thank you
danken to thank
dann then
daran thereon
darbieten, bietet dar, bot dar, dargeboten to offer
darf ich? may I?
darin in it
darstellen to represent
darum therefore
darunter among them
das the, that
dasselbe the same
daß that
Dattel, -n (f) date
gefüllte Datteln stuffed dates
dauern to last
Deckel, - (m) lid
decken to cover
Defekt, -e (m) defect
definitiv definitive
Dekoration, -en (f) decoration
deliziös delicious
denken, dachte, gedacht to think
denn for
dennoch however
der the, this
deren whose
derselbe the same
deshalb therefore
dessen whose
deutlich distinct
deutsch German
Deutschklasse, -n (f) German class
d.h. = das heißt that means; e.g.
Diät, -en (f) diet
diätbewußt diet conscious
dick fat
die the, this, these
Diele, -n (f) den
Dienstag, -e (m) Tuesday
Dienstmann, -er (m) porter
dieser this
diesmal this time
diktieren to dictate

Diplomat, -en (m) diplomat
direkt direct
Dirigent, -en (m) conductor
dirigieren to conduct
Doktor, -en (m) physician
Donnerstag, -e (m) Thursday
Dorf, ⁻er (n) village
dort there
dortig of that place
draußen outside
drei, dreimal, dreizehn, three, three times, thirteen
dreißig thirty
dribbeln to dribble (as in soccer, basketball)
dringend urgent
drinnen inside
drohen to threaten
drohend threatening
Drohung, -en (f) threat
drucken to print
du you (familiar)
duften to smell good
dumm stupid
Dummkopf, ⁻e (m) dumbbell, stupid person
dunkel dark
dünn thin
durch through, by
durchbrechen, bricht durch, brach durch, durchgebrochen to break through
durcheinander pell-mell
dürfen to be allowed to
sich duzen to be on familiar terms with a person

E

eben just now
ebenfalls also
ebenso wie just as
Ecke, -n (f) corner
es ist mir egal it's all the same to me
eher rather
Ehre, -n (f) honor
ehren to honor
Ehrgeiz, -e (m) ambition
Ei, -er (n) egg
eigen - own
eigensinnig stubborn
eigentlich actually
ein a, an
einander one another
Einband, ⁻e (m) cover, binding (of a book)
sich einbilden to imagine
Einbrecher, - (m) burglar
eindringlich emphatic
Eindruck, ⁻e (m) impression
einerseits on the one hand
einfach simple
einfallen: es fällt mir ein it occurs to me
Einführung, -en (f) introduction
eingehend extensive
eingeschüchtert intimidated
eingestellt inclined

Einkauf, ⁻e (m) purchase
einkaufen to purchase
Einkommensquelle, -n (f) source of income
einladen, lädt ein, lud ein, eingeladen to invite
einlangen to arrive
einlullen to lull (into a false sense of security)
einmal once; someday, sometime
einnehmen, nimmt ein, nahm ein, eingenommen to take in
einrichten to furnish
einschalten to turn on
einschlafen, schläft ein, schlief ein, ist eingeschlafen to fall asleep
einschreiben, schrieb ein, eingeschrieben to register (a letter)
einsehen, sieht ein, sah ein, eingesehen to realize
zu früh einsetzen to begin too soon
sich für jemanden einsetzen to stand up for someone
einst at one time
eintragen, trägt ein, trug ein, eingetragen to enter (as in a list)
eintreten, tritt ein, trat ein, ist eingetreten to enter (as into a room)
Einwohner, - (m) inhabitant
einziehen, zieht ein, zog ein, ist eingezogen to move into
einzig only
Eisenbahn, -en (f) railroad
Eisschrank, ⁻e (m) refrigerator
Elfmeter, - (m) a penalty kick in soccer
Eltern (pl.) parents
empfehlen, empfiehlt, empfahl, empfohlen to recommend
emsig busy
Ende, -n (n) end
zu Ende at an end
endlich finally
Energie, -n (f) energy
eng narrow
engagieren to hire
englisch English
entdecken to discover
entfernt distant
entgehen, entging, ist entgangen to escape (a person's attention)
Enthusiasmus, (m) enthusiasm
enthusiastisch enthusiastic
entkorken to uncork
entlang along
entlassen, entläßt, entließ, entlassen to discharge (as from the army)
sich entpuppen to turn out to be
entscheiden, entscheidet, entschied, entschieden to decide
sich entschließen, entschloß, entschlossen to decide, resolve
sich entschuldigen to excuse oneself
entsetzlich dreadful
enttäuscht disappointed

Enttäuschung, -en (f) disappointment
entweder—oder either—or
entwerfen, entwirft, entwarf, entworfen to design
Entwurf, ⁻e (m) design
erdolchen to stab (with a dagger)
Ereignis, -se (n) event
Erfahrung, -en (f) experience
Erfolg, -e (m) success
erfolgreich successful
Ihr sehr ergebener yours very truly
Erhalt (m) receipt
erhalten, erhält, erhielt, erhalten to receive
sich erinnern to remember
sich erkälten to catch a cold
erkennen, erkannte, erkannt to recognize
erklären to explain
erleben to witness
erledigen to bring to a close
ermutigen to encourage
sich ermutigt fühlen to feel encouraged
im Ernst seriously speaking
ernstnehmen, nimmt ernst, nahm ernst, ernstgenommen to take seriously
eröffnen to open
erraten, errät, erriet, erraten to guess
errichten to put up
Ersatz, ⁻e (m) substitute
erschaffen, erschuf, erschaffen to create
erscheinen, erschien, ist erschienen to appear
ersetzen to substitute
erst only
erst recht all the more so; not to mention
erstens firstly
erstklassig first-class
erstaunlich amazing
ersuchen to request
erwarten to expect
Erwartung, -en (f) expectation
erwachsen adult
erwähnen to mention
erwerben, erwirbt, erwarb, erworben to acquire
erwidern to reply
erzählen to tell
erziehen, erzog, erzogen to educate
Erziehungsmethode, -n (f) educational method
es it
essen, ißt, aß, gegessen to eat
das Essen, - (n) meal, food
Eßzimmer, - (n) dining room
Etikett, -e (n) label
etwa maybe, perhaps
etwas something
euer your
Europa (n) Europe
europäisch European (adj)
eventuell perhaps
Exekutivbüro, -s (n) executive office

F

Fach, ̈er (n) field, subject
Fachhochschule, -n (f) specialized college
fahren, fährt, fuhr, ist gefahren to go, travel, drive
Fahrt, -en (f) travel, trip
faktisch for all practical purposes
Fall, ̈e (m) case
fallen, fällt, fiel, ist gefallen to fall
fallenlassen, läßt fallen, ließ fallen, hat fallenlassen to drop
falls in case of
falsch wrong
Familie, -n (f) family
Familienangelegenheiten (f. pl.) family matters, affairs
Familienkonferenz, -en (f) family conference
fanatisch fanatical
fangen, fängt, fing, gefangen to catch
fast almost
fasten to fast
fasziniert fascinated
Faust, ̈e (f) fist
Februar (m) February
fehlen to be lacking
was fehlt ihr? what's wrong with her?
Fehler, - (m) mistake
fehlerlos without a mistake
Feld, -er (n) field
Feldweg, -e (m) country lane
Fenster, - (n) window
Ferien (pl.) vacation
Ferienpläne (pl.) vacation plans
fern distant, apart
Fernseher, - (m) TV set
fertig done
fesch dashing
Fest, -e (n) feast
fest firm
Festessen, - (n) festive meal
festhalten, hält fest, hielt fest, festgehalten to hold onto firmly
festmachen to fasten
fett fat
feucht moist
feuern to fire
Feuerprobe, -n (f) acid test
Fiaker, -s (m) a special Viennese cab
Fiasko, -s (n) fiasco
Fieber, - (n) fever
Figur, -en (f) figure
Film, -e (m) film
finanziell financial
finden, findet, fand, gefunden to find
Finger, - (m) finger
Firma, -en (f) firm
Fisch, -e (m) fish
fischen to fish
Fischer, - (m) fisherman
Fischgeschäft, -e (n) fish market
Flächeninhalt, -e (m) area
Flammenwerfer, - (m) flame thrower
Flasche, -n (f) bottle

Fleisch (n) meat
Fleischbrühe, -n (f) beef broth
Fleischgericht, -e (n) meat dish
fleißig diligent
fliegen, flog, ist geflogen to fly
fließend fluently
Flöte, -n (f) flute
Fluch, ̈e (m) curse
Flug, ̈e (m) flight
Flügel, - (m) wing; grand piano
Flugplatz, ̈e (m) airport
Flugzeug, -e (n) airplane
folgen to follow
die Folgen (f. pl.) consequences
Form, -en (f) form, shape
förmlich practically
fortfahren, fährt fort, fuhr fort, ist fortgefahren to take off
fortfliegen, flog fort, ist fortgeflogen to fly away
fortsetzen to continue
Foul, -s (n) foul (in soccer)
Frack, -s (m) tails
Frage, -n (f) question
fragen to ask
Frau, -en (f) woman
Fräulein, - (n) Miss, Ms.
frei free
im Freien in the open
Freitag, -e (m) Friday
Freizeit, -en (f) spare time
fremd strange, foreign
Fremdenverkehr (m) tourism
ein Fremder, -n (m) a stranger
Fremdwort, ̈er (n) foreign word
fressen, frißt, fraß, gefressen to eat (said of animals; *essen* is used for human beings.)
Freude, -n (f) joy
Freude bereiten to give joy
außer sich vor Freude sein to be beside oneself with joy
Freund, -e (m) friend
freundlich friendly
frieren, fror, gefroren to freeze
frisch fresh
froh glad
Frucht, ̈e (f) fruit
früh early
Frühling. -e (m) spring
Frühstück, -e (n) breakfast
Frühstückstisch, -e (m) breakfast table
fühlen to feel
sich wohl fühlen to feel well
führen to lead, to carry
führend leading
Führerscheinprüfung, -en (f) driver's license test
Führungskraft, ̈e (f) executive
füllen to fill
fünf, fünfzehn, fünfzig five, fifteen, fifty
für for
fürchterlich awful
Fürst, -en, (m) prince
Fuß, ̈e (m) foot
zu Fuß on foot
Fußball (m) soccer
Fußballmannschaft, -en (f) soccer team

Fußballspieler, - (m) soccer player
Fußballstadion, -s (n) soccer stadium
Futter, - (n) lining (as of a coat)

G

ganz complete, very
garantieren to guarantee
garstig nasty
Garten, ̈ (m) garden
Gas, -e (n) gas
Gast, ̈e (m) guest
Gastgeber, - (m) host
Gasthaus, ̈er (n) restaurant
Gaststätte, -n (f) restaurant
Gatte, -n (m) spouse (husband)
Gattin, -nen (f) spouse (wife)
Gebäude, - (n) building
geben, gibt, gab, gegeben to give
gebildet educated
geboren born
gebraucht used
Geburtstag, -e (m) birthday
Gedicht, - (n) poem
gefallen, gefällt, gefiel, gefallen to please
es gefällt mir I like it
Gefahr, -en (f) danger
gefährlich dangerous
Gefrorenes (n) ice cream
gegen at about, toward, against
Gegend, -en (f) area, neighbor, neighborhood
gegenüber opposite
Gegenwart (f) presence
gegenwärtig present
Gegner, - (m) opponent
Gehalt, ̈er (n) salary
Gehaltsaufbesserung, -en (f) increase in salary
Gehaltserhöhung, -en (f) increase in salary
gehen, ging, ist gegangen to go, walk
im Geheimen secretly
Geheimnis, -se (n) secret
gehören to belong
wie es sich gehört as it is fitting
Geiger, - (m) violinist
geizig stingy
Gejammer (n) lamentation, complaining
geläufig fluent
gelb yellow
Geld, -er (n) money
mir ist das Geld ausgegangen I ran short of money
Gelegenheit, -en (f) occasion
gelegentlich occasionally
gemächlich leisurely
Gemüse, - (n) vegetable
gemütlich cosy
genau accurate
General, ̈e (m) general
Generation, -en (f) generation
genießen, genoß, genossen to enjoy
Genossenschaft, -en (f) co-op
genug enough
genügen to be sufficient

geölt oiled
Geplauder (n) small talk
geráde just now
gerécht just
Gericht, -e (n) meal; court
gern gladly
ich habe ihn gern I like him
Gesandtschaftsattaché, -s (m)
  attaché
Geschäft, -e (n) business
Geschäftsbrief, -e (m) business
  letter
geschäftshalber for business reasons
Geschäftskorrespondenz, -en (f)
  business correspondence
Geschäftsleben (n) business life
Geschenk, -e (n) gift
Geschichte, -n (f) story
geschickt skilled
geschieden divorced
Geschirr (n) dishes
Geschirrspülmaschine, -n (f)
  dishwasher
Geschlecht, -er (n) gender, sex
Geschmack, ̈-e (m) taste
das ist Geschmacksache that's a
  matter of taste
geschniegelt und gebügelt spick and
  span
geschraubt stilted
Geschwister (pl.) siblings
geschwollen swollen
Gesellschaft, -en (f) company,
  party, society
Gesicht, -er (n) face
Gesichtszüge (m. pl.) facial features
ich bin gespannt I am anxious to
  know
Gespräch, -e (n) conversation
gesprächig talkative
Gestalt, -en (f) figure
Gestank (m) bad smell
gestehen, gestand, gestanden to
  confess
gestern yesterday
gesund healthy
Getriebe, - (n) works
Gewicht, -e (n) weight
gewinnen, gewann, gewonnen to
  win
gewinnend winning
gewiß certain
Gewissen (n) conscience
gewissenhaft conscientious
Gewitter, - (n) thunderstorm
gewogen favorably inclined
gewöhnlich usual
gierig greedy
Gitarre, -n (f) guitar
glänzend splendid
Glas, ̈-er (n) glass
Glasgefäß, -e (n) glass jar
glauben to believe
Gläubiger, - (m) creditor
gleich similar; immediately
gleichen, glich, geglichen to equal
Gleichgewicht, -e (n) balance
aus dem Gleichgewicht bringen to
  throw off balance
gleichzeitig at the same time

glitzern to glitter
glorreich famous
Glück (n) good luck, happiness
Glück haben to be lucky
zum Glück luckily
glücklich happy
Glückwünsche (m. pl.)
  congratulations
glühend burning, glowing
gnädige Frau, -en (f) Madam
Gold (n) gold
Gott, ̈-er (m) god
Gott sei Dank! thank God
Gramm, -e (n) gram
gräßlich horrible
Gräte, -n (f) fish bone
gratulieren to congratulate
grau gray
Graupensuppe, -n (f) barley broth
grell bright
Grenze, -n (f) border
grob gruff
Groschen, - (m) penny
**groß, big, tall
großartig grand
Großmutter, ̈: (f) grandmother
Großstädter, - (m) city dweller
Großvater, ̈: (m) grandfather
Grübchen, - (n) dimple
grün green
im Grunde genommen basically
gründen to found
Grundlage, -n (f) basis
gründlich thorough
Gruppe, -n (f) group
Gruß, ̈-e (m) greeting
Grüß Gott! a greeting used in
  southern Germany and Austria
Gurkensaft, ̈-e (m) cucumber juice
gut good
das Gut, ̈-er (n) property
gutmütig good-natured
Gymnasium, -ien (n) secondary
  school with emphasis on the
  classics

H

Haar, -e (n) hair
haben, hat, hatte, gehabt to have
Haferschleimsuppe, -n (f) oatmeal
  soup
halb half
Halbzeit, -en (f) half time
hallo hello
Hals, ̈-e (m) neck
halsbrecherisch breakneck
Halsweh (n) sore throat
halt just
halten, hält, hielt, gehalten to
  hold, to block
jemanden dafür halten to consider
  someone as
etwas von jemandem halten to
  think much of someone
Hand, ̈-e (f) hand
Händedruck, ̈-e (m) handshake
Handel (m) commerce
Handelszentrum, -en (n)
  commercial center

Handschuhe (m. pl.) gloves
Handtasche, -n (f) pocketbook
hängen to hang
hänseln to tease
hart hard
Haselnußtorte, -n (f) hazelnut torte
hassen to hate
Hauptsache, -n (f) main thing
hauptsächlich mainly
Hauptsitz, -e (m) main office
Hauptstadt, ̈-e (f) capital
Haus, ̈-er (n) house
zu Hause at home
Hausaufgabe, -n (f) homework
Hausbesitzer, - (m) landlord
Hauseingangstür, -en (f) house
  entrance door
Hausfrau, -en (f) housewife
Hausgehilfin, -nen (f) domestic
hausgemacht homemade
Hauslehrer, - (m) tutor
Hauswirtschaft, -en (f) household
Hebebühne, -n (f) hydraulic lift
Hebel, - (m) lever
alle Hebel in Bewegung setzen to
  do all one can
Heim, -e (n) home
Heimat (f) homeland
Heimatstadt, ̈-e (f) home town
heimbringen to bring home
heimkehren to come home
heiser hoarse
heiß hot
mir ist heiß I am warm
heißen, hieß, geheißen to be called
helfen, hilft, half, geholfen to help
Hemd, -en (n) shirt
heráuskriegen to remove
heráusstellen to set off, to bring out
**heráusziehen, zog heraus,
  heráusgezogen** to draw out
Herbst, -e (m) fall
Hering, -e, (m) herring
**herkommen, kam her, ist
  hergekommen** to come here
herumfuchteln to saw the air
herumklettern to climb around
herumkommandieren to order about
**herumspringen, sprang herum, ist
  herumgesprungen** to jump
  around
**herunterkommen, kam herunter,
  ist heruntergekommen** to
  come down, off
Herr, -en (m) Mr.
herrlich magnificent
hervorragend outstanding
Herz, -en (n) heart
herzig cute
herzlich cordial
Heurige (n), - (m) new wine
Heuschrecke, -n (f) grasshopper
heute today
heutig of today
heutzutage nowadays
Hilfe (f) help
hilfsbereit ready to help
Himmel, - (m) sky, heaven
im siebenten Himmel in Seventh
  Heaven, on cloud nine

hin und her back and forth
hinausschmeißen, schmiß hinaus, hinausgeschmissen to throw out
hineinfahren, fährt hinein, fuhr hinein, ist hineingefahren to drive in
hineinschmuggeln to smuggle into
hineinschneiden, schnitt hinein, hineingeschnitten to cut into
hineintun, tut hinein, tat hinein, hineingetan to put into
hingegen on the other hand
hingehen, ging hin, ist hingegangen to go there
hinhängen to hang there
hinlegen, hinstellen to put there
hinten in the back
nach hinten to the back
hinter behind
hintereinander one after another
Hitze (f) heat
hoch high
hoffen to hope
hoffentlich it is to be hoped
höflich polite
Höflichkeit (f) politeness
Höhe, -n (f) height
Holzbank, ⸚e (f) wooden bench
Honig (m) honey
hören to hear
hör doch auf damit! stop this!
Horn, ⸚er (n) horn
Hotel, -s (n) hotel
Hotelreservierung, -en (f) hotel reservation
hübsch pretty
Humor (m) humor
Hund, -e (m) dog
hundert hundred
Hundertmarkschein, -e (m) hundred mark bill
Hunger (m) hunger
hungrig hungry
hurra! horray!
Husten (m) cough
auf der Hut sein to be on one's guard

I

ich I
Ideal, -e, (n) ideal
Idee, -n (f) idea
ihr you (familiar, pl.)
Ihr your (formal)
illustrieren to illustrate
immer always
importieren to import
imstande sein to be able to
im Wege stehen, stand, gestanden to stand in (someone's) way
in in, inside of, into
indem while
Indien (n) India
Industriezentrum, -en (n) industrial center
innerhalb within
Insel, -n (f) island
Inserat, -e (n) advertisement
insofern (in) so far as

inspizieren to inspect
installieren to install
Institution, -en (f) institution
Instrument, -e (n) instrument
interessant interesting
sich interessieren to be interested
Interpret, -en (m) interpreter
Interview, -s (n) interview
interviewen to interview
Inventur, -en (f) inventory
irgendeinmal sometime
Irrenhaus, ⸚er (n) insane asylum
Italien (n) Italy

J

ja yes
Jacke, -n (f) jacket
Jahr, -e (n) year
Jahrhundert, -e (n) century
jährlich annual
Januar (m) January
japanisch Japanese (adj.)
Jazzkonzert, -e (n) jazz concert
je—desto the—the
je nach der Situation depending on the situation
Jeans (pl.) jeans
jeder every, each
jederzeit anytime
jemand somebody
jetzig of the present time
johlen to yell
jugendlich youthful
jung young
Junge, -n (m) boy
Jungfernkranz (m) the name of a fictitious cheese
Junggeselle, -n (m) bachelor
Juni (m) June
Juli (m) July

K

Kaffee (m) coffee
Kaffee mit Schlag coffee with whipped cream
Kaffeepause, -n (f) coffee break
Kaiser, - (m) emperor
Kaiserreich, -e (n) empire
Kakao (m) cocoa
Kalbsbeuschel, - (n) calf's lung
Kalbsschnitzel, - (n) breaded veal
Kalbszungenfrikassee, -s (n) veal tongue á la king
Kalkulationsaufschlag, ⸚e (m) markup
Kalorie, -n (f) calorie
kalt cold
Kamera, -s (f) camera
Kampf, ⸚e (m) battle
Kandiszucker (m) sugar candy
Kapellmeister, - (m) conductor
Kaper, -n (f) caper
Kapitalanlage, -n (f) investment
kaputt ruined
Kardinalzahl, -en (f) cardinal number
Karikatur, -en (f) cartoon
Karosse, -n (f) coach
Karosserie, -n (f) (car) body

Karriere, -n (f) career
Karriere machen to be quickly promoted
Karte, -n (f) card
Karten spielen to play cards
Kartoffelsuppe, -n (f) potato soup
Käse (m) cheese
Kasse, -n (f) checkout counter
Katze, -n (f) cat
Katzentisch, -e (m) small, separate table
kaufen to buy
Kaufhaus, ⸚er (n) department store
kein not a, not any
kein Anlaß! don't mention it
Keks, -e (m) cookie
Kellner, - (m) waiter
kennen, kannte, gekannt to know
kennenlernen to become acquainted with
Kenntnis, -sse (f) knowledge
Kettenraucher, - (m) chain-smoker
Kilo, -s (n) kilogram
Kind, -er (n) child
kindisch childish
Kino, -s (n) cinema, movies
Kinobesuch, -e (m) going to the movies
Kipfel, - (n) croissant
Kirche, -n (f) church
klagen to complain
klar clear
Klarinette, -n (f) clarinet
Klasse, -n (f) class
Klassenlehrer, - (m) class teacher
Klassiker, - (m) classic
klassisch classical
Klavier, -e (n) piano
Klavierlehrerin, -innen, (f) piano teacher
klebrig sticky
klein small
von klein auf from an early age
Klemme, - (f) pinch
in der Klemme sein to be in a fix
Klient, -en (m) client
Klima, -s (n) climate
klingen, klang, geklungen to sound
Klo, -s (n) toilet
Klub, -s (m) club
Knie, -e (n) knee
knipsen to shoot (a picture)
Knirps, -e (m) midget, shrimp
Knödel, - (m) dumpling
knusprig crisp
Koch, ⸚e (m) cook
viele Köche verderben den Brei too many cooks spoil the broth
kochen to cook
Kohl, -e (m) cabbage
Kohlrabi, -s (m) kohlrabi (a kind of cabbage)
Kölnischwasser, - (n) cologne
komisch funny
kommen, kam, ist gekommen to come
Kommission, -en (f) consignment
Kompliment, -e (n) compliment
kompliziert complicated
komponieren to compose

Komponist, -en (m) composer
Kompott, -e (n) compote
Konditor. -en (m) pastry cook
Konditorei, -en (f) pastry shop
Konferenz, -en (f) conference
König, -e (m) king
königlich like a king
Konkurrenz, -en (f) competition
konkurrieren to compete
können to be able to
Kontinent, -e (m) continent
Kontrakt, -e (m) contract
Kontrollabschnitt, -e (m) ticket
  stub
kontrollieren to check
sich konzentrieren to concentrate
  oneself
Konzert, -e (n) concert
Konzertsaal, -säle (m) concert hall
Kopf, ̈e (m) head
im Kopf herumgehen to go around
  in one's head
köpfen to head (in soccer), to strike
  the ball with one's head
Korb, ̈e (m) basket
Körper, - (m) body
Korrespondenz, -en (f)
  correspondence
korrespondieren to correspond
Kost (f) food
kosten to cost; to taste
Kosten (pl.) costs, expenses
sie kommen auf ihre Kosten they get
  their money's worth
Kostüm, -e (n) woman's tailored suit
Kraft, ̈e (f) strength; labor,
  employee
krank ill
kratzen to scratch
Kraut, ̈er (n) cabbage, weed
Kräutertee, -s (m) herb tea
Kreatur, -en (f) creature
Krebs, -e (m) crab; cancer
Kredit, -e (m) credit
Kreditkarte, -n (f) credit card
Krem, -en (f) cream
Kreta (n) Crete
Krieg, -e (m) war
kriegen to get
Kritik, -en (f) review
Kritiker, - (m) critic
kritisieren to criticize
Krokodil, -e (n) crocodile
Krug, ̈e (m) pitcher
Küche, -n (f) kitchen
Kuchen, - (m) cake
Kugelschreiber, - (m) ball pen
Kühler, - (m) radiator
kulinarisch culinary
Kultur, -en (f) culture
Kulturzentrum, -tren (n) cultural
  center
Kümmel, - (m) kümmel (caraway
  liqueur)
sich kümmern to pay attention
Kunde, -en (m) customer
kündigen to give notice
Kunst, ̈e (f) art
Das ist keine Kunst that's easy;
  there's nothing to it

künstlerisch artistic
Künstlergemeinde, -n (f)
  community of artists
Künstlerkolonie, -n (f) artists'
  colony
Künstlerviertel, - (n) artists' quarter
Kunstwerk, -e (n) work of art
Kupplung, -en (f) clutch
Kurkapelle, -n (f) a band in a
  resort town
Kurs, -e (m) course
kurz short; brief, curt
kurzen Prozeß machen to make
  short work of it
kürzlich recently
Kurzschrift, -en (f) shorthand
Kusine, -n (f) cousin
Kuß, Küsse (m) kiss

L

lachen to laugh
lächerlich ridiculous
Laden, ̈ (m) store
Ladenhüter, - (m) white elephant
Ladentisch, -e (m) counter
Land, ̈er (n) land, state, country
Landkarte, -n (f) map
landwirtschaftlich agricultural
lang(e) long
langjährig of long duration
sich langweilen to get bored
langweilig boring, dull
lassen, läßt, ließ, gelassen to leave;
  to let, to permit, to cause
  (something to happen)
Lärm (m) noise
laufen, läuft, lief, ist gelaufen to
  run
Laune, -n (f) mood
in schlechter Laune sein to be in a
  bad mood
Laut, -e (m) sound
laut loud
Leben, - (n) life
leben to live
Lebensgeschichte, -n (f) biography
Lebensmittel (pl.) foodstuffs
Lebensmittelhändler, - (m) grocer
Lebensweise, -n (f) way of life
Lebkuchen, - (m) ginger bread
Leckerbissen, - (m) delicacy
Lederhosen (f. pl.) leather shorts
Lederwarenabteilung, -en (f)
  leather goods department
ledig single
leer empty
legen to put
Lehrbuch, ̈er (n) textbook
lehren to teach
Lehrer,- (m) teacher
leicht easy, light
es tut mir leid I am sorry
ich kann es nicht leiden I cannot
  stand it
Leidenschaft, -en (f) passion
leider unfortunately
zum Leidwesen to the regret
leihen, lieh, geliehen to lend
leise low, soft

leisten to perform
ich kann Besseres leisten I can do
  better
er kann es sich nicht leisten he
  cannot afford it
Leitung, -en (f) line (as an
  electrical line)
lesen, liest, las, gelesen to read
letzt last
der letztere the latter
letzthin lately
Leute (pl.) people
jemandem die Leviten lesen to give
  someone a dressing down
Libero, -s (m) sweeper (soccer player
  who can play either in the
  offense or the defense)
Licht, -er (n) light (noun)
licht light (adj.)
lieb dear
lieben to love
liebenswürdig kind, affable
lieber preferably, rather
Liebesknochen, - (m) eclair
Liebhaberei, -en (f) hobby
lieblich lovely, smooth
Liebling, -e (m) darling
Lieblingstanz, ̈e (m) favorite dance
Lied, -er (n) song
liefern to deliver
liegen, lag, gelegen to lie
Likör, -e (m) liqueur
Lilie, -n (f) lily
Lineal, -e (n) ruler
Linie, -n (f) line
links left
Linksaußen, - (m) left forward (in
  soccer)
Liste, -n (f) list
Liter, - (m) litre
Löffel, - (m) spoon
Lohnschreiber, - (m) literary hack
Lokal, -e (n) place
was ist los? what is the matter?
Lösung, -en (f) solution
**loswerden, wird los, wurde los, ist
  losgeworden** to get rid of
Lust haben auf to be in the mood
  for
lustig cheerful, jolly

M

machen to do, to make
das macht nichts that doesn't matter
Macht, ̈e, (f) power
mächtig powerful
Mädchen, - (n) girl
Mädchenname, -n (m) maiden name
ich mag nicht I don't like
Magen, ̈ (m) stomach
Magengeschwür, -e (n) stomach
  ulcer
Mahlzeit, -en (f) meal
Mahnbrief, -e (m) request for
  payment
Mai, -e (m) May
Major, -e (m) major
Maler, - (m) painter
man one

Mann, ⁻er (m) man
manchmal sometimes
Mangel, ⁻ (m) shortage
Manieren (pl.) manners
Mantel, ⁻ (m) coat
märchenhaft "fairytale-like," fabulous
Mark, - (f) mark (currency)
Markt, ⁻e (m) market
marktschreierische Reklame ballyhoo
März, -e (m) March
Maschinenschreiben (n) typing
Mathe (f) mathematics
mathematisch mathematical
Mätzchen, - (n) antics
Mauer, -n (f) wall
Maus, ⁻e (f) mouse
Medizin, -en (f) medicine
Meer, -e (n) ocean
Meerrettich, -e (m) radish
Mehlspeiskoch, ⁻e (m) pastry cook
mehrere several
Mehrheit, -en (f) majority
Mehrzahl, -en (f) plural, majority
Meile, -n (f) mile
mein my
meinen to mean, to think
Meisterwerk, -e (n) masterpiece
Menge, -n (f) a lot, crowd
Mensch, -en (m) person, human being
Messer, - (n) knife
mexikanisch Mexican (adj.)
Mezzosopran, -e (m) mezzo soprano
Miene, -n (f) look, facial expression
Miete, -n (f) rent
mieten to rent
Milch (f) milk
Milchprodukt, -e (n) milk product
militärisch military
Minirock, ⁻e (m) miniskirt
Minute, -n (f) minute
miserabel miserable
Mißfallen (n) disapproval
mißfallen, mißfällt, mißfiel, mißfallen to displease
Mission, -en (f) mission
mißtrauisch suspicious
Mist (m) garbage, rubbish (*basic meaning:* manure)
mitbringen, brachte mit, hat mitgebracht to bring along
miteinander together
mithelfen, hilft mit, half mit, mitgeholfen to help
mitkommen, kam mit, ist mitgekommen to come along
mitnehmen, nimmt mit, nahm mit, mitgenommen to take along
mitsummen to hum along
Mittag, -e (m) noon
Mittel (n. pl.) means (as "financial means")
mittelalterlich medieval
Mittelfeld, -er (n) midfield
Mittelgebirge (n) the highlands
mittelgroß medium height
mittendrin in the middle of it

Mitternachtsmesse, -n (f) midnight mass
mittlere Reife (f) a secondary school diploma for students not going on to university
Mittwoch, -e (m) Wednesday
Möbel, - (n) furniture
möblieren to furnish
ich möchte gern . . . I would like to . . .
modern modern
Modezeichnen (n) dress designing
mögen, mag, mochte, gemocht to like, to want
möglicherweise possibly
Möglichkeit, -en (f) possibility, opportunity
sein Möglichstes tun to do his utmost
Mohnkuchen (m) poppy-seed cake
Molkereiprodukt, -e (n) dairy product
momentan right now
Monat, -e (m) month
Mond, -e (m) moon
Monogramm, -e (n) initials
Montag, -e (m) Monday
Mord, -e (m) murder
morgen tomorrow
Morgen, - (m) morning
morgens in the morning
Moskito, -s (m) mosquito
müde tired
Mühe, -n (f) effort
München (n) Munich
Mund, ⁻er (m) mouth
Münze, -n (f) coin
Musik (f) music
musikalisch musical
Musiker, - (m) musician
Musikfest, -e (n) music festival
musikliebend fond of music
Musikstudent, -en (m) music student
Muskel, -n (m) muscle
müssen, muß, mußte, gemußt to have to
Mutter, ⁻ (f) mother
Mütze, -n (f) cap

N

na; na ja well (interj.)
nach to, after
Nachbar, -n (m) neighbor
nachdem after, when
Nachfolger, - (m) successor
nachhelfen, hilft nach, half nach, nachgeholfen to tutor
nachher afterwards
Nachkomme, -n (m) descendant
Nachmittag, -e (m) afternoon
nachsehen, sieht nach, sah nach, nachgesehen to make sure
nächst next
Nacht, ⁻e (f) night
Nachtisch, -e (m) dessert
Nachtlokal, -e (n) night spot, night club
nähen to sew

nahezu almost
nämlich that is (to say)
nahrhaft nutritious
Nahrungsmittelbeilage, -n (f) food supplement
Nase, -n (f) nose
sich die Nase putzen to blow one's nose
naß wet
Natur, -en (f) nature
natürlich of course
neben beside
nebenan next door
nehmen, nimmt, nahm, genommen to take
Neigung, -en (f) inclination
nein no
Nelke, -n (f) carnation
nennen, nannte, genannt to name
nett nice
Nerv, -en (m) nerve
es geht mir auf die Nerven it gets on my nerves
nervös nervous
Nerz, -e (m) mink
Nerzmantel, ⁻ (m) mink coat
neu new
neun, neunzehn, neunzig nine, nineteen, ninety
nicht not
nicht wahr? isn't that so? right?
nichts nothing
nichts besonderes nothing special
nichtsahnend unsuspecting
nichtsdestoweniger nevertheless
Nicken (n) nodding (of the head)
nie never
(sich) niederlassen, läßt nieder, ließ nieder, niedergelassen to settle
sich niedersetzen to sit down
Nierenbraten, - (m) roast loin
noch in addition; still
noch einmal once more
noch immer still
noch nicht not yet
Nordamerika (n) North America
Norden (m) north
Nordsee (f) North Sea
Note, -n (f) grade
Notiz, -en (f) note, memo
notwendig necessary
November (m) November
Nudel, -n (f) noodle
ich gehe auf Numero sicher I want to be absolutely safe
null zero
nun now
nur only
Nuß, Nüsse (f) nut

O

ob whether, if
oben on high
obendrein on top of that, besides, to boot
Ober, - (m) waiter
Oberbuchhalter, - (m) head bookkeeper

die Oberhand gewinnen to gain the upper hand
Oboe, -n (f) oboe
Obst (n) fruit
Ochsenschwanzsuppe, -n (f) oxtail soup
obwohl although
obzwar although
oder or
offen open
öffentlich public
offerieren to offer
Offizier, -e (m) officer
öffnen to open
oft often
ohne without
ohnehin anyway
ohneweiteres readily
Oktober, - (m) October
Öl, -e (n) oil
Olivenöl, -e (n) olive oil
Ölwechsel, - (m) oil change
Onkel, - (m) uncle
Oper, -n (f) opera
Opernaufführung, -en (f) opera performance
Opernkarriere, -n (f) operatic career
Orchester, - (n) orchestra
Orchestermitglied, -er (n) orchestra member
Ordnung, -en (f) order
in Ordnung OK
Organisation, -en (f) organization
Organist, -en (m) organist
Orgel, -n (f) organ
Original, -e (n) original
Originalmusik (f) original music
originell original, amusing, interesting
Osten (m) east
Österreich (n) Austria
Österreicher, - (m) Austrian
Ozean, -e (m) ocean

P

Paar, -e (n) pair, couple
ein paar a few
Paket, -e (n) package
panieren to bread
Panne, -n (f) car breakdown
Papierkorb, ⁻e (m) waste basket
Papiertüte, -n (f) paper bag
Parfümerie, -n (f) cosmetics department
Park, -s (m) park
parken to park
Partitur, -en (f) musical score
Passant, -en (m) passer-by, pedestrian
passen to pass (in soccer)
passieren to happen
es paßt mir gut it suits me to a T
Pause, -n (f) pause, intermission
Pech (n) bad luck
pedantisch pedantic
Pelzmantel, ⁻ (m) fur coat
Pelzwaren (f. pl.) fur goods
pensioniert retired

Person, -en (f) person
persönlich personal
Petersilie, -n (f) parsley
Pfeife, -n (f) pipe
pfeifen, pfiff, gepfiffen to whistle
Pfefferkorn, ⁻er (n) peppercorn
Pferd, -e (n) horse
Pflicht, -en (f) duty
Pflaume, -n (f) plum
Pfosten, - (m) post
Pfund, -e (n) pound
Philharmonie, -ien (f) Philharmonic
Photograph, -en (m) photographer
photographieren to photograph
Pilz, -e (m) mushroom
Pilzbratling, -e (m) fried mushroom
Plan, ⁻e (m) plan
Planet, -en (m) planet
Platz, ⁻e (m) place
nehmen Sie Platz! take a seat
Platzanweiser, - (m) usher
platzen to burst
plaudern to chat
plötzlich sudden
Podium, -s (n) podium
Polka, -s (f) polka
Politik (f) politics
Polstersessel, - (m) easy chair
populär popular
Portion, -en (f) portion
Post (f) mail
Posten, - (m) job
Postkutsche, -n (f) postal coach
Postkutscher, - (m) postal coachman
Postwurfsendung, -en (f) direct mail advertising
praktisch practical
Präsident, -en (m) president
Preis, -e (m) price
um jeden Preis at any cost
Preiselbeeren (f. pl.) cranberries
Presse (f) press
Priorität, -en (f) priority
privat private
Privatsekretärin, -nen (f) private secretary
Probe, -n (f) rehearsal
probieren to try
Problem, -e (n) problem
Programm, -e (n) program
Projekt, -e (n) project
Protest, -e (n) protest
Prozent, -e (n) percent
mit jemandem kurzen Prozeß machen to give short shrift to someone
prüfen to test
Prüfung, -en (f) test, exam
Publikum (n) audience
Pudel, -n (m) poodle
in einem Punkt (m) in one respect
Punkt acht at eight sharp
pünktlich punctual, on time
Punsch, -e (m) punch (beverage)
putzen to clean
Putzmädchen - (n) cleaning woman

Q

Qualität, -en (f) quality

R

Radio, -s (n) radio
Rahm (m) cream
rasch fast
rasieren to shave
Rat (m) advice
raten, rät, riet, geraten to guess
Rathaus, ⁻er (n) city hall
rattern to rattle
rauben to rob
Rauch (m) smoke
rauchen to smoke
Raum, ⁻e (m) room
Rätsel, - (n) puzzle, riddle
Realgymnasium, -ien (n) secondary school emphasizing the natural sciences
Rechnen (n) arithmetic
rechnen to do figures
Rechnung, -en (f) bill, invoice
die Rechnung ohne den Wirt machen to overlook one vital factor
rechts right
recht haben to be right
mit Recht rightfully
Rede, -n (f) speech
eine Rede halten to give a speech
reduzieren to reduce
Regal, -e (n) shelf, set of shelves
Regel, -n (f) rule
regelmäßig regular
Regierung, -en (f) government
regnen to rain
regnerisch rainy
reich rich
Reifen, - (m) tire
Reifenpanne, -n (f) flat tire
Reihe, -n (f) row
ich bin an der Reihe it is my turn
Reimgeklingel, - (n) jingle
rein clean
Reis (m) rice
Reise, -n (f) trip
eine Reise machen to take a trip
Reisebroschüre, -n (f) travel folder
Reisebüro, -s (n) travel agency
Reiseklub, -s (m) travel club
reisen to travel
Reiz, -e (m) appeal, attraction
reizen to tempt
Reklame, -n (f) advertising
rennen, rannte, ist gerannt to run
Repertoire, -s (n) repertory
respektieren to respect
resultieren to result
retten to save, rescue
Rettichlimonade, -n (f) radish lemonade
sich revanchieren to get back at someone
Revolution, -en (f) revolution
Rezept, -e (n) prescription; recipe
Rheinwein, -e (m) Rhine wine
rhythmisch rhythmical
richten to direct
richtig correct
Richtung, -en (f) direction; *also:* trend, school (as in art)
riechen, roch, gerochen to smell

Riese, -n (m) giant
Riesengans, ¨-e (f) giant goose
riesig enormous
Rindfleisch (n) beef
Ring, -e (m) ring
Risiko, Risiken (n) risk
ein Risiko eingehen to take a risk (chance)
Rolle, -n (f) role
das spielt keine Rolle that doesn't matter
Roman, -e (m) novel
Rose, -n (f) rose
rot red
Routine, -n (f) routine
Rübe, -n (f) turnip
Rücken, - (m) back
Rückendeckung, -en (f) rear guard
rückgängig machen to cancel, to rescind
Rucksack, ¨-e (m) backpack
Rückspiegel, - (m) rearview mirror
Ruf (m) reputation
ruhig quiet
sich rühren to stir, move
rührend touching
die Stirn runzeln to frown
Rußland (n) Russia

S

Sache, -n (f) matter, thing
in eine Sackgasse geraten, gerät, geriet, ist geraten to be up against a brick wall
saftig juicy
sagen to say
sag mal! tell me
Sahne, -n (f) cream
Saison, -s (f) season
Salat, -e (m) salad
Salz (n) salt
Salzkartoffeln (f. pl.) boiled potatoes
sammeln to collect
Samstag, -e (m) Saturday
Sänger, - (m) singer
Sängerin, -nen (f) singer
Sardelle, -n (f) anchovy
Sargnagel, ¨ (m) "coffin nail," cigarette
satt satisfied, full
schäbig shabby
Schach (n) chess
schade! too bad!
schaden to hurt
Schaf, -e (n) sheep
schaffen to make (it)
sich schämen to be ashamed
Schärfe (f) rigor, severity
schätzen to value, appraise
ich weiß das zu schätzen I appreciate that
schauen to look
Scheibe, -n (f) slice
Scheidung, -en (f) divorce
scheinen, schien, geschienen to seem, to shine
scheren, schor, geschoren to shear
Scherz, -e (m) joke
Scherz beiseite joking aside

scheußlich dreadful, horrible
schick chic
schicken to send
Schiedsrichter, - (m) referee
schießen, schoß, geschossen to shoot, to score (a goal)
Schild, -er (n) sign
Schinken, - (m) ham
Schlaf (m) sleep
schlafen, schläft, schlief, geschlafen to sleep
Schlafzimmer, - (n) bedroom
Schlagzeile, -n (f) headline
Schlange, -n (f) snake
schlank slender
schlau shrewd
schlecht bad
die Kupplung schleifen to let the clutch slip
schließen, schloß, geschlossen to close
schlimm bad, naughty
Schlinge, -n (f) sling
schlohweiß snow-white
Schluß, ¨-sse (m) end
Mach Schluß! knock it off.
Schlußverkauf, ¨-e (m) final bargain sale
Schmachtfetzen, - (m) tearjerker
schmackhaft tasty
schmal narrow
schmatzen to eat noisily
schmecken to taste
es schmeckt mir gut it tastes good
schmieren to lubricate
Schmierung, -en (f) lubrication
er spricht, wie ihm der Schnabel (beak) gewachsen ist he does not mince words
schneiden, schnitt, geschnitten to cut
schnell fast
es läuft wie am Schnürchen it goes like clockwork, smoothly
schnurstracks direct, in a straight line
schon already
schön beautiful
Schönheit, -en (f) beauty
schöpferisch creative
Schrammelquartett, -e (n) quartet for popular Viennese music: two violins, guitar, accordion
in Schrecken versetzen to terrify
schrecklich terrible
das Schreiben, - (n) letter
schreiben, schrieb, geschrieben to write
Schreibtisch, -e (m) desk
schreien, schrie, geschrien to scream
Schriftsteller, - (m) writer
Schulaufgabe, -n (f) assignment, homework
Schuld, -en (f) debt; fault
schulden to owe
Schule, -n (f) school
Schüler, - (m) pupil, student
Schülerin, -nen (f) pupil, student
Schulkollégin, -nen (f) schoolmate

Schund (m) trash
schwarz black
Schweinebraten, - (m) pork roast
Schweinerouladen (f. pl.) pork roulades
Schweinekotelett, -s (n) pork chop
schwer difficult; heavy
Schwester, -n (f) sister
schwierig difficult
Schwierigkeit, -en (f) difficulty
Schwimmbad, ¨-er (n) swimming pool
schwimmen, schwamm, ist geschwommen to swim
sechs, sechzehn, sechzig six, sixteen, sixty
Seeweg, -e (m) maritime route
sehen, sieht, sah, gesehen to see
sieht ganz so aus! it looks that way
Sehenswürdigkeit, -en (f) sight(s)
sei so gut. . . be so kind. . .
sein, ist, war, ist gewesen to be
sein his, its
seinerseits on his part
(der, die, das) seinige his
seit, seitdem since
Seite, -n (f) page, side
sie zeigen sich von ihrer besten Seite they put their best foot forward
Sekunde, -n (f) second
selbst, selber —self; myself, himself, etc.
Selbstdisziplín (f) self-discipline
selbstverständlich of course
selten seldom, rare
September, - (m) September
servieren to serve
Servus! hello! so long!
Sessel, - (m) chair
setzen to put, to place
alles auf eine Karte setzen to put all one's eggs in one basket
sich (nieder)setzen to sit down
seufzen to sigh
sezieren to dissect
sicher certain, safe
Sie you (formal)
sie they, she, it
sieben, siebzehn, siebzig seven, seventeen, seventy
Siedlung, -en (f) settlement
Sieg, -e (m) victory
siezen to use the polite form (Sie)
Silber (n) silver
Silbermünze, -n (f) silver coin
singen, sang, gesungen to sing
Sinn, -e (m) sense; mind
sinnlos senseless
Situation, -en (f) situation
Sitz, -e (m) seat
sitzen, saß, gesessen to sit
Skandal, -e (m) scandal
Skandinavien (n) Scandinavia
skifahren to ski
Sliwowitz (m) Slivovitz, plum brandy
Smoking, -s (m) tuxedo
so ziemlich pretty well
sobald as soon as

sodaß so that
soeben just now
sofern as far as
sofort right away
Sohn, ⸚e (m) son
solange as long as
sollen to be supposed to
Solo, -s (n) solo
solo alone
Sommer, - (m) summer
sonderbar weird, strange
sondern but, on the contrary
Sonnabend, -e (m) Saturday
Sonne, -n (f) sun
Sonnenaufgang, ⸚e (m) sunrise
Sonnenbrand, ⸚e (m) sunburn
Sonnenbrille, -n (f) sunglasses
Sonnenuntergang, ⸚e (m) sunset
sonnig sunny
Sonntag, -e (m) Sunday
Sonntagsausgabe, -n (f) Sunday
  edition
sonst otherwise
sonst noch etwas? anything else?
sooft as often as
Sopran, -e (m) soprano
dafür sorgen to see to (something)
sich sorgen to worry
Soße, -n (f) sauce, gravy
soso so so
sowohl — als auch as well as
Spanien (n) Spain
sparen to save
Spargel, - (m) asparagus
Sparkonto, -s (n) savings account
Spaß, Spässe (m) joke, jest, fun
es macht ihm Spaß it amuses him
zum Spaß for fun
Spaßvogel, ⸚ (m) joker
spät late
Spätlese (f) wine made from grapes
  gathered late in the fall
Spaziergang, ⸚e (m) walk, stroll
Speck (m) bacon
Speise, -n (f) food, fare
Speisekarte, -n (f) menu
sperren to close
jemanden einsperren to lock
  someone up
Spezialgeschäft, -e (n) specialty
  store
sich spezialisieren to specialize
Spezialität, -en (f) specialty
Spiel, -e (n) game
spielen to play
es spielt keine Rolle it doesn't
  matter
Spinat (m) spinach
Sport (m) sport
Sporthemd, -en (n) sport shirt
Sportkritiker, - (m) sports critic
Sprache, -n (f) language
Sprachspiel, -e (n) language game
**sprechen, spricht, sprach,
  gesprochen** to speak
springen, sprang, ist gesprungen
  to jump
Staat, -en (m) state
großen Staat machen to make a
  grand display

Stadt, ⸚e (f) city
städtisch municipal
stadtbekannt known city-wide
Stadttheater, - (n) city theater
Stadtväter (m. pl.) city fathers
Stammgast, ⸚e (m) regular guest
stampfen to stamp
Standort, -e (m) base (as military
  base)
starten to start
statt, stattdessen instead
Statue, -n (f) statue
Stechmücke, -n (f) mosquito
Stechuhr, -en (f) time clock
stecken to stick, to put
stehen, stand, gestanden to stand
stehlen, stiehlt, stahl, gestohlen to
  steal
kann mir gestohlen werden they
  can keep it
steigen, stieg, ist gestiegen to
  climb, to get into
stellen to place, to put
Stellengesuch, -e (n) job application
Stellung, -en (f) job, position
Stengel, - (m) stalk, stem
Stenotypistin, -nen (f)
  typist-stenographer
Stereoanlage, -n (f) stereo system
steril sterile; (of an animal:
  neutered)
sternhagelvoll dead drunk
Stil, -e (m) style
still quiet
sei still! be quiet!
Stille (f) silence
Stimme, -n (f) voice
mit schallender Stimme at the top
  of his voice
stimmt! true! right!
stinken, stank, gestunken to stink
Stirn, -en (f) forehead
Stock, ⸚e (m) stick
stolz proud
stören to bother, to disturb
Stoßdämpfer, - (m) shock absorber
strahlen to shine
Strand, ⸚e (m) beach
Straße, -n (f) street
Straßenbahn, -en (f) streetcar
sich sträuben to be reluctant, to
  resist
streichen, strich, gestrichen to
  spread
Streichquartett, -e (n) string quartet
streng strict
Strich, -e (m) stroke
Strom (m) electricity
Stück, -e (n) piece
Student, -en (m) student
studieren to study
Stuhl, ⸚e (m) chair
mit Stumpf und Stiel "with root
  and branch," i.e., completely
Stunde, -n (f) hour
Sturm, ⸚e (m) storm
suchen to look for
Südamerika (n) South America
süddeutsch south German
Süden (m) south

Südeuropa (n) southern Europe
südlich southern
süffig very drinkable
sülzen to jelly
summen to hum, to buzz
Suppe, -n (f) soup
Suppenterrine, -n (f) soup tureen
süß sweet
Süßigkeiten (f. pl.) sweets
Symptom, -e, (n) symptom
System, -e (n) system
szenisch scenic

T

Tabelle, -n (f) table, schedule
Tafel, -n (f) blackboard
Tag, -e (m) day
tagaus, tagein day by day
von Tag zu Tag from day to day
tagelang for days
täglich daily
tagsüber during the day
Taktstock, -e (m) baton
Talent, -e (n) talent
Tank, -s (m) tank
Tankstelle, -n (f) service station
Tankwart, -e (m) service station
  attendant
Tante, -n (f) aunt
Tante Emma Laden, ⸚ (m)
  mom-and-pop store
tanzen to dance
Tänzer, - (m) dancer
Taschengeld, -er (n) pocket money
Taschentuch, ⸚er (n) handerchief
Tasse, -n (f) cup
tätig active
tatsächlich actual
taugen to be of use
sich täuschen to be mistaken
Taxichauffeur, -e (m) taxi driver
Tee (m) tea
teilen to share
Teilhaber, - (m) partner
Teilhaberschaft, -en (f) partnership
Telephon, -e (n) telephone
telephonieren to telephone
Teller, - (m) plate
Temperatur, -en (f) temperature
Tempo, s (n) tempo
Tenor, ⸚e (m) tenor
Terrine, -n (f) tureen
teuer expensive
Teufel, - (m) devil
Teufelsbalg, -e (m) "Devil's Brat"
Theater, - (n) theater
Theaterstück, - (n) play
Thema, -en (n) topic
Thermosflasche, -n (f) thermos
  bottle
Thymian, -e (m) thyme
Tiefkühltruhe, -n (f) freezer
Tier, -e (n) animal
Tierfreund, -e (m) animal lover
tippen to type
Tisch, -e (m) table
Tochter, ⸚ (f) daughter
Tod (m) death
Toilette, -n (f) toilet
Tomate, -n (f) tomato

Ton, ¨e (m) tone
Topf, ¨e (m) pot
Tor, -e (n) goal
Torhüter, Tormann, Torwart (m)
    goalkeeper
tot dead
total total
töten to kill
Tourist, -en (m) tourist
Tradition, -en (f) tradition
tragen, trägt, trug, getragen to
    wear; to carry
Tragödie, -n (f) tragedy
Traum, ¨e (m) dream
träumen to dream
traumhaft dreamlike
traurig sad
treu faithful
trinken, trank, getrunken to drink
Trommler, - (m) drummer
tropfen to drip (as of water)
Trottel, -n (m) idiot
trotz in spite of
trotzdem nevertheless
trüb gloomy
in Trümmern in ruins
Truthahn, ¨e (m) turkey
tun, tut, tat, getan to do
Tür, -en (f) door
Turm, ¨e (m) tower
typisch typical

U

üben to practice
über over; across
überall everywhere
überdies besides
überfahren, überfährt, überfuhr,
    überfahren to run over
überhandnehmen, nimmt
    überhand,
    überhandgenommen to spread,
    to increase, to take over (the
    market)
überhaupt at all, altogether
überlassen, überläßt, überließ,
    überlassen to leave (to
    someone)
es sich anders überlegen to change
    one's mind
übermäßig overmuch, excessive
übermenschlich superhuman
übermorgen day after tomorrow
überprüfen to investigate, to
    examine
überreden to persuade
Überraschung, -en (f) surprise
übersetzen to translate
übertreffen, übertrifft, übertraf,
    übertroffen to surpass
ich bin überzeugt I am convinced
üblich usual
übrigens by the way
Uhr, -en (f) clock, watch
um around, at
um . . . zu in order to
umarmen to embrace
sich umdrehen to turn around
Umgang mit Kunden the way one
    deals with customers

Umgebung, -en (f) environs
umrühren to stir
Umsatz, ¨e (m) volume (of sales)
umschulen to retrain
umsonst free of charge
machen Sie keine Umstände! don't
    make a fuss, go out of your
    way
umstritten controversial
umtauschen to exchange
unaufhörlich continuous
nicht unbedingt not necessarily
unbeschränkt unlimited
unbezahlt unpaid
unbeschreiblich indescribable
und and
und zwar namely
undenkbar unthinkable
unerhört unheard of, terrific
unerwartet unexpected
ungebildet uneducated
ungefähr approximate
eine schreiende Ungerechtigkeit a
    crying injustice
ungern reluctantly
ungewöhnlich unusual
Uniform, -en (f) uniform
Universität, -en (f) university
Universitätsspital, ¨er (n) university
    hospital
Universitätskrankenhaus, ¨er
    university hospital
Unkraut, ¨er (n) weed
unlängst recently
eine Unmenge von. . . loads of. . .
unmodern out of fashion
unschön unsightly
unser our
unter under, among
unter uns gesagt between you and
    me
unterbieten, unterbot, unterboten
    to undersell
unterbrechen, unterbricht,
    unterbrach, unterbrochen to
    interrupt
Unterbrechung, -en (f) interruption
sich unterhalten, unterhält sich,
    unterhielt sich, hat sich
    unterhalten to converse, to talk
Unternehmen, - (n) business
eine Reise unternehmen,
    unternimmt, unternahm,
    unternommen to take a trip
unterrichten to teach
zum Unterschied von. . . other
    than. . .
sich unterstehen, unterstand sich,
    hat sich unterstanden to have
    the impudence, to dare
unterstützen to support
untersuchen to examine
Untertasse, -n (f) saucer
unüberwindlich invincible
unverkäuflich unsalable
unvermeidlich unavoidable
unverschämt impudent
Unzahl (f) a great number
unzufrieden dissatisfied
uralt ancient, very old

Urgroßmutter, ¨ (f)
    great-grandmother
Urgroßvater, ¨ (m)
    great-grandfather
Urlaub, -e (m) vacation
auf Urlaub gehen (fahren) to take a
    vacation
keine Ursache! don't mention it
ursprünglich originally

V

Vater, ¨ (m) father
Vegetarier, - (m) vegetarian
vegetarisch vegetarian
Veilchen, - (n) violet
veranstalten to arrange
verantwortlich responsible
Verantwortung, -en (f)
    responsibility
verbergen, verbirgt, verbarg,
    verborgen to hide
sich verbeugen to take a bow
Verbindung, -en (f) connection
verbleiben, verblieb, ist verblieben
    to remain, to stay
verbringen, verbrachte, verbracht
    to spend
verdammt damned
verdanken to owe
Verdauung (f) digestion
verderben, verdirbt, verdarb,
    verdorben to spoil
verdienen to earn
Verdienst, -e (m) salary, earnings
Vereinigte Staaten (pl.) United
    States
verfassen to compose, to write
vergeblich in vain
vergehen, verging, ist vergangen to
    pass
vergessen, vergißt, vergaß,
    vergessen to forget
vergiften to poison
vergleichen, verglich, verglichen to
    compare
Vergnügen (n) pleasure
vergrößern to enlarge
verhauen to muff, to louse up
verheiratet married
verhungern to starve
verkaufen to sell
Verkäuferin, -nen (f) saleslady
Verkaufsschlager, - (m) (big) seller
Verkehr (m) traffic
sich verlassen, verläßt, verließ,
    verlassen to depend, to rely
verläßlich dependable
Verleger, - (m) publisher
verletzen to hurt
verlieren, verlor, verloren to lose
vermerken to make a note of
vermindern to reduce
vermissen to miss (someone)
Vermögen, - (n) fortune
veröffentlichen to publish
verpassen to miss (a train, an event)
verpesten to pollute
verpflanzen to transplant
verraten, verrät, verriet, verraten
    to disclose, to reveal

verrückt crazy
versäumen to miss (an opportunity, a bus)
verschenken to give away
verschieden various, different
verschlechtern to deteriorate
verschmust cuddly
versichern to assure, to insure
versprechen, verspricht, versprach, versprochen to promise
verständig intelligent, sensible
verstärken to strengthen
verstauchen to sprain
verstauen to tuck away
verstellen to obstruct
versuchen to try
Vertrauen (n) confidence
Vetter, -n (m) cousin
Verteidiger, - (m) fullback (in soccer)
Verwandte(r) relative
verwechseln to mistake, to mix up with
verwenden to use
verzeihen, verzieh, verziehen to forgive
viel, viele much, many
vielleicht maybe
vier, vierzehn, vierzig four, fourteen, forty
Viertel, - (n) quarter
Viertelton, -e (m) quarter tone
Villa, -en (f) villa
Violine, -n (f) violin
Violinist, -en (m) violinist
Vitamin, -e (n) vitamin
Volk, -er (n) people
Volkswirtschaft, -en (f) economy
voll full
vollauf, völlig perfectly
Vollmond, -e (m) full moon
von from, of
vor before, in front of
vorbereiten to prepare
Vorbereitung, -en (f) preparation
Vorbereitungen treffen to make preparations
Vorderreifen, - (m) front tire
vorfahren, fährt vor, fuhr vor, ist vorgefahren to drive up
was geht da vor? what is going on here?
vorgestern the day before yesterday
vorhaben to have in mind
Vorhang, -e (m) curtain
vorher before
vorhergehend preceding
vorig last, previous
vorkommen, kam vor, ist vorgekommen to occur
sich jemanden vornehmen to deal with someone
Vorrat, -e (m) supply
Vorrecht, -e (n) right of way
Vorsicht (f) caution
vorsichtig cautious, careful
jemanden vorstellen to introduce someone
stellen Sie sich vor! imagine!
vortrefflich superior

W

Waage, -n (f) scales
wachsen, wächst, wuchs, ist gewachsen to grow
wackeln to wobble
wacker brave, stout; like a trooper
Wagen, - (m) car
Wahl, -en (f) choice
da fällt mir die Wahl schwer this is a hard choice to make
wahr true
währen to last, to take (time)
während during, while
Wahrheit, -en (f) truth
wahrscheinlich probably
Walzer, - (m) waltz
Wand, -e (f) wall
Wange, -n (f) cheek
wann when
Wanze, -n (f) bedbug
Ware, -n (f) merchandise
Warenhaus, -er (n) department store
warnen to warn
warten to wait
wart einmal! wait a minute!
warum why
was what
was für ein what kind of
was übrig bleibt what remains
waschen, wäscht, wusch, gewaschen to wash
Wasser (n) water
Wasserleitung, -en (f) water pipes
wechseln to change
Wecker, - (m) alarm clock
weder—noch neither—nor
weg away
Weg, -e (m) way
im Wege stehen to be in the way
wegen because
wegfahren to leave, to drive away
wegräumen to remove
wehtun to ache, hurt
weiblich female
Weihnachten (f. pl.) Christmas
Weihnachtsabend, -e (m) Christmas Eve
Weihnachtsbaum, -e (m) Christmas tree
Weihnachtslied, -er (n) Christmas carol
Weihnachtssaison, -s (f) Christmas season
weil because
eine Weile a while
Weise, -n (f) tune; manner
weiß white
weit far
weit voraus far ahead
weitergehen to continue
weitertanzen to dance on
welcher which
Welt, -en (f) world
wenn if, when
wenn auch even though
Werbeagentur, -en (f) advertising agency
Werbefirma, -en (f) advertising agency

Werbefachmann, -leute (m) advertising expert
werben, wirbt, warb, geworben to advertise
Werbespot, -s (m) commercial
werden, wird, wurde, geworden to become
werfen, wirft, warf, geworfen to throw
Werk, -e (n) work
Wert, -e (m) value
wertlos worthless
Westbahnhof (m) West Railway Station (in Vienna)
Westen (m) west
Wetter (n) weather
wichtig important
widerstehen, widerstand, widerstanden to resist
wie how, like, as
wie eh und je as always
wie folgt as follows
wie geht's? how are you?
wieder again
Wiedergabe, -n (f) rendition
auf Wiedersehen, auf Wiederhören good-bye
Wien Vienna
Wiener, wienerisch Viennese
wieso how come
wieviel how much
wild wild
willensstark having willpower
willkommen welcome
es wimmelt von Touristen it crawls with tourists
Wind, -e (m) wind
Windschutzscheibe, -n (f) windshield
Winter, - (m) winter
Winterkleider (n. pl.) winter clothes
wir we
wirklich really
wirksam effective
Wirt, -e (m) host
Wirtschaftskrise, -n (f) economic crisis
wispern whisper
wissen, weiß, wußte, gewußt to know
Witwe, -n (f) widow
Witz, -e (m) joke
wo where
wobei whereby
Woche, -n (f) week
Wochenende, -n (n) weekend
wochenlang for weeks
wöchentlich weekly
woher from where
wohin where to
wohl probably, indeed; well
Wohlstand (m) wealth
wohnen, wohnhaft sein to live
Wohnzimmer, - (n) living room
Wolke, -n (f) cloud
Wolle (f) wool
wollen to want to
woran at what
worin in what

wovon of (or from) what
Wort, ⸚er (n) word
in Wort und Bild in words and pictures
Wunder, - (n) wonder, miracle
wunderbar, wunderschön wonderful
sich wundern to be surprised
wünschen to wish
es wurmt ihn it irritates (angers) him
wütend furious

Z

Zahl, -en (f) number
zahlen to pay
zählen to count
Zahn, ⸚e (m) tooth
Zahnweh (n) toothache
Zauberpyramide, -n (f) magic pyramid
zehn ten
Zeichen, - (n) sign
Zeichentrickfilm, -e (m) animated cartoon
Zeichnen (n) drawing
Zeichnung, -en (f) drawing
zeigen to show
Zeit, -en (f) time
um diese Zeit at this time
zeitig early
Zeitschrift, -en (f) magazine
Zeitung, -en (f) newspaper
Zentimeter, - (m) centimeter
Zentrum, -ren (n) center
zerbrechen, zerbricht, zerbrach, zerbrochen to break
zerquetschen to squash, to crush

zerreißen, zerreißt, zerriß, zerrissen to tear apart
sich zerstreiten, zerstreitet sich, zerstritt sich, hat sich zerstritten to have an argument
Zettel, - (m) slip of paper
ziehen, zog, gezogen to draw, to pull
ziemlich pretty, quite
Ziffer, -n (f) number
Zigarre, -n (f) cigar
Zigarette, -n (f) cigarette
Zigarettenstummel, -n (m) cigarette stub
Zimmer, - (n) room
Zimmerpflanze, -n (f) house plant
zimmerrein housebroken
Zitrone, -n (f) lemon
Zögling, -e (m) pupil
zornig angry
zu to, at
zubereiten to prepare
züchten to raise
Zuckerbäcker, - (m) pastry cook
zuerst first
Zufall, ⸚e (m) chance
zufrieden satisfied
Zug, ⸚e (m) train
zugleich at the same time
zuhören to listen
Zuhörer, - (m) listener
zumal da especially since
zunehmen, nimmt zu, nahm zu, zugenommen to gain (weight)
Zungenbrecher, - (m) tongue twister
zurückbringen, brachte zurück, zurückgebracht to bring back

zurückdenken, dachte zurück, zurückgedacht to think back
zurückgeben, gibt zurück, gab zurück, zurückgegeben to return
zurückgehen, ging zurück, ist zurückgegangen to go back
zurückkehren to return
zurücknehmen, nimmt zurück, nahm zurück, zurückgenommen to take back
zurückschicken to send back
zurückverkaufen to sell back
zusammen together
zusammenhalten, hält zusammen, hielt zusammen, zusammengehalten to hold together
zusammenkommen, kam zusammen, ist zusammengekommen to get together
Zuschauer, - (m) spectator
Zuschauerraum, ⸚e (m) auditorium
zuschrauben to screw tight
zuviel too much
Zuwachs (m) addition to the family
zwar it is true, I admit
Zweck, -e (m) purpose
zwei, zwölf, zwanzig two, twelve, twenty
zweitens secondly
zweitrangig second-rate
Zwetschge, -n (f) plum
Zwiebel, -n (f) onion
zwischen between
in der Zwischenzeit in the meantime

English-**German** Vocabulary

Definitions are confined to the context in which the words are used in the text.

A

a, an **ein**
a little **ein bißchen**
about **ungefähr**
accent **Akzent (m)**
to advise against **dagegen raten**
again **wieder**
against **gegen**
a week ago **vor einer Woche**
airplane ticket **Flugkarte (f)**
album **Album (n)**
all **alle, alles**
already **bereits**
also **auch**
although **obwohl**
amazing **erstaunlich**
to amuse oneself **sich unterhalten**
to apologize **sich entschuldigen**
applause **Applaus (m)**
around **um**
to arrange **veranstalten**
to arrive **ankommen**
as **als, wie**
as long as **solange als**
as often as **sooft als**
as well as **sowohl . . . als auch**
aside from **abgesehen von**
to ask **fragen**
to fall asleep **einschlafen**
Atlantic Ocean **atlantischer Ozean (m)**
Australia **Australien (n)**
away **weg**

B

back and forth **hin und her**
bad **schlecht**
ballyhoo **marktschreierische Reklame (f)**
to bathe **baden**
baton **Taktstock (m)**
beautiful **schön**
because **weil**
because of **wegen**
to become **werden**
bedbug **Wanze (f)**
besides **außerdem**
big **groß**
birthday **Geburtstag (m)**
black **schwarz**
blackboard **Tafel (f)**
blond **blond**
to blow **blasen**
book **Buch (n)**
bored **gelangweilt**
born **geboren**
boss **Chef (m)**
to take a bow **eine Verbeugung machen**

boyfriend **Freund (m)**
to bring **bringen**
brother **Bruder (m)**
to brush **bürsten**
I am bursting already **ich platze bereits**
busy **beschäftigt**
to buy **kaufen**
by **durch, mit**

C

cabinet **Kasten (m)**
to call **rufen**
I can **ich kann**
in case **im Falle (m)**
to cancel **annulieren**
car **Wagen (m)**
career **Karriere (f)**
cat **Katze (f)**
to catch cold **sich erkälten**
century **Jahrhundert (n)**
certain **gewiß**
he changes his mind **er überlegt es sich anders**
child **Kind (n)**
Christmas **Weihnachten (pl.)**
classical **klassisch**
clear **klar**
to close **schließen**
coat **Mantel (m)**
coffee **Kaffee (m)**
coincidence **Zufall (m)**
to come **kommen**
to command **kommandieren**
command **Befehl (m)**
comfortable **bequem**
competition **Konkurrenz (f)**
to conduct **dirigieren**
conductor **Dirigent (m)**
confess **gestehen**
conscience **Gewissen (n)**
continent **Kontinent (m)**
to cook **kochen**
cooperative **hilfsbereit**
corner **Ecke (f)**
corsage **Ansteckbukett (n)**
to cost **kosten**
whipped cream **Schlagsahne (f)**
to criticize **kritisieren**
croissant **Kipfel (n)**
cup **Tasse (f)**
cute **herzig**

D

to dance **tanzen**
don't you dare! **unterstehen Sie sich nicht!**
dashing **fesch**
daughter **Tochter (f)**

day **Tag (m)**
day in, day out **Tag für Tag**
death **Tod (m)**
to deceive **täuschen**
to decide **entscheiden**
decoration **Dekoration (f)**
defect **Defékt (m)**
delicious **deliziös**
you can depend on that **Sie können sich darauf verlassen**
dessert **Nachtisch (m)**
to direct **richten**
direction **Richtung (f)**
dishwasher **Geschirrspülmaschine (f)**
Don't mention it! **Kein Anlaß!**
Don't you think so? **Glauben Sie nicht?**
door **Tür (f)**
down **hinunter**
to draw (off blood) **abzapfen**
to draw, sketch **zeichnen**
to dream **träumen**
to drink **trinken**
drummer **Trommler (m)**
during **während**

E

each **jeder**
to earn **verdienen**
easy **leicht**
to eat **essen**
to eat noisily **schmatzen**
either . . . or **entweder . . . oder**
to emigrate **auswandern**
to enlarge **vergrößern**
enough **genug**
to enter **eintreten**
enthusiastic **enthusiastisch**
entrance door **Eingangstür (f)**
every day **jeden Tag (m)**
everywhere **überall**
exactly **genau**
examiner **Prüfer (m)**
to excuse **entschuldigen**
excellent **ausgezeichnet**
expectation **Erwartung (f)**
extra help **Aushilfe (f)**
eye **Auge (n)**

F

face **Gesicht (n)**
famous **berühmt**
fast **schnell**
fat **dick**
to feel **fühlen**
film **Film (m)**
firm **Firma (f)**
first-class **erstklassig**
first **Faust (f)**

245

flight **Flug (m)**
floor **Stock (m)**
flower **Blume (f)**
to fly **fliegen**
on foot **zu Fuß**
for **für**
to forget **vergessen**
fortunately **glücklicherweise**
fortune **Vermögen (n)**
freshly baked **frischgebacken**
from **von**
funny **komisch**
furious **zornig**
future **Zukunft (f)**

G

to gamble **wagen**
garage **Garage (f)**
German **deutsch**
Germany **Deutschland (n)**
to get **bekommen**
girl **Mädchen (n)**
to give **geben**
glad **froh**
glass **Glas (n)**
gloves **Handschuhe (pl.)**
to go back **zurückgehen**
to go on **weitergehen**
goings-on **Getue (n)**
good **gut**
great **groß**
greeting cards **Glückwunschkarten (pl.)**
to grow **wachsen**
guest **Gast (m)**
regular guests **Stammgäste (pl.)**

H

hair **Haar (n)**
half **halb**
hand **Hand (f)**
on the other hand **anderseits**
handkerchief **Taschentuch (n)**
What happened? **Was ist passiert?**
happy **glücklich**
hard **schwer, hart**
to have **haben**
he **er**
to hear **hören**
height **Höhe (f)**
here **hier**
to hide oneself **sich verstecken**
high **hoch**
to hint **andeuten**
to hold **halten**
homemade **hausgemacht**
it is to be hoped **hoffentlich**
horrible **scheußlich**
hotel **Hotel (n)**
hotel reservation **Hotelreservierung (f)**
hour **Stunde (f)**
house **Haus (n)**
How are you? **Wie geht's?**
How much? **Wieviel?**
however **jedoch**

I

I **ich**
I am **ich bin**
it **es**

idealist **Idealist (m)**
if **wenn**
in **in**
inasmuch as **insofern als**
incredible **unglaublich**
inside of **innerhalb von**
in spite of **trotzdem**
instead of **statt**
interested **interessiert**
interruption **Unterbrechung (f)**
interview **Interview (n)**
to invent **erfinden**
investment **Kapitalanlage (f)**

J

job **Job (m)**
joking aside **Scherz beiseite**
just **soeben; gerade**

K

to keep **halten**
they can keep it **es kann mir gestohlen werden**
to keep a diary **ein Tagebuch führen**
kitchen **Küche (f)**
knife **Messer (n)**
to know **kennen; wissen**
I don't know **ich weiß nicht**
Who knows? **Wer weiß?**

L

large **groß**
last **vorig**
the last few days **die letzten paar Tage**
later **später**
leather shorts **Lederhosen (pl.)**
to learn **lernen**
to let **lassen**
letter writer **Briefschreiber (m)**
to lie down **sich niederlegen**
to like **gern haben**
line **Linie (f)**
to listen **zuhören**
little **klein**
to live **wohnen, leben**
living room **Wohnzimmer (n)**
to look **schauen**
lots of. . . **eine Menge von. . .**
lucky **glücklich**

M

mainly **hauptsächlich**
to make **machen**
to make themselves comfortable **es sich bequem machen**
man **Mann (m)**
manners **Manieren (pl.)**
many **viele**
it doesn't matter **es macht nichts**
maybe **vielleicht**
to mean **meinen**
means **Mittel (pl.)**
menu **Menu (n)**
educational method **Erziehungsmethode (f)**
mile **Meile (f)**
What do you have in mind? **Was hast du vor?**

Do you mind? **Hast du was dagegen?**
minute **Minute (f)**
Miss **Fräulein (n)**
modern **modern**
money **Geld (n)**
month **Monat (m)**
she is in a bad mood **sie ist schlechter Laune**
more **mehr**
morning **Morgen (m)**
most **meist**
mother **Mutter (f)**
Mrs. **Frau (f)**
a practicing musician **ein ausübender Musiker (m)**
must **müssen**

N

name **Name (m)**
naughty **schlimm**
necessary **notwendig**
to need **brauchen**
neighbor **Nachbar (m)**
it gets on my nerves **es geht mir auf die Nerven**
never **nie**
nevertheless **nichtsdestoweniger**
new **neu**
next door **nebenan**
nice **nett**
no **nein, kein**
not **nicht**
not too much **nicht zu viel**
nothing **nichts**
nothing else **sonst nichts**
to give notice **kündigen**
nowadays **heutzutage**

O

obviously **offenbar**
ten o'clock **zehn Uhr**
it occurred to me **es fiel mir ein**
of **von**
to offer **antragen**
office **Büro (n)**
office manager **Bürovorstand (m)**
often **oft**
old **alt**
on **auf**
on the other hand **anderseits**
one **ein, man**
only **nur**
to open **öffnen**
open **offen**
opera **Oper (f)**
opinion **Meinung (f)**
opportunity **Gelegenheit (f)**
orchestra **Orchester (n)**
to order **bestellen**
ordering about **das Herumkommandieren (n)**
other **ander**
out **aus**
outside of **außerhalb von**
over **über**

P

to paint **malen**
painter **Maler (m)**

paper **Zeitung (f)**
parents **Eltern (pl.)**
to pass **bestehen; passen**
pastry cook **Zuckerbäcker (m)**
to pay **bezahlen**
penny **Groschen (m)**
people **Leute (pl.)**
person **Person (f)**
personally **persönlich**
photographer **Photograph (m)**
to pick up **abholen**
picture **Bild (n)**
it is a pity **schade!**
plan **Plan (m)**
plate **Teller (m)**
to play **spielen**
please **bitte**
point of departure **Ausgangsort (m)**
to poison **vergiften**
policy, politics **Politik (f)**
popular **populär**
potato **Kartoffel (f)**
practical **praktisch**
to practice **üben**
to prefer **vorziehen**
presence **Gegenwart (f)**
to present **präsentieren**
President **Präsident (m)**
price **Preis (m)**
pride **Stolz (m)**
private **privat**
probably **wahrscheinlich**
problem **Problem (n)**
program **Programm (n)**
prove to be **werden**

R

to ransack **ausrauben**
ready **bereit**
really **wirklich**
to receive **erhalten**
refrigerator **Kühlschrank (m)**
to the regret of. . . **zum Leidwesen von. . .**
relative **relativ**
to remember **sich erinnern**
rent **Miete (f)**
repertory **Repertoire (n)**
reporter **Reporter (m)**
to rest **sich ausruhen**
right of way **Vorrecht (n)**

S

sad **traurig**
the same **dasselbe**
satisfied **zufrieden**
Saturday **Samstag (m)**
to say **sagen**
secretary **Sekretärin (f)**
school **Schule (f)**
sculptor **Bildhauer (m)**
season **Saison (f)**
to see **sehen**
seller, i.e., an item that is selling well **Verkaufsschlager (m)**
to settle **sich niederlassen**
to shave **sich rasieren**
she **sie**
sheep **Schaf (n)**

silly **dumm**
to shine **scheinen**
short **kurz**
to show **zeigen**
shrewd **schlau**
silence **Ruhe (f)**
since **seit**
sister **Schwester (f)**
to sleep **schlafen**
to smoke **rauchen**
so **so**
some **einige**
sometimes **manchmal**
soon **bald**
I am sorry **es tut mir leid**
sound **Laut (m)**
to sound **klingen**
southern **südlich**
to spend **ausgeben**
splendid **glänzend**
spoon **Löffel (m)**
I cannot stand it **ich kann es nicht aushalten**
to start **anfangen**
to stay **bleiben**
Stop it! **Hör auf!**
street **Straße (f)**
strong **stark**
to study **studieren**
suit **Anzug (m)**
sun **Sonne (f)**
Sunday **Sonntag (m)**
sunset **Sonnenuntergang (m)**
superfluous **überflüssig**
to surpass **übertreffen**
stage **Bühne (f)**
still **noch immer**
structural **baulich**
success **Erfolg (m)**
surgeon **Chirurg (m)**

T

to take **nehmen; dauern**
to take along **mitnehmen**
to take a bow **sich verbeugen**
to talk **reden**
tea **Tee (m)**
to tempt **reizen**
terrific! **unerhört!**
to thank **danken**
many thanks **vielen Dank**
that (demon. pronoun) **das**
that (sub. conj.) **daß**
at that time **damals**
the **der, die, das**
there **dort**
there are, there is **es gibt**
therefore **deshalb**
they **sie**
I think **ich glaube**
three **drei**
thirteen **dreizehn**
this **dieser, das**
to threaten **drohen**
through **durch**
to throw out **hinauswerfen**
time **Zeit (f)**
to **zu**
today **heute**

together **zusammen**
tomorrow evening **morgen abend**
toothache **Zahnweh (n)**
topic **Thema (n)**
torte **Torte (f)**
total **total**
it touches him **es berührt ihn**
tourist **Tourist (m)**
toward the end **gegen Ende**
to translate **übersetzen**
travel agency **Reisebüro (n)**
trip **Reise (f)**
to turn around **sich umdrehen**
twenty **zwanzig**
typical **typisch**

U

uncle **Onkel (m)**
to understand **verstehen**
unemployment **Arbeitslosigkeit (f)**
unlimited **unbegrenzt**
usher **Platzanweiser (m)**
his utmost **sein Möglichstes**

V

vehicle **Fahrzeug (n)**
very **sehr**
view **Aussicht (f)**

W

to wait **warten**
waitress **Kellnerin (f)**
to want to **wollen**
warm **warm**
to wash **waschen**
watch **Uhr (f)**
watch out **nehmt euch in acht**
we **wir**
to wear **tragen**
weather **Wetter (n)**
week **Woche (f)**
well-behaved **brav**
what **was**
whenever **wann immer**
where **wo**
which **der; welcher**
while **während**
to whisper **wispern**
who **wer**
whole **ganz**
why **warum**
wind **Wind (m)**
window **Fenster (n)**
with **mit**
without **ohne**
woman **Frau (f)**
No wonder! **Kein Wunder! (n)**
wonderful **wunderbar**
wool trade **Wollhandel (m)**
nothing worth talking about **nicht der Rede wert**
to work **arbeiten**
worth **wert**
year **Jahr (n)**
yesterday afternoon **gestern nachmittag**
yet **noch**
you **du, Sie**
young **jung**

Strong and irregular verbs

INFINITIVE	3RD PERS. SINGULAR	PAST TENSE	PAST PARTICIPLE	ENGLISH MEANING
beginnen	beginnt	begann	begonnen	to begin
bieten	bietet	bot	geboten	to offer
bitten	bittet	bat	gebeten	to ask
blasen	bläst	blies	geblasen	to blow
bleiben	bleibt	blieb	ist geblieben	to stay
brechen	bricht	brach	gebrochen	to break
brennen	brennt	brannte	gebrannt	to burn
bringen	bringt	brachte	gebracht	to bring
denken	denkt	dachte	gedacht	to think
einladen	lädt ein	lud ein	eingeladen	to invite
empfehlen	empfiehlt	empfahl	empfohlen	to recommend
essen	ißt	aß	gegessen	to eat
fahren	fährt	fuhr	ist gefahren	to drive, travel
fallen	fällt	fiel	ist gefallen	to fall
fangen	fängt	fing	gefangen	to catch
finden	findet	fand	gefunden	to find
fliegen	fliegt	flog	ist geflogen	to fly
frieren	friert	fror	gefroren	to freeze
geben	gibt	gab	gegeben	to give
gehen	geht	ging	ist gegangen	to go
genießen	genießt	genoß	genossen	to enjoy
gewinnen	gewinnt	gewann	gewonnen	to win
haben	hat	hatte	gehabt	to have
halten	hält	hielt	gehalten	to hold
helfen	hilft	half	geholfen	to help
kennen	kennt	kannte	gekannt	to know
klingen	klingt	klang	geklungen	to sound
kommen	kommt	kam	ist gekommen	to come
lassen	läßt	ließ	gelassen	to let, allow
laufen	läuft	lief	ist gelaufen	to run
mögen	mag	mochte	gemocht	to like
müssen	muß	mußte	gemußt	to have to
nehmen	nimmt	nahm	genommen	to take
pfeifen	pfeift	pfiff	gepfiffen	to whistle
raten	rät	riet	geraten	to advise
rennen	rennt	rannte	ist gerannt	to run
riechen	riecht	roch	gerochen	to smell
rufen	ruft	rief	gerufen	to call
schaffen	schafft	schuf	geschaffen	to create
scheinen	scheint	schien	geschienen	to shine
scheren	schert	schor	geschoren	to shear
schlafen	schläft	schlief	geschlafen	to sleep
schlagen	schlägt	schlug	geschlagen	to beat
schließen	schließt	schloß	geschlossen	to close
schmeißen	schmeißt	schmiß	geschmissen	to throw
schneiden	schneidet	schnitt	geschnitten	to cut
schreiben	schreibt	schrieb	geschrieben	to write
schreien	schreit	schrie	geschrien	to shout
schwimmen	schwimmt	schwamm	geschwommen	to swim
sehen	sieht	sah	gesehen	to see

sein	ist	war	ist gewesen	to be
singen	singt	sang	gesungen	to sing
sitzen	sitzt	saß	gesessen	to sit
sprechen	spricht	sprach	gesprochen	to speak
springen	springt	sprang	ist gesprungen	to jump
stehen	steht	stand	gestanden	to stand
stehlen	stiehlt	stahl	gestohlen	to steal
steigen	steigt	stieg	ist gestiegen	to climb
sterben	stirbt	starb	ist gestorben	to die
streichen	streicht	strich	gestrichen	to spread
treffen	trifft	traf	getroffen	to meet
treten	tritt	trat	ist getreten	to step
trinken	trinkt	trank	getrunken	to drink
tun	tut	tat	getan	to do
verbergen	verbirgt	verbarg	verborgen	to hide
verderben	verdirbt	verdarb	verdorben	to spoil
vergessen	vergißt	vergaß	vergessen	to forget
vergleichen	vergleicht	verglich	verglichen	to compare
verlieren	verliert	verlor	verloren	to lose
waschen	wäscht	wusch	gewaschen	to wash
werden	wird	wurde	ist geworden	to become
werfen	wirft	warf	geworfen	to throw
wissen	weiß	wußte	gewußt	to know
zerreißen	zerreißt	zerriß	zerrissen	to tear apart
ziehen	zieht	zog	gezogen	to pull, move

Pronunciation Guide

I. Vowels

The symbol ¯ above a vowel will be used to indicate a long vowel.
The symbol ˘ above a vowel will be used to indicate a short vowel.

1. A German vowel is long
   a. if it is followed by a single consonant:
      - ā **Nāme** (as in father), name
      - ē **lēsen** (as in late), to read
      - ī **Maschīne** (as in machine), machine
      - ō **lōben** (as in bone), to praise
      - ū **Schūle** (as in fool), school
   b. if it is doubled; this occurs only with *a, e,* and *o.*
      - **Sāāl** (as in Saab), hall
      - **Mēēr** (as in fair), ocean
      - **Bōōt** (as in load), boat
   c. if it is followed by a silent *h:*
      - **Hāhn** (as in father), rooster
      - **sēhr** (as in share), very
      - **īhn** (as in lean), him
      - **Sōhn** (as in loan), son
      - **Schūh** (as in blue), shoe
   d. if it is followed by a silent *e;* this occurs only after an *i:*
      - **Dīeb** (as in creep), thief
   e. if it is followed by *ß* (scharfes *s*) and another vowel:
      - **Strāße** (as in shah), street
2. A German vowel is short
   a. if it is followed by more than one consonant or a double consonant:
      - ă **dann** (as in con), then
      - ĕ **Gĕld** (as in belt), money
      - ĭ **Lĭnse** (as in pins), lens
      - ŏ **kŏmmen** (as in come, son) to come
      - ŭ **nŭll** (as in bull), zero
   b. if it is an *e* in the last syllable of a word that ends with: *-e, -el, -en, -er:*

allĕ	all
Himmĕl	sky
gehĕn	to go
bittĕr	bitter

   c. if it is an *e* in an inseparable prefix like *be-, emp-, ent-, er-, ge-, ver-, zer-:*

bĕsitzen	to own	**ĕmpfehlen**	to recommend
ĕntlassen	to discharge	**ĕrhalten**	to receive
gĕsehen	seen	**verzeihen**	forgive
zĕrreißen	to tear apart		

Important: German vowels and consonants are pronounced sharply, crisply, with no off-glide sound.

3. An Umlaut is indicated by two dots above the vowel, as in:
   Hănde (hands); this should be pronounced as if spelled *Hende*. There is usually little difference in pronunciation between *ä* and *e.* However, to distinguish between forms like **spreche** and **spräche, sehen** and **sähen,** words with *ä* are given a raspier sound.
   ö **schōn** (beautiful); your lips have to be rounded and pushed forward forcefully. Imagine you're whistling a tune as you pronounce this. Pronounce

English *further* with your lips forward and rounded. Then try the German **fördern** (to further).

ü **grün** (green); do what you did when producing the *ö* only more so. Your mouth has to shrink to a little round hole through which the *ü* has to pass. (Both the *ö* and the *ü* were explained in Chapter 1.)

Please note: The rules as to whether a vowel is long or short apply to the umlauts as well.

4. Diphthongs are pairs of vowels:

au **Haus** (as in mouse), house
äu **Häuser** (as in oil), houses
eu **deutsch** (as in foil), German

Please note: There is absolutely no difference in pronunciation between *äu* and *eu;* they are both pronounced like *oi* in oil or coil.

ai **Mai** (rhymes with lie), May
ei **klein** (rhymes with mine), little.

There is no difference in the pronunciation of *ai* and *ei*.

II. Consonants

b, d, g	are generally pronounced the same way as in English, *except* at the end of a syllable and before a consonant:
b	**gāb** (as if spelled **gāp**), gave
	gībt (as if spelled **gīpt**), gives
d	**Lănd** (as if spelled **Lănt**), land
g	**sāg** (as if spelled **sāk**), say
	sāgt (as if spelled **sākt**), says
c	is used mostly in words that have a *ch* or *sch*. In foreign words before an *e* or *i* it is pronounced *ts*, otherwise like *k*.
f, h, *k, m, n,* *p, t*	are pronounced as in English.
j	**Jāhr** (year); the German *j* is pronounced like the English *y* in year.
l	should be pronounced with the tip of your tongue against the back surface of your upper front teeth. As pointed out in Chapter 1, it should sound like the flat *l* in *William*.
q	As in English, occurs only before *u,* and *qu* is pronounced *kv*.
r	Try to roll the *r* the way a Scotsman does.
s	Before a vowel, *s* sounds like the English *z* in zipper.
	Sommer (as if spelled **zŏmmĕr**), summer
	Nase (as if spelled **Nāzĕ**), nose
	Elsewhere it should sound like an English *s*.
ß (scharfes s)	is pronounced like an English *s*.
	It follows a long vowel or diphthong; it also stands before a consonant and at the end of a word.
	weiß (pronounced like the English *vice*), white.
	läßt (rhymes with guest), lets.
v	is to be sounded exactly like the letter *f:*
	Vater (as if spelled **Fātĕr**), father, *except* in words of foreign origin:
	Vase (**Vāsĕ**), vase
w	is pronounced like the English *v:*
	Winter (pronounced **Vīntĕr**), winter
x	sounds like *ks*.

y	sounds like the umlaut *ü*. If it occurs as the last vowel in a first name, it is sounded like a long *i* (Anny).
z	must be pronounced like the last two letters in *cats*. But it also occurs at the beginning of a syllable: **Zimmer** (as if spelled **Tsĭmmĕr**), room; **Zahn** (as if spelled **Tsān**), tooth

III. Consonant Combinations

ch (the one)	sounds like the *ch* in the Scotch *loch*, and occurs only after the vowels *a, o, u* and the diphthong *au:* **Băch** (brook), **nŏch** (still), **Gerūch** (smell), **Bauch** (belly);
ch (the other)	sounds like an exaggerated *h* in *Hugh*. It occurs after *e, i, n, l, r*, also after *ie, ä, ö, ü, ei*, and *eu.* **Pĕch** (pitch), **mĭch** (me), **München** (Munich), **wĕlcher** (which), **Lĕrche** (lark)
chs	sounds like *ks* **Fuchs** (as if spelled **Fŭx**), fox
sch	sounds the same as the English *sh*.
ck	the same as k
sp, st	at the beginning of words or word stems are pronounced *schp scht:* **Spitze** (as if spelled **Schpĭtse**), point; **Stelle** (as if spelled **Schtĕlle**), place.
th	always like *t:* **Theater** (as if spelled **Tēāter**), theater.